RESISTANCE AND ABOLITION IN THE BORDERLANDS

RESISTANCE AND ABOLITION
IN THE BORDERLANDS

CONFRONTING TRUMP'S REIGN OF TERROR

EDITED BY

ARTURO J. ALDAMA AND JESSICA ORDAZ

FOREWORD BY LEO R. CHAVEZ

AFTERWORD BY KARMA R. CHÁVEZ

THE UNIVERSITY OF
ARIZONA PRESS
TUCSON

The University of Arizona Press
www.uapress.arizona.edu

We respectfully acknowledge the University of Arizona is on the land and territories of Indigenous peoples. Today, Arizona is home to twenty-two federally recognized tribes, with Tucson being home to the O'odham and the Yaqui. Committed to diversity and inclusion, the University strives to build sustainable relationships with sovereign Native Nations and Indigenous communities through education offerings, partnerships, and community service.

ISBN-13: 978-0-8165-5232-0 (hardcover)
ISBN-13: 978-0-8165-5231-3 (paperback)
ISBN-13: 978-0-8165-5233-7 (ebook)

Cover design by Derek Thornton / Notch Design
Cover art via Shutterstock
Typeset by Leigh McDonald in Warnock Pro 10.5/14 and DIN 30640 Std (display)

Publication of this book is made possible in part by support from the Department of Ethnic Studies at the University of Colorado Boulder.

Library of Congress Cataloging-in-Publication Data
Names: Aldama, Arturo J., 1964– editor. | Ordaz, Jessica, editor. | Chavez, Leo R. (Leo Ralph), writer of foreword. | Chávez, Karma R., writer of afterword.
Title: Resistance and abolition in the borderlands : confronting Trump's reign of terror / edited by Arturo J. Aldama and Jessica Ordaz ; foreword by Leo R. Chavez ; afterword by Karma R. Chávez.
Description: Tucson : University of Arizona Press, 2024. | Includes bibliographical references and index.
Identifiers: LCCN 2023024534 (print) | LCCN 2023024535 (ebook) | ISBN 9780816552320 (hardcover) | ISBN 9780816552313 (paperback) | ISBN 9780816552337 (ebook)
Subjects: LCSH: Trump, Donald, 1946– | Immigrants—Violence against—Mexican-American Border Region—History—21st century. | Presidents—United States—Racial attitudes. | United States—Emigration and immigration—Government policy—History—21st century.
Classification: LCC JV6483 .R466 2024 (print) | LCC JV6483 (ebook) | DDC 325.7309/05—dc23/eng/20230909
LC record available at https://lccn.loc.gov/2023024534
LC ebook record available at https://lccn.loc.gov/2023024535

Printed in the United States of America
♾ This paper meets the requirements of ANSI/NISO Z39.48-1992 (Permanence of Paper).

We dedicate this book to all those who fight for a world that does not terrorize, cage, shackle, silence, maim, and shoot at human beings struggling for survival in the U.S./México borderlands and beyond.

CONTENTS

FOREWORD

I, LIKE MANY OTHERS, WATCHED in shock and horror as Donald Trump announced his candidacy for president of the United States with his infamous claim that Mexicans were rapists and murderers. That he went on to win the presidency in 2016 made many of us wary of his policies about the border, the "wall," refugees, "anchor babies," the Deferred Action for Childhood Arrivals (DACA) program, and much more. For four years the nation experienced almost daily tweets that were not just controversial but often filled with invective, threats, bigotry, self-aggrandizement, and, of course, anti-Latinx sentiments. His chief policy adviser, Stephen Miller, was an avowed restrictionist when it came to immigration, except for European immigration. Miller was also an admirer of the alt-right and white nationalist rhetoric, including white replacement theory. Not surprisingly, Stephen Miller was the architect of many of Trump's draconian immigration policies. Trump's four years in office were tumultuous, to say the least.

This volume provides a timely and well-argued history of the present, that is, the Donald Trump era. These scholars provide insightful contributions to our understanding of the impact of Donald Trump's rhetoric and policies on migrants detained and returned, immigrant children separated from their parents and placed in detention centers, and migrant women subjected to sexual and reproductive abuses. The authors document a long list of violences of what the book calls Trump's reign of terror.

Arturo Aldama and Jessica Ordaz have recruited scholars from a range of disciplines—women, gender, and sexuality studies, Mexican American studies, migration studies, sociology, ethnic studies, history, American studies, critical media practices, Spanish, dance studies, media arts, communication, and English—to examine topics not always easy to read but important to engage with, nonetheless. The authors document what happens when a president with an authoritarian and narcissistic personality uses nationalist populism to inflame anti-immigrant and anti-Latinx sentiment. Trump's rhetoric was, and is, often bigoted, misogynistic, xenophobic, and self-interested. The authors provide evidence of the collateral damage of Trump's rhetoric and policies, from the insufferable conditions in migrant detention centers, to the effect of human trafficking laws as a form of state violence, to the lack of concern for refugees and their safety.

This interdisciplinary collection also examines artistic engagements with the border and Trumpism. Through explorations of dance, music, and artistic expression, the authors remind us that migrants and their families are not mere pawns in Trump's political games. They are productive, thinking, and feeling human beings, whose emotions and critiques serve as resistance to Trump and those who so willingly follow his anti-immigrant and anti-Latinx rhetoric. I found compelling the expositions on art and dance that capture the pain and heartache of border crossing and death. In one chapter, a young woman uses her quinceañera to question Trump's zero tolerance policies. An analysis of the tone-deaf Border Patrol Museum resonates well with the other chapters in this collection.

Other chapters examine the media and pop culture. Here Trump's use of the media is well documented, as is his rhetoric's appeal to white nationalism, both in the United States and in Brazil. Trump's obsession with the wall at the U.S.-Mexico border is critiqued as to its eroticization, using metaphors of the anus. The range of topics examined here also includes an analysis of a comic book series on a child's and his mother's incarceration, and the prevalence of gun violence and Trump's use of the invasion metaphor.

In short, the scholars in this volume provide an impressive range and depth of topics on life and social violence experienced during Trump's four years in power. While his one-term presidency may have been relatively short, his legacy continues to influence right-wing politicians and pundits, especially those willing to sustain the trope of immigrant invasions and the alleged threats posed by immigrants and their families. *Resistance and Abolition in the Borderlands* is an essential reader for those wishing to understand the extent of the damage caused by Trump's rhetoric and policies.

I believe this volume should be read widely. It would be particularly useful in college classes, where it would serve as an example of how interdisciplinary approaches can come together to provide insights into issues of concern not just to Latinx communities but to the whole nation. The authors challenge taken-for-granted assumptions about Latinx communities and at the same time speak truth to power.

I am personally grateful to Arturo Aldama and Jessica Ordaz for bringing together such a remarkable group of contributors committed to setting the record straight about the damage caused by Donald Trump's policies. This volume represents a new wave of activist scholarship, one that will be of tremendous use to both academics and the public in general.

Leo R. Chavez
Distinguished Professor of Anthropology
University of California, Irvine

RESISTANCE AND ABOLITION IN THE BORDERLANDS

INTRODUCTION

Terror, Trauma, and Resistance in the U.S./México Borderlands

ARTURO J. ALDAMA AND JESSICA ORDAZ

WE WRITE FROM THE TRADITIONAL territories of the Arapaho, Cheyenne, and Ute Nations and start by calling out the cruelty of U.S. Customs and Border Protection officers (over 50 percent of whom are Hispanic identified).[1] They mocked and humiliated the children, many Indigenous and Afro-Indigenous identified, who cried from pain and trauma and terror when they were taken from their parents as part of Trump's family separation policy, a zero tolerance policy that stole more than 2,500 children from their parents as they attempted to seek asylum in the United States.[2] The 2018 *ProPublica* article "Listen to Children Who've Just Been Separated from Their Parents at the Border" provides leaked audio of ten children sobbing, screaming, and crying out for their "mami and papa." The children were estimated to be between four and ten years old. It is gut wrenching to listen to the "live trauma" of the children trying to process the terror and fear they felt because of Trump's zero tolerance policy. Their feelings were violated further by the border patrol officers who mocked their pain and humiliated them. The audio reveals the baritone voice of an officer yelling above the crying of the children. He says, "Well, we have an orchestra here." "What's missing is a conductor."[3]

It might be easy to dismiss the border patrol officer's traumatizing "humor" as that of a stressed-out officer with poor taste. However, this added cruelty, which makes children into literal abjects, underscores

Trump's presidency, rhetoric, political theater, and policies. His callousness inspired others to enunciate their white supremacist views and actions. To augment further this view of Trump and those who feel "liberated" by his white supremacism, we ask readers to engage with the staff report titled *The Trump Administration's Family Separation Policy: Trauma, Destruction, and Chaos*. The report concludes that the family separation policy—which was piloted in El Paso, Texas, in 2017 and was prepared within weeks of President Trump's inauguration—was "driven by an Administration that was willfully blind to its cruelty" and "determined to go to unthinkable extremes to deliver on political promises," such as stopping migrants from entering the United States.[4]

As editors of this collection, we also recognize, remember, and mourn the countless queer and trans migrants who were incarcerated, deported, or murdered during the Trump era. As the world learned in December 2020, a transgender asylum seeker from Ecuador named C.O. was held in solitary confinement at the Irwin County Detention Center in Georgia for six months due to his gender identity.[5] Immigration authorities held C.O. and denied him hormone treatment as well as other medical resources. Honduran migrant Roxsana Hernandez died due to medical neglect and the traumatizing experience of the detention center or "icebox," so named for its cold temperatures and lack of warm bedding. News reports suggest that when Roxsana was transferred to a private prison, she presented with severe symptoms of "dehydration and pneumonia." Roxsana passed away shortly afterward in a hospital.[6] Johana Medina León, like Roxsana, died due to medical neglect and the depraved indifference shown to her medical needs.[7] May we remember their names and lives, and may they rest in power.

INTENTIONS

The purpose of this volume is to provide a scholarly and creative space for scholars, artists, and activists to share work that examines the violence(s) that inspired, promoted, and were intensified by the Trump regime. Feelings of rage, deep *tristeza* (sadness), and, in some cases, despondency were overwhelming during Trump's regime of terror. These complex feelings were driven by how wantonly cruel Trump's rhetoric and actions were while a large percentage of the voting electorate celebrated his ruthlessness.

Trump had a single-term presidency (2017–21), which he won by the Electoral College vote, not the popular vote. His pathway to the Republican nomination and to the presidential election was kick-started by white supremacists and fans at his campaign rallies, which celebrated the criminalization of Latinx men as drug dealers and rapists, among other nativist stereotypes. Trump supporters advanced the narrative of being invaded by nonwhite people. Such narratives have immense viewing popularity on Fox News and are repeated by people such as Tucker Carlson, who has an enormous fan base and market share of viewers. Many pundits argue that Carlson frequently centers white supremacist theories that are normally found in neo-Nazi circles. One of those theories is the Great Replacement, an anti-Semitic, anti-Black, and anti-Brown conspiracy theory that claims that nonwhite immigrants are replacing white Christian Americans, affecting the voting landscape and political power of the United States. A 2022 blog post by the Anti-Defamation League calls on technology companies to deplatform Carlson, who constantly broadcasts such theories to his social media followers: over 5 million on Twitter, 5 million on Facebook, and 1.8 million on Instagram.[8] According to the blog post, Carlson has recirculated replacement theory diatribes in over four hundred episodes of his Fox News show. The post also references Fox News personality Jeanine Pirro, who disseminates the idea that "illegals" are invading the country to replace true Americans and vote Democrat.

A May 2022 shooting of African American shoppers in Buffalo, New York, evinces the impact and influence of these white supremacist discourses. According to reports, the eighteen-year-old shooter's 180-page manifesto has recognizable tropes of replacement theory.[9] The shooter felt compelled to murder the shoppers to stop the "replacement" of white Christian families and—given the huge support of these racist conspiracy theories in the Republican Party—white Christian Republican voters. The replacement theory parallels the ongoing racist hype of protecting the southern border from "invasion" by nonwhite folks, a refrain heard in Trump's political rallies and from many elected officials. One notable example is the congressman Paul Gosar (R-Ariz.), a former dentist, whose racist misogyny was brought to the fore in an anime video that featured the murder of Alexandria Ocasio-Cortez (AOC) (D-N.Y.). When Gosar was called out for the violence of the anime video in 2021, he defended it by saying that the cartoon "exposes threats to America" and that AOC was "a proud member of the open borders caucus" and a promoter of "the plague of illegal immigration."[10] Replacement theory and the racist hype of "invasion" were also seen as motivators in the horrific mass murder of Latinx people in El Paso, Texas, on August 3, 2019 (a subject of various chapters in this book).

Yet, the criminalization of Latinx communities is neither new nor confined to the Trump administration. The 2017 report "The Obama Record on Deportations: Deporter in Chief or Not?" from the Migration Policy Institute compares Obama's record of deportation to that of previous presidents Bill Clinton and George W. Bush. The report cites U.S. Department of Homeland Security immigration statistics for people detained, removed, returned, or deported under Clinton (1993–2001), Bush (2001–9), and Obama (2009–17), with numbers tallying, respectively, almost 12.3 million people, over 10.3 million people, and almost 5.3 million people.[11] Although Trump's nativist political theater and polices are not unique, however, they are especially virulent, motivating us to design a collection of work that calls out the violence(s) under the Trump administration and that centers the ways Latinx communities push back against and resist the detention and deportation regime.

Trump might have lost his reelection campaign, but he inspired an archipelago of white supremacist, transphobic, and misogynistic laws and statutes. Republican-led states feel emboldened to outlaw critical race theory, pass transphobic legislation, abolish attempts at gender inclusivity in schools and public offices, and pass extreme anti-abortion legalization that criminalizes women's right to choose.[12]

Trump's three appointees to the Supreme Court lied under oath about their willingness to respect precedence in *Roe v. Wade*. Our Supreme Court justices have allowed states to enforce total bans on abortion and women's right to choose. These bans, brutal acts of state-sponsored necropolitical and misogynistic violence, are couched in a type of religiosity about respecting life. However, these bans ensure that many people, especially BIPOC, will die, because medical professionals could face criminal charges for upholding their Hippocratic oath.

We continue to see overfunding of the carceral state and underfunding of public education. States and districts boldly censor public education to promote narratives of white supremacy, settler colonialism, and American exceptionalism. Such narratives maintain a cisgender, white, patriarchal episteme, while classrooms that are extremely diverse in their ethnic and racial makeup don't see themselves in the curriculum.

LITERATURE INSPIRATION

This edited volume was inspired by scholarship that centers border violence, the criminalization of migrants, and resistance narratives. Literature on vigilante violence such as *The Injustice Never Leaves You: Anti-Mexican Violence in Texas* (2018) by Monica Muñoz Martinez reveals the legacies trauma leaves on families that survive vigilante violence. Martinez asserts that vigilante violence functions as a form of state building and securing the border while rendering its victims criminals and enemies of the state. Using oral history and vernacular history making, Martinez also highlights everyday forms of resistance.[13]

The work of Kelly Lytle Hernández and scholars who have written about border policing is also central to this volume. *Migra! A History of the U.S. Border Patrol* (2010) was the first publication to critically examine the border patrol through a transnational, historical lens, using sources from the United States and México. Hernández situates Mexicans as targets of immigration regimes during the twentieth century and argues that they became the iconic illegal alien. She contextualizes the violence of the border region before the creation of the U.S. Border Patrol in 1924 and asserts that early monitoring of the U.S.-México border started with surveillance and unlawful violence by the Texas Rangers. Once the Border Patrol was established, officers were assigned the task of "line watching," or policing political boundaries to identify unauthorized border crossers based on appearance and stereotypical profiles.[14]

Raza Sí, Migra No: Chicano Movement Struggles for Immigrant Rights in San Diego (2017) by Jimmy Patiño discusses antimigrant violence, multiethnic solidarity, and social movements in Southern California. Literature such as this helps us think about the lineage of migrant activism and organizing against the carceral state.[15] Patiño highlights the history of racial profiling, the surveillance state, and the murder of Latinx people. Focusing on a more contemporary period, Martha D. Escobar and others interrogate the limits of the immigrant rights movement. *Captivity Beyond Prisons: Criminalization Experiences of Latina (Im)Migrants* (2016) is crucial in thinking about migrant criminalization, problems with the good/bad immigrant narrative, and connections between migrant struggles and the prison abolition movement.[16]

The work of Leo R. Chavez is essential in thinking about the connections between the media, antimigrant rhetoric, and stereotyping of Latinx migrants as criminals, undeserving individuals, and threats to American society. In *The Latino Threat: Constructing Immigrants, Citizens, and the Nation* (2008), Chavez asserts that Mexican communities are framed as invaders attempting to reclaim the Southwest. More recent scholarship centering the violence of the detention and deportation regime has shown how immigration control is intended to be punitive.[17] This scholarship has been essential in our framing this edited volume as one that thinks about the Trump reign of terror as part of a much longer history of state violence, white supremacy, and policing, an era that also saw community resistance, grassroots organizing, and activism flourish.

CHAPTER OVERVIEW

The book is divided into four sections of original scholarly and creative work. Its chapters include cutting-edge interdisciplinary research from scholars in the fields of women, gender, and sexuality studies, Mexican American studies, migration studies, sociology, ethnic studies, history, American studies, critical media practices, Spanish, dance studies, media arts, communication, and English.

PART I. XENOPHOBIA, ABJECTION, AND STATE VIOLENCE

Part I of this book highlights the brutality that proliferated prior to, during, and beyond Trump's America. Although this book centers on Trump's reign of terror, we view the atrocities that developed between 2017 and 2021 as rooted in a long lineage and history of settler colonialism, racism, xenophobia, white supremacy, and the policing of migration. In "'They're Bringing Drugs!': Reflections on Movement and Migration, the War on Drugs, and the Opioid Crisis in Trump's America," Rebecca

Avalos discusses how the Trump administration reified the archetype of migrant as drug dealer. Framing her argument within the context of neoliberal medicine, the war on drugs, and racial capitalism, Avalos argues that Trump amplified Latinx stereotypes about drug use and criminality while ignoring the very real opioid crisis.

Historian Jennifer Cullison examines the long history of migrant incarceration in Texas to contextualize contemporary antimigrant legislation such as the zero tolerance policy. "Separating and Caging Immigrant Families: Case Studies in South Texas from the Postwar Era Through Trump's Reign of Terror" highlights the brutality and cruelty migrants have experienced in family detention centers across decades. Cullison also charts the transformation from incarcerating women and children in nonprofit institutions to relying on private prisons that promised innovation and efficiency in managing family detention.

In "Human Trafficking and the Politics of State Violence Through Operation Lone Star," Mexican American studies scholar Antonio Vásquez explores the consequences of human trafficking policies on migrants. The discourse used in policies against human trafficking such as Operation Lone Star in Texas (that is, antimigrant policies disguised as national security) has had drastic effects on migrants. Centering migrant criminalization and the militarization of the Texas-México border, Vásquez shows the coded and uncoded ways state violence manifested during the Trump era.

In a comparative history examining reproductive violence in the United States and Guatemala, Alexandria Herrera explores medical abuse of and experimentation on people of color. "The Uterus Collectors: The Lineage of Hemispheric Medical Abuse and Experimentation in the United States and Guatemala" places the practice of forced hysterectomies on incarcerated migrants within the larger context of medical exploitation, including experimentation and sterilizations throughout the Américas.

In "Reflections on Right-Wing Leadership in the United States: From LAPD Chief William Parker to Donald Trump," ethnic studies scholar Roberto A. Mónico compares the Trump administration's antiimmigrant discourse and policies to those of Cold War–era Los Angeles Police Department chief Parker, placing contemporary antimigrant actions within the larger and historical context of the carceral state. This study highlights the nonpartisan nature of policing, criminalizing, and scapegoating of migrants throughout U.S. history. Mónico argues that conservative and liberal administrations have both used law enforcement agencies to assist with migrant apprehensions, detentions, and deportations, complicating how we read and understand the Trump regime.

Lastly, Jasmin Lilian Diab, expert in migration, gender, and conflict studies, discusses the various acts of xenophobia conducted during the Trump era in "Refugees and Human Rights Law During the Trump Administration." Diab shows the many challenges migrants faced during Trump's administration, from the Muslim ban and the detention of asylum seekers to rants about the border wall and the government's pause on temporary protected status for hundreds of thousands of migrants. Together, these chapters contextualize the ideologies, discourse, and policies that shaped, allowed, and legitimized the Trump administration's antimigrant era.

PART II. PERFORMING THE BORDERLANDS: VISUAL ARTS, MUSIC, DANCE, AND COMMUNITY RESISTANCE(S)

The second part of the book features contributions by scholars, artists, and activists who discuss the ways that the Latinx community resists, calls out, and talks back to the intentional suffering and state/vigilante violence that was inflicted by the Trump regime. It begins with a chapter titled "*No Están Solxs*: Mourning Migrant Suffering and Death Through Commemorative Art at the U.S.///Mexico Border," by Alexis N. Meza and Leslie Quintanilla. In this chapter Meza and Quintanilla discuss three case studies of what they call commemorative art in San Diego. One of the acts/sites of commemorative art they consider is *Un Llanto Colectivo: PerformaProtest* by Cherríe Moraga and Celia Herrera Rodriguez, which featured twenty BIPOC artists who performed a script of "sorrow, pain, and resistance outside the walls of the Otay Mesa Detention Center," a script that was grounded in the stories of La Llorona. The second site they consider is *PRESENTE: Children Killed in Border Patrol Custody*, which included seven life-size visual posters commemorating the lives of children who died in border patrol custody. The third site considered is *Vigil for Carlos* by Pueblo Sin Fronteras, which calls out the violence of facing COVID-19 among detained migrants and the lack of safety protocols in what the organization argues became the epicenter of COVID-19 deaths and infection in the United States.

The chapter "'American' Incarceration: Dances That Critique Confinement and Contribute to Prison Abolitionist Possibilities" by dance studies scholar Tria Blu Wakpa considers how dance and performance critique state violence and incarceration, providing abolitionist visions and Indigenous futurisms for incarcerated folks. The chapter focuses on two sites of dance and performance: the short film *This Young Girl Used Her Quinceañera to Protest the Separation of Families,* and a filmed stage performance of *La Hielera* (The Icebox), which features performers expressing what confinement means for people affected by Trump's zero tolerance policies.

The next chapter of this part is by artist, videographer, and media activist Eliseo Ortiz. In "Museum at the Border," he takes a critical look at the Border Patrol Museum in El Paso, Texas, a ten-thousand-square-foot space that opened to the public in 1985. He questions how the museum seeks to normalize state violence by memorializing narratives of invasion and security. The chapter argues that the museum's museology, exhibits, and overall effect sustain a narrative that "justifies" zero tolerance immigration policies and celebrates discrimination against migrants arriving at the U.S.-México border. The chapter then juxtaposes what Ortiz calls a photographic charade with images of border patrol violence. In particular, the chapter discusses the killing of fifteen-year-old Sergio Adrián Hernández Güereca by officer Jesus Mesa Jr., who shot Sergio in the face in 2010. The chapter ends by imagining an alternative Border Patrol Museum, one that calls out the "Border Patrol Museum's abusive celebration of genocidal practices at the southern border."

Finally, the last chapter in this part, "*Canto y Oración* in Juan Gabriel's 'Amor Eterno': A Latin@/x Refusal to Forget Lives Lost to State-Sanctioned Violence" by Kiara Padilla, focuses on the Spanish song "Amor Eterno." Padilla argues that the song serves as an *oración,* or a collective canto that contests social death, premature death, femicides, vigilante killings, and broader state-sanctioned violence in Latin@/x communities. More specifically, the chapter looks at how the Latinx community in El Paso, Texas, used the song in public vigils to mourn the horrific violence of the white supremacist vigilante shooting at a local Walmart on August 3, 2019. The chapter also focuses on the community-building power of this song in a series of vigils that emerged after the April 2020 murder of Vanessa Guillén at Fort Hood, Texas. The chapter concludes by arguing that the vigils and the collective grief inspired by the song "Amor Eterno" allowed communities to "think critically and historically" and "rethink how we understand prayer, solidarity, and resistance through canto, and importantly in an amplified collective voice."

PART III. THE MEDIA AND POPULAR CULTURE

Part III gathers chapters that engage with how the media normalizes Trump's cruelty toward the Latinx community and how popular culture creates sites of resistance and counternarratives. The chapter "Americana White Plight: Bolsotrumpism and the Linear Desire for Westernness" by Renata Carvalho Barreto discusses how the mediascape provides legitimacy to the elections of Donald Trump in 2016 and Jair Bolsonaro in 2018. The chapter considers how both presidencies were driven by nationalist discourses that celebrate white and white-identified heteronormative families undergirded by Christian evangelicals. The chapter considers the ways that Bolsonaro was inspired by Trump to exalt white supremacy and colonial heteropatriarchal state violence and to attack Africana Yoruba-based spiritual and community-building practices through a white supremacist, homophobic, Christian evangelical lens.

The chapter "Trump's Hermeneutics of the Ass: Anal Theory, Gaping Holes, and Backdoor Approaches to the U.S.-Mexico Border" by Sergio A. Macías provides a compelling critique of Trump's fascination with and political promise of building a wall at the southern border to plug up a "gaping hole." Engaging with Trump's own discourse and the way comedians riff off Trump's obsession with the wall, Macías looks at the "metaphoric erotization of the southern border—most notably, the southern border as an anus." Macias builds off earlier work that he called "Trump's Poetics of Caca."

The chapter titled "The Dehumanizing Framing of Central American and Mexican Children and Youth Seeking Refuge in the United States" by Maria Vargas and Heidy Sarabia provides a compelling and incisive critique of media representations of children's trauma under the family separation practices of the zero tolerance policy. They focus on the photography of children from Central America and ground their critiques in Anibal Quijano's ideas of colonialities of power and Sara Ahmed's ideas of recognition and belonging. The chapter examines how images of children in deep trauma provoked minimal public outrage because media outlets referred to the children as "illegal." It also critiques how the media replicated and fomented white supremacist views of the caravans of Central American migrants as criminals and invaders. The focus on the criminalized hypervisible and the invisible calls further attention to the lack of awareness and outrage about the ongoing deaths of people on the border.

The chapter titled "Migrant Children and the Carceral State in the Comic Book *Home*" by José Enrique Navarro discusses how the issues of migration and state violence are reflected in a comic book miniseries titled *Home*. The miniseries follows the "story of Juan, a young Guatemalan boy who seeks asylum with his mother, Mercedes, at the U.S. border in Texas." The series follows how the boy and his mother are incarcerated and separated, and then how Juan gains superpowers to escape the detention center. Navarro argues that *Home*, which was dismissed by mainstream media as anti-Trump propaganda, integrates "images and texts into a narrative that contextualizes a given event, namely the current state of exceptionality at the U.S.-Mexico border."

The final chapter in this section, "I'm the Shooter" by J-M Rivera, is a creative and theoretical intervention into the issues of gun violence and the Latinx community. The chapter starts with calling out the fact that there were seventy thousand deaths from gun violence between 1999 and 2019 under three different administrations: Bush, Obama, and Trump. Rivera then focuses on the brutal carnage of the mass killing in El Paso, Texas, by a white supremacist shooter who felt he needed to do his part to protect the border, stop the "invasion," and "make America great again" by killing Latinx people inside a Walmart. Rivera adds that the term *invasion* became viral in U.S. politics among Trump's voting base, through rally speeches and social media.

PART IV. RESISTANCE AND ABOLITIONIST DREAMS

The final part of the edited volume is dedicated to abolitionist visions and futures. Its first chapter is "Sexual Terror and the Prison/Border Archive: Theorizing a Feminist Abolition Praxis of Migrant Detention" by Cinthya

Martinez. Martinez discusses the rampant sexual violence inside migrant detention facilities and reflects on the limits of archives and historical records. She argues that centers of migrant incarceration are prison/borders, shaped by both carceral and border logics. Furthermore, she asserts that scholars need to think and move beyond state narratives if they are to practice feminist abolition.

Cynthia Bejarano and Diana J. López discuss Trump's border wall, *fronteriza* feminist thought, the surveillance state, and resilience narratives in New Mexico in the chapter titled "Trump's Bellicose Border Wall and the Hateful Rhetoric and Violence It Inspires in the Paso del Norte Region." They highlight the various ways people disrupt and maneuver through border spaces by enacting border politics.

In "White Supremacy and Migrant Advocacy at the U.S.-Mexico Border," Allison Glover interrogates her own positionality as a white ally within the immigrant rights movement. She explores how white supremacy shows up in political assaults against migrants, migrant detention centers, and migrants undergoing asylum during Trump's administration. Glover's exploration further illuminates how Latinx migrants are framed as undesirable, criminal, and unlawful.

The next chapter is an interview about trans abolition. "'Free Them All': A Conversation on Trans Abolitionist Visions with Jordan Garcia" is a transcript of a conversation between ethnic studies scholar Nishant Upadhyay and Garcia, the immigrant ally organizing director for Coloradans for Immigrant Rights. Garcia shares their experiences as someone engaged in queer and trans migrant justice. Central to their conversation are reflections on mutual aid networks, community organizing, and abolition.

In "Resistance Archiving: Reflections on the IMM Print Detention Stories Project," Tina Shull, historian and former Soros Justice Fellow at Freedom for Immigrants, and Jamila Hammami, founder and former executive director of the Queer Detainee Empowerment Project, center the stories of incarcerated migrants while reflecting on the limits of archiving resistance. They focus on IMM Print, an archive of stories that was created when the Trump administration took power, and that calls out antimigrant violence and migrant incarceration by showcasing various manifestations of resistance.

FUTURIST VISIONS

Since January 2021, the world has learned even more about Trump's authoritarian rule. He employed postfactual politics, refused to concede defeat in the 2020 election, and planned an attempted coup during the infamous January 6 insurrection at the Capitol. The period of Trump's reign of terror was difficult to witness and survive. Yet, the community organizing that manifested during this period signals the multitude of ways that criminalized communities and their allies push back against discourses and acts of violence. We center state and vigilante violence to contextualize the past, present, and future, highlight antimigrant rhetoric and policies, chart spaces of cruelty and pain, and feature resistance to breathe life and healing into our imaginations.

Although this book is focused on Latinx migrants, we offer solidarity to BIPOC migrant and refugee communities, who also experience state and vigilante violence. We must also call out the ongoing hate crimes directed at people of Asian descent, especially women. Trump, with afactual and racist tropes of blaming COVID-19 on China (e.g., the China flu), emboldened white supremacist vigilante-like actors to beat, maim, murder, and harass Asian Americans, causing a spike in the long history of hate crimes and xenophobic legislation directed at Asian American and Pacific Islander communities.[18] We were also appalled by what we term a depraved indifference to the families and communities who survived the 2017 Hurricane Maria in Puerto Rico.[19] Trump's callous indifference, extreme incompetence (e.g., the suggestion that one could ingest or inject disinfectant to fight COVID-19), and unwillingness to listen to vetted scientific guidance, coupled with his cisgender patriarchal macho swagger to somehow out-macho COVID, led to preventable deaths, trauma, and suffering of BIPOC communities, especially those without the "luxury" to work remotely.[20] Finally, we call out how Joe Biden's administration continued the anti-Black racism of the detention and deportation regime when he used Title 42 to prevent Haitians from entering the United States so as to "prevent disease" at the border.[21] We were beyond horrified by the published images and video clips of the Texas Rangers chasing after migrants on horses to corral them and push them back across the southern border.[22]

ON ABOLITION

As the editors of this collection, we call for an end to the detention and deportation regime. Although this edited volume largely focuses on the Trump administration, we do not believe that viewing the failures of the Right is enough. We believe in and call for an abolitionist future, "a politics and a practice."[23] We hope this collection inspires new dreams, imaginings, and visions. Inspired by the knowledge, wisdom, and practices of radical Black thinkers and movement makers, we understand abolition "as a concept, process, and reality," as something that is antipolice, antiprison, antiracism, anticapitalism, feminist, and transformative.[24] Or, as Ruth Wilson Gilmore has articulated, "freedom is a place."[25]

The carceral state and its logics—"ideologies and institutions wielding cops, cages, laws, stories, and surveillance"—are all around us, as discussed throughout this edited volume.[26] The practices conducted by "violence workers" throughout the detention and deportation regime have been devasting to migrant communities, but, as many of the chapters detail, they have also engendered what scholar Tina Shull calls "abolitionist imaginaries," or new ideas and possibilities for a future without cages.[27] This process is already unfolding. After all, abolition is not merely about destruction, dismantling, and undoing. Abolition is perhaps more importantly about "presence . . . building life-affirming institutions" and "creative growth."[28] Abolition is about freedom making, liberatory futures, and radical visions. Abolition is both "a revolutionary framework that transforms the way we analyze and understand forces that shape our histories and everyday lives," as Liat Ben-Moshe argues, and a "project that focuses . . . on building a society where it is possible to address harm without relying on structural forms of oppression or the violent systems that increase it," according to Mariame Kaba.[29]

We call for a future "rooted in dignity and care for all people" and hope that the themes highlighted throughout this volume inspire conversations about the power of the carceral system as well as potential solidarities among and between the many communities targeted during Trump's reign of terror.[30] As scholar Megan Ybarra reminds us, "in the face of racial capitalism, freedom is a political project that is a state of becoming. Moreover, if 'freedom is a place,' then immigrants of colour must make it together with both Native people and other people of colour targeted by state violence."[31]

NOTES

1. As of 2021, the Border Patrol workforce was over 50 percent Latinx, but less than 20 percent of those promoted to leadership positions were Latinx. See Cortez, "I Asked Latinos Why They Joined Immigration Law Enforcement"; Giaritelli, "Inside Border Patrol's Struggle to Promote Hispanic Agents."
2. For a timeline of the zero tolerance family separation policies under Trump's presidency, see SPLC, "Family Separation."
3. Thomas, "Listen to Children Who've Just Been Separated from Their Parents at the Border."
4. U.S. House of Representatives, *The Trump Administration's Family Separation Policy*, 21.
5. See MALDEF, "Trump Administration Sued over Intentional Cruelty."
6. See Da Silva, "Who Was Roxsana Hernandez?"
7. See Herrera, "Why Are Trans Women Dying in ICE Detention?," for a discussion of Johana Medina León, Roxsana Hernandez, and patterns of transphobic aggression and neglect by ICE officials.
8. ADL, "Deplatform Tucker Carlson and the 'Great Replacement' Theory."
9. For an overview of the growth of the white supremacist and anti-Semitic replacement theory in mainstream political discourse, and the way that the Buffalo shooter recycled such theories, see Reeve, "How White 'Replacement Theory' Evolved."
10. Anglesey, "Paul Gosar Doubles Down on Cartoon Showing AOC Being Killed."
11. Chishti, Pierce, and Bolter, "The Obama Record on Deportations."
12. See Krishnakumar, "This Record-Breaking Year for Anti-Transgender Legislation," for a discussion on how, between January and April 2021, thirty-one states introduced over a hundred bills to curb and deny the rights of transgender people in the United States. For an overview of state bans of critical race theory and gender inclusivity in public schools (inspired by Trump's executive order banning racial and gender inclusivity trainings in federal agencies), see the interactive map at AAPF, "Welcome to the #TruthBeTold Campaign." And see "Supreme Court Rules on Abortion," *New York Times*, on the conservative-led Supreme Court's 2022 overturn of *Roe v. Wade*.
13. See Martinez, *The Injustice Never Leaves You*; see also Chacón and Davis, *No One Is Illegal*; R. Hernández, *Coloniality of the US/Mexico Border*; Villanueva, *The Lynching of Mexicans in the Texas Borderlands*.
14. See K. Hernández, *Migra!*; see also Andreas, *Border Games*; Kang, *The INS on the Line*; Nevins, *Operation Gatekeeper and Beyond*; Magaña, *Straddling the Border*.
15. See Patiño, *Raza Sí, Migra No*; see also Gonzales, *Reform Without Justice*; Alvarado, Estrada, and Hernández, *U.S. Central Americans*.
16. See Escobar, *Captivity Beyond Prisons*; see also Chávez, *Queer Migration Politics*; Cacho, *Social Death*; Luibhéid and Chávez, *Queer and Trans Migrations*.

17.   See Chavez, *The Latino Threat*; see also Ordaz, *The Shadow of El Centro*; García Hernández, *Migrating to Prison*; Young, *Forever Prisoners*; Lindskoog, *Detain and Punish*; K. Hernández, *City of Inmates*; Speed, *Incarcerated Stories*; Shull, *Detention Empire*.

18.   For a 2021 U.S. Department of Justice report on anti-Asian hate crimes and hostilities, see Comrie, "Combating Hate Crimes." For a pointed critique of how white supremacy and "fears of disease" drives hate crimes toward Asian Americans, see Ho, "White Supremacy Is the Root of All Race-Related Violence in the US."

19.   See Gambino, "Donald Trump Attacked," for Trump's claim that his response to the hurricane was an "unsung success." A 2018 article that cites from the *New England Journal of Medicine* states that the death toll, which was originally estimated to be about three thousand people, was at almost five thousand; see Fleig, "The 5 Deadliest Hurricanes in American History."

20.   On how Trump "weaponizes" masculinity, see Kurtzleben, "Trump Has Weaponized Masculinity as President"; Pauly, "The War on Masks Is a Cover-Up." For an interactive map on how COVID-19 affects BIPOC communities, see Oppel et al., "The Fullest Look Yet at the Racial Inequity of Coronavirus."

21.   See Shear, "Biden Pushes Deterrent Border Policy," for a report on how Biden used Title 42 to prevent the entry of Haitians to the United States.

22.   For the 2021 footage of the Texas Rangers chasing Haitian migrants and an overview of the outrage at Biden's continuation of Trump's inhumane approach, see Sullivan and Kanno-Youngs, "Images of Border Patrol's Treatment of Haitian Migrants."

23.   Davis et al., *Abolition. Feminism. Now*, 13.

24.   Abolition Collective, *Making Abolitionist Worlds*, 9 (qtd); Davis et al., *Abolition. Feminism. Now*, x.

25.   Gilmore, *Abolition Geography*, 474.

26.   Kaba and Ritchie, *No More Police*, 28.

27.   Kaba and Ritchie, 43; Shull, *Detention Empire*, 4.

28.   Davis et al., *Abolition. Feminism. Now*, 51; Abolition Collective, *Making Abolitionist Worlds*, 3.

29.   Ben-Moshe, *Decarcerating Disability*, 116; Kaba, *We Do This 'Til We Free Us*, 2.

30.   Cullors, *An Abolitionist's Handbook*, 8.

31.   Ybarra, "Site Fight!," 39.

BIBLIOGRAPHY

AAPF (African American Policy Forum). "Welcome to the #TruthBeTold Campaign." Accessed May 10, 2023. https://www.aapf.org/truthbetold.

Abolition Collective. *Making Abolitionist Worlds: Proposals for a World on Fire*. New York: Common Notions, 2020.

ADL (Anti-Defamation League). "Deplatform Tucker Carlson and the 'Great Replacement' Theory." May 24, 2022. https://www.adl.org/resources/blog/deplatform-tucker-carlson-and-great-replacement-theory.

Alvarado, Karina Oliva, Alicia Ivonne Estrada, and Ester E. Hernández, eds. *U.S. Central Americans: Reconstructing Memories, Struggles, and Communities of Resistance*. Tucson: University of Arizona Press, 2017.

Andreas, Peter. *Border Games: Policing the U.S.-Mexico Divide*. 2nd ed. Ithaca, N.Y.: Cornell University Press, 2009.

Anglesey, Anders. "Paul Gosar Doubles Down on Cartoon Showing AOC Being Killed: 'Nothing Hateful.'" *Newsweek*, November 15, 2021.

Ben-Moshe, Liat. *Decarcerating Disability: Deinstitutionalization and Prison Abolition*. Minneapolis: University of Minnesota Press, 2020.

Cacho, Lisa Marie. *Social Death: Racialized Rightlessness and the Criminalization of the Unprotected*. New York: New York University Press, 2012.

Chacón, Justin Akers, and Mike Davis. *No One Is Illegal: Fighting Racism and State Violence on the U.S.-Mexico Border*. Chicago: Haymarket Books, 2006.

Chávez, Karma R. *Queer Migration Politics: Activist Rhetoric and Coalitional Possibilities*. Urbana: University of Illinois Press, 2017.

Chavez, Leo R. *The Latino Threat: Constructing Immigrants, Citizens, and the Nation*. Stanford, Calif.: Stanford University Press, 2008.

Chishti, Muzaffar, Sarah Pierce, and Jessica Bolter. "The Obama Record on Deportations: Deporter in Chief or Not?" *Migration Information Source*, January 26, 2017. https://www.migrationpolicy.org/article/obama-record-deportations-deporter-chief-or-not.

Comrie, Nazmia E. A. "Combating Hate Crimes Against Asian American and Pacific Islander Communities." *Community Policing Dispatch* 14, no. 4 (2021). https://cops.usdoj.gov/html/dispatch/04-2021/asian_hate_crimes.html.

Cortez, David. "I Asked Latinos Why They Joined Immigration Law Enforcement. Now I'm Urging Them to Leave." *USA Today*, July 3, 2019.

Cullors, Patrisse. *An Abolitionist's Handbook: 12 Steps to Changing Yourself and the World*. New York: St. Martin's Press, 2021.

Da Silva, Chantal. "Who Was Roxsana Hernandez? Transgender Woman Who Died in ICE Custody Was Beaten Before Death." *Newsweek*, November 28, 2018.

Davis, Angela Y., Gina Dent, Erica R. Meiners, and Beth E. Richie. *Abolition. Feminism. Now*. Chicago: Haymarket Books, 2022.

Escobar, Martha D. *Captivity Beyond Prisons: Criminalization Experiences of Latina (Im)Migrants*. Austin: University of Texas Press, 2016.

Fleig, Shelby. "The 5 Deadliest Hurricanes in American History Now Include Hurricane Maria—with New Death Toll." *USA Today*, May 29, 2018.

Gambino, Lauren. "Donald Trump Attacked for Calling Hurricane Maria Response an 'Incredible Success.'" *Guardian*, September 12, 2018.

García Hernández, César Cuauhtémoc. *Migrating to Prison: America's Obsession with Locking Up Immigrants*. New York: New Press, 2019.

Giaritelli, Anna. "Exclusive: Inside Border Patrol's Struggle to Promote Hispanic Agents." *Washington Examiner*, June 2, 2021.

Gilmore, Ruth Wilson. *Abolition Geography: Essays Toward Liberation*. New York: Verso Books, 2022.

Gonzales, Alfonso. *Reform Without Justice: Latino Migrant Politics and the Homeland Security State*. Oxford: Oxford University Press, 2013.

Hernández, Kelly Lytle. *City of Inmates: Conquest, Rebellion, and the Rise of Human Caging in Los Angeles, 1771–1965*. Chapel Hill: University of North Carolina Press, 2017.

Hernández, Kelly Lytle. *Migra! A History of the U.S. Border Patrol*. Berkeley: University of California Press, 2010.

Hernández, Roberto D. *Coloniality of the US/Mexico Border: Power, Violence, and the Decolonial Imperative*. Tucson: University of Arizona Press, 2018.

Herrera, Jack. "Why Are Trans Women Dying in ICE Detention?" *Pacific Standard*, June 4, 2019. https://psmag.com/social-justice/why-are-trans-women-dying-in -ice-detention.

Ho, Jennifer. "White Supremacy Is the Root of All Race-Related Violence in the US." *Conversation*, April 8, 2021. https://theconversation.com/white-supremacy-is-the -root-of-all-race-related-violence-in-the-us-157566.

Kaba, Mariame. *We Do This 'Til We Free Us: Abolitionist Organizing and Transforming Justice*. Chicago: Haymarket Books, 2021.

Kaba, Mariame, and Andrea J. Ritchie. *No More Police: A Case for Abolition*. New York: New Press, 2022.

Kang, S. Deborah. *The INS on the Line: Making Immigration Law on the US-Mexico Border, 1917–1954*. Oxford: Oxford University Press, 2017.

Krishnakumar, Priya. "This Record-Breaking Year for Anti-Transgender Legislation Would Affect Minors the Most." *CNN*, April 15, 2021. https://edition.cnn.com/ 2021/04/15/politics/anti-transgender-legislation-2021/index.html.

Kurtzleben, Danielle. "Trump Has Weaponized Masculinity as President. Here's Why It Matters." *Weekend Edition Saturday*. NPR, October 28, 2020. https://www.npr .org/2020/10/28/928336749/trump-has-weaponized-masculinity-as-president -heres-why-it-matters.

Lindskoog, Carl. *Detain and Punish: Haitian Refugees and the Rise of the World's Largest Immigration Detention System*. Gainesville: University of Florida Press, 2018.

Luibhéid, Eithne, and Karma R. Chávez, eds. *Queer and Trans Migrations: Dynamics of Illegalization, Detention, and Deportation*. Urbana: University of Illinois Press, 2020.

Magaña, Lisa. *Straddling the Border: Immigration Policy and the INS*. Austin: University of Texas Press, 2003.

MALDEF (Mexican American Legal Defense and Educational Fund). "Trump Administration Sued over Intentional Cruelty at Georgia Immigration Detention Center." News release, December 11, 2020. https://www.maldef.org/2020/

12/trump-administration-sued-over-intentional-cruelty-at-georgia-immigration
-detention-center/.

Martinez, Monica Muñoz. *The Injustice Never Leaves You: Anti-Mexican Violence in Texas*. Cambridge, Mass.: Harvard University Press, 2018.

Nevins, Joseph. *Operation Gatekeeper and Beyond: The War on "Illegals" and the Remaking of the U.S.-Mexico Boundary*. 2nd ed. New York: Routledge, 2010.

New York Times. "Supreme Court Rules on Abortion: Thousands Protest End of Constitutional Right to Abortion." June 24, 2022.

Oppel, Richard A., Jr., Robert Gebeloff, K. K. Rebecca Lai, Will Wright, and Mitch Smith. "The Fullest Look Yet at the Racial Inequity of Coronavirus." *New York Times*, July 5, 2020.

Ordaz, Jessica. *The Shadow of El Centro: A History of Migrant Incarceration and Solidarity*. Chapel Hill: University of North Carolina Press, 2021.

Patiño, Jimmy. *Raza Sí, Migra No: Chicano Movement Struggles for Immigrant Rights in San Diego*. Chapel Hill: University of North Carolina Press, 2017.

Pauly, Madison. "The War on Masks Is a Cover-Up for Toxic Masculinity." *Mother Jones*, October 8, 2020. https://www.motherjones.com/coronavirus-updates/2020/10/trump-masks-covid-toxic-masculinity.

Reeve, Elle. "How White 'Replacement Theory' Evolved from Elderly Racists to Teens Online to the Alleged Inspiration for Another Racist Mass Homicide." *CNN*, May 21, 2022. https://www.cnn.com/2022/05/20/us/replacement-theory-white-supremacist-buffalo-shooter/index.html.

Shear, Michael D., Natalie Kitroeff, Zolan Kanno-Youngs, and Eileen Sullivan. "Biden Pushes Deterrent Border Policy After Promising 'Humane' Approach." *New York Times*, September 22, 2021.

Shull, Tina (Kristina). *Detention Empire: Reagan's War on Immigrants and the Seeds of Resistance*. Chapel Hill: University of North Carolina Press, 2022.

Speed, Shannon. *Incarcerated Stories: Indigenous Women Migrants and Violence in the Settler-Capitalist State*. Chapel Hill: University of North Carolina Press, 2019.

SPLC (Southern Poverty Law Center). "Family Separation—A Timeline." Updated March 23, 2022. https://www.splcenter.org/news/2022/03/23/family-separation-timeline.

Sullivan, Eileen, and Zolan Kanno-Youngs. "Images of Border Patrol's Treatment of Haitian Migrants Prompt Outrage." *New York Times*, September 21, 2021.

Thomas, Ginger. "Listen to Children Who've Just Been Separated from Their Parents at the Border." *ProPublica*, June 18, 2018. https://www.propublica.org/article/children-separated-from-parents-border-patrol-cbp-trump-immigration-policy.

U.S. House of Representatives, Committee on the Judiciary. *The Trump Administration's Family Separation Policy: Trauma, Destruction, and Chaos*. Majority staff report, prepared for Jerrold Nadler. October 2020.

Villanueva, Nicholas, Jr. *The Lynching of Mexicans in the Texas Borderlands*. Albuquerque: University of New Mexico Press, 2017.

Ybarra, Megan. "Site Fight! Toward the Abolition of Immigration Detention on Tacoma's Tar Pits (and Everywhere Else)." *Antipode* 53, no. 1 (2021): 36–55.

Young, Elliott. *Forever Prisoners: How the United States Made the World's Largest Immigrant Detention System.* Oxford: Oxford University Press, 2021.

PART I

XENOPHOBIA, ABJECTION, AND STATE VIOLENCE

PART I

XENOPHOBIA, ABJECTION, AND STATE VIOLENCE

1

"THEY'RE BRINGING DRUGS!"

Reflections on Movement and Migration, the War on Drugs, and the Opioid Crisis in Trump's America

REBECCA AVALOS

When Mexico sends its people, they're not sending their best. They're not sending you. They're not sending you. They're sending people that have lots of problems, and they're bringing those problems with us. They're bringing drugs.
—DONALD J. TRUMP, REMARKS ANNOUNCING CANDIDACY FOR PRESIDENT, JUNE 16, 2015

ENGAGING IN THE AMERICAN TRADITION of condemning foreign racial Others for U.S.-made disasters, the Trump administration animated the archetype of migrant as drug dealer to inflame a culture of Mexican and Latinx xenophobia, expand the legal infrastructure upholding this culture, and, at the same time, avoid tackling a U.S.-made Big Pharma public health catastrophe. In the United States, the constituted spaces, sites, and pathways of neoliberal medicine hide under the normative banality of everyday use, disguised in its ordinary. Innocent due to this ordinary nature, the American underground-yet-aboveground drug economies of opioid painkillers reap capitalist, moral, and innocence-granting benefits by servicing a predominantly white market, an extension of whiteness's service to itself.[1] In their doing so, a racial capitalist cycle continues: whiteness protects what structures white—and Black and Brown—death into being. Yet the dominant narrative of opioid drug addiction in the Trump administration's war on drugs omits American Big Pharma as a central factor. American painkillers have a long medicinal history of (re)legalization, bans, regulations, free market growth, pseudoscience amplification, racial scapegoating, and billions of dollars of profit, to name a few discursive variables. Yet rarely is a racial capitalist critique observed when viewing the ways in which the conjunction of capital and whiteness engage in cannibalism, consumption of an/other, or massive public health corruption. Rather than investigate the ways in which power—animated through the entanglement of American Big Pharma, neoliberal medicine, and whiteness—created our contemporary fluctuation of an opioid crisis, the Trump administration engendered the archetype of migrant as drug dealer to reanimate anti-Latinx sentiment and target Latinx immigration, broadly. In the case study of our contemporary American opioid crisis, assumptions of what moves and migrates within the interior of the country remain undiscussed. The narrative of drugs and addiction continues to center on migrants, in Mexico, at the southern border. At the same time, the United States' internal neoliberal spaces, sites, and pathways of medicine—as well as their origin and movement—remain cloaked in a normative guise of harmlessness and an organic, natural stasis, hiding in their everyday legality.

Central to this project is this: power marks what is to be read and recognized as movement, migration, and that of the underground, what is beneath and what is above, just as power distinguishes what is to be legalized and what is to be illegal. The migrant as drug dealer figure is rhetorically animated as the moving subject/object. American neoliberal medicine is part of the ordinary background, framed as not moving, recognized as a necessary part of everyday life, and so neoliberal medicine is therefore not readily ascribed with criminality or viewed suspect as a possible criminal drug enterprise.[2] The Latinx migrant as drug dealer figure is animated into existence, rhetorically produced as moving, trespassing, and polluting, while American neoliberal medicine, as a meta-organization, maintains refuge under a false stasis, appearing neutral, value free, and law abiding. In centering the migrant as drug dealer figure, coming from the outside in, discourses of migrantness, Brownness, and drugs entangle and come to locate the notion of drugs as native only to external places; matters of drugs stem from, thus, the exterior of the United States, residing outside or on the border. Racializing and reductionist, these same discourses simultaneously construct the white interior spaces of the United States as innocent, crimeless and drugless while also justified and protected by discourses of legality to participate within drug economies. This is the political and rhetorical work of the matterings of drug discourse, racism, and power's ability to demark the punishable and the unpunishable, and the ontological assumptions of what exists and moves on the Brown outside and what cannot possibly be labored, produced, and reside in the white interior. Drugs and drug economies are racialized. Reflecting on these very ideas, this project seeks to understand the ways in which migration and movement are registered ideologically. I ask: What is the (mis)recognition of movement foretelling of power? What is assumed to organically exist in a state of innocence and nonmovement?

A CIVIL WAR REARTICULATED

By the end of the 1990s, U.S.-based pharmaceutical companies successfully lobbied to create a medical consensus that patients, under a patient-first banner in a predominantly white market, could not become addicted to prescription opioid pain relievers. Pharmaceutical giants like Purdue Pharma flourished in an economic culture of neoliberalism aided by American politicians who were willing to look the other way or were willfully ignorant to matters of how addiction and whiteness may converge and continuously hide.[3] In the same decade, hypermilitarized police—armed with tanks, SWAT teams, and high-grade arsenals— swept across the nation in predominantly African American and Latinx neighborhoods, hypercriminalizing such communities under a materialized, beyond metaphor, war on drugs.[4] Established in the Reagan era, such law-and-order and tough-on-crime legal doctrines flourished within the Bush and Clinton administrations of the late 1980s and 1990s, cementing a legalized surveillance matrix composed of federal, state, and local infrastructure, which upheld a racial order of whiteness as innocent and racialized Other as criminal.[5] Racializing drug criminality almost exclusively to Black and Brown communities while simultaneously legalizing white drug usage of opioids as proper medicinal practice despite subsequent addiction, assumptions of race and white privilege reproduced a common sense of drug use and addiction—drug use racialized through white bodies as legal and drug assemblages racialized through the body of nonwhite racial Others as illegal. The time period of the 1990s encompassed two contrived American drug economies: one fueled by the U.S.-Mexico border and another existing through legalized innocent, static, medical opioids. For example, in the late 1990s and early 2000s, when heroin overdose mortality surged in the Black community, zero national outcry resulted outside of the Black community—and there was no restorative or public health agenda. Instead, medical, government, and public agencies labeled victims "superpredators" and "crack babies."[6] Heroin addiction within the Black community was not met with a frame of crisis or compassion; it was configured as a war necessitating combat.

These dominant stories—of external origin on the one hand and legal, inconspicuous circulation on the other—have a substantial and detrimental impact on incarceration rates and articulations of racialized citizenship post-incarceration.[7] From President Ronald Reagan's war on drugs to the contemporary moment, the United States continues to sanction the structured flow of Black and Latinx peoples into the U.S. prison and deportation system.[8] Such restructuring, as noted by criminology scholar Michelle Alexander, helps explain why so many in the Black community are barred from voting—a constitutional right—and why, consequently, so many Black and Brown people have been placed in a position of liminal and abject citizenship.[9] The American drug wars have had a transformative, lifelong, and generational impact, resulting in the uprooting of entire communities, magnification of disparities, intergenerational trauma, and broad structural racial and class implications.[10] All of this is to say that the social decade of the 1990s significantly shaped how the criminalization of drugs, drug usage, and drug economies operate today.

Another tale of drugs centers on the invisiblized and dominant—and kept invisible through its dominance—structure of the medical drug and drug distribution system in the United States. With its wares distributed across the United States in "respectable" neighborhood corners where local Walgreens or CVS stores can be found, American Big Pharma has not been met with the same scrutiny. I point this out not to argue in favor of further criminalization but to highlight the differences in the racialization of drugs and drug use. Under the Trump administration, opioid addiction was framed through the lens of a national health crisis, one that necessitates government intervention through compassionate policy change and criminal reform. The Trump administration's intervention in matters of primarily white public drug addiction contrasts with the hypercriminalized and insensitive legal approach to drug use among racialized communities. Such differences in discourses, approaches, and policies capture the differentiating axiologies of how raced bodies are (to be) valued. Particularly affecting a middle-aged, white male population, the contemporary opioid crisis has been (more than) thirty years in the making: originating in the 1990s, but having a lineage that extends back to the 1971 declaration of the domestic war on drugs.[11]

THE ORIGIN, MOVEMENT, AND ASSUMED INNOCENCE OF AMERICA'S CONTEMPORARY OPIOID ADDICTION

While some scholars disagree on the origin of the modern American opioid epidemic, influential variables for the conditions of opioid abuse and opioid addiction are multifactorial, far reaching, and challenging to reverse. In the 1990s, with the support of doctors, patient-centered pain advocacy groups (which believed that decision-making should not privilege the default authority of a medical professional's judgment) and lobbyists working on behalf of major American pharmaceutical companies pushed for the prescription of opioids to no longer be restricted solely to the treatment of acute pain or terminal conditions such as cancer. As a result, the circulation of medical opioids drastically increased, and the new prescription normal was centered on the patient's perception of pain.[12] The altering of normative prescription practice allowed for broad distribution of medical opioids to patients, the majority of which were white, middle class, insured, and assumed to be law-abiding, respectable citizens. Patient-first advocacy, minimal government regulation, and broad drug dissemination practices introduced a new prescription standard in the legalized drug market of pain relievers. America's brand of medicinal neoliberalism flourished. No longer were opioids dispensed based on a medical doctor's professional evaluation of a patient's established medical condition or restricted to patients who had undergone major surgical procedures. Instead, a new prescription normal was ushered in, one that was backed by the presumed innocence and demand of a predominant white drug user market. Promoting false information, a scientific letter printed in the *New England Journal of Medicine* in 1980 titled "Addiction Rare in Patients Treated with Narcotics" described medically dispensed opioids as unlikely to lead to any addiction.[13] In addition, at this particular juncture, a never-before-seen aggressive marketing campaign originating from Arthur Sackler, cofounder of Purdue Pharma, radicalized the painkiller drug market; Sackler employed an alchemical approach in marketing, enticing surgeons and medical doctors with all-expenses-paid conferences and showcasing Sackler-backed scientific studies. This method of targeted cyclical marketing—disseminating questionable reports like that in the *New England Journal of Medicine* to doctors, and incorporating doctors into the drug infrastructure to then convince and snowball additional medical doctors—is what paved the way for a sweeping success, the promotion and wide distribution of OxyContin, a falsely alleged twelve-hour-release form of oxycodone, a medicalized and legalized highly addictive opioid.[14]

As scientific disinformation, nongovernmental oversight, patient-first advocacy, and aggressive marketing shaped the legalized American white drug market, opioid prescription increased and led to large-scale dependence. As argued by medical professionals, the American opioid crisis is a public health self-inflicted wound; for Nalini Vadivelu and colleagues, the opioid crisis is "the most profound public health crisis our nation has faced."[15] For perspective, in the year 2015, an approximate 240 million opioid prescriptions were dispensed in the United States; this equates to "nearly one for every adult in the general population."[16] Moreover, this figure becomes gravely alarming, as Irfan A. Dhalla and colleagues report that "the burgeoning use of opioids has been accompanied by a steep increase in opioid related mortality."[17] As Rose A. Rudd and colleagues track, trends within public health have shown an increase in opioid-related mortality; for instance, drug overdose deaths nearly tripled from 1999 to 2014.[18] According to the 2017 federal report *The President's Commission on Combating Drug Addiction and the Opioid Crisis*, there are "more than 175 lives lost every day" to the medical opioid epidemic, totaling an estimated 64,000 people per year.[19] As federal attempts at abuse-deterrent opioid formulations and restrictive prescribing have taken effect over recent years, severely restricting opioid prescription practices and broad distribution, underground drug market forces have responded to the increased drug demands. Contrary to their intended effect, restrictive prescribing measures have thickened the connection between opioid use and drug overdoses. For instance, as stated in the 2017 federal report on drugs, the illegal underground markets of heroin and most recently fentanyl have led to an increase in drug overdoses in the wake of legalized opioid restrictions, meaning that underground drug economies have met the massive opioid drug demands created initially by U.S.-based legal medicine. As of late, while there has been a small drop in drug use of medically prescribed opioids, the overall number of opioid-related deaths has not decreased.[20]

Centering a public mental health perspective, Christine E. Grella and colleagues note that more than half of individuals with an opioid use disorder (OUD) meet the DSM criteria for major depressive disorder.[21] Additionally, evidence from Theodore J. Cicero and Matthew S. Ellis indicates that the majority of OUD individuals seeking treatment report that they use opioids to self-medicate for psychological distress.[22] As argued by A. Benjamin Srivastava and Mark S. Gold, the opioid epidemic is largely a matter of diagnosing and treating psychological affective states and other depressive symptoms.[23] Anne Case and Angus Deaton find, similarly, that the multifactorial and multiconsequential opioid epidemic is undergirded by "diseases of despair."[24]

Nevertheless, no critical deconstruction of the modern-day opioid crisis can omit the structural and historical factors of capitalism and racial capitalism. Functioning through the country's medical industry, neoliberalism—that is, structural inequality, wealth disparity, and worsening unemployment and poverty rates—has resulted in compounded disadvantages for certain communities and an ever-increasing inability to survive. Continuing a drug war logic of transplanting culpability onto racialized and noncitizen subjects, the Trump administration identified migration and migrants as its targets.

THE TRUMP ADMINISTRATION AND THE ARCHETYPE OF MIGRANT AS DRUG DEALER

On January 25, 2017, five days after being sworn in as the forty-fifth president of the United States, Donald J. Trump announced two executive orders: "Enhancing Public Safety in the Interior of the United States" and "Border Security and Immigration Enforcement Improvements."[25] "Enhancing Public Safety," executive order 13768, was self-described as ensuring the enforcement of the nation's immigration laws so as to in turn ensure "national security and public safety of the United States."

Specifically, the order calls for: (1) civil fines and penalties to those "who facilitate migrants' presence in the United States," (2) the hiring of an additional ten thousand immigration officers, (3) added federal pressure on sanctuary jurisdictions to comply with federal immigration law, (4) federal-state agreements that would "empower State and local law enforcement agencies across the country to perform the functions of an immigration officer," and (5) the creation of the Office for Victims of Crimes Committed by Removable Aliens. This office, which was later renamed as the Office of Victims of Immigration Crime Engagement (VOICE), existed between February 2017 and June 2021 within U.S. Immigration and Customs Enforcement (ICE). It aimed "to provide proactive, timely, adequate, and professional services to victims of crimes committed by removable aliens and the family members of such victims [and to] provide quarterly reports studying the effects of the victimization by criminal aliens present in the United States."[26] One major project of VOICE was to produce quarterly reports—both quantitative and qualitative data, estimations, and projections—of immigrant criminality, broadly speaking. In collaboration with VOICE, the Trump administration engaged in published and publicized panel discussions on a variety of topics, including the opioid crisis.

"Border Security and Immigration Enforcement Improvements," executive order 13767, was self-described as a legal maneuver to ensure the safety and territorial integrity of the United States by targeting "those who illegally enter . . . [and] seek to harm Americans through acts of terror or criminal conduct" and who are coming from "the recent surge of illegal immigration at the southern border with Mexico." The order's stated justification is that "transnational criminal organizations operate sophisticated drug networks . . . contributing to a significant increase in violent crime and United States deaths from dangerous drugs." For these reasons, the order warrants, "continued illegal immigration presents a clear and present danger to the interests of the United States." The legal architecture of executive order 13767 granted to the executive branch the power to rewrite immigrant law and human rights law in order to (1) "secure the southern border of the United States through the immediate construction of a physical wall on the southern border," (2) immediately construct detention centers to "detain aliens at or near the land border with Mexico," and (3) "issue new policy guidance . . . [on] lawful detention authority under the [Immigration and Nationality Act], including the termination of the practice commonly known as 'catch and release,' whereby aliens are routinely released in the United States shortly after their apprehension for violations of immigration law."[27] Taken together, these two executive orders parallel Donald J. Trump's claim in his first presidential candidate speech that "when Mexico sends its people . . . they're bringing drugs."[28] The Trump administration's legal constructionism followed historical precedent, engaging in the long American tradition of condemning "foreign racial Others" for American-made disasters.

MANUFACTURING TRUTH

Distortion and intentional reconstruction of data are one way, out of the many possible, to manufacture truth. In our post-truth era, there is an understanding that truth claims are a political matter. In political realms, or social for that matter, truth is largely a byproduct of power relations, power structures, and power's materialization through history; power gives shape to what is truth.[29] In mapping the Trump administration's racial discourse that frames the figure of the migrant as drug dealer as the sole cause for America's opioid addiction, one can view a clear example of how power naturalizes and normalizes a discursive meaning structure in the realm of truthfulness. Data is constructed and remade to justify criminalization and exclusion. Such manufacturing of truth must be deconstructed and analyzed. Critical scholarship must map out discourse as data that can materialize in our future.

The Trump administration engaged in the craftwork of discursive reassembling and intentional scaffolding to entangle and scapegoat racial otherness and drugs while at the same time safeguarding whiteness. In our post-truth condition, marked more now than ever by our postmodern realities of social life, data is constructed preemptively to lead the way for legal rematrixing. Paying attention to what is animated, by whom, and for what purposes matters. To make sense of what counts as migration or movement, or what is to be registered as interior or exterior, is of tremendous significance. How matter is rendered legible and how matter is obscured are an expression of political power and indication of ideological design. White drug use and white-serving drug economies were and are widely rendered as something ontologically nonexistent yet also a crisis that necessitates governmental compassion and a massive budget, whereas racialized drug economies are made hyperreal, publicized and meditated with no resolution other than to incarcerate and dehumanize. This is how power works to manufacture truth.

REMARKS AT A LISTENING SESSION ON OPIOIDS AND DRUG ABUSE

Mexican and Central American migrants are scapegoated as the leading cause and actors of opioid mortalities in the United States. As demonstrated by a March 29, 2017, White House listening session on opioids and drug abuse, the Trump administration rhetorically entangled and (re)assembled the figure of the Mexican migrant as drug dealer and the geolocation of social death at the U.S.-Mexico border with opioid criminality. Contriving an image of the opioid crisis as endemic due to the very nature of Mexican migrants, migration, and the border itself, the web of racializing discourse creates the conditions needed to further rationalize the weaponization of legal coding against migrants, refugees, and those rendered abject in Trump's aforementioned executive orders. Speaking at the listening session, the president stated:

> During my campaign, I promised to take action to keep drugs from pouring into our country. And I want to just thank Secretary Kelly; he's done an amazing job. Down 61 percent at the border right now in terms of people, and the drugs that are being stopped. It will take longer, and there's great cooperation with Mexico and others. But we're doing a good job. And we want to help those who have become so badly addicted. Drug abuse has become a crippling problem throughout the United States. Drug overdoses are now the leading cause of accidental death in our country. And opioid overdose deaths have nearly quadrupled since 1999. This is a total epidemic, and I think it's probably almost untalked about compared to the severity that we're witnessing. We want to battle drug addiction and combat opioids, and we have to do it—the crisis.[30]

At the beginning of Trump's oratory, he addresses the subject of America's opioid crisis and associates it with one premise: migration from the southern border. From there, the discourse of migration is discussed as if it correlates to the second verbalized premise, that of the opioid crisis. This intentional conflation of topics—migration from Mexico and the American opioid crisis—causes criminality to stick onto race through tricky (tricking) rhetorical language. Folding together ideas and linking them without explanation of causality—that is, simply attaching ideas together by speaking about them concurrently, without logical attachment or rationale—is one way in which misinformation or the production of truth-like statements occurs within everyday political talk. A poignant exchange revealing how Mexican migration and the U.S.-Mexico border are assembled as already criminal occurred during the listening session:

THE PRESIDENT: Thank you very much . . . you can tell a little bit of your story and how it's turned out so beautifully. We're so proud of you.

TESTIMONY 1: After I left college, I had an injury and was prescribed pain killers, and so quickly, it took off from there. I didn't know anything about heroin. I was never warned, not that it's anybody else's fault.

THE PRESIDENT: So, this all began very innocently with an injury?

TESTIMONY: Absolutely, yes, with a prescription of pain killers.

THE PRESIDENT: And what was it? What was the drug they gave?

TESTIMONY 1: Percocet.

THE PRESIDENT: I see, [Name omitted]. And then, from Percocet, it went to oxy. And then from oxy, it went to heroin, because it is definitely like you said, more accessible and so much cheaper.

Second testimony enters.

TESTIMONY 2: I was a good student. I was an athlete. I found alcohol and other drugs . . . but then I found OxyContin. My dad got in an accident, and I decided that it would be a good idea to try it. And that's really where my story started. You know, now—

THE PRESIDENT: Were you immediately hooked? Because I hear so much about OxyContin. Were you immediately hooked?

TESTIMONY 2: Yes. When I did my first one, I remember doing it and thinking, this is how I want to live the rest of my life. I was always searching for something outside of myself that would make me feel better. People think the drug is the problem, and to some extent, its accessibility is. But addiction is a disease that I always had, and it just had to be unlocked. And that's what I feel OxyContin did for me.[31]

With testimony 1, which frames opioid use as beginning due to an external circumstance of bad luck like an injury, Trump's rhetoric posits a noncriminalizing, compassionate, and understanding tone, approaching the testimony as an innocent (seemingly accidental, mistaken, and happenstance) journey into opioids, a mediated frame commonly found within the conjunction of whiteness and drug use.[32] In contrast, a nonwhite racialized narrative of drug use often details a very different ascription of events and agency, shifting blame onto the individual, an agential actor as opposed to structural forces or bad luck. A racialized narrative of drug use frames a pleasure-seeking and/or malicious subject that deserves no compassion given their intentional entry into the drug world, while a "white good citizen" narrative of opioid drug addiction is met with a nonjudgmental orientation and is viewed as blameless, merciful, and even heroic, as when Trump describes how testimony 1 has "turned out so beautifully."

In Trump's engagement with the testimonies presented, his rhetoric centers on his ample curiosity as he asks direct questions about opioid drugs: who distributed them and what was distributed. Both testimony 1 and testimony 2 directly signal to Big Pharma—Percocet and OxyContin. In the first testimony, their opioid drug addiction origin is, in their telling, best captured by viewing them as a subject pulled into the neoliberal space of medicine via a legal medical prescription. The latter, who took medication that was prescribed for their father, likewise emphasizes that their serious opioid addiction began by consuming legalized opioids. There is a sense, though unstated, that this person may have had some prior knowledge of the psychoactive qualities of OxyContin, hence the statement that "I found alcohol and other drugs . . . but then I found OxyContin . . . and I decided that it would be a good idea to try it." Both panel participants signal their acknowledgment of medically prescribed opioids as addictive substances and as their origins in opioid addiction.

As the listening session continued, Trump began to question when opioid mortalities and addiction began to rise within the United States, prompting both attorney general Jeff Sessions and acting administrator of the Drug Enforcement Administration (DEA) Chuck Rosenberg to respond:

THE PRESIDENT: When did this [opioid crisis] start again? It's so bad. When did it start, would you say—over the last how many years—where it really took the big spike up?

ATTORNEY GENERAL SESSIONS: I think the fentanyl brought the—noticed here—Chuck, maybe—the DEA Director Chuck Rosenberg—

THE PRESIDENT: You would know that. When do you think it really started spiking up, Chuck?

ACTING DIRECTOR ROSENBERG: Mr. President, there have been spikes in the past. We've seen spikes in '05, '06, and '07. I'd say in the last 8 to 10 years, though, the trajectory has been awful. And there's a number of pieces to it. One is that we consume, as Americans, most of the world's supply of hydrocodone and oxycodone [medically prescribed opioids]. And as these good folks have attested to, once you get hooked on that, heroin is cheaper and more plentiful. And folks just make that transition. . . .

THE PRESIDENT: So [opioid addiction has] been really spiked over the last 8 to 10 years. Would that have anything to do with the weakening of the borders? Because a lot of it comes from the southern border.[33]

Asking a question only to end where he wishes to end, regardless of feedback or quality of evidence in response, Trump begins this section of the session by probing: "When did this [opioid crisis] start again?" Responding to this question, Rosenberg states that there has been not one rise in opioid addiction in the United States but multiple over time, most recently in 2005, 2006, and 2007, gesturing to the not-new quality of opioid drug addiction and mortality. Moreover, stating that although the root causes for opioid addiction are multiple, Rosenberg begins to address the larger question of why an opioid addiction crisis exists in the United States by asserting that "we consume, as Americans, most of the world's supply of hydrocodone and oxycodone."[34] In this response, what Rosenberg does not directly state or allude to is Big Pharma's responsibility, the United States' lack of governmental regulation and drug oversight, or the propagating of a culture and market of neoliberalized medicine to make a profit. The choice to be willfully ignorant, to selectively target and shelter medical neoliberalism by the American government remains unacknowledged—and perhaps acknowledgeable only to whiteness—because whiteness is presumed innocent, nonagential, and nonseeking in matters of drug use. Thus, the statement "we consume, as Americans, most of the world's supply of hydrocodone and oxycodone" is delivered with a matter-of-fact, uncritical tone. Rosenberg does not name the neoliberal medical industry or factors that have led to Americans' consumption of so much hydrocodone and oxycodone, and thus he normativizes neoliberal medicine through silence and omission, strategies of whiteness.

Omitting key variables that have led to our contemporary opioid crisis, Rosenberg continues, reiterates, and strengthens the narrative of a good citizen: "And as these good folks have attested to." The good white citizen narrative shifts attention from the frame of an agential subject to external circumstances, bad luck, or the probability of chance. In the good white citizen tale of drug use, one falls into drugs—as opposed to an agent-focused racialized narrative of criminality, wherein a nonwhite racial criminal pursues opioids based on personal choice, desire, or expression of self-agency. Rosenberg continues: "once you get hooked on that [hydrocodone and oxycodone or prescribed opioids], heroin is cheaper and more plentiful. And folks just make that transition." Describing the ways in which good citizens "just" transition from medical opioid use to heroin as understandable, commonsense, and even rational, Rosenberg does not speak to what a priori structures pipeline Americans into underground opioid ecologies. To put it plainly: the United States' opioid public health crisis, which affects a largely white population, is rooted in actions by American Big Pharma, aided by a government obsessed with imprisoning Black and Brown communities while simultaneously protecting—through ignoring—a legalized white drug market. The rhetoric Rosenberg echoes, from his position as a leading government official and representative, is that of racial and neoliberal ignorance. Finally, Rosenberg centers the now normalized and justified effect of medical opioid addiction: "And folks just make that transition."[35]

The origins of neoliberal medicine and whiteness remain undiscussed in matters of what moves and migrates. Capital's role in medicine and racist and racializing policing remain disguised as normative and harmless societal practices of everyday life. Given such suppositions, this project questions the assumed rhetoricity of movement and animation of the American opioid crisis. Of particular interest is the question of what is ontologically animated as moving, trespassing, and polluting: what hides in a false state of stasis, appearing neutral, value free, and law abiding? The mattering of drugs, crime, and regressive morality is discursively figured as existing outside U.S. borders by dominant U.S. culture. This project therefore investigates what is assumed about the pathways of movement and circulation of neoliberal medicine and whiteness. The sense-making, tracking, and surveilling of movement are themselves political and discursive. What is registered as migratory and how such migration is described as ontological can also be fabricated. American opioid addiction is American made, strengthened by pipelines of poverty, trauma, economic impossibility, a mental health public need, and racial capitalism.

The psychological effects and affects of poverty, the ever-shrinking possibility of living a life on minimum wage, the growing gap between the rich and poor, and the near impossibility of a debt-free life in the United States today are some ways in which neoliberalism organizes and structures social (dis)order. Depression and sicknesses of sadness caused by capital are structured into American life. The effects and movements of neoliberalization are everywhere, within legalized medicinal ecologies, constituting our many social spaces. The sheltering of whiteness and whiteness's ability to shelter medical opioid markets through legalization safeguard and (re)produce opioid drug addiction. At the same time, nonwhite racialized subjects and the archetype of the migrant as drug dealer remain saturated with condemnation for a war that cannot ever end. The Trump administration projected criminality onto external or foreign Others while preserving the movements of capital and whiteness. Within the (rarely recognized) world of neoliberal medicine, U.S. politicians do very little to intervene in neoliberal medicine's structuration of pathologies; they are coconspirators of massive public disinformation and are active collaborators in the making of public disasters.[36] These are the moves of power, almost never registered as moving at all: feigning innocence, hiding in the ordinary, conspiring internally, and scapegoating the all-too-perfect figure of the migrant as drug dealer, an already constructed rhetorical figure. Without the structural recognition of racial capitalism and the feelings of alienation produced within American society, matters of addiction and human-structured suffering will continue to rearticulate—shifting in names, scapegoats, and administrations.

Migrants—and, as this project specifically addresses, migrants entering from the U.S.-Mexico border—remain emplaced in a discursive
space of rhetorical crisis. Against those always already othered, the non-
citizen-subject, the United States continues to declare war. The migrant
body is a U.S. target, and the United States remains convinced of the
overdetermined rhetoric of migrant criminality. By operating in a state
of public health crisis, the United States can justify, manufacture, and
export punishment to migrants while evading internal examination. As
stated by then presidential candidate Donald J. Trump, "When Mexico
sends its people . . . they're not sending you. . . . They're sending people
that have lots of problems. . . . They're bringing drugs."[37]

NOTES

1. Herzberg, *White Market Drugs*.
2. Bartilow, *Drug War Pathologies*.
3. Netherland and Hansen, "White Opioids"; Herzberg, "Entitled to Addiction?"
4. Lynch, "Theorizing the Role of the 'War on Drugs' in US Punishment."
5. Romero, "Racial Profiling and Immigration Law Enforcement"; Agozino, "Theorizing Otherness."
6. Logan, "The Wrong Race, Committing Crime, Doing Drugs, and Maladjusted
for Motherhood."
7. Alexander, *The New Jim Crow*.
8. Johnson, "Racial Profiling in the War on Drugs"; Johnson, "U.S. Border Enforcement"; Yates, Collins, and Chin, "A War on Drugs or a War on Immigrants."
9. Sered, "Diminished Citizenship in the Era of Mass Incarceration"; Alexander,
The New Jim Crow.
10. Rosino and Hughey, "The War on Drugs, Racial Meanings, and Structural
Racism."
11. Case and Deaton, "Rising Morbidity and Mortality in Midlife."
12. Rummans, Burton, and Dawson, "How Good Intentions Contributed to Bad
Outcomes."
13. Porter and Jick, "Addiction Rare in Patients Treated with Narcotics."
14. Keefe, "The Family That Built an Empire of Pain."
15. Vadivelu et al., "The Opioid Crisis."
16. Makary, Overton, and Wang, "Overprescribing Is Major Contributor to Opioid
Crisis."
17. Dhalla, Persaud, and Juurlink, "Facing Up to the Prescription Opioid Crisis."
18. Rudd et al., "Increases in Drug and Opioid-Involved Overdose Deaths."

19. Christie et al., *The President's Commission on Combating Drug Addiction and the Opioid Crisis*, 5.
20. Christie et al., 23.
21. Grella et al., "Gender and Comorbidity Among Individuals with Opioid Use Disorders."
22. Cicero and Ellis, "Understanding the Demand Side of the Prescription Opioid Epidemic."
23. Srivastava and Gold, "Beyond Supply."
24. Case and Deaton, "Mortality and Morbidity in the 21st Century."
25. Only two days later, on January 27, 2017, the Trump administration announced another executive order, "Protecting the Nation from Foreign Terrorist Entry into the United States," which would later be referred to as the first proposed "Muslim Ban."
26. Trump, "Enhancing Public Safety in the Interior of the United States."
27. Trump, "Border Security and Immigration Enforcement Improvements."
28. Trump, "Remarks Announcing Candidacy for President in New York City."
29. Foucault, *The History of Sexuality*; Foucault, *Discipline and Punish*.
30. Trump, "Remarks at a Listening Session on Opioids and Drug Abuse."
31. Trump.
32. Netherland and Hansen. "The War on Drugs That Wasn't."
33. Trump, "Remarks at a Listening Session on Opioids and Drug Abuse." The last half of Rosenberg's commentary is omitted from this extract due to it not being topically relevant; Trump soon recentered the conversation on the spike in the opioid crisis. However, to summarize what is omitted here, Rosenberg addressed (1) the necessity of changing American drug culture, (2) education as a tool for prevention, and (3) the DEA's heroic efforts in combating the opioid crisis.
34. Trump.
35. Trump.
36. Nik-Khah, "Neoliberal Pharmaceutical Science and the Chicago School of Economics."
37. Trump, "Remarks Announcing Candidacy for President in New York City."

BIBLIOGRAPHY

Agozino, Biko. "Theorizing Otherness, the War on Drugs and Incarceration." *Theoretical Criminology* 4, no. 3 (2000): 359–76.

Alexander, Michelle. *The New Jim Crow: Mass Incarceration in the Age of Colorblindness*. New York: New Press, 2012.

Bartilow, Horace A. *Drug War Pathologies: Embedded Corporatism and U.S. Drug Enforcement in the Americas*. Chapel Hill: University of North Carolina Press, 2019.

Case, Anne, and Angus Deaton. "Mortality and Morbidity in the 21st Century." *Brookings Papers on Economic Activity*, Spring 2017, 397–476.

Case, Anne, and Angus Deaton. "Rising Morbidity and Mortality in Midlife Among White Non-Hispanic Americans in the 21st Century." *Proceedings of the National Academy of Sciences of the United States of America* 112, no. 49 (2015): 15078–83.

Christie, Chris, Charlie Baker, Roy Cooper, Patrick J. Kennedy, Bertha Madras, and Pam Bondi. *The President's Commission on Combating Drug Addiction and the Opioid Crisis*. November 2017.

Cicero, Theodore J., and Matthew S. Ellis. "Understanding the Demand Side of the Prescription Opioid Epidemic: Does the Initial Source of Opioids Matter?" *Drug and Alcohol Dependence* 173, no. S1 (2017): S4–10.

Dhalla, Irfan A., Navindra Persaud, and David N. Juurlink. "Facing Up to the Prescription Opioid Crisis." *BMJ* 343 (2011): d5142. https://doi.org/10.1136/bmj.d5142.

Foucault, Michel. *Discipline and Punish: The Birth of the Prison*. Translated by Alan Sheridan. New York: Vintage, 1995.

Foucault, Michel. *The History of Sexuality: An Introduction*. New York: Vintage, 1990.

Grella, Christine E., Mitchell P. Karno, Umme S. Warda, Noosha Niv, and Alison A. Moore. "Gender and Comorbidity Among Individuals with Opioid Use Disorders in the NESARC Study." *Addictive Behaviors* 34, no. 6–7 (2009): 498–504.

Herzberg, David. "Entitled to Addiction? Pharmaceuticals, Race, and America's First Drug War." *Bulletin of the History of Medicine* 91, no. 3 (2017): 586–623.

Herzberg, David. *White Market Drugs: Big Pharma and the Hidden History of Addiction in America*. Chicago: University of Chicago Press, 2020.

Johnson, Kevin R. "Racial Profiling in the War on Drugs Meets the Immigration Removal Process: The Case of *Moncrieffe v. Holder*." *University of Michigan Journal of Law Reform* 48, no. 4 (2015): 967–99.

Johnson, Kevin R. "U.S. Border Enforcement: Drugs, Migrants, and the Rule of Law." *Villanova Law Review* 47, no. 4 (2002): 897–920.

Keefe, Patrick Radden. "The Family That Built an Empire of Pain." *New Yorker*, October 23, 2017.

Logan, Enid. "The Wrong Race, Committing Crime, Doing Drugs, and Maladjusted for Motherhood: The Nation's Fury over 'Crack Babies.'" *Social Justice* 26, no. 1 (1999): 115–38.

Lynch, Mona. "Theorizing the Role of the 'War on Drugs' in US Punishment." *Theoretical Criminology* 16, no. 2 (2012): 175–99.

Makary, Martin A., Heidi N. Overton, and Peiqi Wang. "Overprescribing Is Major Contributor to Opioid Crisis." *BMJ* 359 (2017): j4792. https://doi.org/10.1136/bmj.j4792.

Netherland, Julie, and Helena B. Hansen. "The War on Drugs That Wasn't: Wasted Whiteness, 'Dirty Doctors,' and Race in Media Coverage of Prescription Opioid Misuse." *Culture, Medicine, and Psychiatry* 40, no. 4 (2016): 664–86.

Netherland, Julie, and Helena B. Hansen. "White Opioids: Pharmaceutical Race and the War on Drugs That Wasn't." *BioSocieties* 12, no. 2 (2017): 217–38.

Nik-Khah, Edward. "Neoliberal Pharmaceutical Science and the Chicago School of Economics." *Social Studies of Science* 44, no. 4 (2014): 489–517.

Porter, Jane, and Hershel Jick. "Addiction Rare in Patients Treated with Narcotics." *New England Journal of Medicine* 302, no. 2 (1980): 123.

Romero, Mary. "Racial Profiling and Immigration Law Enforcement: Rounding Up of Usual Suspects in the Latino Community." *Critical Sociology* 32, no. 2–3 (2006): 447–73.

Rosino, Michael L., and Matthew W. Hughey. "The War on Drugs, Racial Meanings, and Structural Racism: A Holistic and Reproductive Approach." *American Journal of Economics and Sociology* 77, no. 3–4 (2018): 849–92.

Rudd, Rose A., Puja Seth, Felicita David, and Lawrence Scholl. "Increases in Drug and Opioid-Involved Overdose Deaths—United States, 2010–2015." *Morbidity and Mortality Weekly Report* 65, no. 50–51 (2016): 1445–52.

Rummans, Teresa A., M. Caroline Burton, and Nancy L. Dawson. "How Good Intentions Contributed to Bad Outcomes: The Opioid Crisis." *Mayo Clinic Proceedings* 93, no. 3 (2018): 344–50.

Sered, Susan Starr. "Diminished Citizenship in the Era of Mass Incarceration." *Punishment and Society* 23, no. 2 (2021): 218–40.

Srivastava, A. Benjamin, and Mark S. Gold. "Beyond Supply: How We Must Tackle the Opioid Epidemic." *Mayo Clinic Proceedings* 93, no. 3 (2018): 269–72.

Trump, Donald J. "Border Security and Immigration Enforcement Improvements." Exec. order 13767, January 25, 2017. American Presidency Project. https://www.presidency.ucsb.edu/node/322155.

Trump, Donald J. "Enhancing Public Safety in the Interior of the United States." Exec. order 13768, January 25, 2017. American Presidency Project. https://www.presidency.ucsb.edu/node/322157.

Trump, Donald J. "Protecting the Nation from Foreign Terrorist Entry into the United States." Exec. order 13769, January 27, 2017. American Presidency Project. https://www.presidency.ucsb.edu/node/322204.

Trump, Donald J. "Remarks Announcing Candidacy for President in New York City." June 16, 2015. American Presidency Project. https://www.presidency.ucsb.edu/node/310310.

Trump, Donald J. "Remarks at a Listening Session on Opioids and Drug Abuse and an Exchange with Reporters." March 29, 2017. American Presidency Project. https://www.presidency.ucsb.edu/node/326499.

Vadivelu, Nalini, Alice M. Kai, Vijay Kodumudi, Julie Sramcik, and Alan D. Kaye. "The Opioid Crisis: A Comprehensive Overview." *Current Pain and Headache Reports* 22, no. 3 (2018): article 16. https://doi.org/10.1007/s11916-018-0670-z.

Yates, Jeff, Todd A. Collins, and Gabriel J. Chin. 2005. "A War on Drugs or a War on Immigrants—Expanding the Definition of Drug Trafficking in Determining Aggravated Felon Status for Noncitizens." *Maryland Law Review* 64 (3): 875–909.

2

SEPARATING AND CAGING IMMIGRANT FAMILIES

Case Studies in South Texas from the Postwar Era Through Trump's Reign of Terror

JENNIFER CULLISON

IN APRIL 2018, WHEN U.S. attorney general Jeff Sessions announced the Zero Tolerance policy, which allowed U.S. Immigration and Customs Enforcement (ICE) agents to openly separate over three thousand undocumented immigrant parents from their children, it seemed that U.S. immigration policy had stooped to a new low.[1] Though for many years ICE had been detaining undocumented families at detention centers riddled with human rights problems—the largest ones being in Dilley and Karnes City, Texas—the new policy promised worse nightmares for these immigrants.[2] With the planned prosecution of all unlawful entry at the U.S.-Mexico border by the U.S. Department of Justice (DOJ), ICE officials transferred fewer of the mostly Central American arrivals to these detention centers to await immigration hearings. Instead, under Zero Tolerance, ICE sent these parents through a series of what we can call cages: U.S. Marshals Service pretrial detention to await DOJ court prosecution, then federal prison, and ultimately ICE detention centers (not necessarily those designated for family) to await possible deportation. The official program was short lived; Trump canceled it in June 2018. But the reality proved more unsettling: as first reported in November 2017, Zero Tolerance had begun as a pilot program in July of that year. And following a court-initiated accounting process in

January 2020, we now know that between July 2017 and June 2018, ICE officials separated at least 4,368 children from their parents.[3] The immigrant minors, the children of many of the immigrants sent to federal trial, were taken through state-sanctioned abduction and detained with "unaccompanied alien children," despite having arrived with at least one parent.

The Zero Tolerance policy was meant to deter migration and punish those who crossed without authorization—with no real regard on the part of the government to international conventions pertaining to the best interests of refugees, asylum seekers, or children, or even the U.S. Refugee Act of 1980.[4] DOJ prosecution of unlawful entry, along with the corresponding implication that migrant parents were illegitimate or unfit caretakers, was a thinly veiled effort to deter not all possible migrants coming from all corners of the world but only those Brown people at the southwest border of the United States, the majority of whom were Central Americans. Yet, the U.S. immigration system has been in the business of this kind of racialized injustice since its founding. Zero Tolerance is not evidence that the U.S. immigration system broke under Donald Trump. The speed with which the policy was put into place, if not its very form, is evidence that the system has always been broken, especially with regard to treatment of BIPoC immigrants.

A HISTORY OF SENDING PARENTS TO JAILS AND PRISONS

To fully understand Zero Tolerance, one must first know some of the history of immigrant detention writ large for adults in the United States. Since the early twentieth century, immigrants unlawfully crossing the U.S. border have not always been detained by U.S. immigration enforcement regimes alone, but instead have often been incarcerated in a hydra of jails, prisons, and detention centers. Parents, especially fathers, have long been charged with unlawful entry and then incarcerated in the criminal justice system, separated not only from family but also from structures of immigration law and policy that could benefit them.

The caging of undocumented immigrants outside of the immigration regime has played out in at least two distinct and troubling ways. First, despite the fact that the 1896 Supreme Court ruling in *Wong Wing v.*

United States determined that deportation was a civil matter (and that therefore immigrants awaiting deportation could be detained but not sentenced to prison), the Undesirable Aliens Act of 1929 criminalized unlawful entry into the United States. The 1929 act gave the U.S. Immigration and Naturalization Service (INS) the option to use the U.S. criminal justice system's infrastructure of pretrial detention and, for those found "guilty" of unlawful crossing, post-trial incarceration.[5] Just as the 1790 federal statute on immigration, which reserved naturalization for white people, was shaped by white supremacy, xenophobia, and nativism, so too was this act.[6] The 1929 law against unlawful entry was put in place to preserve a sense of the nation as white. Though prosecution data does not appear to exist for the first two decades after the implementation of the law, border patrol agents reported use of it against Mexicans during the mass repatriation program Operation Wetback of the early 1950s (with between 10,000 and 16,000 prosecutions annually between 1950 and 1955, according to the INS). One administrator in INS commissioner Joseph Swing's office noted in July 1954, toward the end of Operation Wetback, that "the bulk of the 'wetbacks' prosecuted in the courts are repeaters. They are flagrant cases. A prison sentence is the principal means we have of discouraging these continuing violations. We are employing this procedure in connection with the special operation [Operation Wetback] in California by weeding out the flagrant violators to be held for prosecution."[7] In later years, though INS annual reports and archives do not break down federal prosecutions by demographics, concerns about undocumented Mexican entries continued to inform INS enforcement policy.[8] In the years after Operation Wetback, there were increasing numbers of federal prosecutions and convictions. For example, though prosecutions declined to 3,500 in number between 1956 and 1969, they steadily increased between 1970 and 1994, to around 19,000 or 20,000.[9] Since historical deportation demographics show that Mexicans made up about 62 percent of yearly deportations between 1952 and 1994, we can infer that the majority of those prosecuted were likely Mexicans and then Central Americans. Other evidence since then suggests that for many years, most people charged with unlawful entry have been Latin American. A large data study of 3,121 unlawful entry prosecution cases over a single week in May 2018, for example, confirms that the vast majority of these were for Latin Americans.[10]

Criminalizing undocumented border crossing did not have to happen in 1929, in the early 1950s, or today. The U.S. law, as written in 1929, punished with additional incarceration people already subject to administrative detention (which typically only lasted a month). It deemed first-time violations of the border crossing law as misdemeanors punishable with one year of imprisonment and/or a $1,000 fine; repeated entries were deemed felonies punishable with two years of imprisonment and/or a $2,000 fine.[11] The law offered INS officials what they saw as a solution to the problem at the U.S.-Mexico border.[12] Sending "flagrant" migrants to the courts meant that INS officials could bypass their own typical six-month limit on detention.[13] In 1953, as part of Operation Wetback, when migration surges outsized the capacity of both immigration and criminal cages, INS officials collaborated with the federal courts and the Office of the U.S. Marshal (later, the U.S. Marshals Service or the USMS) to facilitate short sentences for increased numbers of first-time and repeat "border jumpers": respectively, three- and six-month imprisonments through the Federal Bureau of Prisons.[14] Ultimately, administration of the law has been arbitrary and punitive in a context that, at least per due process ideals, should be neither. Not all countries criminalize and punish unlawful entry; instead, fifteen countries including Spain, Mexico, Portugal, and Brazil consider it only a civil violation, just as the United States did before 1929. As of 2019, the United States was among 124 countries that still held border crossing to be a criminal offense.[15] Reversing this law (as Mexico did in 2011) would be an important step for any country seeking a future that separates immigration policy from punishment and caging.

A second way in which migrant caging has occurred outside the U.S. immigration regime predates the 1929 law and arises out of interagency agreements with various branches of the criminal justice system. U.S. immigration officials have long resorted to contracting with county prisons to take "overflow" populations of immigrants. Despite the penal cells they are transferred to, these individuals do not officially serve time as pretrial detained migrants but instead are still, on paper, "administratively" detained by the immigration enforcement regime. When outside the "civil" holding conditions of the INS/ICE, migrants who are not actually being charged in a federal court have ended up contracted out to county jails. Again, when migration surges occur, this kind of transfer increases. Interestingly, migrants who have served time for unlawful entry in a federal prison could, under such interagency agreements for ICE detention, find themselves still in carceral conditions in a county jail or, more recently, in a mixed-use prison for the USMS and ICE, even once they have completed their sentence.

A TEXAS CASE STUDY

To demonstrate the difference between immigrant detention and criminal detention for individuals transferred between the two (whether by the 1929 law or simply by interagency contract), it is worth looking at a historical case study in Texas, a longtime epicenter of immigration enforcement. I do this with an anonymous migrant's story that was detailed in a 1989 report from the U.S. Committee for Refugees. I am giving him the name "Salvador." Salvador, a husband and father from El Salvador, was probably apprehended by the U.S. Border Patrol before being handed over to the warden at the Webb County Detention Center (WCDC) in Laredo, Texas. He may have been held there as a USMS migrant to face federal trial for an immigration offense—for unlawful entry or some form of immigration fraud—or as a material witness to a coyote who may have guided his entry into the United States. Or he may have been there on an interagency contract as, simply, an INS detained migrant. In any case, the regular INS detention center in the area was certainly full at that point. It was 1989. In fact, the flagship Texas INS detention center, at Port Isabel, was bursting at the seams, with bunk beds added to the regular barracks and temporary circus-tent dorms erected. Instead of paroling the people they apprehended, INS officers were transferring folks to remote jails and detention facilities.

These officers usually reserved the WCDC for those migrants they believed should face trial and criminal sentencing for immigration offenses. But in 1989, most of those individuals incarcerated at the WCDC were migrants, whether they were there on an interagency contract, were detained pretrial by the USMS, or otherwise were convicted and serving their time. The WCDC was a real prison with barred barracks, barbed wire fences, and guard towers. The WCDC had been a regular site for detaining migrants since at least the 1970s. For incarcerated migrants, its conditions had only worsened over the past two decades.

Speaking in 1989 from behind the bars lining the halls of the WCDC barracks, Salvador explained to a local reporter that upon his booking, "They only asked me if I came with a smuggler. . . . When they gave the papers, they said 'Sign here, sign here, sign here.' A uniformed person asked how many kids I have, about my wife, my work, birthdate, school, religion. He did not ask me why I left [my country]. The only thing he explained was the list of attorneys."[16]

Indeed, the WCDC was remotely located and thus fraught with legal challenges for the immigrants incarcerated there. Salvador, for example, felt completely disregarded legally. He wanted to be asked why he had left El Salvador. He shared with a visiting commission in 1989 that he had fled his home in El Salvador late the previous year, after being forced to join the Civil Guard but then receiving an anonymous note advising him to disappear (apparently the writer believed that the guard would act against Salvador).[17] According to his account, nobody from the USMS, the INS, or the county had asked him about this. Instead, since they were usually in the business of detaining material witnesses and thus helping prosecute human traffickers, they asked whether he had been guided to the United States by a coyote. As with so many others from El Salvador, what he really needed was not the questioning but instead legal assistance to apply for asylum in the United States. Due to its remote location, Laredo only had immigration judges on loan from other areas. And there were no free legal services for migrants anywhere in Laredo through at least 1989.[18] In 1991, for example, there were only six lawyers and four nonprofits helping incarcerated migrants in Brownsville-Harlingen, one of the nearest metropolitan areas.[19] Few if any of those lawyers and staffers could travel 150 miles to Laredo. Further, there was no courtroom at the WCDC or anywhere nearby. Ultimately, in Laredo there was only a chimera of immigration law.

Worse than the lack of legal process or legal help was that, according to reports of local immigrant rights organization Proyecto Libertad, conditions at the WCDC in 1989 were not simply overcrowded and legally deprived; they were abusive. Detained migrants had prohibitively high bonds (at $7,500, these were between $3,000 and $4,000 higher than those set in Harlingen) and little to no information about the legal process (including bond reduction and political asylum). Also, according to migrants interviewed by Proyecto Libertad, county staff threatened noncompliant Central Americans with physical harm, including transfer to Barracks 148, where "Mexican and Cuban detainees" would allegedly beat them. Finally, they had limited access to the outside world, with only two phones for each barracks.[20] Under these conditions at the WCDC, then, Salvador and other asylum seekers usually found no avenue to properly request safe harbor in the United States and instead were caged as criminals before their deportation.

EXPANDING USE OF IMMIGRANT "SHADOW PRISONS"

Use of federal prisons and county jails in the project of prosecuting unlawful entry as well as other immigration offenses picked up significantly in the 1980s and 1990s and was a norm by the start of the Trump administration. The stage was set in 1986 with the Immigration Reform and Control Act, which required that the U.S. attorney general, "in the case of an alien who is convicted of an offense which makes the alien subject to deportation . . . begin any deportation proceeding as expeditiously as possible after the date of the conviction."[21] In 1999, to accommodate the growing number of people sentenced for immigration offenses (then at ten thousand annually), the Federal Bureau of Prisons authorized the first contracts for "shadow prisons" or "criminal alien requirement" prisons. Fairly steady yearly increases thereafter, coupled with the establishment of the expedited federal court hearings known as Operation Streamline in 2005, led to a peak of nearly twenty-four thousand people entering federal prisons for immigration offenses (and another eight thousand immigrants being incarcerated for other offenses) in 2011.[22] At the time of the 2018 Zero Tolerance policy, though the number of people entering the federal prison system (for any kind of offense) was on the decline, thirteen shadow prisons were at the disposal of ICE officials.[23] With Zero Tolerance, adult migrants were caged in these fully carceral prisons, often hundreds and thousands of miles away from their children, who were sent to any of a hundred different Office of Refugee Resettlement (ORR) shelters across the country.

Outcomes of federal prosecution of unlawful border crossing have included ultimately unfair criminalization of migrants, separation of families, and a lack of due process (exacerbated by the fact that the facilities are often located far from urban centers with enough immigration attorneys). Additionally, further legislation in 1996 on expedited deportation of "criminal aliens" means that immigrants who serve time for crimes unrelated to immigration law are regularly transferred directly to ICE, where they face further injustice—effectively serving additional time in immigrant detention for those same crimes, even before deportation.[24]

In 2016, even though U.S.-Mexico border apprehensions were declining (by 2018 they would fall 75 percent from the most recent peak of 1,643,679 in 2000), Trump promised to increase ICE removals of "illegals" at the southern border.[25] During the first months of his administration, ICE officials worked to not only transfer more of those they apprehended to the U.S. justice system from the start but also contract with increased numbers of county and federal prisons to house immigrants still facing only immigration (not criminal) courtrooms. This started in April 2017, when the Trump administration began planning significant increases to ICE detention.[26] Though Trump ultimately did not issue an executive order to this end, two officials from the U.S. Department of Homeland Security (DHS) told a *New York Times* journalist that they were looking to quickly add as many as twenty-two thousand people to the ICE average daily population (ADP), meaning an increase from about thirty-four to fifty-six thousand people caged.[27] Without sufficient beds available within ICE-owned or ICE-contracted facilities to meet this goal, the two officials planned for interagency agreements with additional county jails and prisons to hold more alleged "illegals." They had new, simpler contract templates ready for vetting. With this approach, Trump and ICE officials apparently intended to curtail the specialized standards that had been in place for immigrant detention since 2001. The DHS officials suggested that new contracts would make far fewer guarantees for immigrants on interagency transfers. These migrants might lose, for example, separate detention, translation services, regular mental health evaluations, or strict limitations on solitary confinement.

Trump delivered on his xenophobic campaign promises to fight undocumented immigration. Under his watch, ICE detention spiked for the first time since the last years of the George W. Bush administration (2001–9).[28] The ICE ADP for fiscal year 2017 reached thirty-eight thousand, about 15 percent or five thousand people over the average of the previous few years.[29] And though the ICE and USMS ADP declined some in 2018 (about 11 and 19 percent, respectively), the number of prosecutions for immigration offenses reached a two-decade high, rising 66 percent between 2017 and 2018, from sixty thousand to ninety-nine thousand, with the prosecutions for unlawful entry among those doubling.[30] Many of those deported were parents who were lucky enough to have the ORR return their children to them, and thus families departed together. Many other parents, after facing caging in any number of ICE or USMS detention centers, county jails, or federal prisons, were deported without their children.

A HISTORY OF DETAINING IMMIGRANT FAMILIES AND CHILDREN

Though the 2018 Zero Tolerance policy and its pilot predecessor shocked much of the nation with their state-sanctioned abduction of more than four thousand children from immigrant families, the atrocity was not entirely new for the U.S. immigration regime. Neither was the caging of families and children. Since at least the 1980s, to check for potential human trafficking, the INS (and later ICE) had separated children from caretakers and family members who were not legal guardians. The Trump administration, however, set a new precedent by authorizing the separation of children from legal guardians and parents. Separating immigrant children from their parents is fundamentally unjust per the Convention on the Rights of the Child, signed by UN member nations in November 1989.[31]

Due to the blatant disregard for the best interests of children, advocates quickly protested this new level of family separation in early 2018. Even before the policy was announced, in February, journalists condemned family separation.[32] Also in February, the American Civil Liberties Union (ACLU) filed a writ of habeas corpus in a California federal district court in response to a November 2017 case of family separation; by the next month, the ACLU had filed to modify the case into a class action.[33] Following Jeff Sessions's April announcement of the Zero Tolerance policy, journalists released photos of separations and reported on the abusive conditions under which the hundreds and then thousands of separated children were contained. They exposed scenes in makeshift fenced cages at the border patrol stations where crowds of children under foil blankets were apparently shivering on the floor from (famously) excessive air conditioning if not suffering from hunger, sickness, or deprivation-induced filth; where older children were changing diapers of younger ones; and where many cried for their parents. They also drew attention to the plight of the children in the ORR facilities (often tent cities or giant converted stores), which were not initially equipped to deal with children under the age of thirteen and, due to the prolonged trauma of family separation and no-hug policies (even between siblings), imposed great psychological tolls on many incarcerated there. The journalists reported that increasing numbers of advocates were unable to reunite the families.[34] From Geneva, on June 5, the United Nations condemned the forced separations and called the practice child abuse.[35] And even within Trump's Republican Party, on June 17, former First Lady Laura Bush published an editorial pointing to the cruelty.

Public opinion and protest led to the end of Zero Tolerance, though not abolition of the structures that had allowed the injustices. Following a June 19 poll showing that most of the nation opposed family separation, on June 20, Trump terminated the practice and instead focused on family detention.[36] Not trusting the president's words, activists continued to organize. Within the week, nearly six hundred protesters were arrested in Washington, D.C. Seventeen states sued Trump for the cruel practice of Zero Tolerance, calling it unconstitutional.[37] And in response to the ACLU case, Judge Dana M. Sabraw concluded on June 26 that the U.S. government had "no system in place" for keeping track of the separated children and their parents and thus ordered that the Trump administration immediately put together one and reunite the families.[38] Finally, on June 30, though Trump had discontinued the separation policy and Judge Sabraw had ordered reunions, activists from dozens of organizations including the ACLU and MoveOn organized protests nationwide. The activists had reason to keep agitating: family reunions were going slowly, U.S. law still allowed separating children from designated caretakers at the border, and conditions of confinement in family detention remained detrimental.[39]

Investigations over the ensuing years have demonstrated that the problem persists. Studies later in 2018 revealed how chaotic and cruel the process was and that many of the children had been sexually abused within the shelters.[40] And it was only in January 2020 that officials under

Judge Sabraw's court order determined that in fact 1,556 children had been separated from their families earlier, in 2017, bring the combined total of separated families in 2017 and 2018 to 4,368.[41]

Use of family detention and separate detention for "unaccompanied" minors has an even longer precedent in the United States. Until the arrival of Central American refugees in the 1980s, INS officials in the postwar era had fragmented experience detaining children. Though border patrol officers sometimes apprehended unaccompanied Mexican minors and detained a few of them by contract at local juvenile facilities, in many cases apprehension, detentions, and deportations of children were few.[42] With the Central American refugee crisis of the 1980s and early 1990s, INS officials had to consider what to do with the greater numbers of families migrating across the border, as I will discuss. From the beginning, the growth of the enterprise, unsurprisingly, proved problematic.

In the 1980s and early 1990s, many Central American family groups escaped their war-torn homelands, confronted trying circumstances in their exile, and headed toward the United States together. For INS officers, the problem in these years was not simply that Central Americans were arriving undocumented in the United States, but that they were arriving in family groups (whether these resembled the nuclear family or had less traditional configurations). Central American minors also arrived in the United States unaccompanied. Detaining Central American populations proved to be a different challenge than detaining Mexican children and family groups. INS officers could not easily remove Central Americans from the United States, especially since many of these migrants applied for asylum. With an interest in using detention as deterrence, INS officers faced a matter not merely of finding beds, but of providing services particular to family and minor needs. The situation for children proved the most sensitive.

Seeking to house the large numbers of Central American family groups arriving in the early 1980s, South Texas INS officers initially contracted with juvenile detention centers and churches. Examples of the latter contractors include Casa Oscar Romero in Brownsville/San Benito, Catholic Charities in Houston, and the Catholic Diocese of Corpus Christi.[43] The Catholic Church's support of the sanctuary movement, however, led to the demise of these contracts, especially once INS officers began persecuting sanctuary activists for escorting and harboring unauthorized migrants in 1984.[44] With the move away from churches in the mid-1980s, INS officers then contracted more regularly with large nonprofits such as International Education Services, as well as private prison companies.

Before INS officers made their first private prison contracts for family detention, they often detained fathers in INS facilities but left women and children together under the care of the nonprofits. This choice restricted the issue of bail bonds to the father and avoided the question of caregiving, since mothers would remain with their children. It also left the problem of education to the local public schools. Because these organizations provided shelter and sometimes services for the newly arrived migrants, this choice also appeared, on the surface, to be the most humanitarian way to promote appearances for immigration hearings. Migrants at Brownsville church shelters in the early 1980s, for example, could come and go. Unaccompanied minors, on the other hand, were often contracted to county juvenile detention centers. The National Center for Immigrants' Rights (NCIR) estimated that the INS detained eight hundred children under these various conditions over the course of 1984. By the next year, however, the NCIR estimated that the INS was detaining two thousand children per year.[45] With an apparent interest in further limiting the freedoms of undocumented families, the INS moved that year toward private prisons to detain children with their caregivers.

When INS officials sent out their call for bids on a Laredo family detention center in early 1984, Patrick M. Hughes, an attorney at Proyecto Libertad in South Texas, was in shock. "It's unheard of here in Harlingen that [immigrant] children be detained," he said. And he was upset that the INS was considering private prison companies to do that. "It just blisters me that no one cares about the children. . . . It's wrong."[46] Hughes and probably most migrant advocates in South Texas had heard of the opening of a new INS-contracted "private prison" for immigrants in Houston that spring and understood the implications. This would be the first family prison. The 1984 call outlined the need for a secure facility of 175 beds in Laredo—suitable for families. Though Hughes was apparently unaware of the patchy history of families within the INS detention system, he was right to note a shift in INS practice. Indeed, the 1980s marked an overt INS turn to caging women and children.

Unlike nonprofits, Corrections Corporation of America (CCA, now CoreCivic) and other private prison companies offered the INS the ability to hold more kinds of migrants—and to confine them if necessary.[47] They could hold immigrants awaiting federal trial for unlawful entry. Beginning in 1985, under contract with the local criminal justice system and per new Texas law, they could even hold "criminal aliens" serving their last six months of a court-ordered sentence.[48] Under these conditions, the "criminal aliens" were caged and ready for a paper transfer to INS custody for deportation. Private prisons could detain these individuals on the same property (though segregated from the incarcerated population) as noncriminal migrants awaiting hearings or deportation. Private prisons could even house children, if they met state institutional codes (the same used for halfway houses and the like). Private prison companies, therefore, offered the "convenience" of taking on state code compliance for minors, so that INS officials did not have to.

Private prison officials were wooing federal and county officials at the time with promises that competition-driven innovation and efficiency would allow them to operate detention centers of a higher quality and at a lower cost. At about this time, CCA cofounder Richard G. Crane, for example, promised that CCA could provide humane treatment and quality guards.[49] CCA also claimed in an early brochure, "Other benefits include reduced pressure from the courts for reforming and upgrading."[50] What CCA was really offering was a private prison model of decreased transparency, fewer hours of training, reduced salaries (kept low due to serious turnover), and "voluntary" labor extracted from the people detained in its system. Though the nation would learn later that the model was ultimately a drain on the local tax base, CCA won its first contract in 1983 for operations in Houston.[51] In April 1984, it opened its newly constructed, one-story, fully carceral property with 350 beds. The site, located near the George Bush Intercontinental Airport, offered an immigration court with three judges as well as glass-partitioned visiting space.[52] To get to the court or the visiting space, however, lawyers, family members, and the public still needed to pass a flank of barbed wire fencing, secure sally ports, metal detectors, and guards. Most likely due to the abbreviated training provided to the staff, evidence of mismanagement and abuse quickly arose. Various hunger strikes and demonstrations were reported over the first few years of operation.[53]

Unsurprisingly, CCA put in a bid and won the INS contract for the first family detention center in the nation, to be built in Laredo in 1985.[54]

Much like in Houston, CCA Laredo was built with security in mind. It was made of fortresslike cinder block walls, had only a few iron-barred, bulletproof, chicken-wire carceral windows, and, beyond the entrance, was surrounded by fourteen-foot barbed wire fencing and sally ports. Except for special suites for mothers and their children, the main open-bay dormitories and bathrooms offered little privacy. Though INS officials contracted for only 175 beds, CCA Laredo opened with 210 beds; about 40 of these were for unaccompanied children or for infants.[55] With cribs in the men's dormitories and special suites for mothers with children, the facility could potentially detain 50 children.

ANOTHER TEXAS CASE STUDY

Celia Valdés was one of the first children detained in CCA's Laredo prison. Celia, a teenager, had traveled with her sister and brother-in-law through extreme conditions from their home in El Salvador, through Guatemala and Mexico, and finally across the U.S.-Mexico border in South Texas. The *Texas Observer* published the story of their 1985 journey to Laredo.[56] After Celia and her family arrived, they were apprehended for "entry without inspection." Soon INS judges ordered her sister and brother-in-law (both adults) to be deported to El Salvador, but Celia remained at what she called "a jail . . . [that] wasn't a jail," with a desire to obtain asylum. Without a parent to claim her in the United States, INS official policy required that she remain detained until her deportation was accomplished or her asylum approved. Like with many Central American children escaping the violence and massacres of military governments, the detention center provided no mercy to her. Despite its "family" designation, staff there offered neither counseling nor safeguards from mistreatment and instead followed the Texas precedent: they handled children like prisoners, subjecting them to strip search and solitary confinement. But Celia was lucky. When INS officers held fast to their "parent" rule, a lawyer convinced an INS judge that Celia would not miss her hearings while with a sponsor family. The family (a two-parent, two-lawyer household) not only offered shelter to Celia while she awaited her asylum but also helped facilitate her escape from prison. Eventually, the family adopted her.

Over her stay at CCA Laredo, Celia witnessed how, on behalf of the INS, privately contracted officials tackled new detention management issues. The first of these was the question of when to bond out children. Though Celia was able to leave CCA after a short period, officially children were held without a bond and thus INS officers effectively held migrant children hostage in Laredo.[57] Under instruction by the INS, CCA officers in 1985 would usually not release children to anybody but the minors' parents—what critics found to be a trap for undocumented parents. The parents feared that if they were to pick up their children, they would be subject to INS apprehension, detention, and deportation. Most undocumented parents, therefore, did not try to claim their children, and consequently the children remained in INS custody. In 1987, following the initial injunctions in the landmark kids-in-cages case *Flores v. Meese*, INS officers had to release children as quickly as possible, though the conditions of release remained the same.[58] At this time, however, due to advocacy by local residents and lawyers such Celia's adoptive parents, INS officers seemed to release children more frequently to shelters and legal guardians. Meanwhile, as previously mentioned, INS officers in Laredo had by this point set the average bond rate for adults at $7,500.[59] The high bond rate prevented many families from exercising any freedom or mobility while awaiting their hearings. And, even with the new detention center, Laredo still had no legal services. Most detained immigrants at this time had no community support in Laredo at all.[60]

The second management problem related to the provision of education for the children at CCA Laredo. By the time CCA Laredo was opened, and while Celia was there, it had already been three years since the *Plyler v. Doe* Supreme Court decision relating to the education of undocumented youth.[61] This case, in response to nativist resistance in Texas, had challenged public school districts that were denying undocumented children admittance to their schools or were otherwise requiring tuition. The 1982 decision guaranteed public education to all children, regardless of their immigration status. Yet at CCA Laredo, children were systematically denied access to education, whether on site or via passes to off-site public schools.

Overall, however, the carceral environment and punitive discipline of children at CCA Laredo remained the most pressing problem. Like the adults, the children were monitored by guards, held to stringent rules, and forced to live with their time and movement highly regimented. The environment also proved excessively punitive. According to journalist Robert Kahn, "a semicircle with a radius of about one meter had been drawn on the floor under each window. Many children who stood within that semicircle to look out the window were punished with solitary confinement."[62] Meanwhile, CCA officials severely limited children's outdoor exposure and sunlight. The initial CCA-INS contract stated that children would have access to indoor and outdoor recreation space, including supervised play. Yet, there was no special recreational space contracted for the children, at least per the documentation drafted and updated through early March 1985.[63] Like typical CCA adult prisoners, incarcerated children might play board games but were unlikely to receive learning materials.

And, with training no different than that provided in private prisons for adults, staff at CCA Laredo acted much more like guards than like counselors, mentors, and allies. Many Central American refugee children like Celia arrived at CCA Laredo needing counseling and support. Celia herself had experienced a series of traumas, including deaths of family members. Escaping repression by the government and military of their homelands, migrants like her arrived in the United States with a heightened fear of authority. With such a history, many Central American children and adults needed translators, lawyers, and emotional support. Usually receiving none, they tried to learn the rules of behavior and navigate the foreign carceral and legal system. But when provoked or frustrated, they sometimes found themselves in conflict with the guards. If they misbehaved, those guards often sent them to solitary confinement without a hearing.[64] The children and adults eventually called the solitary confinement chamber "El Pozo" or "the hole."[65]

Finally, CCA guards violated children's bodies and souls. Strip searches became normal operating procedure by late 1985 for all children meeting with lawyers.[66] According to Patrick Hughes, an attorney at Refugee Legal Services in Laredo, adult and child migrants were regularly strip-searched for visits with him and other attorneys. In spring 1985, he gathered affidavits from adults and children who had faced such experiences. He sent the affidavits along with a letter to INS regional commissioner Ed O'Connor in Dallas. According to Hughes and others, none of these searches had ever resulted in the discovery of contraband.[67] Though

O'Connor promised to curb the searches, the complaints continued through at least the summer.[68] Older girls seemed to be disproportionately represented among the children strip-searched. Further, advocates reported that CCA Laredo guards sexually threatened and pressured the children.[69]

Children who could turn to legal help to respond to the abuses at CCA Laredo had some benefits from recent case law. The Supreme Court decision in *Flores v. Meese* made a big difference, as the courts ordered in 1988 that INS or INS-contracted officers discontinue performing body cavity searches on children.[70] Meanwhile, however, the children at CCA Laredo were misled and fed disinformation. At Laredo, Kahn met with several detained immigrants who had been forced by guards (impersonating judges) to sign I-274s (requests for deportation). Officers at CCA Laredo also violated standing case law (the 1988 *Orantes-Hernandez v. Meese* case) by providing a list of rights but then telling children that they could only choose one among them ("the right to be represented by an attorney, the right to a deportation hearing, the right to request political asylum, and the right to request voluntary [departure] repatriation").[71]

There were so many problems for children at CCA Laredo that in 1989 INS officials moved unaccompanied children from the CCA Laredo facility to nonprofit shelters dedicated to minors.[72] This was an attempt to meet some of the concerns of confinement and education brought up in *Flores v. Meese*. Today, CCA Laredo continues to operate, but it is no longer a family detention center. Despite the failures there, however, INS and then ICE officials did not give up on detaining children and families. Unaccompanied minor detention persisted with companies like International Education Services. Then, in 2001—in response to anti-immigrant legislation from 1996 and 9/11-related fears of large numbers of migrants "threatening" national security—INS officials turned to private prison companies to build family detention centers, first with one in Berks County, Pennsylvania, and then at other sites across much of the Southwest.

In 2018, when it was evident that the crowded shelters were not meeting the standards of ORR and *Flores* mandates, it became clear that ICE officials had very little legal ground on which to continue their brutal practice of family separation and child abduction. And yet, the crisis continues today as ICE officials still separate children from trusted caregivers at the border.

This chapter has reviewed the traumatic history of the prosecuting and caging of immigrant parents and the state-sanctioned abduction of their children. The immigration regime has turned to the U.S. criminal system to expand its caging footprint, to criminalize undocumented border crossing, and to house its "charges" in penal confinement. The detention of families and children has long jeopardized the health and safety of an at-risk population and created abusive liminal spaces in what is already a trying process of being displaced from their homes. Though Zero Tolerance ended, the crisis is not over. President Biden began sunsetting federal contracts for privately operated criminal detention facilities with an executive order issued on January 26, 2021, but prison companies have simply begun transitioning the shadow prisons to the unaffected immigrant detention system and immigrants are still facing criminal prosecution for immigration code violations.[73] In February 2023, more than five years after the pilot separations, across the United States nearly a thousand separated children were yet to be reunited with their deported parents.[74] As this book goes to press, at the border, children are still being separated from parents who have committed even the most minor of transgressions or are listed on problematic gang databases, and they are still being separated from trusted caregivers.[75] The detention facilities continue to be less like shelters and more like prisons. Still too, far from the border, even U.S. citizen children continue facing another hell as they are separated from their immigrant parents through ICE interior enforcement.[76] And these processes, though less draconian since the end of June 2018, remain national atrocities while still affecting mostly Brown undocumented immigrants and their families.

NOTES

1. U.S. Department of Justice, Office of Public Affairs, "Attorney General Announces Zero-Tolerance Policy for Criminal Illegal Entry."
2. Even before Zero Tolerance, reports and news stories of wrongful or prolonged detention, neglect, and abuse at Dilley and Karnes were many. See, e.g., National Immigrant Justice Center, "Children Detained by the Department of Homeland Security"; Speed, "The US Is Jailing Immigrant Women and Children Under Appalling Conditions."
3. Kriel, "Trump Moves to End 'Catch and Release'"; Davis, "U.S. Officials Say They Are Highly Confident."

4. Though not a signatory of the 1951 Convention Relating to the Status of Refugees, the United States did sign the related 1967 protocol, which widened the applicability of the original convention. See UNHRC, *Convention and Protocol Relating to the Status of Refugees*. The United States has signed but not ratified the Convention on the Rights of the Child. See UN General Assembly, Resolution 44/25, Convention on the Rights of the Child, A/RES/44/25 (November 20, 1989). See also U.S. Congress, Refugee Act of 1980, Pub. L. No. 96–212, 94 Stat. 102 (1980).

5. U.S. Congress, Undesirable Aliens Act of 1929, Pub L. No. 70–1018, 45 Stat. 1551 (1929).

6. U.S. Congress, Naturalization Act of 1790, 1 Stat 103 (1790).

7. RHR, Office of the Commissioner of Immigration and Naturalization, memo to administrative assistant of the attorney general, "Handling of 'Wetbacks' After Court Has Pronounced Judgment," July 2, 1954, RG 85, INS Records 1920–57, box 20286, document 56336/276, 1, National Archives and Records Administration; Cullison, "The Growth of Immigrant Caging in Postwar America," figure I.7.

8. See, e.g., Chapman, "How Millions of Illegal Aliens Sneak into the U.S."

9. Cullison, "The Growth of Immigrant Caging in Postwar America," figures I.7, I.12, I.17.

10. See "Most Came from Latin America" in Solon et al., "3,121 Desperate Journeys Exposing a Week of Chaos." For similar tables on deportations by nation, see Cullison, "The Growth of Immigrant Caging in Postwar America," figures I.4, I.9, I.14.

11. For more on this aspect of the 1929 immigration law, also known as Blease's Law because it was written by the "proud and unreconstructed white supremacist" US senator Coleman Livingston Blease (D-S.C.), see Hernández, *City of Inmates*, 137–45 (137 qtd.).

12. According to an INS examiner, most detention sentences were for a maximum of one month; see B. R. Murdock, letter to R. C. Jackson, acting chief examiner, Department of Justice, June 5, 1954, RG 85, INS Records 1920–57, box 20286, document 56336/276, 2, National Archives and Records Administration.

13. Since the Immigration Act of February 5, 1917 (and as amended on September 22, 1950, by the Internal Security Act), barring exceptional processing circumstances, the INS/Border Patrol limited migrant detention to six months or less. See U.S. Department of Justice, Immigration and Naturalization Service, *1952 Annual Report*, 49. This clause was written into the 1952 Immigration and Nationality Act, section 242(c). See U.S. Congress, Immigration and Nationality Act of 1952, Pub. L. No. 82–414, 66 Stat. 163 (1952).

14. The prison system could not accommodate such efforts for long. After about three weeks of intensive prosecutions of unauthorized entries in 1953, for example, the county jails were overflowing. With district judges holding kangaroo court hearings with eighty to a hundred migrants each day, the judges quickly

surpassed an average of two hundred prisoners (of which 40 percent were for immigration cases) in custody with the U.S. Marshals in Arizona. In the third week, the total in custody with the U.S. Marshals was five hundred. See U.S. Department of Justice, Immigration and Naturalization Service, *INS Information Bulletin*, 5–6.

15. Global Legal Research Directorate, "Criminalization of Illegal Entry Around the World."

16. For narrative purposes, I am calling this incarcerated migrant "Salvador." The original source provided his testimony anonymously. See Frelick, *Refugees at Our Border*, 9.

17. Frelick, 9.

18. Proyecto Libertad, "Orantes Contempt Action Seeks to Counter Massive Rights Violation."

19. Proyecto Libertad, "The Numbers Are Down."

20. Proyecto Libertad, "A Report from Laredo."

21. U.S. Congress, Immigration Reform and Control Act of 1986, Pub. L. No. 99–603, 100 Stat. 3359 (1986).

22. For statistics on the numbers of people entering the federal prison system by violation and citizenship status between 1998 and 2021, see Bureau of Justice Statistics, "Federal Criminal Case Processing Statistics."

23. American Civil Liberties Union, *Warehoused and Forgotten*, 3.

24. See U.S. Congress, Illegal Immigration Reform and Immigrant Responsibility Act of 1996, Pub. L. No. 104–208, 110 Stat. 3009–546 (1996); U.S. Congress, Antiterrorism and Effective Death Penalty Act of 1996, Pub. L. No. 104–132, 110 Stat 1214 (1996).

25. See Gramlich, "Far More Immigration Cases Are Being Prosecuted Criminally," table titled "Despite Recent Uptick . . ."

26. Dickerson, "Trump Plan Would Curtail Protections for Detained Immigrants."

27. The 2016 ICE ADP was 34,376. See U.S. Department of Homeland Security, *US Immigration and Customs Enforcement: Budget Overview*, ICE-14.

28. The single greatest spike in immigrant detention ADP in the postwar era occurred between 2006 and 2007, when ADP jumped from 20,148 to 30,295. For INS/ICE ADP in 1997–2006, see Congressional Research Service, "Immigration Enforcement Within the United States," figure 7; for 2007–11, see U.S. Department of Homeland Security, "ICE Total Removals." With the Department of Homeland Security Appropriations Act of 2010, Senate Appropriations Committee chair Robert Byrd (D-W.V.) put into place a temporary ICE "bed quota" of 33,400 beds (until September 30, 2010), though by this point ICE had maintained an ADP over 30,000 since 2008. See U.S. Congress, Department of Homeland Security Appropriations Act of 2010, Pub. L. No. 111–83, 123 Stat. 2149 (2009). The bed mandate was entrenched in law in 2015; see U.S. Congress, Department of Homeland Security Appropriations Act of 2015, Pub. L. No. 114–4, 129 Stat. 39 (2015).

29. Wamsley, "As It Makes More Arrests, ICE Looks for More Detention Centers."

30. Gramlich, "Far More Immigration Cases Are Being Prosecuted Criminally," esp. table titled "Federal Criminal Prosecutions . . ."

31. UN General Assembly, Resolution 44/25, Convention on the Rights of the Child, A/RES/44/25 (November 20, 1989).

32. See, e.g., Wynn, "The Detention Archipelago"; Long, "The False Choice Between Family Separation and Detention"; Galacatos, Shapiro, and Stark, "The Cruel Ploy of Taking Immigrant Kids from Their Parents."

33. The case started with a Congo family and then expanded with a Brazilian one. See *Ms. L. v. U.S. Immigration and Customs Enforcement*, 3:18-cv-00428 (S.D. Cal. 2018).

34. Dickerson, "Hundreds of Immigrant Children Have Been Taken from Parents at U.S. Border"; Rosenberg, "Nearly 1,800 Families Separated at U.S.-Mexico Border in 17 Months"; Goodwin, "Children Are Being Used as a Tool"; Reigstad, "Records Reveal Southwest Key Cited for Hundreds of Violations."

35. UN News, "UN Rights Chief Slams 'Unconscionable' US Border Policy"; Cumming-Bruce, "Taking Migrant Children from Parents Is Illegal."

36. Sides, "The Extraordinary Unpopularity of Trump's Family Separation Policy"; Trump, "Affording Congress an Opportunity to Address Family Separation."

37. Shear et al., "Federal Judge in California Halts Splitting of Migrant Families at Border."

38. *Ms. L. v. U.S. Immigration and Customs Enforcement*, 3:18-cv-00428 (S.D. Cal. 2018).

39. On the continued problem of separating children from their designated caretakers at the border, see Long, "More Action Is Needed to End Family Separations."

40. See, e.g., Solon et al., "3,121 Desperate Journeys Exposing a Week of Chaos"; Reigstad, "Records Reveal Southwest Key Cited for Hundreds of Violations"; Kilani, "Thousands of Migrant Children Allegedly Sexually Abused in US Custody."

41. Davis, "U.S. Officials Say They Are Highly Confident."

42. For a look at ways in which the INS treated unaccompanied Mexican immigrant children, see Cullison, "The Growth of Immigrant Caging in Postwar America," 406–16.

43. Proyecto Libertad, "A Child's Nightmare in Laredo."

44. Kahn, "Detention Camps More Horrendous for Young Inmates."

45. Proyecto Libertad, "Children Held Hostage."

46. Quoted in Danini, "Prisons for Profit."

47. INS officers continued, however, to parole and bond most families through the 1980s and 1990s, due to a lack of space. During the 1989 asylum crisis, for example, many families were paroled from the Port Isabel Detention Center in Los Fresnos, Texas, and then sent to the Red Cross shelter in Brownsville, Texas. Critics say, however, that the Red Cross operated under the direction of the INS. See Proyecto Libertad, "A Legal Primer."

48. Warren, "Counseling Plan Initiated for Inmates Awaiting Parole."

49. *Privatization of Corrections: Hearings Before the Subcommittee on Courts, Civil Liberties, and the Administration of Justice of the Committee on the Judiciary, House of Representatives*, 99th Cong. 28–29 (1985–86).

50. Tolchin, "Jails Run by Private Company Force It to Face Question of Accountability."

51. AFSCME Corrections United, *Don't Be a Prisoner to Empty Promises*; Culp, "The Failed Promise of Prison Privatization."

52. Fixler, "Behind Bars We Find an Enterprise Zone"; Tolchin, "Jails Run by Private Company Force It to Face Question of Accountability"; Quan, "Don't Rush to Immigration Services Yet."

53. See Cullison, "The Growth of Immigrant Caging in Postwar America," chap. 4 and figure I.19.

54. Ramon, "Strip Searches at Laredo Facility."

55. Fixler, "Behind Bars We Find an Enterprise Zone"; Roberto Rodríguez H., letter to Secretario de Relaciones Exteriores (SRE), Dirección General de Protección, April 3, 1985, Fondo Laredo, caja 18, expediente 73–26/732.84, Nuevo Centro de Detención Condad de Webb, SRE, Mexico City; Kahn, *Other People's Blood*, 117.

56. For more on Celia's story, see Dubose, "Central American Children of War."

57. Proyecto Libertad, "Children Held Hostage."

58. *Flores v. Meese*, 681 F. Supp. 655 (C.D. Cal. 1988).

59. Kahn, *Other People's Blood*, 117–18.

60. Proyecto Libertad, "A Child's Nightmare in Laredo."

61. *Plyler v. Doe*, 457 U.S. 202, 225 (1982).

62. Kahn, *Other People's Blood*, 119.

63. Fernando Tafoya, telephone interview. Kahn searched ten contracts (a total of seventy-one pages) for Laredo, from the March 7, 1984, solicitation offer to the last amendments to the contract, dated March 10, 1985, and found no mention of an agreement for children's recreational space; see Kahn, *Other People's Blood*, 183.

64. Kahn, "Detention Camps More Horrendous for Young Inmates."

65. Kahn, *Other People's Blood*, 118.

66. Ramon, "Strip Searches at Laredo Facility."

67. Kahn, "Detention Camps More Horrendous for Young Inmates."

68. Ramon, "Strip Searches at Laredo Facility."

69. Kahn, *Other People's Blood*, 118, 126.

70. *Flores v. Meese*, 681 F. Supp. 655 (C.D. Cal. 1988).

71. Kahn, *Other People's Blood*, 120; and see *Orantes-Hernandez v. Meese*, 685 F. Supp. 1488 (C.D. Cal. 1988).

72. Proyecto Libertad, "Update: Refugee Children in the Valley."

73. Biden, "Reforming Our Incarceration System"; Franzblau, "Phase Out of Private Prisons."

74. Hesson, "Close to 1,000 Migrant Children Separated by Trump."
75. Human Rights Watch, "Groups Urge US End Discriminatory ICE 'Gang' Prioritization"; "ACLU: 911 Children Split at Border since 2018 Court Order," AP News.
76. Rozensky, "The Biden Administration Routinely Separates Immigrant Families."

BIBLIOGRAPHY

AFSCME Corrections United (American Federation of State, County and Municipal Employees). *Don't Be a Prisoner to Empty Promises: Prison Privatization, The Five Empty Promises*. Pamphlet, n.d.

American Civil Liberties Union. *Warehoused and Forgotten: Immigrants Trapped in Our Shadow Private Prison System*. New York: American Civil Liberties Union, 2014.

AP News. "ACLU: 911 Children Split at Border Since 2018 Court Order." July 31, 2019.

Biden, Joseph R. "Reforming Our Incarceration System to Eliminate the Use of Privately Operated Criminal Detention Facilities." Exec. order 14006, January 26, 2021. American Presidency Project. https://www.presidency.ucsb.edu/node/347867.

Bureau of Justice Statistics. "Federal Criminal Case Processing Statistics." U.S. Department of Justice. Accessed July 10, 2023. https://bjs.gov/fjsrc/.

Chapman, Leonard F. "How Millions of Illegal Aliens Sneak into the U.S." Interview. *US News and World Report*, July 22, 1974.

Congressional Research Service. "Immigration Enforcement Within the United States." Report RL33351, April 6, 2006.

Cullison, Jennifer L. "The Growth of Immigrant Caging in Postwar America: National Immigration Policy Choices, Regional Shifts Toward Greater Carceral Control, and Continuing Legal Resistance in the US and South Texas." PhD diss., University of Colorado, 2018.

Culp, Richard. "The Failed Promise of Prison Privatization." *Prison Legal News* (blog). Human Rights Defense Center, October 15, 2011. https://www.prisonlegalnews.org/news/2011/oct/15/the-failed-promise-of-prison-privatization/.

Cumming-Bruce, Nick. "Taking Migrant Children from Parents Is Illegal, U.N. Tells U.S." *New York Times*, June 5, 2018.

Danini, Carmina. "Prisons for Profit: Detention Center Needs Beckon Private Enterprise." *Laredo Morning Times*, April 26, 1984.

Davis, Kristina. "U.S. Officials Say They Are Highly Confident to Have Reached Tally on Separated Children: 4,368." *Los Angeles Times*, January 18, 2020.

Dickerson, Caitlin. "Hundreds of Immigrant Children Have Been Taken from Parents at U.S. Border." *New York Times*, April 20, 2018.

Dickerson, Caitlin. "Trump Plan Would Curtail Protections for Detained Immigrants." *New York Times*, April 13, 2017.

Dubose, Louise. "Central American Children of War." *Texas Observer*, November 22, 1985.

Fixler, Philip E. "Behind Bars We Find an Enterprise Zone." *Wall Street Journal*, November 29, 1984.

Franzblau, Jesse. "Phase Out of Private Prisons Must Extend to Immigration Detention System." National Immigrant Justice Center, January 28, 2021. https://immigrantjustice.org/staff/blog/phase-out-private-prisons-must-extend-immigration-detention-system.

Frelick, Bill. *Refugees at Our Border: The US Response to Asylum Seekers*. Washington, D.C.: U.S. Committee for Refugees, 1989.

Galacatos, Dora, Alan Shapiro, and Brett Stark. "The Cruel Ploy of Taking Immigrant Kids from Their Parents." *New York Times*, February 28, 2018.

Global Legal Research Directorate. "Criminalization of Illegal Entry Around the World." Law Library of Congress, August 2019.

Goodwin, Liz. "'Children Are Being Used as a Tool' in Trump's Effort to Stop Border Crossings." *Boston Globe*, June 10, 2018.

Gramlich, John. "Far More Immigration Cases Are Being Prosecuted Criminally Under Trump Administration." Pew Research Center, September 27, 2019. https://www.pewresearch.org/fact-tank/2019/09/27/far-more-immigration-cases-are-being-prosecuted-criminally-under-trump-administration/.

Hernández, Kelly Lytle. *City of Inmates: Conquest, Rebellion, and the Rise of Human Caging in Los Angeles, 1771–1965*. Chapel Hill: University of North Carolina Press, 2017.

Hesson, Ted. "Close to 1,000 Migrant Children Separated by Trump Yet to Be Reunited with Parents." Reuters, February 2, 2023. https://www.reuters.com/world/us/close-1000-migrant-children-separated-by-trump-yet-be-reunited-with-parents-2023-02-02/.

Human Rights Watch. "Groups Urge US End Discriminatory ICE 'Gang' Prioritization." Letter to Alejandro Mayorkas, U.S. Department of Homeland Security. April 1, 2021. https://www.hrw.org/news/2021/04/01/groups-urge-us-end-discriminatory-ice-gang-prioritization.

Kahn, Robert. "Detention Camps More Horrendous for Young Inmates." *Ottawa Citizen*, May 18, 1985.

Kahn, Robert. *Other People's Blood: US Immigration Prisons in the Reagan Decade*. Boulder, Colo.: Westview Press, 1996.

Kilani, Hazar. "Thousands of Migrant Children Allegedly Sexually Abused in US Custody." *Guardian*, February 27, 2019.

Kriel, Lomi. "Trump Moves to End 'Catch and Release,' Prosecuting Parents and Removing Children Who Cross Border." *Houston Chronicle*, November 25, 2017.

Long, Clara. "The False Choice Between Family Separation and Detention: ICE Has Abandoned an Effective Alternative That Keeps Families Free." Human Rights Watch, June 26, 2018. https://www.hrw.org/news/2018/06/26/false-choice-between-family-separation-and-detention.

Long, Clara. "More Action Is Needed to End Family Separations and Protect Children at the Border." Human Rights Watch, February 13, 2021. https://www.hrw.org/news/2021/02/13/more-action-needed-end-family-separations-and-protect-children-border.

National Immigrant Justice Center. "Children Detained by the Department of Homeland Security in Adult Detention Facilities." Fact sheet, May 2013.

Proyecto Libertad. "Children Held Hostage." Newsletter (Harlingen, Tex.), September 1985.

Proyecto Libertad. "A Child's Nightmare in Laredo." Newsletter (Harlingen, Tex.), December 1986.

Proyecto Libertad. "A Legal Primer." Newsletter (Harlingen, Tex.), October 1989.

Proyecto Libertad. "The Numbers Are Down." Newsletter (Harlingen, Tex.), Spring 1991.

Proyecto Libertad. "Orantes Contempt Action Seeks to Counter Massive Rights Violation." Newsletter (Harlingen, Tex.), June 1989.

Proyecto Libertad. "A Report from Laredo." Newsletter (Harlingen, Tex.), June 1989.

Proyecto Libertad. "Update: Refugee Children in the Valley." Newsletter (Harlingen, Tex.), June 1989.

Quan, Gordon. "Don't Rush to Immigration Services Yet." *Southwest Chinese Journal*, July 1, 1984.

Ramon, Dora. "Strip Searches at Laredo Facility." Proyecto Libertad newsletter (Harlingen, Tex.), July 1985.

Reigstad, Leif. "Records Reveal Southwest Key Cited for Hundreds of Violations in the Last Three Years." *Texas Monthly*, June 28, 2018. https://www.texasmonthly.com/news-politics/records-reveal-southwest-key-cited-hundreds-violations-last-three-years/.

Rosenberg, Mica. "Nearly 1,800 Families Separated at U.S.-Mexico Border in 17 Months Through February." Reuters, June 8, 2018. https://www.reuters.com/article/us-usa-immigration-children-exclusive/exclusive-nearly-1800-families-separated-at-us-mexico-border-in-17-months-through-february-idUSKCN1J42UE.

Rozensky, Jordyn. "The Biden Administration Routinely Separates Immigrant Families." National Immigration Justice Center, January 19, 2022. https://immigrantjustice.org/staff/blog/biden-administration-routinely-separates-immigrant-families.

Shear, Michael, Julie Hirschfeld Davis, David Kaplan, and Robert Pear. "Federal Judge in California Halts Splitting of Migrant Families at Border." *New York Times*, June 26, 2018.

Sides, John. "The Extraordinary Unpopularity of Trump's Family Separation Policy (in One Graph)." *Washington Post*, June 19, 2018.

Solon, Olivia, Julia Carrie Wong, Pamela Duncan, Margaret Katcher, Patrick Timmons, and Sam Morris. "3,121 Desperate Journeys Exposing a Week of Chaos Under Trump's Zero Tolerance." *Guardian*, October 14, 2018.

Speed, Shannon. "The US Is Jailing Immigrant Women and Children Under Appalling Conditions." *The World*. PRX, October 10, 2014. https://theworld.org/stories/2014 -10-10/us-jailing-immigrant-women-and-children-under-appalling-conditions.

Tolchin, Martin. "Jails Run by Private Companies Force It to Face Question of Accountability." *New York Times*, February 19, 1985.

Trump, Donald J. "Affording Congress an Opportunity to Address Family Separation." Exec. order 13841, June 20, 2018. American Presidency Project. https://www .presidency.ucsb.edu/node/333089.

UNHRC (UN Refugee Agency). *Convention and Protocol Relating to the Status of Refugees*. Geneva: UNHRC, 2010.

UN News. "UN Rights Chief Slams 'Unconscionable' US Border Policy of Separating Migrant Children from Parents." June 18, 2018. https://news.un.org/en/story/ 2018/06/1012382.

U.S. Department of Homeland Security. "ICE Total Removals, Through August 25, 2012." August 25, 2012. https://www.ice.gov/doclib/about/offices/ero/pdf/ero -removals1.pdf.

U.S. Department of Homeland Security. *U.S. Immigration and Customs Enforcement: Budget Overview*. Fiscal year 2018. October 2017. https://www.dhs.gov/sites/ default/files/publications/ICE%20FY18%20Budget.pdf.

U.S. Department of Justice, Immigration and Naturalization Service. *1952 Annual Report of the Immigration and Naturalization Service*. Washington, D.C.: U.S. Government Printing Office, 1952.

U.S. Department of Justice, Immigration and Naturalization Service. *INS Information Bulletin*, June 24, 1953.

U.S. Department of Justice, Office of Public Affairs. "Attorney General Announces Zero-Tolerance Policy for Criminal Illegal Entry." News release, April 6, 2018. https://www.justice.gov/opa/pr/attorney-general-announces-zero-tolerance -policy-criminal-illegal-entry.

U.S. Department of Justice, Office of the Inspector General. *Review of the Department of Justice's Planning and Implementation of Its Zero Tolerance Policy and Its Coordination with the Departments of Homeland Security and Health and Human Services*. January 2021, rev. April 2022. https://oig.justice.gov/sites/default/files/ reports/21-028_o.pdf.

Wamsley, Laurel. "As It Makes More Arrests, ICE Looks for More Detention Centers." *The Two-Way*. NPR, October 26, 2017. https://www.npr.org/sections/thetwo-way/ 2017/10/26/560257834/.

Warren, Susan. "Counseling Plan Initiated for Inmates Awaiting Parole." *Houston Chronicle*, July 9, 1987.

Wynn, Maksim. "The Detention Archipelago: Immigrant Prisons and the Companies That Run Them." *Kennedy School Review*, June 22, 2018. https://ksr.hkspublications .org/2018/06/22/.

3

HUMAN TRAFFICKING AND THE POLITICS OF STATE VIOLENCE THROUGH OPERATION LONE STAR

ANTONIO VÁSQUEZ

IN 2000, THE UN GENERAL Assembly adopted the Protocol to Prevent, Suppress and Punish Trafficking in Persons as a supplement to the Convention Against Transnational Organized Crime. There were three clear objectives. The first was to "prevent and combat trafficking in persons," especially women and children. Second, the protocol emphasized the need to "protect and assist the victims of such trafficking." And third, the protocol sought to promote cooperation among participating nations. Support for the protocol, which went into effect in 2003, was strengthened by legislation passed among participating member nations. In the United States, this support was realized through the signing of the Victims of Trafficking and Violence Protection Act of 2000, which has subsequently been renewed in 2003, 2006, 2008, 2013, and 2018. One underlying message behind this legislative support is that human trafficking is an important issue and political leadership will use whatever resources available to counter, combat, and stop it.[1]

This essay complicates this view by examining how the language of human trafficking has also been used to perpetuate conditions of exploitation and vulnerability for recent migrants subjected to anti-immigrant policies and rhetoric in the United States. Operation Lone Star (OLS) in Texas serves as the case study in this essay. Announced by

Texas governor Greg Abbott on March 4, 2021, OLS is a state-funded multibillion-dollar business that deploys state law enforcement officials to "high-threat" areas along the Texas-Mexico border to deter migration to the United States. The success of OLS is due in part to the normalization of xenophobia as promulgated by the Trump campaign and presidency, including the conflation of human trafficking with immigration enforcement. Abbott employed this same approach to justify the purpose and expansion of OLS, within a framework of national security. From his perspective, OLS is a necessary counter to stop human trafficking and to keep communities safe, especially children. This essay challenges this view by demonstrating how OLS, justified partly through the human trafficking narrative, builds on and accentuates the continued criminalization of Black and Brown migrants and the militarization of the Texas-Mexico border. OLS should thus be positioned and opposed as the most recent rendering of state violence.

To contextualize this discussion, the next section describes how the human trafficking narrative emerged and became conflated with a restrictive immigration enforcement agenda at the federal level during the Trump administration. The second section examines the relationship between the Trump presidency and the Abbott governorship vis-à-vis human trafficking and immigration enforcement. Finally, the last part provides a critique of Operation Lone Star through a critical lens of human trafficking.

"IT IS INDEED A CRISIS"

Donald Trump made human trafficking one of his highest priorities during his presidency. In January 2020, in commemoration of the twentieth anniversary of the Victims of Trafficking and Violence Protection Act, Trump declared that his administration was "100 percent committed to eradicating human trafficking from the earth." On this occasion, he created a new seat on the Domestic Policy Council to tackle this matter and signed an executive order called Combating Human Trafficking and Online Child Exploitation in the United States. He also released a National Action Plan to Combat Human Trafficking, with the charge of directing the federal government to end human trafficking in the United

States. As early as 2017, Trump signed an executive order to target transnational criminal organizations that use human trafficking. In April 2018, he signed legislation to combat online sex trafficking. The U.S. Department of Health and Human Services also modernized the National Human Trafficking Hotline, and the U.S. Department of Homeland Security (DHS) established the Center for Countering Human Trafficking to coordinate human trafficking investigations among law enforcement agencies. Other examples of legislation signed by Trump around this issue include the Trafficking Victims Protection Reauthorization Act of 2017, the Trafficking Victims Protection Act of 2017, the Abolish Human Trafficking Act of 2017, and the Frederick Douglass Trafficking Victims Prevention and Protection Reauthorization Act of 2018. In 2019, Trump designated January as National Slavery and Human Trafficking Prevention Month. By January 2020, he declared that he had "never seen such enthusiasm for a single issue as [he had] for human trafficking."[2]

A corollary to Trump's embrace of human trafficking as part of his platform was his active pursuit of an immigration enforcement agenda that exacerbated conditions of precarity and exploitation for persons subjected to human trafficking. The deepening of federal immigration enforcement was also part and parcel of the George W. Bush and Barack Obama administrations. The Trump administration diverged in two slight ways, however. First, Trump openly employed anti-Mexican and anti-immigrant rhetoric during his 2016 presidential campaign and entire presidency, positioning Black and Brown "foreigners" as threats to the nation. This rhetoric was complemented by policies throughout his administration, from the Muslim Ban, which sought to deny refugee migrants from specific countries, to the use of Title 42 to expel asylum-seeking migrants in the United States in the wake of COVID-19.

A second distinction was Trump's incorporation of the language around human trafficking to build support for his immigration enforcement agenda. One key issue that defined the Trump campaign and administration, for example, was the call to build a wall between the United States and the Republic of Mexico. In February 2019, Trump pitched his support for the wall as a necessary physical barrier to the trafficking of persons across the geopolitical border. He argued that human trafficking by airplane was not possible. He asserted that "human trafficking by van and truck, in the backseat of a car, and going through a border where there's nobody for miles and miles, and there's no wall to protect—it's very easy. They make a right, then they make a left. They come into our country. And they sell people. And we cannot let it go on." The building of a wall was also necessary, Trump further argued, to protect national security. "Our progress will be limited if we don't secure our porous border and put an end to the human trafficking and humanitarian crisis that is taking place at the southern border," he declared. "It is indeed a crisis. And, you know, we have right now an invasion."[3] Of course, it is difficult to visualize the crossing of vehicles through the imposed geopolitical border between the United States and Mexico, which includes a river as well as desert, mountainous terrain, and other physical impediments. Accordingly, based on statistics from 2019, nearly 80 percent of migrants subjected to conditions of human trafficking had crossed through legal ports of entry. The call for a physical barrier did not address this concern. A wall between the two countries would also be ineffective for persons subjected to conditions of human trafficking within the United States, citizens and noncitizens alike. These and other points of contention to Trump's distortions, however, are moot. More visible and damaging here was Trump's conflation of human trafficking with unauthorized immigration in order to justify more enforcement, especially the militarization of the border.[4]

This link has been harmful to persons subjected to conditions of abuse and exploitation in the United States. According to Saket Soni from the National Guestworker Alliance, for example, "criminalising immigrants makes them more vulnerable to forced labour, human trafficking, and modern-day slavery." Likewise, Sarah Mehta from the American Civil Liberties Union (ACLU) cautioned that heightened immigration enforcement pushes people further underground and creates "a significant chilling effect on reporting labour abuses."[5] Persons without legal status become more afraid to come forward because of the threat of deportation. Such was the case in February 2017, when an undocumented transgender woman appeared in a domestic violence court to request a protective order in El Paso, Texas. The presiding judge granted the order, but, subsequently, U.S. Immigration and Customs Enforcement (ICE) came forward and arrested her for deportation. In defense of this practice, a DHS spokesperson declared, "Just because they're a victim in a certain case does not mean there's not something in their background that could cause them to be a removable alien." And so, as Eric Schwartz from Refugees International claimed in January 2020, the Trump immigration enforcement agenda fosters conditions of abuse and exploitation by decreasing the use of extant legal protections.[6]

One key protection available to immigrants is the T visa, which was established with the passing of the Victims of Trafficking and Violence Protection Act in 2000. Through the T visa, noncitizens seeking protection from human trafficking and assisting law enforcement with an investigation can attain legal status and remain in the United States for a period, with work authorization and benefits. At the very least, the T visa provides stability for survivors of human trafficking. The Trump administration made the stipulations for receiving approval for the T visa stringent. For example, the U.S. Citizenship and Immigration Services (USCIS), which facilitates the process, sought out further evidence "that a person was indeed trafficked or that their trafficking history is the reason they are still in the U.S." According to USCIS data, in 2019 the United States had more T visa denials and fewer approvals than at any time in the preceding decade. The processing time for T visa applications was also extended, from 7.9 months in 2016 to 2.4 years in 2019. As a result, there is a large backlog of T visa applications. In addition, in November 2018, Trump announced that persons being denied a T visa may instead be issued a notice to appear by the federal government, to begin deportation proceedings. Jean Bruggeman from the Freedom Network USA— the largest coalition of anti-trafficking service providers and advocates in the country—noted in October 2020, "We've got at least four years, if not eight, of harmful policies that are making it easier for traffickers, pushing survivors further into the shadows and causing service providers who are most likely to be able to identify trafficking victims to not trust federal agencies."[7]

"THE LONE STAR STATE IS SECURING THE BORDER"

Since taking office in January 2015, Texas governor Greg Abbott has condemned his state to a growing political nativism. In May 2017, he signed Texas Senate Bill 4 (SB4), which targets local jurisdictions that do not cooperate with federal immigration enforcement. Initiated by state senator Charles Perry (R-Lubbock), SB 4 allows the state government to charge local officials with a crime, remove them from office, and impose fines. Abbott has also supported state legislation that restricts how race relations can be discussed in classrooms, enables citizens to buy and carry handguns without a license, changes election rules to increase voter suppression, and bars most abortions from being performed in the state. Abbott's platform benefited greatly from the Trump presidency. Speaking at the White House in May 2020, then-president Trump described Abbott as a "very special governor."[8] Their highly publicized special relationship stems partly from Abbott's expanding political ambitions, including an endorsement by Trump for Abbott's 2022 reelection bid (the former president held a political rally near Houston, Texas, in February of that year, during which the governor took center stage). There is also a synchronization of policies and approaches. For this reason, as early as October 2017, Manny Garcia from the Texas Democratic Party astutely observed that "Donald Trump is pushing the policies that Greg Abbott has crafted in Texas." That is, the "Greg Abbott playbook is what Donald Trump is trying to do." This observation certainly reflects Abbott's active push for immigration enforcement, which has continued beyond the Trump presidency, with equally damaging results.[9]

One key element that has defined Abbott's political career to date was the launching of OLS in early March 2021. Under OLS, Texas Department of Public Safety (DPS) troopers and agents, Texas Rangers, and Texas National Guard members—in collaboration with local police— are deployed to "high-threat" areas along the Texas-Mexico border. This operation follows the Prevention Through Deterrence model enacted under Bill Clinton in the 1990s, which included Operation Gatekeeper, Operation Hold the Line, and the like. The intention was that law enforcement personnel deployed to the border would, through their mere presence, act as a deterrent to migration. "From deterring illegal immigration, to preventing the smuggling of drugs and weapons, to curtailing human trafficking," according to Abbott, "the deployment of resources and personnel needed to arrest and jail criminals along the border is imperative to our comprehensive border security strategy under Operation Lone Star."[10] When Abbott took office in January 2015, roughly 1,000 Texas National Guard members were already activated along the border by then-governor Rick Perry. Abbott authorized the soldiers to remain there. In March 2021, after Joe Biden's administration reported 173,000 migrants at the border, roughly 70,000 more than in March 2019, Abbott announced his own state-run operation (that is, OLS) in the same month. As of January 2022, Abbott has deployed around 10,000 Texas National Guard members and law enforcement officers to the border under OLS. In addition, OLS funding has included resources such as a grant program to encourage city and county government collaboration and the placement of more physical barriers along the border, like fencing and steel shipping containers. In November 2022, Texas Military Department officials ordered an unknown number of military M113 armored personnel carrier vehicles to be positioned along the Texas-Mexico border as part of OLS. The Texas legislature to date has allocated more than $4 billion to support the operation, with an additional $1 billion announced by the governor in December 2021 (along with $54 million in private donations) for the construction of a border wall, to begin in Starr County. Abbott has adopted and expanded a key provision from the Trump presidency through the solicitation of private funds and state taxpayer money.[11]

Like Trump, Abbott has justified his approach through a lens of national security. That is, he uses his platform to portray immigrants as foreigners and threats to the nation to advance his immigration enforcement agenda. As one example, in the wake of COVID-19 in early March 2021, Abbott criticized the Biden administration for causing physical harm to the health and well-being of citizens in his state. In an interview with CNBC, Abbott stated without providing evidence, "The Biden administration has been releasing immigrants in South Texas that have been exposing Texans to COVID." In another statement in late June 2021, Abbott claimed that "homes are being invaded" and farmers were losing their livestock and crops because of the "carnage that is being caused by the people who are coming across the border." And in an interview on the Fox Business show *Mornings with Maria* in late January 2022, Abbott further criticized the Biden administration for failing to keep communities safe from threats of violence. Abbott first cautioned against immigrants who come from more than 150 countries around the globe to the Texas-Mexico border. "We have a president who's in charge," he then declared, "who's not protecting . . . [our] national security by allowing people from terrorist[-]based nations [to] come across the border."[12] At the very least, these statements create a sense of fear and loathing toward immigrants. In this view, immigrants do not come to the United States out of necessity, to better their lives and the lives of others. They come to invade, cause harm, and destroy. This false anti-immigrant narrative has been used to demonstrate a need for border immigration enforcement in general and OLS specifically.[13]

Another key component in Abbott's justification for OLS has been the issue of human trafficking. This focus is not particular to the current governor. As early as 2003, three years after the UN Protocol to Prevent, Suppress and Punish Trafficking in Persons was adopted, state leadership in Texas passed its first legislation that defined human trafficking. In subsequent years, state legislators from both political parties provided additional support to raise awareness and stop human trafficking. Texas has consistently been one of the most active states in the nation with respect to legislation around this issue. Abbott, too, supported efforts against human trafficking in his previous role as state attorney general. During his 2014 gubernatorial campaign, he also identified sex trafficking, what he termed "modern-day slavery," as one of his top ten issues.[14]

Abbott's promotion of human trafficking awareness has continued in his role as governor. As recently as January 2022, he proclaimed, "we must stand unified against human trafficking in Texas and work to end the exploitation of women and children in our state."[15] Pertinent to this study, his call to stand against human trafficking has taken place alongside his push for immigration enforcement. This convergence was most visible when Abbott announced the expansion of OLS to include anti–human trafficking efforts in late March 2021. The occasion was the establishment of temporary shelters by the Federal Emergency Management Agency (FEMA) to house unaccompanied minors apprehended at the border, primarily from Central America. President Biden charged FEMA and the U.S. Department of Health and Human Services with the task of expanding shelter capacity and providing necessities to the youth on a temporary basis. Localities were identified for this purpose, including the Kay Bailey Hutchison Convention Center in Dallas, the Freeman Coliseum in San Antonio, and a former camp for oil field workers in Midland.[16]

Speaking about this development at a news conference in Dallas, Abbott again criticized the Biden administration, accusing it of creating a humanitarian crisis at the border by "enriching the cartels, smugglers, and human traffickers who often prey on and abuse unaccompanied minors." The new initiative within OLS would be supported by the Child Sex Trafficking Team in the Office of the Governor. Abbott further announced that DPS troopers, DPS agents, and Texas Rangers under OLS would interrogate the minors to identify persons subjected to human trafficking and gather intelligence. OLS is necessary, according to Abbott, "to keep these children safe, root out human trafficking or other criminal activity, and prevent more children from being trafficked and abused."[17] In one response, Dallas County judge Clay Jenkins criticized the governor for politicizing the plight of these youth as a distraction from his failed leadership with respect to the COVID-19 vaccine and the devastating winter storm that shut down the state's power grid in February 2021. "There is work to be done to fix our broken immigration system," Jenkins further stated. "Traumatized kids are not a proxy for this issue or anyone's viewpoint."[18] Immigrant rights advocates also challenged the sincerity of the governor's concern for the safety and well-being of minors. In a press release, for example, the Refugee and Immigrant Center for Education and Legal Services (RAICES) noted that Abbott's political rhetoric has consistently contributed to the dehumanization of and attacks against migrant children and their families. His support of anti-immigrant laws in Texas has also created conditions in which sponsors and parents are unable or afraid to go through the process of reuniting with their children in detention. Furthermore, RAICES pointed out that the governor was not using measures currently available to him to protect these children: "if the Governor is serious about his concerns regarding the safety of migrant children, he can ensure that any victims of possible abuse are given a U Visa," a document that (similar to the T visa) is available to those who "fall victim to certain crimes, including sexual assault."[19] Jessica Azua from the Texas Organizing Project cautioned against the governor's attempt to use the dire situation of unaccompanied migrant children to advance his push for immigration enforcement. "To address this moment in the most humane way possible," Azua stated, "we need ample funding and resources from our federal government, including more social workers, trauma specialists, medical professionals, and human rights specialists who can provide direct, needed assistance—NOT more militarization along our southern border."[20]

HUMAN TRAFFICKING REVISITED

In January 2022, a Travis County judge ruled that OLS was unconstitutional because the operation violates the Supremacy Clause of the U.S. Constitution. The case involved the arrest of a migrant originally from Ecuador who had traversed the geopolitical border without authorization to seek asylum in the United States. When he crossed the border, the man was arrested and incarcerated in Kinney County on a criminal trespass charge. Lawyers on his behalf argued that their client was jailed rather than being considered for asylum, which was within his right. "The Texas government is restraining the liberty of thousands under the guise of criminal trespass prosecutions," they further argued, "in an attempt to usurp federal immigration legislation and strong arm the federal government into enacting policies that Gov. Abbott would prefer." The Travis County district attorney, acting on behalf of the state, partly supported this contention. That is, part of OLS does represent "an impermissible attempt to intrude on federal immigration policy," according to the district attorney. As a result, the defendant has applied for asylum and is awaiting trial in the United States.[21] Ironically, OLS has provided an opportunity for defendants to circumvent federal immigration policies from the Trump administration, specifically Title 42 and the Migrant Protection Protocols. Title 42 authorizes federal officials to automatically expel refugee migrants before they can make an asylum claim in the United States, if this action is justifiable due to a public health concern. Trump used Title 42 to expel thousands of migrants in the wake of COVID-19. Migrant Protection Protocols, or the Remain in Mexico policy, requires asylum seekers to wait in Mexico for their U.S. immigration hearings. In the case of the Ecuadoran defendant, federal law would have meant that he was automatically expelled under Title 42, rather than arrested and held in Texas. In this way, "Operation Lone Star has allowed our clients to avoid a federal program where they would have not only been expelled but would have had to remain in Mexico (amid) pending asylum proceedings," stated attorney Kristin Etter from Texas RioGrande Legal Aid.[22]

In December 2021, attorneys from the ACLU of Texas, the Texas Civil Rights Project, the Texas Fair Defense Project, and others called for a full investigation by the U.S. Department of Justice into OLS for federal civil rights violations. Title VI of the Civil Rights Act of 1964 bars discrimination based on race, color, or national origin. The purpose of OLS is not simply to act as a deterrent for migration, as promoted by the governor. OLS also exists to punish migrants for coming to the United States. "It's plain that the trespass program is a pretextual use of state criminal law," according to their request, "with the underlying interest of harming Black and Brown migrants." For example, at the time that the attorneys submitted their request, more than 2,200 people had been arrested on misdemeanor state criminal trespass charges under OLS. Most if not all of those arrested were Latinx and Black migrant men. This view is consistent with 168 arrest affidavits across two counties provided by DPS troopers under OLS: 72 in Val Verde County, and 96 in neighboring Kinney County. From these arrests, DPS troopers noted approximately 98 percent as "H/M" (Hispanic male) and 2 percent as "B/M" (Black male). OLS thus exists in practice as a form of "state-sanctioned targeting" of immigrants. "There is an urgent need for federal action to protect the rights of Black and Brown migrants targeted by this unlawful system," the attorneys further noted, "and to ensure that this kind of pretextual discriminatory program does not flourish in Texas or spread to other states."[23]

Building on these critiques and others, this essay calls for a reexamination of the significance of OLS from the perspective of human trafficking. In other words, the language of human trafficking provides a useful lens to understand the complexity and severity of this state operation. As defined in the UN Protocol to Prevent, Suppress and Punish Trafficking in Persons, human trafficking refers to "the recruitment, transportation, transfer, harboring or receipt of persons, by means of the threat or use of force or other forms of coercion, of abduction, of fraud, of deception, of the abuse of power or of a position of vulnerability or of the giving or receiving of payments or benefits to achieve the consent of a person having control over another person, for the purpose of exploitation." Whether persons are enticed into their predicament or recruited by force or coercion, the key matter here is that one person has complete control over another person, for the purpose of exploitation.[24]

Several resonances exist between the meaning of human trafficking and practices of apprehension and detention under OLS. There is, first, the recruitment and enticement of migrants into the operation. In some instances, OLS officers encourage migrants to break the criminal trespass law only to then arrest and incarcerate them. In one testimony, for example, a refugee migrant originally from Venezuela describes walking with other migrants along a road near Del Rio and noticing two officials dressed in camouflage. The two officials signaled for the man and other migrants to go to them. According to the man, "so, obeying their hand signals, we walked through the gate to talk to them. I told them I was seeking asylum, and they said to me in English, 'sit down here.'" He was then told that he and the others had committed a crime and were to be arrested because they had trespassed onto private property. "I walked towards the officials because I thought they would help us seek safety. I had no idea I was on private property."[25] Similarly, in another testimony, a migrant originally from Nicaragua was arrested and jailed with his brother under OLS after being invited to walk through an open gate by law enforcement:

> My brother and I arrived at an open gate with a sign that said "no trespassing" in English. On the other side of the gate, we saw two young men wearing tan and gray uniforms. The two appeared to be American soldiers and they had a little camp set up. . . . We called out to them from outside the gate, said "we are here to apply for asylum" and waved our blue and white Nicaraguan flag to try to get their attention. The soldiers invited us to come to the other side of the gate. They started to approach us and said in Spanish, "Vengan aquí" (come over here) and "tranquilo" (stay calm). We hesitated at first because of the "no trespassing" sign, but as the soldiers continued to insist and walked to meet us at the gate, eventually we followed their instructions and went to meet them on the other side of the gate. We felt safe entering the gate because they had invited us.[26]

These excerpts reflect the degree of deception and abuse of power exercised by OLS officers to entrap migrants into their business. The migrants would not have committed a "criminal" act if they had known about the consequences.

A second resonance involves the way that migrants are arrested and held captive against their will. Hundreds of those arrested under OLS have been incarcerated for weeks and months without a court date or a defense attorney. They are completely dependent on law enforcement officials. The two migrants whose testimony I excerpted earlier, from Venezuela and Nicaragua, were jailed for sixty-three days and thirty-seven days, respectively. This inclination to extend jail time speaks to the governor's promotion of OLS as an "arrest and jail" system, as opposed to the "catch and release" system associated with federal immigration policy.[27]

This also speaks to the third and final resonance, which is exploitation reflected in the generation of revenue. As the ACLU and civil rights attorneys noted in December 2021, the purpose of OLS is to deter migration and to punish migrants from coming to the United States. From the perspective of human trafficking, there is an economic benefit to be gained from the business of arresting and incarcerating primarily Black and Brown male migrants under OLS. In September 2021, for example, Abbott signed into law Texas House Bill 9 (HB9), thereby funneling $1.8 billion from state taxpayer funds to border security over the next two years. This included $32.5 million to the Office of Court Administration, $301 million to the Texas Military Department, $154.8 million to DPS, $273.7 million to the Texas Department of Criminal Justice, $214,785 to the Texas Commission on Jail Standards, $3.75 million to the Border Prosecution Unit, $16.4 million to the Texas Department of State Health Services, and $1.02 billion to local grants, processing centers, and the construction and placement of more barriers. The bill earmarked funds for three distinct OLS jail booking facilities, including one in Jim Hogg County, and approximately $74 million from OLS was diverted to assist border cities and countries near the Texas-Mexico border. Also in December 2021, Abbott's Public Safety Office awarded an additional $38.4 million for jail operations and court administrative activities in direct support of OLS. This included $16 million for additional income to peace officers, jailers, prosecutors, indigent defense counsel, and administrative court staff; $19.5 million for the purchase of equipment and supplies like more patrol vehicles, radios, surveillance equipment, bulletproof vests, and thermal/night vision technology; $1.9 million for the construction and maintenance of radio towers; and $800,000 for travel costs to nonborder counties that provide law enforcement assistance to "border disaster-declared counties." In short, like other human trafficking endeavors, OLS is a business that thrives on the exploitation of human beings.[28]

In one respect, Operation Lone Star represents a continuation of an immigration enforcement agenda espoused by the Trump administration. Abbott expressed this sentiment when he announced in June 2021 the solicitation of private donations and the allocation of state funds to be used for the completion of Trump's multibillion-dollar wall between the United States and Mexico. Abbott made his case then while using descriptives like homes "being invaded" and "carnage . . . being caused by the people who are coming across the border." In this way, he picked up where the former president left off. In December 2021, the Texas governor even declared that the state cost for building the wall was "going to cost less than it did for the Trump administration."[29]

Certainly, Abbott's own political nativism, including in his role as governor, precedes the Trump presidency, and he would have plausibly continued in this direction without Trump's successful election. It is clear, however, that he greatly benefited from and amplified a politics that he has sought to parallel with the Trump brand at the federal level, one that promotes fear and dehumanization of the Other and policies that disproportionately affect Black and Brown working-class communities. The formation and expansion of OLS partly reflect the successful culmination of this confluence on the part of Abbott. The governor's reliance on the language of human trafficking to build consent for his operation, within a Gramscian framework, was also a strategy employed by Trump at the federal level.[30]

This recognition, however, also poses a challenge. On the one hand, the language of human trafficking has become integrated into global political discourse over the past two decades. The adoption of the Protocol to Prevent, Suppress and Punish Trafficking in Persons by the UN General Assembly in 2000 was paramount. Participating member nations, including the United States, created and adopted their own legislation in concert with the United Nations. Since 2003, state leadership in Texas has also actively pursued legislation to raise awareness and combat human trafficking. There is thus a greater sensibility regarding and abhorrence toward human trafficking. At the same time, the modern era of globalization has facilitated the proliferation of human trafficking, and nations have played a role in fomenting conditions of exploitation. Part of the challenge in the current political moment is to remove the legitimacy of the state as the sole authority on what constitutes "human trafficking." At the very least, this removal is necessary to shed light on the complicity of the state in creating and perpetuating the violent conditions of human trafficking. Such is the case with Abbott's Operation Lone Star, the most recent manifestation of state violence in Texas.

NOTES

1. UN General Assembly, Resolution 55/25, Protocol to Prevent, Suppress and Punish Trafficking in Persons Especially Women and Children (November 15, 2000).

2. Trump, "Combating Human Trafficking and Online Child Exploitation"; Superville, "Trump Signs Order Creating Post Focused on Human Trafficking"; White House, "President Donald J. Trump Is Fighting to Eradicate Human Trafficking"; Abrams, "I Thought I Was Going to Die."

3. White House, "Remarks by President Trump in Meeting on Human Trafficking on the Southern Border."

4. Long, "AP Fact Check"; Shooster, "Trump Isn't Fighting Human Trafficking, He's Facilitating It."

5. Soni and Mehta quoted in Shooster, "Trump Isn't Fighting Human Trafficking, He's Facilitating It."

6. "Undocumented Transgender Woman Filing Domestic Violence Claim Arrested," *CBS News*; DHS spokesperson quoted in Shooster, "Trump Isn't Fighting Human Trafficking, He's Facilitating It"; Schwartz quoted in Superville, "Trump Signs Order Creating Post Focused on Human Trafficking."

7. Quoted material from Abrams, "I Thought I Was Going to Die"; see also Shooster, "Trump Isn't Fighting Human Trafficking, He's Facilitating It"; "Undocumented Transgender Woman Filing Domestic Violence Claim Arrested," *CBS News*; Superville, "Trump Signs Order Creating Post Focused on Human Trafficking."

8. Trump, "Remarks in a Meeting with Governor Gregory W. Abbott of Texas."

9. Garcia quoted in Svitek, "Abbott Chases Bigger Share of Hispanic Vote in 2018"; see also Walsh, "Gov. Greg Abbott Signs SB 4"; O'Hanlon, "Why These Texas Republicans Say They Won't Vote for Gov. Greg Abbott."

10. Office of the Texas Governor, "Governor Abbott Announces an Additional $38.4 Million in Funding."

11. Winkie and Barragán, "Deplorable Conditions, Unclear Mission"; Bartiromo, McDowell, and Concha, "Fed Signals Rate Hike in March to Cool Inflation"; Lepore and Phillips, "Lone Star State Goes It Alone"; Edgar Sandoval, "Texas Says It Will Build the Wall"; Winkie and Melhado, "Texas Guard to Send Tank-Like Military Vehicles."

12. Quoted, respectively, in Alvarez, "Texas Gov. Abbott Stalled Federal Offers to Test Migrants Then Blamed Them for Spreading COVID"; Weber, "Texas' Abbott Lead GOP Push for Trump-Style Border Measures"; Bartiromo, McDowell, and Concha, "Fed Signals Rate Hike."

13. Office of the Texas Governor, "Governor Abbott Provides Update on Operation Lone Star in Weslaco."

14. Smith, Satija, and Walters, "How Hollow Rhetoric and a Broken Child Welfare System Feed Texas' Sex-Trafficking Underworld"; Abbott for Governor, "Issues."

15. *Governance, Risk, and Compliance Monitor Worldwide*, "Gov. Greg Abbott Urges Denton County Leaders to Stand Unified."

16. "Gov. Abbott Signs Border Security Funding into Law," *Athens (Tex.) Daily Review*; Office of the Texas Governor, "Governor Abbott Announces Expansion of Operation Lone Star"; Garnham, "Gov. Greg Abbott Says Texas Will Target Human Traffickers."

17. Office of the Texas Governor, "Governor Abbott Announces Expansion of Operation Lone Star."

18. Quoted in Garnham, "Gov. Greg Abbott Says Texas Will Target Human Traffickers."

19. RAICES, "Gov. Abbott: If You Care About Migrant Children, Stop Persecuting Their Sponsors."

20. Quoted in Garnham, "Gov. Greg Abbott Says Texas Will Target Human Traffickers." See also RAICES, "RAICES in Bexar County Freeman Coliseum."

21. Quoted material from Lepore, "Texas Judge Rules Apprehension of Illegal Immigrant by Soldiers."

22. Quoted in Scherer, "How Gov. Abbott's Border Crackdown Is Backfiring."

23. Quoted material from Huddleston et al., "Texas Migrant Arrest Program Under 'Operation Lone Star,'" 4, 21, 2.

24. UN General Assembly, Resolution 55/25, Protocol to Prevent, Suppress and Punish Trafficking in Persons Especially Women and Children (November 15, 2000).

25. Quoted in Huddleston et al., "Texas Migrant Arrest Program Under 'Operation Lone Star,'" 18.

26. Quoted in Huddleston et al., 18.

27. Quoted in Huddleston et al., 14.

28. Huddleston et al.; Office of the Texas Governor, "Governor Abbott Thanks Tennessee Governor Bill Lee"; Office of the Texas Governor, "Texas Gov. Abbott Announces an Additional $38.4 Million in Funding"; "Gov. Abbott Signs Border Security Funding into Law," *Athens (Tex.) Daily Review*; Office of the Texas Governor, "Governor Abbott Opens Operation Lone Star Jail Booking Facility."

29. Weber, "Texas' Abbott Leads GOP Push for Trump-Style Border Measures"; Lepore and Phillips, "Lone Star State Goes It Alone."

30. Sandoval, "Texas Says It Will Build the Wall."

BIBLIOGRAPHY

Abbott for Governor (website). "Issues." Accessed February 14, 2022. https://www
.gregabbott.com.

Abrams, Abigail. "'I Thought I Was Going to Die': How Donald Trump's Immigration
Agenda Set Back the Clock on Fighting Human Trafficking." *Time*, October 30,
2020.

Alvarez, Priscilla. "Texas Gov. Abbott Stalled Federal Offer to Test Migrants Then
Blamed Them for Spreading Covid." *CNN*, March 5, 2021. https://www.cnn.com/
2021/03/04/politics/abbott-migrants-covid-testing/index.html.

Athens (Tex.) Daily Review. "Gov. Abbott Signs Border Security Funding Into Law."
September 22, 2021.

Bartiromo, Maria, Dagen McDowell, and Joe Concha. "First-Hand Look at Biden's
Border Crisis." *Mornings with Maria*, Fox Business, January 28, 2022. LexisNexis.

CBS News. "Undocumented Transgender Woman Filing Domestic Violence Claim
Arrested at El Paso Courthouse by ICE, Official Says." February 16, 2017. https://
www.cbsnews.com/news/undocumented-transgender-woman-filing-domestic
-violence-claim-arrested-at-el-paso-courthouse-by-ice-official-says/.

Garnham, Juan Pablo. "Gov. Greg Abbott Says Texas Will Target Human Traffickers
in Response to 'Humanitarian Crisis' at the Border." *Texas Tribune*, March 17,
2021.

Governance, Risk, and Compliance Monitor Worldwide. "Gov. Greg Abbott Urges
Denton County Leaders to Stand Unified Against Human Trafficking and Fentanyl." January 12, 2022. LexisNexis.

Huddleston, Kathryn, Savannah Kumar, Andre Segura, Maya Chaudhuri, Camilla
Hsu, Amanda Woog, Laura Peña, Kassandra Gonzalez, and Alexis Bay. "Texas
Migrant Arrest Program Under 'Operation Lone Star'—Urgent Need for Investi-
gation into Race and National Origin Discrimination by Texas Agencies." Letter
to Merrick Garland, Lisa Monaco, Vanita Gupta, Kristen Clarke, and Christine
Stoneman, December 15, 2021.

Lepore, Stephen M. "Texas Judge Rules Apprehension of Illegal Immigrant by Soldiers During Gov. Greg Abbott's 'Operation Lone Star' along Rio Grande Was
Unconstitutional." *Daily Mail*, January 13, 2022. https://www.dailymail.co.uk/
news/article-10400299/.

Lepore, Stephen M., and Morgan Phillips. "Lone Star State Goes It Alone: Texas Gov.
Greg Abbott Announces Work Has Started on $1B State-Funded Wall After Biden
Ended Federal Money." *Daily Mail*, December 19, 2021. https://www.dailymail.co
.uk/news/article-10325533/.

Long, Colleen. "AP Fact Check: Trump on Human Trafficking." AP News, February
5, 2019.

Office of the Texas Governor. "Governor Abbott Announces an Additional $38.4
Million in Funding for Operation Lone Star." Press release, December 20, 2021.

Office of the Texas Governor. "Governor Abbott Announces Expansion of Operation Lone Star to Include Anti–Human Trafficking Efforts." Press release, March 17, 2021.

Office of the Texas Governor. "Governor Abbott Opens Operation Lone Star Jail Booking Facility in Jim Hogg County." Press release, February 8, 2022.

Office of the Texas Governor. "Governor Abbott Provides Update on Operation Lone Star in Weslaco." Press release, April 1, 2021.

Office of the Texas Governor. "Governor Abbott Thanks Tennessee Governor Bill Lee for Operation Lone Star Support." Press release, December 7, 2021.

O'Hanlon, Morgan. "Why These Texas Republicans Say They Won't Vote for Gov. Greg Abbott." *Texas Tribune*, February 3, 2022.

RAICES (Refugee and Immigrant Center for Education and Legal Services). "Gov. Abbott: If You Care About Migrant Children, Stop Persecuting Their Sponsors." Press release, April 13, 2021.

RAICES (Refugee and Immigrant Center for Education and Legal Services). "RAICES in Bexar County Freeman Coliseum: The Facts." Press release, April 8, 2021.

Sandoval, Edgar. "Texas Says It Will Build the Wall, and Asks Online Donors to Pay for It." *New York Times*, June 16, 2021.

Scherer, Jasper. "How Gov. Abbott's Border Crackdown Is Backfiring, Giving More Migrants a Clearer Path to the U.S." *Houston Chronicle*, January 19, 2022.

Shooster, Jay. "Trump Isn't Fighting Human Trafficking, He's Facilitating It." *Just Security*, May 2, 2017. https://www.justsecurity.org/40461/trump-fighting-human -trafficking-facilitating/.

Smith, Morgan, Neena Satija, and Edgar Walters. "How Hollow Rhetoric and a Broken Child Welfare System Feed Texas' Sex-Trafficking Underworld." *Texas Tribune*, February 13, 2017.

Superville, Darlene. "Trump Signs Order Creating Post Focused on Human Trafficking." AP News, January 31, 2020.

Svitek, Patrick. "Abbott Chases Bigger Share of Hispanic Vote in 2018." *Texas Tribune*, October 7, 2017.

Trump, Donald J. "Combating Human Trafficking and Online Child Exploitation in the United States." Exec. order 13903, January 31, 2020. American Presidency Project. https://www.presidency.ucsb.edu/node/340057.

Trump, Donald J. "Remarks in a Meeting with Governor Gregory W. Abbott of Texas and an Exchange with Reporters." May 7, 2020. American Presidency Project. https://www.presidency.ucsb.edu/node/341931.

Walsh, Sean Collins. "Gov. Greg Abbott Signs SB 4: 'Texas Has Now Banned Sanctuary Cities.'" *Austin American-Statesman*, May 8, 2017.

Weber, Paul J. "Texas' Abbott Leads GOP Push for Trump-Style Border Measures." AP News, June 24, 2021.

White House (archived website). "President Donald J. Trump Is Fighting to Eradicate Human Trafficking." Press release, January 9, 2019. https://trumpwhitehouse

.archives.gov/briefings-statements/president-donald-j-trump-fighting-eradicate
-human-trafficking/.

White House (archived site). "Remarks by President Trump in Meeting on Human
Trafficking on the Southern Border." Press release, February 1, 2019. https://
trumpwhitehouse.archives.gov/briefings-statements/remarks-president-trump
-meeting-human-trafficking-southern-border/.

Winkie, Davis, and James Barragán. "Deplorable Conditions, Unclear Mission: Texas
National Guard Troops Call Abbott's Rushed Border Operation a Disaster." *Texas
Tribune*, February 1, 2022.

Winkie, Davis, and William Melhado. "Texas Guard to Send Tank-Like Military Vehicles to the Border." *Texas Tribune*, November 18, 2022.

4

THE UTERUS COLLECTORS

The Lineage of Hemispheric Medical Abuse and
Experimentation in the United States and Guatemala

ALEXANDRIA HERRERA

IN THE SUMMER OF 2020, at the height of the COVID-19 pandemic, whistleblower nurse Dawn Wooten came forward with allegations of gross medical neglect at the Irwin County Detention Center (ICDC) in Ocilla, Georgia. Wooten, a licensed nurse employed by ICDC, filed in collaboration with the advocacy group Project South a twenty-seven-page whistleblower report. Wooten explained, "We've [the nurses] questioned among ourselves like goodness he's taking everybody's stuff out.... That's his specialty, he's the uterus collector."[1] The report prompted national outcry, countless news articles, U.S. congressional inquiries, and federal investigations.[2] Wooten and detained women who spoke to Project South detailed atrocious instances of hysterectomies without informed consent. The majority of women that had undergone unnecessary gynecological procedures at ICDC were Black or of Latin American descent, from the Caribbean, Africa, and Latin America.[3] Wooten told Project South, "I've had several inmates tell me that they've been to see the doctor and they've had hysterectomies and they don't know why they went or why they're going."[4] Instead of using the medical interpretation line required to explain medical procedures to patients, nurses would try to simply google Spanish or ask another detained migrant to help translate. One woman told Project South that after talking to five others who had undergone a hysterectomy at ICDC between October and December 2019, "I thought this was like an experimental concentration camp. It was like they're experimenting with our bodies."[5]

The forced sterilizations at ICDC occurred during President Donald Trump's time in office (2017–21). The ICDC case is just one of countless atrocious actions committed during Trump's presidency. The Trump administration enacted policies that exposed migrants and BIPOC to physical harm and mental trauma. The Zero Tolerance policy, for example, spurred outrage against family separations at the U.S.-Mexico border, and the Stay in Mexico policy made it more challenging for migrants to claim asylum. The Trump administration's relentless attacks on migrants were cruel and racist. However, it would be misguided to claim that the administration's actions were unprecedented. Instead, the Trump administration's inhumane policies have a longer historical trajectory.

THE LEGACY OF REPRODUCTIVE MEDICAL EXPERIMENTATION

The events at ICDC are not the first time that the United States has been accused of performing unnecessary medical treatments and medical experimentation on Black, Latin American–descended, and Indigenous peoples' bodies. Academics, news outlets, activists, and public organizations have connected the events at ICDC to numerous acts of medical abuse in U.S. history. In the nineteenth century, enslaved persons were used during medical school training for autopsies, and their bodies and physical features were measured to justify their enslavement. Notoriously, J. Marion Sims, known as the "Father of Gynecology," used enslaved women for gynecological experimentation and research without anesthesia.[6] The events at ICDC have also been connected to the 1970s *Madrigal v. Quilligan* case, where ten Mexican American women filed a class-action lawsuit after they were coerced into undergoing sterilization surgery without informed consent. Less commonly, the ICDC case is compared to earlier cases of sterilizations, such as the sterilizations of poor women of color between 1929 and 1975 in North Carolina.[7] Other examples include sterilizations and birth control pill testing in the 1950s in Puerto Rico, and the infamous Tuskegee experiment (1932–72), which failed to treat Black men suffering from syphilis in Alabama.[8]

There has also been significant research on reproductive medical experimentation, birth control experimentation, and forced sterilizations in Latin America. Much of the research focuses on Chile and Peru. Still, there were other considerable cases of forced sterilizations in Colombia, Costa Rica, Mexico, the Dominican Republic, El Salvador, Panama, and Guatemala.[9] While the United States was not always directly involved in supporting and funding sterilizations in these countries, the ideological framework that supported sterilizations as a form of birth control for low-income women in these countries was inspired by U.S. Cold War–era neo-Malthusian beliefs that attributed poverty to rising birth rates.[10] Before the Cold War, sterilization was used by government officials to rid their nations of "undesirables" and the "feebleminded."

The use of the bodies of women of color for reproductive medical experimentation, including forced sterilizations, experimental birth control, and treatments for sexually transmitted infections (STIs), was global, but there was a concentration in the western hemisphere. This chapter addresses a connection that academics, journalists, and politicians have failed to make: the ICDC case in the United States and the U.S.-funded Guatemalan syphilis experiments of the 1940s.

During the Guatemalan syphilis experiments, John Cutler, the assistant surgeon general of the U.S. Public Health Service (USPHS) and the deputy director of the Pan American Sanitary Bureau (a precursor to the Pan American Health Organization), under the direction of Dr. John F. Mahoney and with funding from the U.S. National Institutes of Health, infected approximately two thousand people with syphilis without informed consent.[11] Cutler's victims were some of the most marginalized populations in Guatemala, including sex workers, asylum patients, orphans, and men in Guatemala's mostly Indigenous army. The U.S. officials behind the Guatemalan syphilis experiments used Latin America as a laboratory and then returned to the United States to conduct more extensive research using the lessons they had learned.

After Cutler's experiments in Guatemala, he returned to the United States and worked on the later stages of the Tuskegee experiment.[12] Cutler used Guatemala as his preliminary experimental site so that when he returned to the United States, he could ensure that his experiments were efficient. With support from Guatemalan officials, Cutler gained access to government institutions and marginalized individuals in Guatemalan society. Cutler and the Guatemalan government knowingly allowed infected sex workers to enter prisons and sleep with prisoners to infect them, and he used members of the Guatemalan Army for his experiments because they were a readily available, large population of mostly Indigenous men.[13] Conducting such an experiment necessitated sophisticated communication networks between U.S. and Guatemalan government officials, scientists, and doctors. The ICDC sterilization events are a direct legacy of the lessons that U.S. officials learned internationally and then returned to use domestically.

The ICDC cases of forced sterilization and the 1946–48 Guatemalan syphilis experiments demonstrate the importance of transnational and hemispheric research on sterilizations and reproductive medical abuse. The U.S. and Latin American government officials, scientists, and doctors co-constructed the arguments for using Central and Latin American women's bodies for medical research and experimentation.

The Guatemalan syphilis experiments and the cases of forced sterilization at ICDC are examples of medical professionals, scientists, and politicians that viewed the bodies of people of color as fit for medical experimentation. In the process, they left a trail of trauma that continues to affect Indigenous Mayans' willingness to undergo medical treatment. Indigenous people in Guatemala continue to express mistrust of non-Indigenous medical providers, especially for obstetrics and gynecological medical care.[14]

MEDICAL EXPERIMENTATION IN GUATEMALA

During the colonial period, the Spanish Empire was fascinated with its new territory and sent out countless expeditions searching for botanicals, animals, minerals, precious stones, and other goods to bring wealth to the Spanish Crown. Spanish doctors and naturalists worked tirelessly to discover how items from the New World could be applied to treat diseases and ailments. By the eighteenth century, what had been a search for curiosities had become a search for utilitarian goods that could make Spain competitive intellectually and economically with the rest of Europe and the world market, thus expanding the empire's influence.[15]

Early Spanish expeditions and experiments helped form Latin America into an important location for scientific and medical knowledge creation and dissemination. Specifically, Guatemala has long been at the center of medical knowledge production and education in Latin America. The contemporary Universidad de San Carlos in Guatemala City is one of the region's oldest and most prestigious medical schools. For U.S. scientists, Guatemala was a favorable site because it was viewed as exotic and remote enough to not be of concern to the average American, it had general freedom from regulations and legal constraints compared to the United States, and it was close enough to the United States for the easy movement of people, documents, tools, and research samples. Well-established United Fruit Company steamship routes used to transport shipments of bananas between port cities in Puerto Barrios and Livingston, Guatemala, and the United States helped facilitate the movement of goods and people.

Additionally, the legacy of Spanish colonial beliefs that Indigenous Central Americans were savage, backward, and dirty meant that Latin American government and public health officials in the twentieth century blamed diseases on Indigenous people, instead of acknowledging the lack of infrastructure or access to health care that made disease possible.[16] Colonial-era beliefs that Indigenous people were less-than-human "disease vectors" served as justification for treating Indigenous people as "acceptable" for experimentation by international and local medical researchers and as justification for conducting medical research in Guatemala.

Between 1943 and 1944, two years before conducting the Guatemalan syphilis experiments, John Cutler conducted failed experiments at the Terre Haute Federal Penitentiary in Indiana. During the Terre Haute experiments, the USPHS deliberately injected prisoners with gonorrhea but found it difficult to get the prisoners to exhibit signs of infection. Pressure in the United States about the ethics of the experiments forced the USPHS and Cutler to look for another suitable location to continue their work and extend it to include syphilis.[17] To justify the move to Guatemala, to secure financial support from the U.S. government, and to gain the approval of the Guatemalan government, Cutler had to explain that Guatemala was the ideal location for his experiment. He required a precedent for successful research on syphilis and gonorrhea in the country.

And he found it: between 1929 and 1933, Harvard Medical School tropical medicine professor George C. Shattuck and Harvard School of Public Health instructor of bacteriology Kenneth Goodner had traveled to southern Mexico and Guatemala to study the effects of syphilis and gonorrhea on the human body. Their pseudo-eugenic research argued that Indigenous people either experienced limited side effects from an infection or might be immune to the STIs.[18] Shattuck and Goodner claimed that Central America was a "suitable place" to study the impact of STIs on the body because racial differences between white and Indigenous people had to be responsible for the "milder cases" of syphilis experienced by Indigenous Central Americans, and they concluded that "the more Indian the blood, the milder the syphilis."[19] In Cutler's final report on his own experiments in Guatemala, he cited Shattuck and Goodner's studies, demonstrating how they served as a research precedent for his work.[20] Cutler also made use of the critical connections he had within Guatemala, including to the Ministry of Health, the National Army of the Revolution, the National Mental Health Hospital, and the Ministry of Justice. The USPHS had trained Dr. Juan Funes, Guatemala's leading venereal disease public health official, who helped organize access to test subjects.[21] The precedent set through earlier research, changing perceptions about the ethics of research in the United States, and the USPHS connections in Guatemala contributed to the country's selection for continued STI research by the USPHS.

Changing political conditions in Guatemala also made it the perfect location for such an experiment. At the end of the nineteenth century, the United Fruit Company was created through a merger of various shipping lines, railroads, plantations, and distribution networks. The company became immensely powerful over the twentieth century and was responsible for shaping political and social conditions in Latin America through purchases of large tracts of land that once belonged to Indigenous farmers, the use of violence to suppress union movements, and its ability to take advantage of coups against governments that failed to acquiesce to United Fruit's desires.[22] In 1931, backed by the United States, dictator general Jorge Ubico came to power in Guatemala and expanded the reach of United Fruit in the country. In October 1944, however, a movement spearheaded by students, teachers, military reformers, and the emerging middle class overthrew Ubico. Across the next decade, known as the Ten

Years of Spring, Guatemala had two democratically elected presidents, Juan José Arévalo and Jacobo Árbenz Guzmán. These presidents consolidated constitutional rule; extended the franchise to women, the poor, and Maya; established state-run social security and health care; enacted a labor code; ended forced labor on coffee plantations; and implemented land reforms. Árbenz Guzmán was overthrown in 1954 by the U.S. Central Intelligence Agency (CIA); his land reforms had challenged the control of United Fruit and U.S. governmental interests (many top U.S. officials had financially invested in United Fruit). The overthrow of Árbenz Guzmán was the CIA's first extensive Latin American coup of the Cold War. It allowed the United States to take control once again over Guatemalan political affairs. In the background of the changing social and political dynamics in the country, Cutler and the USPHS conducted the Guatemalan syphilis experiments.

THE LEGACIES AND LESSONS OF EXPERIMENTATION

The summer of 2020 saw political and social upheaval due to a global pandemic and protests in the United States and worldwide, which served as the backdrop as the first reports detailing the ICDC case were released to the public. Many of the countless news articles asked a similar question: how could this have occurred in the United States in 2020? But, given the history of the United States in conducting similar experiments abroad and domestically, some we may even still be unaware of, it does not seem as much out of the range of possibility.

The Trump administration drew on existing conservative U.S. rhetoric to fan flames of anger about failures in border policy and a so-called flood or siege of migrants at the U.S. border that spread disease and criminal activity, and that took jobs and social resources from white Americans. At the core of this rhetoric was racism, fear of the Other, and a general unwillingness to take responsibility for having created the conditions that made migration a necessity for survival. There is no coincidence that Cutler, Funes, and the USPHS viewed Indigenous Central Americans in the same light that the Trump administration and countless other officials have viewed contemporary migrants from Mexico, Central America, Latin America, and, more recently, Haiti and countries on the African continent.

Understanding how such atrocious acts of medical malpractice could have occurred domestically during the ICDC event requires a comprehensive understanding of the United States' involvement in reproductive abuse abroad. U.S. officials and medical personnel used Latin America as an experimental testing ground to explore questions they could not have answered in the United States due to the unethical nature of their research. Having left a trail of violence and abuse in Guatemala, U.S. officials then returned to the United States and used the knowledge they had gained abroad to underpin their domestic research, adapting it ever so slightly to meet the minimum ethical constraints in the United States. The ICDC event is the direct legacy of the Guatemalan syphilis experiments. The knowledge about how to conduct an experiment, including who to use as experimental subjects, was realized in Guatemala and then brought back to the United States.

It is important to understand why U.S. Immigration and Customs Enforcement (ICE) officials and the doctor they hired to provide medical care to detained migrants at ICDC deemed sterilization appropriate and necessary. Based on a precedent set by previous forced and coerced sterilization cases in the United States, it is plausible that the procedure was considered a form of population control. If the women were granted asylum or were deported but found a way to return to the United States, they would not be able to have children and thereby put a strain on U.S. social services. Another reason could be to stop the perceived threat of "anchor babies." Or, possibly, the sterilization of female migrants could be a form of deterrence to stop Central American, Latin American, and African migrants from coming to the United States: migrants sterilized in U.S. ICE detention centers might, upon deportation and return to their communities, warn other women about what awaits them in U.S. detention facilities.

The inhumane experiments at ICDC and in Guatemala are not isolated cases but are part of a larger transnational movement with interlocking ideologies and practices of racist science, medicine, and disrespect for the autonomy and reproductive capacity of racialized women. The trauma of these events continues to exist within localized and national communities across the United States and Latin America. For example, Indigenous communities in Guatemala are extremely skeptical of the Western medical community and non-Indigenous medical providers. Continued academic research on cases of medical abuse and experimentation has important practical applications for improving how medical providers educate and inform their patients, addressing the trauma caused by medical malpractice, and empowering communities to gain access to health care.

NOTES

1. Project South, "Lack of Medical Care, Unsafe Work Practices, and Absence of Adequate Protection," 19.
2. For just a sampling of articles published by significant news outlets, see Manian, "Immigration Detention and Coerced Sterilization"; Moore, "ICE Is Accused of Sterilizing Detainees"; Treisman, "Whistleblower Alleges 'Medical Neglect'"; see also 166 Cong. Rec. H5123–36 (daily ed. October 1, 2020).
3. O'Toole, "19 Women Allege Medical Abuse in Georgia Detention Center."
4. Project South, "Lack of Medical Care, Unsafe Work Practices, and Absence of Adequate Protection," 19.
5. Project South, 20.
6. Briggs, "The Race of Hysteria."
7. Schoen, *Choice and Coercion*; *Madrigal v. Quilligan*, Civ. no. 75–2057 (C.D. Cal. 1978). Another intervention that should be included in the discussion of the ICDC case is the news coverage that presented the use of sterilizations as a black-and-white issue, claiming that women were always the victims of coercion and forced sterilizations. Considerable feminist research has investigated the many, complex reasons why poor women would opt for sterilization. This research challenges the perceived notion that sterilizations are always forced on women. Importantly, however, the concept of "choosing" to be sterilized as a form of birth control is just as complex for women who do not have other viable options. For more on feminist discussions of choice, see López, "Agency and Constraint"; López, *Matters of Choice*.
8. Briggs, *Reproducing Empire*; Hartmann, *Reproductive Rights and Wrongs*; Colón Warren et al., *Políticas, visiones y voces en torno al aborto en Puerto Rico*; Mass, "Puerto Rico"; CARASA, *Women Under Attack*.
9. On less commonly researched countries that have had widespread use of sterilizations for birth control, see Stycos, "Sterilization in Latin America." For more on Guatemala, specifically, see Santiso G., Bertrand, and Pineda, "Voluntary Sterilization in Guatemala"; IPPF WHR, "Male Sterilization in Guatemala"; Kestler et al., "Humanizing Access to Modern Contraceptive Methods."
10. For more on Peru and Chile, see Pieper Mooney, "Re-Visiting Histories of Modernization, Progress, and (Unequal) Citizenship Rights"; Pieper Mooney, *The Politics of Motherhood*; Walsh, "The Executioner's Shadow." On the transna-

tional conversations about birth control, see Pieper Mooney, "Of 'Zipper Rings' and 'Tatum Ts,' Chile–USA."

11. Sporadic recordkeeping during Cutler's experiments means that there is currently not an objective, agreed-on total number for the experimental subjects. Numbers typically range between 1,300 and 3,000 people.

12. There is a common misconception that officials involved with the Tuskegee experiment infected African American men with syphilis. Instead, they failed to provide proper medical care and treatment to patients who were already suffering from the disease. See Reverby, "'Normal Exposure' and Inoculation Syphilis," 7.

13 Cutler was specifically testing the use of penicillin among soldiers suffering from STIs in the U.S. Army. For this reason, using soldiers from the Guatemalan Army made sense.

14. Cerón et al., "Abuse and Discrimination Towards Indigenous People in Public Health Care Facilities."

15. On the use of flora and fauna as utilitarian goods, see Clark, "Appealing to the Republic of Letters"; Goodman, "Science, Medicine, and Technology in Colonial Spanish America."

16. Briggs and Mantini-Briggs, *Stories in the Time of Cholera*.

17. Reverby, "'Normal Exposure' and Inoculation Syphilis," 10–11.

18. Cutler, *Final Syphilis Report*, part 7 and bibliography; Shattuck and Goodner, "Preliminary Communication on Syphilis in Yucatan."

19. Shattuck and Goodner, "Have the Maya a Partial Immunity to Syphilis?," 262.

20. Cutler, *Final Syphilis Report*, part 1, fs. 7; Cutler, *Final Syphilis Report*, part 7 and bibliography.

21. Reverby, "'Normal Exposure' and Inoculation Syphilis," 11.

22. Adams, "Conquest of the Tropics," 144.

BIBLIOGRAPHY

Adams, Frederick U. "Conquest of the Tropics." In *The Guatemala Reader: History, Culture, Politics*, edited by Greg Grandin, Deborah T. Levenson, and Elizabeth Oglesby, 144–50. Durham, N.C.: Duke University Press, 2011.

Briggs, Charles L., and Clara Mantini-Briggs. *Stories in the Time of Cholera: Racial Profiling During a Medical Nightmare*. Berkeley: University of California Press, 2004.

Briggs, Laura. "The Race of Hysteria: 'Overcivilization' and the 'Savage' Women in Late Nineteenth-Century Obstetrics and Gynecology." *American Quarterly* 52, no. 2 (2000): 246–73.

Briggs, Laura. *Reproducing Empire: Race, Sex, Science, and U.S. Imperialism in Puerto Rico*. Berkeley: University of California Press, 2002.

CARASA (Committee for Abortion Rights and Against Sterilization Abuse). *Women Under Attack: Abortion, Sterilization Abuse, and Reproductive Freedom*. New York: Photo Comp Press, 1979.

Cerón, Alejandro, Ana Lorena Ruano, Silvia Sánchez, Aiken S. Chew, Diego Díaz, Alison Hernández, and Walter Flores. "Abuse and Discrimination Towards Indigenous People in Public Health Care Facilities: Experiences in Rural Guatemala." *International Journal for Equity in Health* 15 (2016): article 77. https://doi.org/10.1186/s12939-016-0367-z.

Clark, Fiona. "Appealing to the Republic of Letters: An Autopsy of Anti-Venereal Trials in Eighteenth-Century Mexico." *Social History of Medicine* 2, no. 1 (2013): 2–21.

Colón Warren, Alice E., Ana Luisa Dávila, Maria Dolores Fernós, and Esther Vicente. *Políticas, visiones y voces en torno al aborto en Puerto Rico*. San Juan: Universidad de Puerto Rico, 1999.

Cutler, John. *Final Syphilis Report*. 7 parts, c. 1940s. CDC record group 442, Hollinger Box 1a, folders 1–7, John Cutler Papers, National Archives and Records Administration. https://www.archives.gov/research/health/cdc-cutler-records.

Goodman, David. "Science, Medicine, and Technology in Colonial Spanish America: New Interpretations, New Approaches." In *Science in the Spanish and Portuguese Empires, 1500–1800*, edited by Daniela Bleichmar, Paula De Vos, Kristin Huffine, and Kevin Sheehan, 9–34. Stanford, Calif.: Stanford University Press, 2008.

Hartmann, Betsy. *Reproductive Rights and Wrongs: The Global Politics of Population Control*. Boston: South End Press, 1995.

IPPF WHR (International Planned Parenthood Federation, Western Hemisphere Region). "Male Sterilization in Guatemala." *IPPF/WHR News Service*, no. 4–5 (1976): 19–40.

Kestler, Edgar, Beatriz Barrios, Elsa M. Hernández, Vinicio del Valle, and Alejandro Silva. "Humanizing Access to Modern Contraceptive Methods in National Hospitals in Guatemala, Central America." *Contraception* 80, no. 1 (2009): 68–73.

López, Iris. "Agency and Constraint: Sterilization and Productive Freedom Among Puerto Rican Women in New York City." *Urban Anthropology and Studies of Cultural Systems and World Economic Development* 22, no. 3–4 (1993): 299–323.

López, Iris. *Matters of Choice: Puerto Rican Women's Struggle for Reproductive Freedom*. New Brunswick, N.J.: Rutgers University Press, 2008.

Manian, Maya. "Immigration Detention and Coerced Sterilization: History Tragically Repeats Itself." American Civil Liberties Union, September 29, 2020. https://www.aclu.org/news/immigrants-rights/immigration-detention-and-coerced-sterilization-history-tragically-repeats-itself/.

Mass, Bonnie. "Puerto Rico: A Case Study of Population Control." *Latin American Perspectives* 4, no. 4 (1977): 66–81.

Moore, Steven. "ICE Is Accused of Sterilizing Detainees: That Echoes the U.S.'s Long History of Forced Sterilization." *Washington Post*, September 25, 2020.

O'Toole, Molly. "19 Women Allege Medical Abuse in Georgia Detention Center." *Los Angeles Times*, October 22, 2020.

Pieper Mooney, Jadwiga E. "Of 'Zipper Rings' and 'Tatum Ts', Chile–USA: Intrauterine Devices, Men of Science, and Women in Need." *Comparativ* 28, no. 3 (2018): 14–32.

Pieper Mooney, Jadwiga E. *The Politics of Motherhood: Maternity and Women's Rights in Twentieth-Century Chile.* Pittsburgh, Pa.: University of Pittsburgh Press, 2009.

Pieper Mooney, Jadwiga E. "Re-Visiting Histories of Modernization, Progress, and (Unequal) Citizenship Rights: Coerced Sterilization in Peru and in the United States." *History Compass* 8, no. 9 (2010): 1036–54.

Project South. "Lack of Medical Care, Unsafe Work Practices, and Absence of Adequate Protection Against COVID-19 for Detained Immigrants and Employees Alike at the Irwin County Detention Center." Letter to Joseph V. Cuffari, Cameron Quinn, Thomas P. Giles, and David Paulk, September 14, 2020. https:// projectsouth.org/wp-content/uploads/2020/09/OIG-ICDC-Complaint-1.pdf.

Reverby, Susan. "'Normal Exposure' and Inoculation Syphilis: A PHS 'Tuskegee' Doctor in Guatemala, 1946–1948." *Journal of Policy History* 23, no. 1 (2011): 6–28.

Santiso G., Roberto, Jane T. Bertrand, and Maria Antonieta Pineda. "Voluntary Sterilization in Guatemala: A Comparison of Men and Women." *Studies in Family Planning* 14, no. 3 (1983): 73–82.

Schoen, Johanna. *Choice and Coercion: Birth Control, Sterilization, and Abortion in Public Health and Welfare.* Chapel Hill: University of North Carolina Press, 2005.

Shattuck, George C., and Kenneth Goodner. "Have the Maya a Partial Immunity to Syphilis?" In *The Peninsula of Yucatan: Medical, Biological, Meteorological, and Sociological Studies,* by George C. Shattuck, 259–63. Washington, D.C.: Carnegie Institution of Washington, 1933.

Shattuck, George C., and Kenneth Goodner. "Preliminary Communication on Syphilis in Yucatan." In *The Peninsula of Yucatan: Medical, Biological, Meteorological, and Sociological Studies,* by George C. Shattuck, 217–20. Washington, D.C.: Carnegie Institution of Washington, 1933.

Stycos, J. Mayone. "Sterilization in Latin America: Its Past and Its Future." *International Family Planning Perspectives* 10, no. 2 (1984): 58–64.

Treisman, Rachel. "Whistleblower Alleges 'Medical Neglect,' Questionable Hysterectomies of ICE Detainees." NPR, September 16, 2020. https://www.npr.org/ 2020/09/16/913398383/whistleblower-alleges-medical-neglect-questionable -hysterectomies-of-ice-detaine.

Walsh, Sarah. "The Executioner's Shadow: Coerced Sterilization and the Creation of 'Latin' Eugenics in Chile." *History of Science* 60, no. 1 (2018): 18–40.

5

REFLECTIONS ON RIGHT-WING LEADERSHIP IN THE UNITED STATES

From LAPD Chief William Parker to Donald Trump

ROBERTO A. MÓNICO

TRUMP'S DEHUMANIZING IMMIGRATION POLICIES WERE not the first of their kind in the United States. The George W. Bush and Barack Obama administrations, for example, both utilized the 287(g) program, which deputizes local police departments to act as de facto federal immigration agents, to detain unauthorized immigrants within the borders of the United States.[1] Numerous sitting presidents—regardless of their party affiliation—have conducted some form of deterrence, detainment, or deportation to sway immigrants from entering the United States. However, most presidents have focused their deportation efforts on Latin American immigrants. In 1994, President Bill Clinton enacted Operation Gatekeeper during his first term to appear tough on unauthorized immigration and appeal to the conservative electorate.[2] Moreover, in 1996, the Illegal Immigration Reform and Immigrant Responsibility Act expanded aggravated felonies and mandated that undocumented immigrants serve their prison sentence in the United States before being deported.[3] Regardless of the administration in power, liberal and conservative presidents have hyperpoliced immigrant communities and scapegoated them as the source of crime and economic woes while ignoring decades of colonialism, imperialism, and U.S. efforts to overthrow democratically elected governments.[4] Such foreign policies led immigrants to flee their countries to search for basic living standards and a semblance of dignity. These foreign issues are hardly discussed within the American context of its purported greatness. Instead, the narrative is reframed to give the appearance that the United States is a nation where immigrants are unquestionably welcomed.

Since the 1950s, politicians have advocated for enhanced deportation strategies to target people of Latina/o/x descent. In 1953, for example, U.S. attorney general Herbert Brownell expressed concern that people of Mexican descent were a problem for the American workforce.[5] In the 1990s, California governor Pete Wilson supported the ballot initiative Proposition 187 ("Save Our State"), which would have precluded undocumented people from receiving education, health care, and access to social programs. Wilson wanted local law enforcement professionals, such as Los Angeles Police Department (LAPD) officers, to act as deputized immigrant agents to investigate the status of undocumented people.[6] Brownell and Wilson are examples of individuals who used draconian anti-immigrant policies to target undocumented immigrants. This chapter discusses two leading proponents of such polices: LAPD chief William H. Parker and former president Donald Trump. Parker and Trump exerted their authority in the press by producing and reproducing old narratives that criminalized undocumented communities while attempting to avoid appearing racist. They presented themselves as steadfast leaders of a deportation regime punishing and deporting undesirable immigrants. The history of deporting unwanted immigrants is long, but to understand its current manifestation, I examine how the federal government worked with local municipalities throughout the 1950s, at a time when police departments like the LAPD became de facto federal border patrol agencies.[7]

This article compares Parker and Trump, two right-wing leaders who used specific rhetoric to criminalize undocumented Latin American immigrants. Parker was the chief of the LAPD between 1950 and 1966. He joined the force in 1927 and reshaped the LAPD. For example, in 1934, he was a co-architect of the rewritten Los Angeles Charter Amendment Section 202, which protected police officers from public scrutiny and disciplinary actions unless doled out internally. Parker transformed the LAPD from a local disgrace replete with scandals to the best professionally trained police force in the United States. He has been lauded for increasing police salaries, instituting a paramilitary apparatus, and installing a corruption-free police department. His authoritarian rule emphasized military analogies, such as "police science" derived from criminologist August Vollmer.[8] When Parker was appointed chief in 1950, the LAPD radically changed, becoming a quasi-military centralized bureaucracy. The newly transformed department was unleashed onto the streets of Los Angeles as a tightly structured paramilitary apparatus, an occupying battalion entrenched in nonwhite neighborhoods, targeting individuals who appeared "suspicious." Parker's policies are critical to understanding the similarities he shared with Trump because both men advocated for the repatriation of people of Latina/o/x descent by using this paramilitary structure of policing. They did so by positioning themselves as saviors who could restore law and order. The Parker era left a blueprint later taken up by men like Trump. Their rise to power was predicated on villainizing and further marginalizing undocumented communities.

Anti-immigrant sentiment toward the Latina/o/x community has a long history, but one pivotal moment can be traced to the midcentury, when the U.S. Immigration and Naturalization Service (INS) conducted an operation to deport unauthorized people of Mexican descent from the interior of the United States: Operation Wetback.[9] Today, many conservatives and ultra-right-wingers champion the fifties as an era when white people were at the apex of a racial hierarchy that attempted to obscure the overt and institutional racism embedded within our social structures. Trump capitalized on this era as a marketing strategy during his campaign and presidency, as was clearly apparent to his detractors. His followers, however, saw this form of capitalist production as a reinforcement of their beliefs, expressed through fashion in MAGA ("Make America Great Again") products.

Much has rightfully been said about the Trump administration's draconian stance on immigration, but his presidency was not the first to implement anti-immigrant policies. Older anti-immigrant legacies—stemming from an era that readily produced fabricated moral threats to the white power structure—have become the framework used to criminalize undocumented populations. In taking up this legacy, both Parker and Trump relied on a savior complex, representing themselves as sober-minded leaders who were concerned for the safety of their supporters while scapegoating immigrants as the source of high crime rates.

Many politicians in the United States have positioned immigrants as undeserving to be citizens. With limited access to legal recourse, immigrants remain vulnerable to a mode of punishment that includes deportation and separation from loved ones.[10] Conservative discourse perpetuates the false narrative that criminalizes immigrants, with right-wing media operatives often employing misrepresentations of immigrants as unfit to be Americans. This, in turn, fosters public consensus regarding a need to apprehend, incarcerate, and forcefully remove immigrants from the United States. Regrettably, the United States has a disturbing history of people of Mexican descent enduring this deportation regime. During the 1950s, according to the INS, millions of Mexicans were repatriated to Mexico (current research argues that the INS figures were likely exaggerated to prove success, but families were still torn apart). With the aid of the LAPD, people of Mexican descent, regardless of documented status, were criminalized. Such partnerships continue to operate today between local agencies and the U.S. Immigration and Customs Enforcement (ICE).[11] With this history in mind, this chapter argues that these two eras are crucial to understanding the long trajectory of deportations in the United States: the 1950s, when local and federal law enforcement agencies worked in concert to deport people of Mexican descent in Los Angeles, and the years of the Trump presidency (2017–21), when the president and other officials extended these exclusionary policies by falsely claiming that immigrants committed more "crime" than American citizens.[12]

In his leadership of the LAPD, Parker's use of anti-immigrant rhetoric was strikingly similar to Trump's own, many decades later. With the help of the press, people of Mexican descent were villainized as political subversives. Local newspapers such as the *Los Angeles Times* promoted this narrative to scare their white readership. Trump's anti-immigrant policies are merely an extension of the way immigrant communities have been criminalized in the media. Today's young generation may have never witnessed such cruelty, specifically the separation of children from their parents, but this was also executed during so-called liberal administrations, such as with Bill Clinton and Barack Obama.[13]

CONSERVATIVES AND LIBERALS: UNDERSTANDING
THE DEPORTATION REGIME

During the years of the Trump presidency, the Republican Party's stance on undocumented immigrants became a focal point for liberals. The racist rhetoric employed by Trump during his presidential bid in 2015–16 emboldened white supremacists' beliefs of racial superiority and nationalism, two key components of fascism. Liberals were astonished to discover that over sixty million people voted for Trump in 2016 and then, four years later, over seventy million. Stunned by his victory, liberals began using platitudes of resistance, attempting to counter Trump's rhetoric. The so-called postracial society that liberals espouse obfuscates the racism within our social institutions, including police departments and the unions that support Trump. His administration promoted efforts to hyperbolize what has been called a precarious demarcation between chaos and order.[14] It is worth pausing to reevaluate what each side represents. In this regard, "chaos" was associated with leftist organizations that support undocumented communities and a slew of social issues, such as abolishing ICE and defunding the police, whereas "order" reflected police power and people who supported fabricated causes, such as an opposition to the "siege" of American cities by immigrants, leftists, and criminals. However, those who were astounded by Trump's victory have seemingly been immersed in a life that shields them from the day-to-day racism that nonwhite communities endure regularly.[15] Local law enforcement and federal agents have long worked together to criminalize nonwhite and undocumented communities.

Liberals who exalted the Clinton and Obama administrations as a framework of progress must acknowledge their role in advancing criminal justice in this country: the Clinton administration passed the Violent Crime Control and Law Enforcement Act of 1994, which created the Office of Community Oriented Policing Services (COPS), and the Obama administration significantly increased funding to this office.[16] Both administrations also gave local police departments more money to acquire military-style equipment. It would be used to patrol poor and working-class neighborhoods. Clinton deployed 350 military troops to help with immigration law enforcement along the California and Arizona border, with the sole purpose of deterring immigrants from entering the country.[17] Obama, for his part, expanded Secure Communities, a database used by the U.S. Department of Homeland Security to determine whether immigrants are living in the country unauthorized (by 2013, a record 3,181 jurisdictions were using the program).[18] These technological advancements, accelerated by bloated budgets, are not used to patrol white, affluent communities. Rather, they have been utilized to target vulnerable immigrant communities.

Criminalization has long been a major component of the racial formation of the United States. Scholars such as Khalil Gibran Muhammad have astutely noted that crime has historically been ascribed to race, beginning in the late nineteenth century.[19] In the production of racial formation, the ascription of criminal activity to certain racial and ethnic groups such as people of Mexican descent can mold public opinion. This is a useful analytic when discussing how unauthorized border crossing has been associated with Latina/o/x people. Right-wing media helps perpetuate this narrative of criminality. Unauthorized immigrants have been falsely portrayed as criminals who have entered the country "illegally," by a media that simultaneously ignores the reasons that force them to emigrate. In this view, because of the unauthorized route they embarked on, people who live in the United States without proper documentation can only be of Latina/o/x descent. Making the production of "illegality" worse, Trump began his 2016 campaign with racist and false allegations such as, "Mexico sends their worst . . . rapists and such." This salvo of politically and racially charged language shocked liberals, but for the right-wingers, Trump was simply reinforcing their racist beliefs, which culminated in his presidential victory.[20]

The Trump presidency is the result of white resentment that has been festering since the gains of the civil rights movement. This strategy was first applied when Richard Nixon won the presidency in the late sixties, and again with Ronald Reagan in the eighties.[21] It is worth noting that both Republican presidents won two terms, which reflects the white anger seen in the United States across those decades. Racist white people have fallaciously depicted themselves as the true victims in a country where nonwhite people are striving to regain their power after years of abandonment, violence, and discriminatory practices in schools, work sites, and the criminal legal system. Claiming that Latina/o/x immigrants are draining economic resources and that they are the source of rising crime has become a focal point for Trump, who exploits white anxieties. The narrative that criminalizes (undocumented) Latina/o/x immigrants as a public nuisance can be understood more clearly when seen in tandem with the one that declares white Americans to be the true victims, robbed of legal entitlements.[22] White lives are provided with sanctioned protections akin to the commodification of private property, as critical race theorist Cheryl Harris explains: "Whiteness defined the legal status of a person as slave or free. White identity conferred tangible and economically valuable benefits, and it was jealously guarded as a valued possession, allowed only to those who met a strict standard of proof. Whiteness—the right to white identity as embraced by the law—is property if by 'property' one means all of a person's legal rights."[23] Immigrants are not seen as Americans in the eyes of Trump supporters. This was made evident when millions of white Americans embraced Trump as their president in 2016, and again in 2020. Furthermore, to disguise their racism, many claimed that they accept immigrants entering the United States, but only through a legal pathway. A repeated claim recalls how their European ancestors arrived in the United States, while omitting their family's participation in genocidal warfare against Native Americans.[24]

The American myth of Manifest Destiny, which saw North America as vacant lands awaiting white settlement, plays into this false narrative that has been widely exploited by conservative leadership to garner support from racist white people. The genocidal warfare aimed at Native Americans and the enslavement of Africans falsely propagated a chauvinistic representation of American individualism, characterizing white Americans as rugged individuals who built a society out of sheer hard work, while the surrounding population was portrayed as uncivilized and without history. This characterization of American identity led to the othering of people who were considered to be racially impure based on blood quantum. The hypodescent rule stipulated that any drop of nonwhite blood—usually but not always African—was deemed to be contaminated.[25] As violence and blood spilled across the North American continent, the social construction of hypodescent seeped into the consciousness of millions of Europeans, and the ideology that arose was racial superiority and nationalism. European descendants believed that the land preordained them, justifying their murderous rampage. The racialized project of the United States is grounded in acts of violence that persist today. Vigilante violence and military conquest under the guise of Manifest Destiny and the doctrine of discovery were followed by the rise of local police departments to not only annihilate unwanted populations, but criminalize them in the process.[26] This diluted history foregrounds North America as a land where Europeans created an advanced civilization, with large swaths of land becoming the private property of those individuals who toiled to achieve them.[27]

The history of the United States often omits the horrific experiences of nonwhite communities. Shameful acts of violence, conquest, and imperialism distort the myth of American exceptionalism, revered by conservatives and liberals alike. The Trump presidency was criticized for detaining undocumented immigrants and refugees at the border, and rightfully so. The separation of children from their families was an appalling act and a form of psychological abuse. However, when the Obama administration broke deportation records and itself separated families, liberals were silent on the issue, redirecting their attention to executive orders like Deferred Action for Childhood Arrivals (DACA), announced in 2012. Marveled at as a great achievement, the policy did not provide a pathway to citizenship for undocumented families. According to political scientist Alfonso Gonzales, the Obama administration pacified the immigrant rights movement in order to temporarily garner support for social reforms thought to protect undocumented individuals who contributed to the United States economically and militarily.[28] DACA was a step in the right direction but left millions without legal protections from work raids and deportations. As Malcolm X once shrewdly pointed out regarding the lack of progress in the United States, "If you stick a knife in my back nine inches and pull it out six inches, there's no progress. If you pull it all the way out there's no progress. The progress is healing the wound that the blow made."[29] In this case, the wound that is in dire need of healing can be traced back to the 1950s, when the deportation regime sought to exclude people of Mexican descent from the United States through Operation Wetback. Liberals are quick to blame the Trump administration's anti-immigrant policies because of the appalling language he used to galvanize his base during campaigning—but they shouldn't overlook that this language was simply not as digestible as the furtive raids and deportations overseen by the Obama administration.[30] The fact of the matter is that deportation policies—regardless of who sits in the White House—are racist law enforcement tools that have been wrought to detain and eradicate people of Mexican and Latina/o/x descent since the 1950s.

THE PARTNERSHIP BETWEEN THE LAPD AND INS: OPERATION WETBACK

In 1954, people of Mexican descent were exposed to what was advertised as one of the largest sweeps in American history, aimed at deporting one million people in the Southwest region of the United States. Though current scholarship refutes the historical figures, arguing that the numbers were exaggerated to induce panic, historian Kelly Lytle Hernández writes that eight hundred border patrol agents were deployed to the southwestern United States to conduct a series of raids that were believed to be successful by then attorney general Herbert Brownell.[31] The sweep, which sought to deport people of Mexican descent from the interior, regardless of their citizenship status, was labeled with a pejorative term, Operation Wetback.[32] With the full cooperation of the LAPD, the deportation process was a racialized project to segregate people of Mexican descent from the white population in Los Angeles. The remnants of racial segregation can still be felt in Los Angeles as the city is still separated into ethnic and racial enclaves that sprang up in this era.[33] Operation Wetback arose in part as a reaction to the Bracero Program. Though thousands of families of Mexican descent already called Los Angeles their home in the first half of the twentieth century, the creation of the Bracero Program in 1942 invited Mexican nationals (mostly men) to the United States to work as farmhands to support the agriculture industry. The guest worker program lasted for two decades, hiring approximately four million men.[34] Braceros were initially viewed positively because they filled wartime labor shortages. But nine years after World War II ended, the mood had soured. It was in this context that the LAPD, mostly composed of white men, partnered with the INS to conduct one of the largest deportation operations in U.S. history.[35]

The LAPD willfully participated in the removal of people of Mexican descent. The operation could not have happened without the leadership of William Parker, who was named chief in 1950. Parker was a staunchly conservative Catholic who was admired by the John Birch

Society, a right-wing organization that embodied (and continues to embody) a brand of Christian values mixed with white supremacist nationalism purportedly predicated on American patriotism. Among its other stances, the society supported racial segregation, opposed women's right to abortions, and called for prayer in public schools. In the 1960s, the official publication, *American Opinion*, posted Parker on the cover multiple times as a savior amid the supposed social disorder occurring in Los Angeles. He was a recurring guest on a radio program hosted by a right-winger named Clarence Manion, who was also a member of the John Birch Society's National Council. Parker used the radio program to denounce the courts as being too lenient toward alleged criminals and to downplay civil liberties during the nascent civil rights movement.[36] This sentiment parallels Trump's law-and-order rhetoric today, with both Parker and Trump epitomizing a type of hypermasculinity in their performances as protectors amid fabricated crises (whether communist or antifa). In the 1960s, the members of the John Birch Society thought of themselves as ideological warriors in the fight to save America from a growing, fictitious Red Menace. With the Cold War as a backdrop, far-fetched allegations from the society included that a "Soviet Negro Republic" would emerge in the southern states and be controlled by Soviet Union. The segregationist politician George Wallace was a close ally to the society, and one hundred chapters sprang up across southern states.[37] Promoting itself as aligned with Christian principles, the society criticized anyone who went against its right-wing values.

When Parker's LAPD began cooperating with the U.S. Border Patrol in the early fifties under Operation Wetback, it deepened social fissures between the white population of Los Angeles and the Mexican community. As the INS descended on Los Angeles, its presence exasperated the social anxieties felt by people of Mexican descent. These law enforcement agencies set their sights on all Mexicans, whose actual citizenship status was of little concern to federal officials.[38] The partnership between the agencies meant that racism was institutionalized and put into practice within both local and federal law enforcement agencies. This operation occurred amid a race-based immigration quota system that was enacted by the Calvin Coolidge administration in 1924 and that lasted until 1965. The law favored northern and western European immigrants over those who hailed from southern and eastern European countries,

Asia, or Africa.[39] Though immigrants from the western hemisphere were exempted from this quota system, Mexican nationals were seen as unwelcome by so-called nativists.

The U.S. Border Patrol was used as an institution of social control. At its 1924 advent, Congress allocated $1 million to the Immigration Bureau of the Department of Labor, in part to enforce immigration quotas through the National Origins Act of 1924. The establishment of the U.S. Border Patrol set a precedent on how federal agents would be used to thwart immigrants migrating from Mexico. The novel federal law enforcement agency used its equipment funding to procure horses and guns and to construct buildings. Most expenditures, however, went to salaries to kick-start careers for white men.[40] The National Origins Act meant that Nordic immigrants were the primary immigrants welcomed to the United States; it imposed restrictions on immigration using a quota system (set at 150,000 total immigrants annually in 1929), with country-specific quotas based the number of people from those countries who were living in the United States in 1890.[41] At the time, the country was mostly composed of "Anglo-Saxons."[42]

In 1950, Chief Parker called Los Angeles the "white spot of the great cities of America today. It is to the advantage of the community that we keep it that way."[43] Parker claimed that people of Mexican descent committed five times more crimes per capita than the white community and that they had a genetic propensity toward violence because of their ancestry.[44] He stated, "The Latin population that came here in great strength were here before us and presented a great problem because I worked over on the East Side when men had to work in pairs . . . and it's because some of these people being not too far removed from the wild tribes of the district of the inner mountains of Mexico. I don't think you can throw the genes out of the question when discussing behavior patterns of people." When Mexican American councilman Edward Roybal demanded an apology for his racist comments, Parker refused.[45]

Though Mexican immigrants were allowed to enter the United States to work in the agriculture fields, they were surveilled and criminalized through newspapers. So-called nativists opposed the flow of Mexican workers entering the country and wanted them to be placed in the same quota system used to exclude undesired immigrants. Nativists characterized Mexico as a nation of mongrels that would destroy the social fabric of the United States. As such, Mexican workers began demanding better living wages, which raised alarm among the business elites and summoned the police to quell strikes. As the workers struggled to attain livable wages by protesting, local newspapers seized on the opportunity to depict Mexicans as a threat to U.S. capitalism.

In the early twentieth century, newspapers such as the *Los Angeles Times* played a pivotal role in criminalizing people of Mexican descent. With headlines like, "Brownell Pledges Wetback Action" and "U.S. Increased Guard Against 'Wetback' Horde," the *Los Angeles Times* deliberately assisted the deportation regime's efforts to remove people of Mexican descent.[46] The endeavor can be traced to 1934, when Mexican farmworkers went on strike in the Imperial Valley for better wages. The LAPD's notorious Red Squads claimed that the disturbances in the agricultural community stemmed from Communist agitation.[47] The *Times* depicted Mexican farmhands as disobedient laborers looking to beset the U.S. government. Although Mexican laborers clashed with the LAPD during these strikes, the *Times* reported that Mexican workers were responsible for the hostilities and framed them as the culprits who initiated the violence. LAPD officers were represented as the true victims of these skirmishes, as men who were simply trying to enforce the law against Mexican workers who refused to comply. The *Times* ignored the violence that was endemic to the culture of the LAPD.[48] By consistently misinforming the public, it used the Mexican Revolution as a backdrop to conjure up moral panics among its readers. It was a maneuver that helped control public opinion by embedding fear within articles. White people living in Los Angeles began feeling anxious over the political leanings that people of Mexican descent held and worried that the Mexican Revolution would inspire the local population to rise up. The potential overthrow of the U.S. government was enough to imbue panic among local white people and convince them that people of Mexican descent needed to be contained at any cost, even if that meant exercising violence over them.[49] Their safety was of low priority. Whatever violence was exerted by the LAPD on the Mexican community was a justifiable act. The fear tactics that were used in the *Times* convinced white people that violence was a justifiable measure to prevent an uprising among people of Mexican descent. In this capacity, the LAPD was only doing its job, which set the stage for its consorting with the U.S. Border Patrol.

Both Parker and Brownell, like many other high-ranking officials in the U.S. government and law enforcement, wanted the United States to remain a white nation. The country was rapidly changing as more and more people of Mexican descent were entering. The partnership was an enforcement tool that created a legal apparatus to help keep America white. In 1949, five years before Operation Wetback was launched, James Butterfield, district commissioner of the Vermont division of the INS, sent twenty patrol officers to the border to hinder the "traffic influx" of people of Mexican descent entering the United States.[50] This precursor to Operation Wetback followed a similar logic to Trump's executive order no. 13767, which he issued in his first week of office. Falsely claiming that the country's national security was in dire jeopardy, the executive order stated that the job of federal law enforcement was "to deploy all lawful means to secure the Nation's southern border, to prevent further illegal immigration into the United States, and to repatriate illegal aliens swiftly, consistently, and humanely." Parker and Brownell used much the same rhetoric of national security as a pretext to detain people of Mexican descent under Operation Wetback.[51] This collaboration between local and federal officials was a powerful current that swept the Mexican community. It was a paramilitarized strategy that relied on local police departments to apprehend and bolster anxieties, but the operation could not have advanced without the support of right-wing ideology.

Right-wing ideology dovetails with law enforcement policies. In the United States, such ideology has historically been intertwined with white supremacy, capitalism, and policing. It has largely existed to place non-white and working-class communities in subordinate positions, leaving many to feel unprotected by the law. Men like Trump and Parker are the personification of this ideology. Yet this ideology relies on falsehoods that are made evident when certain groups are portrayed as enemies. Propaganda is used with the intention of inciting feelings of a nationalist traditional past; this propaganda positions enemies as hordes of invaders and criminals "illegally" circumventing immigration laws. Conversely, positioned as the true patriots of the land are so-called nativists, particularly those who live outside the city. Philosopher Jason Stanley explains, "resources that flow to cities must be directed to the rural communities instead, to preserve this vital center of the nation's values. And the rural communities, as the source of the pure blood of the nation, cannot be polluted by outside blood via immigration."[52] The racist rhetoric that Trump spewed toward immigrant communities during his presidency attempted to position Mexicans and Central Americans as foreign criminals. Trump declared that he could fix the "broken" border. Like Parker, he positioned himself as an ideological savior, willing to protect his supporters and the country's national security. For both men, their egos emerged while they were espousing rhetoric grounded in right-wing ideology that censures oppositional groups while asserting their authority.

CREDIBILITY VIA EGOTISM

Many right-wing leaders have shown this egocentrism, using it to propel a false sense of their credibility. As Dawn F. Colley describes, "Trump is credible not because he understands and is capable of handling the issues that we face as a nation but because his words are, ostensibly, not clothed in the colors of rhetoric." Colley continues, "As such, his targeted audience is invited to accept what he says at face value; his words are believable for the very fact they are not well considered."[53] Parker used a similar strategy by invoking his credibility whenever he spoke on the concerns of rising crime. Often, Parker cloaked his racism by eschewing race in his speeches, but he still understood how to exploit social anxieties by using his position as a trusted police chief. He stated, "we do not control economic cycles; we are not equipped to deal with racial, religious, or political prejudice; we are not arbiters of right and wrong. In short, we are not healers of social ills. Our job is to apply emergency treatment to society's surface wounds; we deal with effects, not causes."[54] Here, Parker could absolve himself and the LAPD of any responsibility for the violence committed by his department on nonwhite, working-class communities because it was the duty of the LAPD to curb crime. In a 1956 article on the role of the police in the community, Parker wrote, "Deployment is often heaviest in so-called minority sections of the city. The reason is statistical—it is a fact that certain racial groups, at the present time, commit a disproportionate share of the total crime."[55] Parker was careful in how he stated his assertions. By inserting the phrase "at the present time," he removed himself from potential accusations of racism. If only these communities would simply rectify their behavior, then "social ills" such as poverty, unemployment, and crime would cease to exist. The statement evades race as a motivator for higher crime rates and refocuses our attention on police deployment to arrest the criminals living in nonwhite communities. Moreover, Parker used statistical evidence to advance his claim and thus gain public support. This incorporation of data establishes his credibility and validates his authority in matters concerning crime. Race is not a central concern; instead, crime redirects our attention, becoming the main issue. As a police officer, Parker used his position to dole out information in whatever modus he needed to persuade the (white) public. The data cited in this statement gives credence to his position as chief of police and allows him to be observed as a concerned police officer working tirelessly to protect the public's safety.

For Trump, his credibility relied on the aggrandizement of his intelligence, the below-average nature of which was made evident every time he spoke or tweeted. Regularly referring to himself as a "stable genius," he compensated for his inferior intellect by highlighting his devoted supporters in his interviews and on social media.[56] Trump gloated that his followers would never refute him as they were personally committed to his nonsensical pomposity. He demonstrated this in 2016 by stating, "They say I have the most loyal people—did you ever see that? Where I could stand in the middle of 5th Avenue and shoot somebody, and I wouldn't lose any voters."[57] But the notion that anyone would follow Trump blindly has its origins in him appearing on reality television. His popularity did not materialize out of nowhere. Trump had been in the public eye for years and used his celebrity status to eventually cross over into mainstream politics and get himself elected, even though he had no previous political experience. For right-wingers, he spoke a language that resonated with them, a language grounded in racism and fear, overcompensation and arrogance, that demonized nonwhite people and the Left.

This sort of showmanship among right-wing politicians can be traced back to Parker and an earlier generation of television: the short-lived television show *The Thin Blue Line*, which Parker produced for the local NBC station in 1952. This panel show aired weekly in Los Angeles and featured purported experts on political and police affairs. The show was broadcast as a form of resistance to the barrage of criticism that the LAPD received for its violent and racist tactics in nonwhite communities. According to LAPD historian Edward J. Escobar, "Parker argued that criticism of the police hindered officers' ability to fight crime, thus leaving law-abiding citizens defenseless against the depredations of gangsters and criminals who sought to overrun the city."[58] Though it only aired for one season, the program served as a vehicle for right-wing propaganda in a period characterized by Cold War politics, which stigmatized leftists.

Though Trump's television persona did not tackle political issues in this same way, his media platform allowed him to ascend into the political theater, where he drummed up fear among his base, leaving many to believe that leftists—specifically antifascist and antiracist activists— were the source of the violence occurring on the streets during the 2020 uprisings. Here, too, Trump was following a template earlier used by Parker. Seeking to attack the civil rights movement—on the belief that civil rights organizations had caused his officers to doubt themselves in their interactions with nonwhite communities—Parker falsely claimed that the movement was controlled by the Soviet Union. In 1957 he wrote, "this is a situation long sought by the Masters in the Kremlin. The bloody revolution, long the dream of the Comintern, cannot be accomplished in the face of a resolute police."[59] The Comintern refers to the Third International of Communists, which sought to overthrow the capitalist structure that exploited workers worldwide in 1919.[60] Both Parker and Trump, then, were vehemently against leftists and demonstrated it by redirecting their base's ire at the civil rights and antifascist movements, respectively.

MAGA: PROFITING OFF OF HISTORICAL RACISM

When Trump introduced his campaign slogan "Make America Great Again" in 2015, it became not only a catchphrase, but also an opportunity to profit. Trump must have understood this opportunity when he chose a slogan that harked back to Reagan's declaration amid the 1980 presidential campaign, "Let's Make America Great Again."[61] Despite what some political pundits have said about the administrations functioning differently, both the Reagan and Trump administrations are rooted in white supremacy. Reagan began his 1980 campaign at the virtually all-white Neshoba County Fair in Mississippi.[62] (Neshoba is known for this fair, which dates back to 1889, and also for the notorious 1964 murders of civil rights organizers James Earl Chaney, Michael Schwerner, and Andrew

Goodman by police officers in the Ku Klux Klan.) Reagan launched his campaign at the fair, covertly signaling to the racists of the nation that he was the president who would represent their interests in the White House. MAGA, for its part, was not just a product that could be purchased on Trump's website; it was an attempt to reproduce an era when women, African Americans, Native Americans, people of color, the queer community, and leftists were all in danger of being violently attacked by angry white mobs. Indeed, Trump's hard-line followers viewed the mid-twentieth century—a time when men like Chief Parker enforced de facto racial segregation through violent policing methods—as the ideal "great" era in America's past.[63] MAGA represented a nostalgia for racists who wanted to reproduce an era in which Parker and LAPD officers were able to operate with impunity. We saw this when Trump's followers supported Blue Lives Matter and battled antifascist activists on the streets of Charlottesville, Virginia.[64] Trump wanted to remake old racist policies that many on the Right hope to re-create, but he is also a snake oil salesman who profited off of a motto that deceived his followers into believing that he would cure their social problems by traveling back to this era. If people supported him, then all the social disorders transpiring in the United States would miraculously disappear by his prescriptions.

Though Trump's pronouncements were absurd, the reality is that millions of people agreed with his racist and nonsensical rants. On January 6, 2021, white supremacists and fascists stormed the U.S. Capitol, believing Trump's rhetoric that the election was unfairly stolen from him. He convinced them that they, too, were cheated. We laughed at his childish behavior while he threw a tantrum, but this was premature—as we learned when his supporters engaged in violent acts to try to reinstate him as their leader. What is no laughing matter is how the Trump administration can be compared to the Nazi regime in Germany during the 1920s and 1930s, when antifascists and the Brownshirts fought each other on the streets.[65] Moreover, the Black Lives Matter movement can be compared to how the John Birch Society used the "Soviet Negro Republic" language, and the antifascist protestors to the alleged Red Menace. Parker never rejected these bombastic allegations. Instead, he used them to promote his right-wing ideology of supporting the police. This type of language is what created the violent atmosphere that allowed Trump's supporters to physically assault anyone who disagreed with him. Historian and journalist Jelani

Cobb expressed a crucial point via a tweet on the day of the insurrection: "We should never forget that barely two months ago 70 million people voted for a man this unstable to be president for another term. The problem is not and never has been Donald Trump. It's the fact that he is the embodiment of a deep and resilient set of American values."[66]

While Trump's incendiary language angered many liberals and close allies alike, he was not the first to criminalize immigrant communities. Democratic presidents have also contributed to the deportation regime. Both political parties are culpable in the use of local law enforcement departments as federal agents to apprehend, detain, and deport unauthorized immigrants residing in the United States. Such policies and actions date back to the 1950s, when the INS collaborated with the LAPD under Operation Wetback. They have their roots in the actions of right-wing police chief William Parker, the racial segregationist organizations that supported him, a base of supporters willing to accept the false notion that they needed protection from fictitious criminals, and local newspapers that criminalized people of Mexican descent through disparaging language, portraying them as deviants threatening the white supremacist, capitalist structure. This has continued right through the Trump presidency. Trump capitalized on a manufactured crisis, claiming that only he could save America. As such, today we are faced with our own crisis: the rise of a new fascist movement in the United States. There will certainly be more right-wing leaders following in the footsteps of both Parker and Trump. It is up to us to challenge them at every turn; the police have certainly proven that they will not intervene to thwart this dangerous movement.

NOTES

1. Illegal Immigration Reform and Immigrant Responsibility Act of 1996, Pub. L. No. 104–208, 110 Stat. 3009–546 (1996).
2. Romero, "Keeping Citizenship Rights White."
3. Hagan, Castro, and Rodriguez, "The Effects of U.S. Deportation Policies on Immigrant Families and Communities."
4. Prashad, *Washington Bullets*, 14.
5. "Brownell Pledges Wetbacks Action," *Los Angeles Times*.
6. Foley, *Mexicans in the Making of America*, 204–5.
7. "Brownell Pledges Wetbacks Action," *Los Angeles Times*.

8.   Woods, "The Progressives and the Police," 428.

9.   Hernández, *Migra!*

10.   Cacho, *Social Death*, 95.

11.   Noriega, "The LAPD Says It Won't Work with Fed on Deportations."

12.   Lee, "Donald Trump's False Comments Connecting Mexican Immigrants and Crime."

13.   Hagan, Castro, and Rodriguez, "The Effects of U.S. Deportation Policies on Immigrant Families and Communities."

14.   Serwer, "The Authoritarian Instincts of Police Unions."

15.   Kushner, "Is Prison Necessary?"

16.   Balko, "7 Ways the Obama Administration Has Accelerated Police Militarization."

17.   Dunn, "Border Militarization via Drug and Immigration Enforcement."

18.   Gonzales, *Reform Without Justice*, 148.

19.   Muhammad, *The Condemnation of Blackness*, 4.

20.   Lee, "Donald Trump's False Comments Connecting Mexican Immigrants and Crime."

21.   Taylor, *From #BlackLivesMatter to Black Liberation*, 55.

22.   Cacho, *Social Death*, 27.

23.   Harris, "Whiteness as Property," 278, 280 (qtd.).

24.   Estes, *Our History Is the Future*, 13.

25.   Gotanda, "A Critique of 'Our Constitution Is Color-Blind.'"

26.   Estes, *Our History Is the Future*, 75; Martinez, *The Injustice Never Leaves You*, 27.

27.   Treuer, *The Heartbeat of Wounded Knee*, 254.

28.   Gonzales, *Reform Without Justice*, 122.

29.   Quoted in Askaripour, "Falling in Love with Malcolm X."

30.   "Deportations from U.S. Hit a Record High," *New York Times.*

31.   Hernández, "The Crimes and Consequences of Illegal Immigration."

32.   Molina, *How Race Is Made in America*, 112.

33.   Davis, *City of Quartz*, 294.

34.   Molina, *How Race Is Made in America*, 112.

35.   "Brownell Pledges Wetbacks Action," *Los Angeles Times.*

36.   Donner, *Protectors of Privilege*, 248.

37.   Terry, "Bringing Back Birch."

38.   Molina, *How Race Is Made in America*, 134.

39.   J. Wilson, *Hitler's American Model*, 35.

40.   Hernández, *Migra!*, 33.

41.   Hagan, Castro, and Rodriguez, "The Effects of U.S. Deportation Policies on Immigrant Families and Communities."

42.   Muhammad, *The Condemnation of Blackness*, 33.

43.   O. Wilson, *Parker on Police*, 11.

44.   Woods, "The Progressives and the Police," 464.

45. "Parker Claims Negro 'Provoked' Racial Slur," *California Eagle*.
46. "U.S. Increases Guard Against 'Wetback' Horde," *Los Angeles Times*.
47. Escobar, *Race, Police, and the Making of a Political Identity*, 82.
48. Woods, "The Progressives and the Police," 417.
49. Escobar, *Race, Police, and the Making of a Political Identity*, 69.
50. "U.S. Increases Guard Against 'Wetback' Horde," *Los Angeles Times*.
51. Galbraith, "Trump Administration Tightens Procedures with Respect to Asylum Seekers"; Trump, "Border Security and Immigration Enforcement Improvements"; "Brownell Pledges Wetbacks Action," *Los Angeles Times*.
52. Stanley, *How Fascism Works*, 144.
53. Colley, "Of Twit-Storms and Demagogues," 38.
54. O. Wilson, *Parker on Police*, 12.
55. Parker, "The Police Role in Community Relations," 377.
56. Colley, "Of Twit-Storms and Demagogues," 35.
57. Reilly, "Donald Trump Says He 'Could Shoot Somebody and Not Lose Voters.'"
58. Escobar, "Bloody Christmas and the Irony of Police Professionalism," 194.
59. Parker, "California Crime Rise," 723.
60. Lenin, "The Third International and Its Place in History."
61. Morgan, "Make America Great Again."
62. Anderson, *White Rage*, 118.
63. O'Connor, "The Negro and the Police in Los Angeles," 62.
64. Thompson, "Police Stood by as Mayhem Mounted in Charlottesville."
65. Testa, *Militant Anti-Fascism*, 84.
66. Jelani Cobb (@jelani9), "We should never forget . . . ," Twitter, January 6, 2021, 9:52 p.m., https://twitter.com/jelani9/status/1347043302793768960 (tweet no longer accessible).

BIBLIOGRAPHY

Anderson, Carol. *White Rage: The Unspoken Truth of Our Racial Divide*. New York: Bloomsbury, 2017.

Askaripour, Mateo. "Falling in Love with Malcolm X—and His Mastery of Metaphor." *Literary Hub*, April 10, 2019. https://lithub.com/falling-in-love-with-malcolm-x -and-his-mastery-of-metaphor/.

Balko, Radley. "7 Ways the Obama Administration Has Accelerated Police Militarization." *Huffington Post*, July 10, 2013. https://www.huffpost.com/entry/obama -police-militarization_n_3566478.

Cacho, Lisa Marie. *Social Death: Racialized Rightlessness and the Criminalization of the Unprotected*. New York: New York University Press, 2012.

California Eagle. "Parker Claims Negro 'Provoked' Racial Slur." February 4, 1960.

Colley, Dawn F. "Of Twit-Storms and Demagogues: Trump, Illusory Truths of Patriotism, and the Language of Twittersphere." In *President Trump and His Political Discourse*, edited by Michele Lockhart, 33–51. New York: Routledge, 2018.

Davis, Mike. *City of Quartz: Excavating the Future in Los Angeles*. New York: Verso Books, 1992.

Donner, Frank. *Protectors of Privilege: Red Squads and Police Repression in Urban America*. Berkeley: University of California Press, 1990.

Dunn, Timothy J. "Border Militarization via Drug and Immigration Enforcement: Human Rights Implications." *Social Justice* 28, no. 2 (2001): 7–30.

Escobar, Edward J. "Bloody Christmas and the Irony of Police Professionalism: The Los Angeles Police Department, Mexican Americans, and Police Reform in the 1950s." *Pacific Historical Review* 72, no. 2 (2003): 171–99.

Escobar, Edward J. *Race, Police, and the Making of a Political Identity: Mexican Americans and the Los Angeles Police Department, 1900–1945*. Berkeley: University of California Press, 1999.

Estes, Nick. *Our History Is the Future*. London: Verso Books, 2019.

Foley, Neil. *Mexicans in the Making of America*. Cambridge, Mass.: Belknap Press, 2014.

Galbraith, Jean, ed. "Trump Administration Tightens Procedures with Respect to Asylum Seekers at the Southern Border." *American Journal of International Law* 113, no. 2 (2019): 377–86.

Gonzales, Alfonso. *Reform Without Justice: Latino Migrant Politics and the Homeland Security State*. New York: Oxford University Press, 2014.

Gotanda, Neil. "A Critique of 'Our Constitution Is Color-Blind.'" In *Critical Race Theory: The Key Writings That Formed the Movement*, edited by Kimberlé Crenshaw, Neil Gotanda, Gary Peller, and Kendall Thomas, 257–75. New York: New Press, 1995.

Hagan, Jacqueline, Brianna Castro, and Nestor Rodriguez. "The Effects of U.S. Deportation Policies on Immigrant Families and Communities: Cross-Border Perspectives." *North Carolina Law Review* 88, no. 5 (2010): 1799–1823.

Harris, Cheryl. "Whiteness as Property." In *Critical Race Theory: The Key Writings That Formed the Movement*, edited by Kimberlé Crenshaw, Neil Gotanda, Gary Peller, and Kendall Thomas, 276–91. New York: New Press, 1995.

Hernández, Kelly Lytle. "The Crimes and Consequences of Illegal Immigration: A Cross-Border Examination of Operation Wetback, 1943 to 1954." *Western Historical Quarterly* 37, no. 4 (2006): 421–44.

Hernández, Kelly Lytle. *Migra! A History of the U.S. Border Patrol*. Berkeley: University of California Press, 2010.

Kushner, Rachel. "Is Prison Necessary? Ruth Wilson Gilmore Might Change Your Mind." *New York Times Magazine*, April 17, 2019.

Lee, Michelle Ye Hee. "Donald Trump's False Comments Connecting Mexican Immigrants and Crime." *Washington Post*, July 8, 2015.

Lenin, Vladimir I. "The Third International and Its Place in History." In *Lenin's Collected Works*, 4th English ed., vol. 29, 305–13. Moscow: Progress, 1972.

Los Angeles Times. "Brownell Pledges Wetbacks Action: Attorney General Says U.S. Will Seek Quick Solution of Mexican Alien Problem." August 16, 1953.

Los Angeles Times. "U.S. Increases Guard Against 'Wetback' Horde." July 24, 1949.

Martinez, Monica Muñoz. *The Injustice Never Leaves You: Anti-Mexican Violence in Texas*. Cambridge, Mass.: Harvard University Press, 2018.

Molina, Natalia. *How Race Is Made in America: Immigration, Citizenship, and the Historical Power of Racial Scripts*. Berkeley: University of California Press, 2014.

Morgan, Iwan. "Make America Great Again: Ronald Reagan and Donald Trump; From Campaign Trail to World Stage." In *The Trump Presidency: From Campaign Trail to World Stage*, edited by Mara Oliva and Mark Shanahan, 59–82. New York: Springer, 2019.

Muhammad, Khalil Gibran. *The Condemnation of Blackness: Race, Crime, and the Making of Modern Urban America*. Cambridge: Harvard University Press, 2010.

New York Times. "Deportations from U.S. Hit a Record High." October 6, 2010.

Noriega, David. "The LAPD Says It Won't Work with Fed on Deportations, but It Already Does." *Buzzfeed News*, December 8, 2016. https://www.buzzfeednews.com/article/davidnoriega/the-lapd-says-it-wont-work-with-feds-on-deportations-but-it.

O'Connor, George M. "The Negro and the Police in Los Angeles." Master's thesis, University of Southern California, 1955.

Parker, William. "California Crime Rise." *Journal of Criminal Law, Criminology, and Police Science* 47, no. 6 (1957): 721–29.

Parker, William. "The Police Role in Community Relations." *Journal of Criminal Law, Criminology, and Police Science* 47, no. 3 (1956): 368–79.

Prashad, Vijay. *Washington Bullets: A History of the CIA, Coups, and Assassinations*. New York: Monthly Review Press, 2020.

Reilly, Katie. "Donald Trump Says He 'Could Shoot Somebody and Not Lose Voters.'" *New York Times*, January 23, 2016.

Romero, Mary. "Keeping Citizenship Rights White: Arizona's Racial Profiling Practices in Immigration Law Enforcement." *Law Journal for Social Justice* 1, no. 1 (2011): 97–113.

Serwer, Adam. "The Authoritarian Instincts of Police Unions." *Atlantic*, July/August 2021.

Stanley, Jason. *How Fascism Works: The Politics of Us and Them*. New York: Random House, 2020.

Taylor, Keeanga-Yamahtta. *From #BlackLivesMatter to Black Liberation*. Chicago: Haymarket Books, 2016.

Terry, Don. "Bringing Back Birch." *Intelligence Report*, March 1, 2013.

Testa, M. *Militant Anti-Fascism: A Hundred Years of Resistance*. Chico, Calif.: AK Press, 2014.

Thompson, A. C. "Police Stood by as Mayhem Mounted in Charlottesville." Pro-Publica, August 12, 2017. https://www.propublica.org/article/police-stood-by-as-mayhem-mounted-in-charlottesville.

Treuer, David. *The Heartbeat of Wounded Knee: Native America from 1890 to the Present*. New York: Riverhead Books, 2019.

Trump, Donald J. "Border Security and Immigration Enforcement Improvements." Exec. order 13767, January 25, 2017. American Presidency Project. https://www.presidency.ucsb.edu/node/322155.

Wilson, James Q. *Hitler's American Model: The United States and the Making of Nazi Race Law*. Princeton, N.J.: Princeton University, 2018.

Wilson, O. W. *Parker on Police*. Springfield, Ill.: Charles C. Thomas, 1957.

Woods, James. "The Progressives and the Police: Urban Reform and the Professionalization of the Los Angeles Police." PhD diss., University of California, Los Angeles, 1973.

6

REFUGEES AND HUMAN RIGHTS LAW DURING THE TRUMP ADMINISTRATION

JASMIN LILIAN DIAB

REFUGEES AND MIGRANTS FLEEING PERSECUTION were faced with a difficult reality under the Trump presidency—a reality where significant numbers of those who fled tyranny and risked their lives to reach the United States feared deportation on several grounds from their newly adopted country. Rhetoric regarding refugees has underwritten an uneasy atmosphere for those living in the United States under temporary protected status (TPS) and created unprecedented logistical tension between long-allied Canada and the United States, tension that has dealt a major blow to Canada's Immigration and Refugee Board, further challenging the Safe Third Country Agreement (STCA) between the two states.[1] While the United States' refugee concerns have often fluctuated throughout the country's history, recent developments on the international level have increased policymakers' focus on arrivals. Amid these developments and in line with his electoral campaign, Donald Trump introduced a ban on refugees from several conflict-ridden countries, ultimately renewing the discussion over the national security consequences and concerns of refugee policy. The focus on refugees, immigration, and border control throughout Trump's electoral campaign, as well as during the first hundred days of his presidency, led to inadvertent consequences in Canada. A message posted by Canadian prime minister Justin Trudeau's Twitter page in January 2017 illustrated the emerging rhetorical but perhaps not ideological differences between the two heads of state, reading: "To those fleeing persecution, terror and war, Canadians will welcome you, regardless of your faith. Diversity is our strength #WelcomeToCanada."[2] The Trump administration had clamped down on migration as soon as he took office. In addition to President Trump signing multiple executive orders that negatively affected refugees directly, the administration ignited mass anti-immigrant and anti-foreign sentiments across the country. These sentiments even inspired protests against refugees and asylum seekers in areas such as Charlottesville, Virginia.[3]

VIOLATIONS OF INTERNATIONAL MIGRATION AND REFUGEE LAW UNDER TRUMP

The U.S. refugee system does not comply with the obligations outlined in the 1951 Refugee Convention or the associated 1967 Protocol Relating to the Status of Refugees. Although this had been the case prior to the election of Donald Trump, the decline in refugee protection rights worsened under his administration.[4] Writing in the *Health and Human Rights Journal*, Katherine C. McKenzie and colleagues insist that "President Donald Trump has made abolishing most immigration a priority of his administration, and his policies have resulted in the de facto dismantling of asylum in the United States. These changes have impacted the lives and health of countless individuals attempting to seek safety from persecution."[5] The Trump administration was severely criticized for publicly "demonizing asylum-seekers."[6] The administration adopted a policy of persecuting any individual who crossed the U.S. border irregularly. This resulted in the criminal prosecution of asylum seekers, a clear violation of article 31 of the Refugee Convention. Under article 31, the "Contracting States shall not apply to the movements of such refugees restrictions other than those which are necessary and such restrictions shall only be applied until their status in the country is regularized or they obtain admission into another country."[7]

In 2018, 396,448 individuals were booked into U.S. Immigration and Customs Enforcement (ICE) custody. Of this number, 242,778 were detained by U.S. Customs and Border Protection (CBP) and 153,670 by

ICE's independent enforcement operations. A daily average of 42,188 immigrants (40,075 adults and 2,113 adults and children in families) were held by ICE in that same year. Between May and June 2019, 14,000–18,000 individuals were held by CBP each night.[8] In July 2020, multiple news outlets reported that migrants had been gassed with "disinfectant and tear gas," leading to multiple injuries.[9] There have been additional claims of women being illegally sterilized, and of migrant children being isolated from their families.[10] In the 2020 report *Justice-Free Zones: U.S. Immigration Detention Under the Trump Administration*, the American Civil Liberties Union, Human Rights Watch, and National Immigrant Justice Center address immigration detention under the Trump administration. The report looks at the growth of the immigration detention system since 2017, the miserable conditions and medical care in detention centers (even prior to the COVID-19 outbreak), and the due process hurdles faced by immigrants held in remote locations.[11] The report combines quantitative and qualitative data from visits to five detention centers across Louisiana, Mississippi, and Arizona, and it encompasses interviews with 120 detained individuals as well as documents Human Rights Watch received through Freedom of Information Act (FOIA) requests.[12]

The report's key findings relevant to the purpose of this study include: (1) for fiscal year 2021, the Trump administration requested that taxpayers fund ICE at $4.1 billion, with the intent to expand ICE's detention capacity to 60,000 individuals per day; (2) individuals are detained in conditions that are inhumane, and access to medical care and mental health support is scarce, even before the pandemic; (3) detained immigrants spoke about facilities taking a week to set a broken bone and said that necessary medication, such as inhalers for asthma, was often not available; (4) immigrants in detention centers opened under the Trump administration were extremely isolated from access to counsel; (5) facilities opened before 2017 had four times as many immigration attorneys available within a hundred-mile radius as those opened under the Trump administration. The report additionally found that more than 70 percent of individuals held in detention centers built under the Trump administration were under the mandate of the New Orleans field office. This office denied 99.1 percent of all asylum seekers' applications for release on parole between March and December 2019.[13]

Not only do these detention conditions violate the Refugee Convention and international law, they are also in violation of ICE policy drafted in 2009, which states: "asylum-seekers who are not at risk of flight and do not pose a danger to society should be released on parole while their asylum process unfolds." The instructions for detention and removal operations (DRO) according to that measure state that: "When an arriving alien found to have credible fear establishes to the satisfaction of DRO his or her identity and that he or she presents no flight risk nor danger to the community, DRO should, absent additional factors, parole the alien on the basis that his or her continued detention is not in the public interest." Additionally, critics and lawmakers have stated that the government's "blanket detention" of asylum seekers violated the Fifth Amendment's due process clause, because it did not consider each parole claim separately. The due process clause clearly states that no individual shall "be deprived of life, liberty, or property, without due process of law."[14]

Moreover, ICE was reportedly denying parole to the vast majority of asylum seekers who were found to have "credible fear."[15] As per the U.S. Department of Homeland Security (DHS), "an individual will be found to have a 'credible fear' of persecution if he or she establishes that there is a 'significant possibility' that he or she could establish in a full hearing before an Immigration Judge that he or she has been persecuted or has a well-founded fear of persecution or harm on account of his or her race, religion, nationality, membership in a particular social group, or political opinion if returned to his or her country."[16] On June 15, 2020, a joint notice issued by the DHS and the Executive Office for Immigration Review outlined proposed amendments to the regulations governing "credible fear" for immigration officials responsible for making these determinations. The departments proposed changes to the regulations regarding asylum, withholding of removal, and deferral of removal under the 1984 Convention Against Torture and Other Cruel, Inhuman or Degrading Treatment or Punishment. They further proposed amendments related to the standards for adjudication of applications for asylum and statutory withholding.[17]

Under these new guidelines, the likelihood of the refoulement of refugees increased substantially. By the June 2020 notice, if there was reasonable doubt about the credibility of an asylum seeker, immigration officials were authorized to make their own final judgment before an asylum seeker had access to legal counsel or a hearing before a judge.[18] The amendments to these guidelines fell directly in line with the Trump administration's approach toward asylum three years earlier, when he took office. In a tweet shared exactly two years prior to these amendments, in June 2018, President Trump insisted that "we cannot allow all of these people to invade our Country. When somebody comes in, we must immediately, with no Judges or Court Cases, bring them back from where they came."[19]

ON BUILDING WALLS: THE U.S.-MEXICAN BORDER PARADIGM

MIGRANT PROTECTION PROTOCOLS AND HUMAN RIGHTS VIOLATIONS

Under a Trump administration policy called the Migrant Protection Protocols (MPP), asylum seekers were forced to wait in dangerous circumstances at the U.S.-Mexican border for court proceedings that could drag on for months. By 2019, the MPP had outlined that foreign individuals entering or seeking admission to the United States from Mexico—irregularly or without proper documentation—could be returned to Mexico for the duration of their immigration proceedings, with Mexico responsible for providing them with all appropriate humanitarian protections during their stay. The MPP was branded as a "comprehensive approach" for the DHS, in connection with regional partners, to manage unauthorized migration by streamlining U.S. removal proceedings.[20] However, as an associate reporting officer at the UN High Commissioner for Refugees (UNHCR) explains, asylum seekers typically waited for lengthy periods (to no end) prior to being able to submit their application, even sleeping for prolonged periods of time at the border while waiting.[21] In September 2019, Human Rights Watch reported that under the MPP (also referred to as the "Remain in Mexico" program), asylum seekers awaiting hearings in the United States were being returned to cities in Mexico that had "a shortage of shelter." Human Rights Watch additionally found that asylum seekers faced "new or increased barriers to obtaining and communicating with legal counsel; increased closure of MPP court hearings to the public; and threats of kidnapping, extortion, and other violence while in Mexico."[22]

A decision by U.S. attorney general Jeff Sessions in 2018 overturned asylum protections for domestic and gang violence.[23] A precedent set by the Obama administration in 2009 had cleared the way for women who have experienced severe domestic beatings and sexual abuse to receive asylum in the United States.[24] The attorney general explained his decision by insisting that the "prototypical refugee flees her home country because the government has persecuted her," adding that "an alien may suffer threats and violence in a foreign country for any number of reasons relating to her social, economic, family or other personal circumstances. Yet the asylum statute does not provide redress for all misfortune."[25] Following this decision, the bar was set so high for victims of violence that not only did the government of the home country need to be unable or unwilling to assist or take on the case, but the applicant had to "show that the government condoned the private actions or demonstrated an inability to protect the victims."[26]

FAMILY SEPARATION, CHILDREN, AND THE ZERO TOLERANCE POLICY

Criminal prosecution of asylum seekers under the Trump administration also led to the separation of children from their parents, and to the use of separation as a deterrent measure. According to the UN Human Rights Council, this separation policy was classified under international legal frameworks as "torture." UN experts insisted that "the executive order signed by the US President on 20 June 2018 fails to address the situation of thousands of migrant children forcibly separated from their parents and held in detention at the border. In addition, it may lead to indefinite detention of entire families in violation of international human rights standards." They added, "detention of children is punitive, severely hampers their development, and in some cases may amount to torture."[27] Amnesty International called the separation policy "nothing short of torture." Amnesty International's Americas director stated, "this is a spectacularly cruel policy, where frightened children are being ripped from their parent's arms and taken to overflowing detention centers, which are effectively cages. The severe mental suffering that officials have intentionally inflicted on families for coercive purposes means that these acts meet the definitions of torture under both US and international law."[28]

While the Trump administration repeatedly insisted that this was not a new policy, and that the separation policy had been in place during the Obama administration, this claim is in fact misleading and untrue. Although separations did sometimes happen under Obama and other past administrations, there was no blanket policy to prosecute parents prior to the Trump presidency. Under the Obama administration, a child and an adult who arrived together at the border could possibly be separated, but only when border officials could not establish the custodial relationship; when they believed the custodian to be a threat to the child; or when the custodian was being detained for prosecution.[29] In contrast, under the Trump administration's Zero Tolerance policy, over two thousand children were separated from their parents between April and May 2018—many of whom were anticipated to still not be reunited with their parents by the end of his term (this remains true as of early 2023 under the Biden administration).[30] The Trump administration insisted that this policy was a deterrent to illegal migration, although the separation of children from their families was rejected by the U.S. Supreme Court as early as 1982, in the case of *Plyler v. Doe*. In this decision, the court held that a state government could not punish the child for the actions of the parents—something the Trump administration openly did.[31]

The Zero Tolerance policy, which applied to anyone caught crossing the border irregularly, meant that anyone crossing the border was referred to the U.S. Department of Justice and prosecuted for the misdemeanor of "illegal entry," without exception. This unjustly included asylum seekers fleeing persecution and those crossing the border with their children.[32] Throughout this process, when parents were transferred to criminal custody, their children were treated as "unaccompanied minors," as if they had crossed the border on their own or by their own will.[33] Unaccompanied minors, also referred to as "unaccompanied alien children," were governed under a program operated by the Office of Refugee Resettlement (a division of the U.S. Department of Health and Human Services), which houses them.

The Homeland Security Act of 2002 defines "unaccompanied alien children" as unauthorized immigrants under the age of eighteen without legal guardians in the United States. However, DHS practice is to only define children traveling with their parents or legal guardians as part of "family units," relegating all other children to the status of "unaccompanied minors." In contradiction to the practices outlined in the 2002 act, children separated from their parents under the Trump administration's Zero Tolerance policy were referred to the Unaccompanied Alien Children program (now the Unaccompanied Children program).[34] From the time this program began in 2003, until 2011, it housed fewer than 8,000 children per year. In contrast, in fiscal year 2018, under the Trump administration, 49,100 children were referred to the program, more than 130 per day. This rate increased to an estimated 287 daily referrals in April 2019.[35] CBP holds unaccompanied children after their initial arrest. Though CBP is legally obligated to refer them to the Unaccompanied Children program within seventy-two hours of their arrest, 2,081 children were reportedly being held for weeks or months in CBP custody, according to multiple 2019 reports.[36]

The Zero Tolerance policy violated international law relating to children, which requires that the best interest of the child be considered when applying government policy, and that children only be detained as a final resort. Article 9 of the 1990 Convention on the Rights of the Child states: "State Parties shall ensure that a child shall not be separated from his or her parents against their will, except when competent authorities subject to judicial review determine, in accordance with applicable law and procedures, that such separation is necessary for the best interests of the child. Such determination may be necessary in a particular case such as one involving abuse or neglect of the child by the parents, or one where the parents are living separately, and a decision must be made as to the child's place of residence."[37]

THE MUSLIM BAN AND THE "THREAT TO NATIONAL SECURITY"

President Trump worked on cementing his anti-immigrant and anti-Muslim rhetoric in government policy throughout the duration of his term. Ignoring the U.S. Constitution's guarantee of freedom of religion, and in breach of the 1952 Immigration and Nationality Act's prioritization of family reunification, his administration issued multiple executive orders that imposed indefinite, sweeping immigration bans targeting Muslims and people from the Middle East and North Africa.[38] The U.S. Department of Justice and DHS issued a report characterizing Muslim immigrants as "terrorism threats" under the Trump administration.[39] The

U.S. Department of State even went as far as permitting for the development of regulations that created a "digital infrastructure" through the "ideological screening" of immigrants.[40] In December 2015, while still on the campaign trail, Trump called for a "total and complete shutdown of Muslims entering the United States."[41] Just one week after assuming office, in January 2017, President Trump banned migrants from seven Muslim countries: Iran, Iraq, Libya, Somalia, Sudan, Syria, and Yemen.[42] Under the so-called Muslim Ban, more than seven hundred travelers were detained, and up to sixty thousand visas were revoked.[43] Federal courts across the United States viewed the ban as discriminatory, with the Fourth Circuit finding that the measure "dripped 'with religious intolerance, animus, and discrimination,'" and that "'vague words of national security' were supported by evidence that the excluded foreigners posed a danger to Americans."[44]

Though "the ban was withdrawn and replaced twice as the administration sought to strip out overtly discriminatory elements," the U.S. Supreme Court issued a 5–4 ruling in June 2018 that its third version could stand. The majority in the court accepted the Trump administration's claim that it had carefully selected the banned countries by evaluating each of them against the same baseline standards: (1) whether they issued electronic passports, and (2) whether they shared lists of suspected terrorists.[45] The Trump administration insisted that the selected countries on this list just "happened to be predominantly Muslim."[46] Often compared to the Zero Tolerance policy, the Muslim Ban also led to family separation by preventing Americans' family members from coming to the United States. Approximately one year after the decision, the U.S. Department of State published a report illustrating the devastating impact on American citizens and their families. According to the report, at least 42,650 individuals had been barred from the United States because of their country of origin, despite the fact that no other concerns existed in their files.[47]

After the third anniversary of the Muslim Ban, the Trump administration further barred immigrants from Kyrgyzstan, Myanmar, Eritrea, Nigeria, Sudan, and Tanzania. Five of the added countries have populations that range between 30 percent and 85 percent Muslim. As it stood after this addition, the ban included thirteen countries, over half a billion people, and a quarter of the population of Africa. The Trump administration continuously depicted refugees, particularly those fleeing Muslim countries, as a threat to "national security"—despite the fact that a 2015 Migration Policy Institute report showed that of the one million refugees resettled in the United States since 9/11, not a single refugee had been responsible for any act of violence that resulted in the death of a U.S. citizen.[48] At the beginning of his presidency, Trump set a cap of 45,000 refugees for the 2017 fiscal year, despite the global refugee crisis.[49] Of the estimated 65 million refugees in the world at the time, the United States admitted only eleven Syrian refugees in 2018.[50]

Among the executive orders President Donald Trump signed soon after his inauguration was "Protecting the Nation from Foreign Terrorist Entry into the United States" (no. 13769), which suspended the U.S. Refugee Admissions Program and banned travel from seven African and Middle Eastern countries.[51] In response, immigrant and civil rights advocacy groups across Canada called for the federal government to suspend the Safe Third Country Agreement.[52] These groups included Amnesty International, the Canadian Civil Liberties Association, the Association québécoise des avocats et avocates en droit de l'immigration, the British Columbia Civil Liberties Association, the Canadian Association of Refugee Lawyers, and the Canadian Council for Refugees, as well as two hundred law professors from universities across Canada.[53]

The United States and Canada entered the STCA in 2004, as part of the Smart Border Action Plan. The STCA is intended to "better manage the flow of refugee claimants at the shared land border" between the two countries.[54] Individuals who seek refugee protection must make a claim in the first country they enter, and at a designated port of entry. If a claimant is found to be a refugee in the United States, they can be deported from Canada, with the reverse scenario also applying. There are four types of exceptions to this agreement: (1) if asylum seekers have family members in Canada who have some sort of legal status; (2) if they are unaccompanied minors (under the age of eighteen years old); (3) if they have another form of legal document such as a valid Canadian visa; and (4) if certain public interest issues apply, such as if they have been convicted of an offense that could lead to a death penalty sentence in the United States (the death penalty was de facto abolished in Canada in 1972).

Though reviews of the STCA issued by the Canadian government determined that "the United States meets a high standard with respect to

the protection of human rights"—citing independent courts, the separation of powers, and an open democracy as the reasons for its determination as a safe third country—the current political climate challenges such
a finding. For example, the separation of powers purportedly helps ensure
that the country's policies and practices are in line with the Convention
Against Torture and the Refugee Convention: Canada determined that
the United States has an "extensive administrative system subject to
judicial checks and balances," and that its refugee determination system
offers a high degree of protection to potential refugees.[55] There is no data,
however, as to how this was determined, and critics have long argued
that U.S. migration laws and policies constitute several procedural bars
that exclude significant groups of refugees. The United States continues
to have one of the most grueling and complex refugee determination
systems in the world. Furthermore, refugees who ultimately seek asylum
in the United States must bear longer wait times and face a heightened
risk of refoulement under the system.

THE DIRECT IMPACT OF TRUMP'S POLICIES ON MEXICAN, LATINX, AND CENTRAL AMERICAN COMMUNITIES

While the contours of a "shared" Latinx identity are still evolving, racism
and xenophobia targeting the Latinx population endure. Racism under
the Trump era was guided by a "white racial frame," wherein whiteness was deemed superior and other groups were deemed inferior.[56]
After Trump took office in 2017, the racial ideologies plugged into the
campaign trail that had portrayed Mexican immigrants and Latinxs as
criminals were translated into racist policies that augmented existing
structures of enforcement and inhumane treatment of this category of
immigrants.[57] Two executive orders that Trump signed during his first
week in office unduly targeted Latinxs through heightened interior and
exterior enforcement. The first order, "Border Security and Immigration Enforcement Improvements" (no. 13767), intended to uphold his
infamous campaign promise of "building a wall" along the U.S.-Mexico
border, though the militarization of the southern border had already
proven ineffective in deterring undocumented migration. The executive
order additionally authorized hiring additional border patrol agents and

directed DHS to build more detention facilities and significantly restrict access to asylum.[58]

The second executive order Trump signed into effect, called "Enhancing Public Safety in the Interior of the United States" (no. 13768), outlined Trump's internal priorities. The order revived and extended efforts to bridge local and federal law enforcement agencies and increased the number of ICE agents. Two decades before Trump assumed office, the Illegal Immigration Reform and Immigrant Responsibility Act (1996) and the Personal Responsibility and Work Opportunity Reconciliation Act (1996) laid the foundation for states and cities to implement immigration policies by encouraging police officers to question individuals about their immigration status during stops.[59] A noncitizen could subsequently be transferred to ICE custody and eventually deported. In 2008, ICE launched the Secure Communities and 287(g) programs, which facilitated data sharing between local police officers, DHS, and the FBI, and significantly increased deportations, earning Obama the moniker "Deporter-in-Chief." Trump's executive order resuscitated Secure Communities. As scholars have demonstrated, the definition of people considered to be "priorities" was expanded to include undocumented immigrants charged with minor offenses or suspected of committing a crime.[60] In Trump's first one hundred days in office, the number of civil immigration arrests increased 38 percent compared to the year prior. Reports have shown that dark-skinned Latinx and Black men were disproportionately targeted by enforcement efforts, eventually yielding a "gendered racial removal program."[61]

According to Stephanie L. Canizales and Jody Agius Vallejo, "Trump drew on the migration and apprehension trends at the U.S. Southern border to manufacture a Latino immigration crisis from a humanitarian one, resulting in increasingly draconian policies targeting Latino immigrants."[62] Trump's racist and dehumanizing rhetoric and policy actions continued to increase Latinxs' experiences of everything from institutionalized legal violence to the expansion of the detention and deportation regime, to state-sponsored abuse against children, the stripping of civil rights, and racial violence on a national scale. In late 2019, the FBI reported that anti-Latinx hate crimes had increased over 21 percent the previous year.[63]

CHANGES TO THE DEFERRED ACTION FOR CHILDHOOD ARRIVALS AND TEMPORARY PROTECTED STATUS

The Deferred Action for Childhood Arrivals, more commonly referred to as DACA, is directed at individuals who entered the United States as children, frequently without any legal status, and who meet the guidelines for protection under U.S. immigration law. As of 2017, 690,000 young adults were enrolled in DACA.[64] This made them eligible to reside and work in the United States, obtain valid driver's licenses, pay income taxes, and enroll in academic institutions. Noteworthy, however, is that DACA does not provide legal status.[65] It does not offer any legal pathway to becoming lawful U.S. citizens or permanent residents; it only defers an individual from deportation or removal for a certain period of time, with prospects of renewal.[66] Individuals who were originally eligible for protection under DACA had to be under the age of thirty-one as of June 15, 2012.[67] They must have come into the United States before the age of sixteen and have resided continuously in the country since their arrival. They should not have any previous lawful status in the United States and must currently be in school or must have completed high school or its equivalent. These individuals also must have not committed any felonies or be considered a threat to national security or overall public safety. DACA recipients were mostly Mexican nationals, with Salvadorans, Guatemalans, Hondurans, and South Koreans rounding out the top five nationalities in recent years.[68] In September 2017, the Trump administration announced a rescission of the program, with a six-month grace period for review.[69] On August 31, 2018, district court judge Andrew Hanen of Texas ruled that DACA was likely unconstitutional. However, he let the program remain in place as litigation proceeded.[70]

Temporary protected status (TPS) is another form of humanitarian protection. It is available to nationals of designated countries as chosen by DHS on the basis of protracted or ongoing armed conflict, environmental disasters, or other extraordinary and temporary circumstances. Those who are granted TPS may not be removed from the United States while their country holds this status, are eligible to obtain an employment authorization document, are granted travel authorization, and are protected from detainment by DHS. By 2020, ten countries had TPS designations: El Salvador, Haiti, Honduras, Nepal, Nicaragua, Somalia,

Sudan, South Sudan, Syria, and Yemen.[71] The Trump administration explored the possibility of ending TPS for Central Americans and Haitians in general, but this decision did not materialize. Should the TPS designation of a state end, and individual visas expire, individuals who had TPS designations may be forced to return to their country of origin even if it is still in conflict.[72]

MAIN TAKEAWAYS

While the STCA requires certain claimants to seek protection in the United States rather than Canada, it did not consider the fact that the United States was not necessarily the safest for refugees under the Trump administration, and in the past as well. Hundreds of thousands of asylum seekers, including minors, continue to be held in detention centers along U.S. borders, sometimes for months or even years. Many reported cases confirm that irregular migrants are at times even detained in prisons.[73] Irregular migrants that are placed in detention centers have reduced chances of receiving refugee protection, because of the difficulties in accessing adequate legal counsel and assistance in presenting their refugee claims. Ill treatment and poor conditions that violate human rights standards and principles have been reported in detention centers and immigration jails across the United States.[74]

The United States does not have a consistent history of providing protection to refugees. In the past, many claimants were recognized as refugees by the Canadian government after having been refused this status in the United States, where the category of refugee was subject to stricter interpretation. Eligibility requirements and U.S. policy restrictions essentially mean that asylum seekers who apply after having been in the United States for more than one year may be denied a hearing. Unlike in Canada, U.S. immigration and asylum laws under Trump did not necessarily provide protection for individuals who face a risk to their livelihoods or who are at risk for cruel and unusual treatment or punishment. If the Canadian government returns a refugee or asylum seeker to the United States and they are deported and sent back to persecution, Canada will need to assume a significant part of the responsibility for the harm this individual may face. U.S. policies and practices under Trump additionally discriminated based on country of origin, nationality, ethnicity, and religion denomination.

Proposed amendments to the STCA put forth by the Trudeau Parliament budget bill in August 2019 include a pre-removal assessment to adequately evaluate whether asylum seekers will face any immediate or foreseeable danger if deported.[75] This, however, is not necessarily an amendment that would be in the interest of refugees. This amendment would impose limitations on asylum seekers' legal right to a full trial. No such amendment has been approved to date, as of early 2023. The Canadian Council for Refugees has warned in the past that such amendments would place asylum seekers and refugees at a heightened risk of deportation back to their countries of origin, where their livelihoods, well-being, and safety could be threatened on multiple fronts. On different occasions, the Trump administration pursued the imposition of inhumane and discriminatory policies and practices toward the refugee community, threatening the provision of human rights and basic standards of human dignity.

The Biden administration has much to prove. After all, the Obama administration (for which Biden served as vice president) was responsible for the deportation of millions of individuals from the United States.[76] Canada must hold the United States accountable for the violations committed under the Trump administration and regularly inform Canada's Federal Court, the public, and the national refugee protection community about whether the STCA is effective in ensuring that the rights of asylum seekers are upheld and maintained.

NOTES

1. The STCA is a treaty that entered into force on December 29, 2004, with the aim of better managing the flow of refugee claimants at the shared land border between Canada and the United States. Under the STCA, persons seeking refugee status in either country must make their claim in the first country in which they arrive, unless they qualify for an exception.
2. On the tweet, see Smith, "Trudeau Tweet Caused Influx of Refugee Inquiries."
3. Keneally, "What to Know About the Violent Charlottesville Protests and Anniversary Rallies."
4. Snow and Watson, "Under Trump, US No Longer Leads World on Refugee Protections."

5.   McKenzie et al., "Eliminating Asylum."
6.   Roelofs, "Trump Demonizes Refugees."
7.   See UNHRC, *Convention and Protocol Relating to the Status of Refugees*, 29.
8.   U.S. Immigration and Customs Enforcement, "Fiscal Year 2018 ICE Enforcement and Removal Operations Report."
9.   Swetlitz, "Suddenly They Started Gassing Us."
10. D. Brooks, "Sterilization of Migrant Women in U.S. Detention Centers Causes Outrage."
11. Human Rights Watch, "US: New Report Shines Spotlight on Abuses and Growth." *Due process* is the legal requirement that the state must respect all legal rights that are owed to a person. Due process balances the power of the law of the land and protects the individual person from it.
12. The FOIA is a federal law that requires, upon request, the full or partial disclosure of previously unreleased information and documents controlled by the U.S. government.
13. Cho, Tidwell Cullen, and Long, *Justice-Free Zones*, 5–6.
14. ICE policy and other material quoted from Campoy, "Nielsen Says It's the Law to Detain Asylum Seekers." See also ICE directive 11002.1, Parole of Arriving Aliens Found to Have a Credible Fear of Persecution or Torture (December 8, 2009).
15. Campoy, "Nielsen Says It's the Law to Detain Asylum Seekers."
16. U.S. Department of Homeland Security, "Credible Fear Cases Completed."
17. Procedures for Asylum and Withholding of Removal; Credible Fear and Reasonable Fear Review, 85 Fed. Reg. 36264 (June 15, 2020).
18. Procedures for Asylum and Withholding of Removal.
19. Reuters, "Trump Says Undocumented Immigrants Should Be Deported."
20. U.S. Department of Homeland Security, "Migrant Protection Protocols."
21. Pers. comm., June 2020.
22. Human Rights Watch, "US Move Puts More Asylum Seekers at Risk."
23. Selby, "Why Jeff Sessions' Ruling on Domestic Violence and Asylum Matters."
24. McGreal, "Obama Moves to Grant Political Asylum to Women Who Suffer Domestic Abuse."
25. Quoted in New Humanitarian, "Executive Summary for June 12th."
26. Quoted in Kopan, "Trump Admin Drops Asylum Protections for Domestic Violence Victims."
27. UN OHCHR, "UN Experts to US."
28. Amnesty International, "USA: Policy of Separating Children from Parents."
29. Cummings, "Trump Defends Conditions for Detained Migrant Kids"; Valverde, "Trump Wrong on Obama Family Separation Policy."
30. Aguilera, "Here's What to Know About the Status of Family Separation at the U.S. Border."
31. *Plyler v. Doe*, 457 U.S. 202 (1982).
32. Human Rights Watch, "Q&A: Trump Administration's 'Zero-Tolerance' Immigration Policy."

33. Congressional Research Service. "The Trump Administration's 'Zero Tolerance' Immigration Enforcement Policy."

34. Congressional Research Service.

35. U.S. Department of Health and Human Services, "Latest UC Data—FY2019."

36. Lind, "The Horrifying Conditions Facing Kids in Border Detention."

37. UN General Assembly, Resolution 44/25, Convention on the Rights of the Child, A/RES/44/25 (November 20, 1989).

38. The First Amendment of the U.S. Constitution guarantees freedom of religion in two clauses: the "establishment" clause, which prohibits the government from establishing an official church, and the "free exercise" clause, which allows people to worship as they please. The 1965 INA, also known as the Hart-Celler Act, abolished an earlier quota system based on national origin and established a new immigration policy based on reuniting immigrant families and attracting skilled labor to the United States.

39. Jackson et al., *Practical Terrorism Prevention*, 30, 141, 215.

40. Patel, "Deference to Discrimination."

41. Taylor, "Trump Calls for 'Total and Complete Shutdown of Muslims Entering' U.S."

42. Gladstone and Sugiyama, "Trump's Travel Ban."

43. "Up to '60,000 Visas Revoked' After Trump's Travel Ban," *Al Jazeera*.

44. Buckley, "The Federal Courts Just Joined 'the Resistance.'"

45. Patel, "Deference to Discrimination."

46. Cole, "'So-Called Judges' Trump Trump."

47. Panduranga, "The Muslim Ban."

48. Kanno-Youngs, "Trump Administration Adds Six Countries to Travel Ban"; Newland, "The U.S. Record Shows Refugees Are Not a Threat."

49. Rose, "Trump Administration to Drop Refugee Cap to 45,000, Lowest in Years."

50. Gelardi, "The US Is Resettling the Fewest Number of Refugees in 40 Years."

51. UNC Global, "Information and Resources."

52. Proctor, "Fleeing to Canada on Foot."

53. Amnesty International, "Canada: End the Safe Third Country Agreement."

54. Canada Border Services Agency, quoted in Barrett, "Seeking Asylum Across the International Boundary," 68.

55. Immigration, Refugees and Citizenship Canada, quoted in Barrett, 71.

56. Turcott and Boykoff, "The White Racial Frame in Sport Media."

57. Canizales and Agius Vallejo, "Latinos and Racism in the Trump Era."

58. BAL, "Trump Signs Executive Orders on Border Wall, Sanctuary Cities."

59. LII, "Illegal Immigration Reform and Immigration Responsibility Act."

60. "Obama Leaves Office as 'Deporter-in-Chief,'" *Latino USA*.

61. Golash-Boza and Hondagneu-Sotelo, "Latino Immigrant Men and the Deportation Crisis."

62. Canizales and Agius Vallejo, "Latinos and Racism in the Trump Era," 154.

63. B. Brooks, "Victims of Anti-Latino Hate Crimes Soar in U.S."
64. López and Krogstad, "Key Facts About Unauthorized Immigrants Enrolled in DACA."
65. Cabrera and Patler, *From Undocumented to DACAmented*, 6.
66. Boundless, "What Is DACA?"
67. López and Krogstad, "Key Facts About Unauthorized Immigrants Enrolled in DACA."
68. Icenhower, "Top 5 Countries of Origin of DACA Immigrants."
69. "Trump Ends DACA Program & Gives 6 Month Grace Period," YouTube.
70. Rose, "Texas Judge Says DACA Is Probably Illegal."
71. U.S. Citizenship and Immigration Services, "Temporary Protected Status."
72. Castillo, "Internal Documents Capture Trump Administration Debate."
73. Global Detention Project, "United States."
74. Austin-Hillery and Long, "We Went to a US Border Detention Center for Children."
75. Wright, "Refugee Advocates 'Shocked and Dismayed' over Asylum Changes in Budget Bill."
76. Wolf, "Yes, Obama Deported More People Than Trump but Context Is Everything."

BIBLIOGRAPHY

Aguilera, Jasmine. "Here's What to Know About the Status of Family Separation at the U.S. Border, Which Isn't Nearly Over." *Time*, October 25, 2019.

Al Jazeera. "Up to '60,000 Visas Revoked' After Trump's Travel Ban." February 3, 2017. https://www.aljazeera.com/news/2017/2/3/up-to-60000-visas-revoked-after-trumps-travel-ban.

Amnesty International. "Canada: End the Safe Third Country Agreement." Petition. Accessed August 7, 2023. https://takeaction.amnesty.ca/page/103088/action/1.

Amnesty International. "USA: Policy of Separating Children from Parents Is Nothing Short of Torture." Press release, June 18, 2018. https://www.amnesty.org/en/latest/news/2018/06/usa-family-separation-torture/.

Austin-Hillery, Nicole, and Clara Long. "We Went to a US Border Detention Center for Children. What We Saw Was Awful." Human Rights Watch, June 24, 2019. https://www.hrw.org/news/2019/06/24/we-went-us-border-detention-center-children-what-we-saw-was-awful.

BAL (Berry Appleman and Leiden LLP). "Trump Signs Executive Orders on Border Wall, Sanctuary Cities." Press release, January 25, 2017. https://www.bal.com/bal-news/trump-signs-executive-orders-on-border-wall-sanctuary-cities/.

Barrett, Sarah E. "Seeking Asylum Across the International Boundary: Legal Terms and Geopolitical Conditions of Irregular Border Crossing and Asylum Seeking

Between the United States and Canada, 2016–2018." Undergraduate honors thesis, University of Vermont, 2018.

Boundless. "What Is DACA? Everything You Need to Know." Accessed August 7, 2023. https://www.boundless.com/immigration-resources/what-is-daca.

Brooks, Brad. "Victims of Anti-Latino Hate Crimes Soar in U.S.: FBI Report." Reuters, November 12, 2019.

Brooks, David. "Sterilization of Migrant Women in U.S. Detention Centers Causes Outrage." *Struggle La Lucha*, September 22, 2020. https://www.struggle-la-lucha .org/2020/09/22/.

Buckley, F. H. "The Federal Courts Just Joined 'the Resistance.'" *New York Post*, May 31, 2017.

Cabrera, Jorge A., and Caitlin Patler. *From Undocumented to DACAmented: Impacts of the Deferred Action for Childhood Arrivals (DACA) Program*. Los Angeles: Institute for Research on Labor and Employment, 2015. http://www.chicano.ucla .edu/files/Patler_DACA_Report_061515.pdf.

Campoy, Ana. "Nielsen Says It's the Law to Detain Asylum Seekers. It's Not, According to These Rules." *Quartz*, June 19, 2018. https://qz.com/1309188/trumps-family -separation-policy-nielsens-detainment-claim-is-challenged-by-two-rules/.

Canizales, Stephanie L., and Jody Agius Vallejo. "Latinos and Racism in the Trump Era." *Daedalus* 150, no. 2 (2021): 150–64.

Castillo, Andrea. "Internal Documents Capture Trump Administration Debate About Ending Temporary Immigrant Protections." *Los Angeles Times*, October 4, 2018.

Cho, Eunice Hyunhye, Tara Tidwell Cullen, and Clara Long. *Justice-Free Zones: U.S. Immigration Detention Under the Trump Administration*. American Civil Liberties Union research report, 2020.

Cole, David. "'So-Called Judges' Trump Trump." *Washington Post*, February 10, 2017.

Congressional Research Service. "The Trump Administration's 'Zero Tolerance' Immigration Enforcement Policy." Report R45266, February 2, 2021.

Cummings, William. "Trump Defends Conditions for Detained Migrant Kids, Blames Obama for Family Separations; Fact Checkers Call Foul." *USA Today*, June 23, 2020.

Gantt Shafer, Jessica. "Donald Trump's 'Political Incorrectness': Neoliberalism as Frontstage Racism on Social Media." *Social Media and Society* 3, no. 3 (2017). https://doi.org/10.1177/2056305117733226.

Garrett, Taylor H. "Refugee Protection in International Law: UNHCR's Global Consultations on International Protection." *Michigan Journal of International Law* 25, no. 3 (2004): 751–54.

Gelardi, Chris. "The US Is Resettling the Fewest Number of Refugees in 40 Years." *Global Citizen*, April 26, 2018. https://www.globalcitizen.org/en/content/us -accepted-refugees-2018/.

Gladstone, Rick, and Satoshi Sugiyama. "Trump's Travel Ban: How It Works and Who Is Affected." *New York Times*, July 1, 2018.

Global Detention Project. "United States." Accessed December 29, 2020. https://www
.globaldetentionproject.org/countries/americas/united-states.

Golash-Boza, Tanya, and Pierrette Hondagneu-Sotelo. "Latino Immigrant Men and
the Deportation Crisis: A Gendered Racial Removal Program." *Latino Studies* 11,
no. 3 (2013): 271–92.

Human Rights Watch. "Q&A: Trump Administration's 'Zero-Tolerance' Immigration Policy." August 16, 2018. https://www.hrw.org/news/2018/08/16/qa-trump
-administrations-zero-tolerance-immigration-policy.

Human Rights Watch. "US Move Puts More Asylum Seekers at Risk." September
25, 2019. https://www.hrw.org/news/2019/09/25/us-move-puts-more-asylum
-seekers-risk.

Human Rights Watch. "US: New Report Shines Spotlight on Abuses and Growth in
Immigrant Detention Under Trump." April 30, 2020. https://www.hrw.org/news/
2020/04/30/us-new-report-shines-spotlight-abuses-and-growth-immigrant
-detention-under-trump.

Icenhower, Alexandria. "Top 5 Countries of Origin of DACA Immigrants." Brookings
Institution, June 9, 2015. https://www.brookings.edu/blog/brookings-now/2015/
06/09/top-5-countries-of-origin-of-daca-immigrants/.

Immigration Equality. "DACA (Deferred Action for Childhood Arrivals)." Last
updated August 30, 2020. https://immigrationequality.org/legal/legal-help/other
-paths-to-status/deferred-action-for-childhood-arrivals-daca/.

Jackson, Brian A., Ashley L. Rhoades, Jordan R. Reimer, Natasha Lander, Katherine
Costello, and Sina Beaghley. *Practical Terrorism Prevention: Reexamining U.S.
National Approaches to Addressing the Threat of Ideologically Motivated Violence.*
Santa Monica, Calif.: Homeland Security Operational Analysis Center, 2019.

Kanno-Youngs, Zolan. "Trump Administration Adds Six Countries to Travel Ban."
New York Times, January 31, 2020.

Keneally, Meagan. "What to Know About the Violent Charlottesville Protests and
Anniversary Rallies." *ABC News*, August 8, 2018.

Kopan, Tal. "Trump Admin Drops Asylum Protections for Domestic Violence Victims." AP News, June 12, 2018.

Latino USA. "Obama Leaves Office as 'Deporter-in-Chief.'" NPR, January 20, 2017.
Audio file, 11 min. https://www.npr.org/2017/01/20/510799842/.

LII (Legal Information Institute). "Illegal Immigration Reform and Immigration
Responsibility Act." Cornell Law School. Accessed August 7, 2023. https://www.law
.cornell.edu/wex/illegal_immigration_reform_and_immigration_responsibility
_act.

Lind, Dara. "The Horrifying Conditions Facing Kids in Border Detention, Explained."
Vox, June 25, 2019, https://www.vox.com/policy-and-politics/2019/6/25/18715725/.

López, Gustavo, and Jens Manuel Krogstad. "Key Facts About Unauthorized Immigrants Enrolled in DACA." Pew Research Center, September 25, 2017. https://www
.pewresearch.org/fact-tank/2017/09/25/.

McGreal, Chris. "Obama Moves to Grant Political Asylum to Women Who Suffer Domestic Abuse." *Guardian*, July 24, 2009.

McKenzie, Katherine C., Eleanor Emery, Kathryn Hampton, and Sural Shah. "Eliminating Asylum: The Effects of Trump Administration Policies." *Health and Human Rights Journal*, August 24, 2020. https://www.hhrjournal.org/2020/08/eliminating-asylum-the-effects-of-trump-administration-policies/.

New Humanitarian. "Executive Summary for June 12th." Posted June 12, 2018. https://deeply.thenewhumanitarian.org/refugees/executive-summaries/2018/06/12.

Newland, Kathleen. "The U.S. Record Shows Refugees Are Not a Threat." Migration Policy Institute, October 2015. https://www.migrationpolicy.org/news/us-record-shows-refugees-are-not-threat.

Panduranga, Harsha. "The Muslim Ban: A Family Separation Policy." Brennan Center for Justice, June 26, 2019. https://www.brennancenter.org/our-work/analysis-opinion/muslim-ban-family-separation-policy.

Patel, Faiza. "Deference to Discrimination: Immigration and National Security in the Trump Era." *Human Rights* 45, no. 2 (2020). https://www.americanbar.org/groups/crsj/publications/human_rights_magazine_home/immigration/deference-to-discrimination/.

Proctor, Benn. "Fleeing to Canada on Foot: Reviewing the Canada-U.S. Safe Third Country Agreement." Wilson Center Canada Institute, April 5, 2017. https://www.wilsoncenter.org/article/fleeing-to-canada-foot-reviewing-the-canada-us-safe-third-country-agreement.

Reuters. "Trump Says Undocumented Immigrants Should Be Deported with 'No Judges or Court Cases.'" *The World*. PRX, June 25, 2018. https://theworld.org/stories/2018-06-25/trump-says-undocumented-immigrants-should-be-deported-no-judges-or-court-cases.

Roelofs, Tom. "Trump Demonizes Refugees. Biden Wants More. Whose Plan Will Michigan Back?" *Bridge Michigan*, September 15, 2020. https://www.bridgemi.com/quality-life/trump-demonizes-refugees-biden-wants-more-whose-plan-will-michigan-back.

Rose, Joel. "Texas Judge Says DACA Is Probably Illegal, but Leaves It In Place." NPR, August 31, 2018. https://www.npr.org/2018/08/31/643814735/.

Rose, Joel. "Trump Administration to Drop Refugee Cap to 45,000, Lowest in Years." NPR, September 27, 2017. https://www.npr.org/2017/09/27/554046980/.

Selby, Daniele. "Why Jeff Sessions' Ruling on Domestic Violence and Asylum Matters." Global Citizen, June 12, 2018. https://www.globalcitizen.org/de/content/jeff-sessions-domestic-gang-violence-asylum/.

Smith, Marie-Danielle. "Trudeau Tweet Caused Influx of Refugee Inquiries, Confusion Within Government, Emails Reveal." *National Post*, April 3, 2018.

Snow, Anita, and Julie Watson. "Under Trump, US No Longer Leads World on Refugee Protections." AP News, October 26, 2020.

Swetlitz, Ike. "'Suddenly They Started Gassing Us': Cuban Migrants Tell of Shocking Attack at ICE Prison." *Guardian*, July 2, 2020.

Taylor, Jessica. "Trump Calls for 'Total and Complete Shutdown of Muslims Entering' U.S." NPR, December 7, 2015. https://www.npr.org/2015/12/07/458836388/.

Trump, Donald J. "Protecting the Nation from Foreign Terrorist Entry into the United States." Exec. order 13769, January 27, 2017. American Presidency Project. https://www.presidency.ucsb.edu/node/322204.

"Trump Ends DACA Program & Gives 6 Month Grace Period." YouTube, video uploaded October 2, 2017, by Rahgozar Law Firm, PLLC, 6:43. https://www.youtube.com/watch?v=z5sdyFPlh2U.

Turcott, Ryan, and Jules Boykoff. "The White Racial Frame in Sport Media: Framing of Donald Trump and LaVar Ball's Public Feud Following the UCLA Basketball Player Arrests in China." *Journal of Sport and Social Issues* 46, no. 1 (2020). https://doi.org/10.1177/0193723520962953.

UNC Global (University of North Carolina International Student and Scholar Services). "Information and Resources Regarding Presidential Proclamations and Executive Orders on Immigration." Updated June 29, 2018. https://isss.unc.edu/sample-page-2/executiveorders/.

UNHRC (UN Refugee Agency). *Convention and Protocol Relating to the Status of Refugees.* Geneva: UNHRC, 2010.

UNHCR (UN Refugee Agency). *Monitoring Report: Canada–United States "Safe Third Country" Agreement.* June 2006. https://www.unhcr.org/uk/455b2cca4.pdf.

UN OHCHR (UN Human Rights Office of the High Commissioner). "UN Experts to US: Release Migrant Children from Detention and Stop Using Them to Deter Irregular Migration." News release, June 22, 2018. https://www.ohchr.org/EN/NewsEvents/Pages/DisplayNews.aspx?NewsID=23245.

U.S. Citizenship and Immigration Services. "Temporary Protected Status." Last updated March 13, 2023. https://www.uscis.gov/humanitarian/temporary-protected-status.

U.S. Department of Health and Human Services. "Latest UC Data—FY2019." Last reviewed February 1, 2021. https://www.hhs.gov/programs/social-services/unaccompanied-alien-children/latest-uac-data-fy2019/index.html.

U.S. Department of Homeland Security. "Credible Fear Cases Completed and Referrals for Credible Fear Interview." Last updated December 12, 2022. https://www.dhs.gov/immigration-statistics/readingroom/RFA/credible-fear-cases-interview.

U.S. Department of Homeland Security. "Migrant Protection Protocols." Posted January 24, 2019. https://www.dhs.gov/news/2019/01/24/migrant-protection-protocols.

U.S. Department of State. "Department of State Report: Implementation of Presidential Proclamation 9645, December 8, 2017, to March 31, 2019." c. April 2019. https://travel.state.gov/content/travel/en/us-visas/visa-information-resources/presidential-proclamation-archive/presidential-proclamation9645.html.

U.S. Immigration and Customs Enforcement. "Fiscal Year 2018 ICE Enforcement and Removal Operations Report." December 2018. https://www.ice.gov/doclib/about/offices/ero/pdf/eroFY2018Report.pdf.

Valverde, Miriam. "Trump Wrong on Obama Family Separation Policy." *Austin American-Statesman*, June 25, 2019.

Wolf, Zachary B. "Yes, Obama Deported More People Than Trump but Context Is Everything." *CNN*, July 13, 2019. https://edition.cnn.com/2019/07/13/politics/obama-trump-deportations-illegal-immigration/index.html.

Wright, Teresa. "Refugee Advocates 'Shocked and Dismayed' over Asylum Changes in Budget Bill." *CBC News*, April 9, 2019. https://www.cbc.ca/news/politics/refugee-asylum-federal-budget-1.5091397.

PART II

PERFORMING THE BORDERLANDS

Visual Arts, Music, Dance, and Community Resistance(s)

7

NO ESTÁN SOLXS

Mourning Migrant Suffering and Death Through
Commemorative Art at the U.S.///Mexico Border

ALEXIS N. MEZA AND LESLIE QUINTANILLA

IN THE LAST FEW YEARS, the topic of immigration has been portrayed by the mainstream media in the United States as "crisis" after "crisis." This chapter covers the period from the arrival of the Central American migrant caravans at the U.S.///Mexico border in 2018 to the outbreak of the COVID-19 pandemic in 2020, two recent moments when the theme of immigration garnered national attention as "crisis."[1]

In April 2018, the Trump administration implemented a Zero Tolerance policy, directing U.S. attorneys' offices along the southwest border to detain and prosecute, as a crime, all cases involving "illegal entry," defined as entering the United States without authorization and outside of an official port of entry. This policy created conditions of increased danger and precarity by leaving asylum seekers to wait in Mexico and produced the infamous family separations that sparked widespread outrage and remain a legacy of the Trump administration.[2] However, as expressed by members of the San Diego Migrant and Refugee Solidarity Coalition (SDMRSC), antimigrant violence did not begin with and cannot be reduced to the Trump administration. Instead, in response to these policies, SDMRSC stated that this administration has been "emboldened by the last few decades of bipartisan militarization of the border, mass raids, expansion of for-profit detention centers, and mass deportations. . . . Further, these policies are a continuation of a long history of anti-Indigenous colonial violence and genocide."[3] Given San Diego's proximity to the U.S.///Mexico border, the San Ysidro Port of Entry, and Otay Mesa Detention Center, a regional articulation of an Abolish ICE movement—centering collective grassroots organizing against migrant suffering and death and condemning the broader hegemonic normalization of border-military-detention violence—was reinvigorated in 2018 in the San Diego–Tijuana region.

By November 2018, widespread media coverage ensured that most Americans were aware of a recent mass movement of people making their way northward with the intention to reach the U.S.///Mexico border and claim asylum: the so-called migrant caravan.[4] The migrants in this caravan departed from Honduras in mid-October and traveled together to protect themselves from the increasing dangers associated with migration in recent decades, due, in part, to the rise of regimes of mobility control and the externalization of border controls. On-the-ground social media coverage, lawyers, and human rights activists accompanied the caravan and, some have argued, added a layer of safety as they reported daily on the migrants' experiences. As they made their way north, they were welcomed by many with food, shelter, and support along their route. A popular saying emerged: *abrazamos a los que caminan* (we hug those who walk), gesturing toward the sense of joint struggle that emerged throughout their journey north. This spirit of support and grassroots humanitarianism, however, took a turn toward discrimination after thousands more, in the new "caravans" that subsequently formed, arrived at the U.S.///Mexico border near Tijuana, Mexico. The arrival of men, women, and children to Tijuana each day and the expanding encampments became increasingly visible, resulting in mass media spectacularization as Tijuana municipality instructed them to temporarily reside at Unidad Deportiva Benito Juárez, a sports complex that was repurposed to temporarily house what became a caravan of an estimated five to eight thousand people.

As we walked toward Unidad Deportiva we were approached in the streets by women and children who shared that they had just arrived the night before. They had traveled for weeks only with what they could carry. Within minutes we gave away all the donations we had brought with us to transport: tents, blankets, and clothing.

When I arrived back at my apartment late that night, all I felt was sadness, numbness, and shock. I broke down in tears. It was the heaviness of witnessing dire need, what within days became deemed a humanitarian "crisis" yet was met with neglect. As far as we witnessed, there were no NGOs, no UNHCR [UN High Commissioner for Refugees], or even the local Mexican state; worse yet, the news had begun reporting on the Trump administration's nativist and militaristic response to the "caravans."

It was the migrants' testimonies, the señoras cooking and distributing food, local organizers mobilizing donation drives and providing legal resources, and the outpouring of care and support sent from near and far—expressions of the collective belief in the right to asylum and the freedom of migration—that in these moments restored hope to continue to do what each of us could to respond.

—Alexis, a memory

As the attacks on migrants and asylum seekers escalated in rhetoric and in policy changes further restricting rights to asylum, San Diego and Tijuana transborder networks mobilized in many ways to support migrant and asylum seeker communities. This included holding mass donation drives, providing legal assistance, coordinating volunteer-based medical care, and organizing advocacy and actions to demand political change. To complement these efforts, the local community also engaged in creative forms of mourning the pain, violence, and death experienced by migrants. As they struggled against the rhetoric, policies, and practices contributing to these conditions, they produced and participated in cocreating commemorative art actions. The word *commemorate* derives from the Latin root *memor*, meaning "mindful."[5] We conceptualize the production and participation in commemorative art praxis, then, as spatial and temporal, activated in community, in mindfulness. As a community-based practice, commemorative art within movement spaces has the potential to transform collective grief, trauma, and violence into spaces of encounter and intimacies that can cultivate solidarity and the conviction necessary to build an Abolish ICE movement.

Commemorative art is intricately bound to the regenerative politics of San Diego grassroots organizing, which performs, we argue, a countersurveillance tactic revealing what we call the *compounded violence* migrant and asylum seekers experience under U.S. Immigration and Customs Enforcement (ICE) and Customs and Border Protection (CBP) custody. We name the everyday inhumane conditions and practices of immigrant incarceration—including the infamous "iceboxes"—that induce and worsen health conditions among detained migrants, along with rampant medical negligence while in ICE and CBP custody, as compounded violence.[6] There exists extensive research, reports, and testimonies of ICE and CBP abuses, human rights violations, and deaths.[7] The cases we focus on in this chapter include those affected by family separation, the inhumane conditions of immigration incarceration, and deaths related to medical negligence while in ICE or CBP custody. While these deaths and injustices garnered national attention and outrage, the commemorative art and mourning reveal the routine and layered compounded violence experienced by migrants and asylum seekers. These acts of violence must be recognized as such and as compounded: not isolated or unique, as Estela Schindel explains in the European context, they typically only receive attention when they result in death obscuring the "invisible, daily, silent forms of harm that criminalized travelers are exposed to on their journeys."[8]

To describe compounded violence, we draw on a 2020 American Friends Service Committee report titled *Compounding Suffering During a Pandemic*, Rob Nixon's concept of *slow violence*, and Cecilia Menjívar and Leisy J. Abrego's concept of *legal violence*. Through his concept of slow violence, Nixon complicates conventional definitions of violence. He explains,

> By slow violence I mean a violence that occurs gradually and out of sight, a violence of delayed destruction that is dispersed across time and space, an attritional violence that is typically not viewed as violence at all, . . . a violence that is neither spectacular nor instantaneous, but rather incremental and accretive, its calamitous repercussions playing out across a range of temporal scales. In [engaging with this concept], we also need to engage the representational, narrative, and strategic challenges posed by the relative invisibility of slow violence.[9]

While Nixon's work is on environmental crises, his rethinking of violence is useful in conceptualizing violence within the detention center as an ecology itself, beyond the media-driven spectacle and toward the "calamities that are slow and long lasting."[10] We use the phrase *compounded violence* to suggest that the deaths in ICE and CBP custody are violence, as is the everyday negligence experienced by migrants and asylum seekers. These everyday occurrences—whose impacts may not be seen immediately but that cause delayed effects—often result in worsened health and, at times, death. Menjívar and Abrego coin the term *legal violence* to reconceptualize conventional understandings of violence as physical and also to include how violence is enacted in seemingly "normalized" ways. When studied collectively, they explain, legal violence reveals immigrant vulnerabilities and "legally sanctioned social suffering." The accumulation of these harmful effects is what Menjívar and Abrego refer to as legal violence.[11] These reconceptualizations of violence based on Nixon's concept of slow violence and Menjívar and Abrego's concept of legal violence inform our use of *compounded violence* to describe the violations that occur in ICE and CBP custody, a slow and legal hiddenness that shields them from accountability for their abuses and violences.

San Diego migrant justice activists' analysis of the border and the modern border control apparatus is shaped by the historical struggle against state violence of racialized communities in the borderlands.[12] While humanitarian aid and direct service to migrant and asylum seeker communities derives from diverse sectors of society, this chapter largely focuses on the organizations, autonomous and nongovernmental, that express an explicit abolitionist politics. At marches, actions, and vigils, it is commonly acknowledged that the San Diego///Tijuana border is a settler colonial boundary on unceded Kumeyaay territory, a boundary that continues to divide Kumeyaay communities in what is called the San Diego–Tijuana region. As Benjamin Prado of the local Unión del Barrio stated during a march, "that's an illegitimate border."[13] This is a common sentiment shared among those dedicated to exposing the violence perpetrated by the continued existence of the border and the agents who surveil it. This analysis of the border is key to understanding San Diego migrant justice politics, which is premised on abolitionism and, thus, deviates from traditional reformist and assimilation-based immigration rights politics. Detention Resistance, for example, describes itself as "an abolitionist, non-institutional, autonomous collective organizing in accompaniment with migrants, refugees, and those who have been criminalized by the state."[14] As part of its human rights documentation, it runs a seven-day-a-week hotline to support people detained and document violations in detention, including rampant medical neglect and negligence. As part of its abolitionist goals, Detention Resistance strives to shut down Otay Mesa Detention Center and states that it organizes to end "the terrorizing by Border Patrol, 'United States Immigration and Customs Enforcement ("ICE"),' police in BIPOC communities, and an end to the military bases and ineffectual local and national governments which prop up inhumane systems of oppression." The American Friends Service Committee, San Diego, is a long-standing human rights organization that monitors and documents instances of civil and human rights abuse and publishes reports such as the aforementioned *Compounding Suffering During a Pandemic*. Pueblo Sin Fronteras (PSF), a transborder organization made up of human rights defenders, also engages in monitoring and raising awareness of human rights abuses against migrants and refugees in Mexico and the United States.[15] These human rights–oriented organizations, along with many others not listed, closely monitor the actions of ICE and CBP as a form of community-based countersurveillance. This monitoring and documentation work contribute to advancing policy change, to pursuing lawsuits, and to raising awareness via media coverage. By extension, commemorative art and the practice of grassroots collective mourning complement this countersurveillance in effective visual and auditory ways to rehumanize those who have been "criminalized by the state" and reweave the social fabric of the community from below and to the left.

The rest of this chapter centers three commemorative art case studies, all of them examples of countersurveillance tactics in joint struggle with migrants in transit, in detention, and in death.

CASE 1. *UN LLANTO COLECTIVO: PERFORMAPROTESTA* BY CHERRÍE MORAGA AND CELIA HERRERA RODRIGUEZ

On Sunday, September 16, 2018, a group of about twenty women of color *teatristas* convened by Chicana feminist writers Cherríe Moraga and Celia Herrera Rodriguez, all dressed in white, performed a script of sorrow, pain, and resistance outside the walls of the Otay Mesa Detention

Center (OMDC).[16] The act was an ode to the myth of La Llorona, the wailing woman, the Indigenous mother whose children were taken from her by colonizers. Asylum seekers inside OMDC heard the cries from the performance—a *llanto* in solidarity, where commemorative theater became an avenue to voice the pain of the families' compounded violence by ICE, borders, and detention family separations.[17] At the performance's conclusion, a phone call from the inside expressed gratitude for this *performaprotesta* (figure 7.1).

It was an exhausting two full days of rehearsal at the Centro Cultural de la Raza, where Cherríe Moraga, Celia Rodriguez, and an ensemble of about twenty women of color rehearsed an original and evolving live script: the performaprotesta to commemorate the lives of children, adults, seniors, who have been separated by border and detention walls. Reading the script, repeatedly, with embedded testimonies from migrants and refugees themselves currently trapped within the triad of the border-military-detention industrial complexes in San Diego, was a gut-wrenching exercise to perform. Just days

Figure 7.1. *Un Llanto Colectivo* at Otay Mesa Detention Center. September 16, 2018. Photo by Leslie Quintanilla.

before, I had been at the camps in Tijuana doing my best to serve my people—those that came from my parents' lands, geographies, historical contexts. I was to the limit of my emotions, exhaustion, and energy, but I needed to be a part of this facilitated space of performance—to cry, to wail, and to ensure there was a Central American presence in the ensemble. For all that I had been witnessing at the border, for all that my parents endured in their crossing, for the intergenerational suffering I was trying to rectify and heal. The performaprotesta wasn't just for those currently trapped behind walls, but for feeling the pain of my parents' experiences. This was a cry for their (border) crossing in the past, in relation to the (border) crossings happening in this very instant.

—Leslie, a memory

While there has been an important critique of "trauma porn" and its (mis)uses, particularly within the realm of police brutality and social media circulation of public executions in racialized communities, we contend with acts of pain and registrars of trauma that we do not frame within the bounds of "trauma porn," though they might be seen as such. Theater performances that reintroduce audiences or witnesses to deep feelings of pain, hurt, and trauma are not spectacles for voyeuristic gazes, or for mainstream attention. This *performaprotesta*, a "performance" in/of "protest," was in direct conversation with frontline communities in struggle and in border transit. While Cherríe Moraga and Celia Herrera Rodriguez proposed the story, scenes, and script to be performed in solidarity and for those trapped inside the detention walls, many of the stories and script lines are direct quotes from refugees and migrants themselves. Grassroots organizations that had been working directly with asylum seekers at OMDC were able to share the testimonies of those inside the walls for the purpose of the *performaprotesta*. This collaboration beyond caged walls shows that commemorative art can and must be coproduced in conversation between those outside and those inside the walls of state violence. It solidified the fact that our politics, in all their manifestations, whether they are artistic or not, are driven by the collective care and love for humans criminalized and demonized by the state.[18]

The performance-making process and production were intimate in order to bear witness to the compounded border violence of those currently trapped, and the making of this theater *performaprotesta* brought healing to those who participated, trained performers or not. Performance studies scholar and San Diego artist-scholar Jade Power-Sotomayor writes that it is important to

> engage border studies in a way that not only theorizes bodies at the border but also theorizes the border through the body, as [Gloria] Anzaldúa and a legion of Chicana feminists have insisted. As borders transform space into place, they necessitate theories of embodiment, and performance as both an act and an optic. . . . Not only does the border as a "scriptive thing" direct the movement of bodies, relationships, and the flow of power but it is constituted by movement itself. Conversely, the daily desires, needs, and pull toward relational networks of belonging drive the border-crossing bodies in these movement rituals.[19]

Extending Power-Sotomayor's call to theorize the border through bodily movements, we understand the *performaprotesta* as a space of encounter of grassroots movement building through the deep affect that moves through bodies during the performance protest. At this *performaprotesta*, the *llanto* is a theorization of the border through the wailing, screaming, crying body. Its affective power rests in the way those performing and those witnessing the *performaprotesta* had to listen to and contend with refugee and migrant narratives that were written into the script yet were direct quotes from migrants and refugees who had recently crossed many borders to be trapped in detention centers. In the rehearsal process, the women of color participants varied in their engagements with the script and border context. Experiences of border violence, displacement, and capitalist imperialism as they relate to different geographies are the rhizomes through which these women of color performers were able to theorize the border and its violence through their *llantos* and cries at the *performaprotesta*. Each person cried for their histories of compounded violence, in relation to the present one at OMDC, even if they were themselves positioned differently from the specificities of Central American geographies, calendars, and embodiments within the current exodus. Thus, theater, as a space and praxis of theorization, aided in the embodiment of commemorative art that speaks against transhistorical and transterritorial implications of border and detention violence in the specificity of San Diego///Tijuana as a region. Ethnic studies and activist scholar Fatima El-Tayeb writes that "shared interests and experiences rather than ethnic identity provided the material from which to build cross-nation discourses" in the context of hip-hop in Europe, and we extend El-Tayeb's analysis to this space of women of color theater and performance as an encounter in which cross-border discourses are at the center of multiracial joint struggle spaces in San Diego///Tijuana.[20]

Abuses and deaths in ICE and CBP custody are hidden to the public because the imprisonment/warehousing of migrants takes place in remote regions of the city; OMDC is far away from the population center, tucked into an eastern corner of San Diego.[21] Juxtaposing this remote and hidden location with the collective wail from a group of theater performers allows us to understand that this form of art is another way of hypervisibilizing and theorizing border violence through bodies that shout the pain that is endured by those inside detention walls, through the wailing bodies of those who are outside the detention centers. In this way, what is unseen inside detention walls is made to be felt, and heard, outside these walls. The *performaprotesta* as commemorative art channels the collective, intergenerational, and cross-geographic analyses of state violence that has continuously targeted migrant and refugee bodies for death. More importantly, the *performaprotesta* channels the grassroots ethos of joint struggle, to make sure that those inside OMDC know that they are not alone.

CASE 2. *CHILDREN KILLED IN BORDER PATROL CUSTODY* POSTERS BY ANTONIA DAVIS

Mariee Juarez

Claudia Patricia Gomez Gonzalez

Darlyn Cristabel Cordova-Valle

Jakelin Caal Maquin

Felipe Alonzo Gomez

Juan de Leon Gutierrez

Wilmer Jose Ramirez Vazquez

PRESENTE.

These seven youth and children shared something in common; they had all made the difficult trek from Central America to the U.S.-Mexico border to seek asylum in the United States. They share something else in common; they all died due to medical negligence experienced in CBP and ICE custody, except for Claudia, who was shot by a Border Patrol agent.

Since 2019 seven life-size visual posters commemorating the lives of seven children who died in border patrol custody have been present at various migrant and refugee rallies, vigils, and events throughout San Diego. The presence of these posters, we suggest, marks the ongoing collective mourning and artistic healing practices of grassroots organizing efforts to resist compounded state violence that uses health negligence that is embedded within the infrastructure of the detention-industrial complex (figure 7.2).

On Friday, January 11, 2019, the San Diego Migrant and Refugee Solidarity Coalition hosted an event called "March on DHS, CBP & ICE! In Solidarity with the Migrant Caravan," where participants marched from

Figure 7.2. *Children Killed in Border Patrol Custody*, posters at Federal Building, downtown San Diego. January 11, 2019. Photo by Leslie Quintanilla.

the Mexican Consulate to rally at the Federal Building in support of the dignified right to migration by Central American peoples in the 2018–19 large-scale caravans.[22] In the rally, local speakers from the SDMRSC and its affiliated organizations, as well as national members of the International Migrants Alliance from New York, New Jersey, and Connecticut, spoke thoroughly about the systemic and systematic injustices that have forced the displacement of Central American communities. Several speakers connected the context of capitalist and imperialist interventions in the region, including the climate and environmental injustices that degrade land and water systems and make Central America uninhabitable for the working class, campesinos, and Indigenous people in the region. These rallies have pedagogical purposes; they are community-building methods of creating larger networks, with conviction, of resistance praxis. When it comes to resistance organizing at the San Diego–Tijuana border, borderization tactics that include violent displays of tear gas, military guards, rubber bullets, and barbed wire coil fencing all directly point and shoot at the thousands of Central American caravan members. Those who seek a dignified life in the face of homeland violence and, in their migratory journeys, border violence must first face the spectrum of borderization violences across the hemisphere—from internal Central American border militarization regimes up to the U.S.-Mexico border policies that deny asylum seekers entry to the United States.

The connection between the context of Central American land dispossession, neoliberal capitalism, and imperial intervention directly upholds the violence of the U.S.-Mexico border regime. The spectrum of border violence extends beyond and below the fabric of border militarization, into the very reasons why Central American migrants have fled. This historical correlation of violence was a focal point at the SDMRSC rally, where one speaker, Benjamin Prado, a longtime organizer in San Diego, stated the following: "We are witnessing the symptoms of a sick system that must be abolished. And that's why we not only say that we need to abolish ICE, not only do we say that we need to abolish that terrible border that is the policy of calculated death. Not only do we need to abolish the sick system that creates a situation where our young people are held in concentration camps . . . but we need to abolish this economic system known as capitalism."[23]

This statement, which connects ICE, the U.S.-Mexico border, concentration camps, and capitalism, are a means to educate the collective consciousness to fine-tune an analytic framework as border communities continue to create networks and strategies of resistance from multiple fronts. It is through this statement that we can anchor simultaneous and connected strategies of resistance against the structures of death-making and toward structures of life-making networks for migrants and refugees in the San Diego–Tijuana region. San Diego's own scholar-activist Justin Akers-Chacon similarly writes in *The Border Crossed Us* that "re-forming the migra-state while the capitalist mode of production is intact is not possible; so, dismantling and abolishing the migra-state requires full-scale confrontation with the capitalist mode of production itself."[24] Both Prado's statement and Akers-Chacon's analysis of the capitalist economic system are central to San Diego–Tijuana's grassroots activism against the border as a death-making infrastructure.

At the rally in front of the Federal Building, currently detaining migrants and refugees, where speakers continued to speak about the structures of migrant injustice, there stood an art display of posters that showcased black-and-white silhouettes of migrant youth who were killed by these very structures. Here, rally participants were able to listen to the speeches while reconciling the very names and bodies of seven migrant youth with the medically compounded violence that had caused their deaths at the hands of CBP:

Mariee Juarez (one year old, Guatemala) was detained by CBP in "icebox" with her mother, where Mariee got sick and died on Mother's Day 2018; Felipe Alonzo Gomez (eight years old, Guatemala) died of flu and infection while in CBP custody on Christmas Eve 2018; Claudia Patricia Gomez Gonzalez (twenty years old, Guatemala) was shot by CBP agent; Jakelin Caal Maquin (seven years old, Guatemala) died of a bacterial infection after being in border patrol custody December 8, 2018; Wilmer Josue Ramirez Vasquez (two years old, Guatemala) died of intestinal and respiratory infectious diseases and died of pneumonia; Juan de León Gutiérrez (sixteen years old, Guatemala) died on April 30 after being apprehended by border patrol agents near El Paso on April 19; the Guatemalan Foreign Ministry said Gutiérrez died of complications from an infection in the frontal lobe of his brain; Darlyn Cristabel Cordova-Valle (ten years old, El Salvador) suffered from a congenital heart defect that led her to a comatose state, dying of fever and respiratory issues.[25]

Each child's death must be analyzed in the context of the built-in structure of medical and health negligence of the prison and detention infrastructures of violence. In an analysis of the medical-industrial complex's COVID-19 response, alongside simultaneous calls to "Free Them All" from unsafe prisons and jails, feminist and abolitionist scholar-activists Jess Whatcott and Liat Ben-Moshe say that "under an ableist and neo-eugenicist common-sense, the pandemic has made apparent that hege-monic medical discourse requires that some lives continue to be sacrificed in order to preserve the lives of others."[26] Thus, if we extend an analysis of the relationship between the prison-industrial complex and medical-industrial complex, the steps that lead to deaths inside detention centers are all too common: medical negligence and a disregard for migrant life. However, opposed to this structural disregard and negligence are princi-pled care for, attention to, and reverence for the dignity of migrant life, forces that simultaneously confront the state on its death-making tactics.

The artwork—and the posters' meaning as an archive of memory—allows those that are coming to the rallies/events to say *no están solos* (the children are not alone). Their deaths take on new meaning and, for that, reinvigorate the ways migrant justice communities imagine a world that values the right to live, to migrate, and to stay. On one side of each of the seven life-size portraits, the name of a Central American youth killed while in custody by CBP is written on the foreground of a black silhou-ette that outlines the murdered child. On the other side of the portraits are colorful depictions of the youth, with full faces, eyes, ears, mouths, and smiles, and with halos made of flowers on their heads and feet. In their concept and their production, these portraits, which formed part of this and many other migrant and border justice rallies in San Diego, are the work of artist and activist Antonia Davis. In a commentary piece written for the *San Diego Union-Tribune*, Davis describes her purpose in conceptualizing these portraits and the purpose she wanted them to serve. She states, "in contrast to the hateful speech demonizing desperate people seeking asylum in this country, I wanted to portray them as the beautiful, hopeful people they were. Each and every one is deserving of our compassion and respect."[27]

More than a humanization project, this art piece commemorates the lives, stories, and bodies of Central American children, who continue to be targets of death by the illegitimate border regime. Pedro Rios writes, "just a week before the Border Patrol tear gassed migrants at the border, a Border Patrol agent was found not guilty for shooting and killing 16-year-old Jose Antonio Elena Rodríguez through the Nogales border fence in 2012, solidifying a message that Border Patrol agents can operate with impunity. And just days ago, a 7-year-old girl from Guatemala died in Border Patrol custody from dehydration and shock."[28]

The architecture of the border regime, from tear gas, to bullets, to medical and health neglect, becomes the context on which grassroots activism creates its antithesis of border regimes, with sites of hope, life, and dignity for those killed by the state. Because Davis's purpose and practice are directly connected to the rallies, marches, and public outcries against state violence, the seven posters become the method through which commemorative art builds conviction in these spaces of education, outcry, and community building. Much like holding a candle at a religious procession, holding these posters or signs at various "Abolish ICE" events is part of the practice and embodiment of commemorating and honoring those who have been killed by the state. More than an act of remembrance, these posters become participants and subjects themselves, bringing the lives and spirits of Central American migrants to the fight against ICE, the very reason why we have assembled in the first place.

As the main purpose of the rallies and marches is to use education and commemoration to denounce the state's targeted killing of Central Americans, the seven children actively form a part of the movement against ICE. Their deaths are not in vain because through their memory, they become seven spirits of joint struggle that embolden San Diego–Tijuana grassroots organizing against the death-making border regime. Thus, it is crucial to think about the depth and possibility of commemorative art beyond the posters' symbolic presence but also to see the functionality of the posters as active agents of joint struggle movement building, where they are anchors for public resistance to state violence. Most importantly, these posters are countersurveillance strategies against agents of violence such as the border, detention, and the military-industrial complex because, in order to honor the lives of Central American children, one must also be keenly aware of the tactics and strategies of state surveillance projects—not just to become aware of border surveillance histories and tactics, but also to actively counter them and prevent further deaths in the present and future migratory contexts. .

CASE 3. *VIGIL FOR CARLOS* BY PUEBLO SIN FRONTERAS

As schools closed, millions lost their jobs, and the death toll surged following the World Health Organization's declaration of COVID-19 as a pandemic in mid-March 2020, persons incarcerated in ICE detention centers found themselves immediately in high-risk settings. In the early months of the pandemic, OMDC emerged as an epicenter, the ICE facility with the highest confirmed COVID-19 cases nationwide. After establishing regular communication with detained migrants, Detention Resistance (along with other organizations, including Pueblo Sin Fronteras) began documenting personal testimonies to monitor the conditions and health of persons detained at OMDC. Through this documentation the community was informed of the lack of implementation of COVID-19 protocols, the closing of the kitchens at the facility (which had led to detained migrants being fed cold packaged sandwiches for every meal), and an April 10 incident in which incarcerated folks had been pepper-sprayed by guards after refusing to sign waivers releasing CoreCivic of liability for health problems related to COVID-19 (the waivers were a condition to receive face masks).[29] A week after that incident, on April 17, a group calling themselves "Inmigrantes unidos de la detención de Otay Mesa," consisting of over a hundred imprisoned people, recorded and announced that they would be joining a general hunger strike alongside others taking place in nearby detention centers. In their collectively written statement, they requested to be released on parole or bond to be with their families as they awaited their immigration proceedings. In their plea, they also affirmed their humanity and warned, "if we continue in detention, many lives can be lost. . . . Release us before it is too late. We are parents, children, brothers, and grandfathers."[30] In response and in support, a call to action was announced at the end of April 2022. An ad hoc coalition formed, joining local grassroots activists, nongovernmental organizations, lawyers from Al Otro Lado, doctors from Doctors for Camp Closure, faith-based humanitarian groups, and other migrant rights– and social justice–oriented individuals and organizations across San Diego. All came together to demand that detained immigrants be released before the detention center became a death camp.

Despite the migrant-led efforts, community support, and statements of caution issued by physicians, the first prisoner in ICE custody nationwide to die from COVID-19 was at OMDC.[31] On May 6, 2020, Carlos Ernesto Escobar Mejia died after contracting COVID-19 at OMDC. The death of Mr. Mejia quickly received national attention. The *San Diego Union-Tribune* published one of the first articles confirming Mr. Mejia's death, while immigrant rights organizations posted commemorative photos, graphics, and art on social media, capturing the attention of many news and media outlets. Mr. Mejia was fifty-seven years old. He originally fled the Salvadoran Civil War in 1980. His death was felt deeply by a San Diego community that had been tirelessly demanding the release of those detained even before news broke that someone had died at OMDC, and the heaviness of community grief made it difficult for organizers to immediately respond to external calls to action. With Mejia's death, the warning was no longer a threat; it seemed to herald more deaths at the hands of CoreCivic, ICE, and all those who had the power to release more folks but chose not to.

A vigil was held at OMDC on May 9, 2020 (with a Día de los Muertos altar built later that year), to honor Mejia's life as a commemorative practice of community remembrance and as countersurveillance "to provide witness," as Pedro Rios from American Friends Service Committee states. As many of his fellow migrants or incarcerated folks, his sister, Rosa, and local community organizations argued, Mejia's death was preventable. On April 30, 2020, following the *Rodriguez Alcantara v. Archambeault* class-action lawsuit led by the American Civil Liberties Union Foundation of San Diego and Imperial Counties, the court had certified a class of medically vulnerable people at OMDC for immediate release, resulting in the release of an estimated one hundred people.[32] Despite preexisting medical conditions including hypertension and diabetes, which placed him at heightened risk of serious illness or death due to COVID-19, Mr. Mejia had not been released. The day she was notified of his passing, Rosa, who resides in Los Angeles, sobbed, asking, "where was the 'justice'?"[33]

As we arrived, masked and socially distanced, and saw from afar those we had only been connecting with virtually for months, it felt difficult to mourn in these circumstances, unable to hold or hug due to the pandemic. As we mourned, we listened to the testimony of those who had witnessed Mejia's last days of medical neglect and declining health. One witness in Mr. Mejia's pod stated,

> It was gross negligence on behalf of [CoreCivic] staff, administration, and medical. Señor Escobar, to begin with, had underlying medical conditions, and he had almost a month complaining to medical staff about how he felt. And for about three weeks, the last three weeks, he didn't really come out of his room anymore because of how he felt. He would keep telling medical, I think he went a couple of times to medical and they never really took him to the hospital to check him out. Number one, they know that this COVID-19 is going around and that they have to take special care of people with underlying medical conditions. I'm not a doctor, but I believe that anybody in this situation, in their right mind, right and correct sane mind, would have taken him to the doctor, to the hospital, or would have actually done a real checkup.[34]

Local community speakers condemned ICE, CoreCivic, and everyone who "profit from human suffering," and they recommitted to the fight against antimigrant violence. While this vigil, altar, and subsequent events in honor of Mejia were about his specific experience of injustice, his experience also exposes the compounded violence in the form of neglect, negligence, and abuse that occurs daily in ICE detention centers.[35] We were there to acknowledge that this death had occurred, and that this death was preventable, to share space in these heavy moments of grief and to reaffirm that migrants' and asylum seekers' lives will not go unaccounted for. The vigil told ICE and CoreCivic that they were being watched. Our presence, as a community, was to state that this would not go unchallenged and, in the words of Alex Mensing, "that's why we have to continue coming to this place."[36] Mensing was referring to OMDC, but "this place" can be also interpreted metaphorically, referring to spaces such as the vigil that bring people together, in presence with one another, to build a movement that has the potential to end these violences. With chants, the vigil also communicated to those still detained behind the

Figure 7.3. *Vigil for Carlos* at Otay Mesa Detention Center. May 9, 2020. Photo by Pedro Rios.

prison's walls that they were not alone or forgotten. Honking to signal our solidarity and departure for the evening as we drove down the one-way exit street along the detention center "pods," we heard noise in return, acknowledging that they heard us. And as we drove off, we whispered to ourselves as if somehow, they could hear us, *no están solos* (figure 7.3).

NOTES

1.   To mark the multiplicity of borders that currently exist in the San Diego/// Tijuana border region, we take inspiration from Roberto D. Hernández's use of /// in *Coloniality of the US/Mexico Border*, with which he marks a visual protest against the "triple fence strategy" that started with Operation Gatekeeper in San Ysidro. We expand the meaning of the triple slashes to account for the evolving material and physical borders that migrants physically confront in the San Diego and Tijuana region. During this moment of multiple caravans, more borderization techniques, like additional barbed wiring, are embedded in the compounding triple-slash marker.

2.   In *The Border Crossed Us* (2021), Justin Akers-Chacón describes the Zero Tolerance family separation policy as an order that "required the prosecution of all adult migrants and refugees apprehended trying to cross the US-Mexico

border, and the separation of all children who were turned over to state custody. Over this period, more than 5,500 children, including babies and toddlers, were separated from their detained and sometimes deported parents, and moved through the detention-to-shelter process within the United States. By October 2020, the whereabouts of the parents of 545 children remain unknown" (218).

3. San Diego Migrant and Refugee Solidarity Coalition, "A Call to Action to Support the Caravan."

4. As journalists and scholars have noted, the November 2018 caravan was not the first, but it received more attention than previous ones had because of the larger size of the group. Earlier, in March 2018, a caravan of more than a thousand people, mostly women and children, had traveled together to the U.S./// Mexico border with the intention of applying for asylum; see Semple, "Inside an Immigrant Caravan."

5. *Merriam-Webster*, s.v. "commemorate," accessed October 1, 2021, https://www.merriam-webster.com/dictionary/commemorate.

6. Our understanding and analysis of medical negligence are informed by the knowledge shared at the "Medical Neglect and Abuse" virtual event hosted by the Free Them All San Diego Coalition in February 2021. We would also like to credit the knowledge and analysis of Detention Resistance collective members and volunteers—particularly Ruth Mendez and Jess Whatcott—who have tirelessly documented medical neglect at Otay Mesa Detention Center and in their medical advocacy have concluded that medical negligence is a more appropriate way to categorize the incarcerated migrant experience with medical and health-related care at this facility.

7. See, e.g., Freedom for Immigrants, *Persecuted in U.S. Immigration Detention*; International Human Rights Clinic, *Neglect and Abuse of Unaccompanied Children*; Southern Border Communities Coalition, "Fatal Encounters with CBP since 2010."

8. Schindel, "Border Matters."

9. Nixon, *Slow Violence and the Environmentalism of the Poor*, 2.

10. Nixon, 6.

11. Menjívar and Abrego, "Legal Violence," 1413.

12. See Martinez, *The Injustice Never Leaves You*; K. L. Hernández, *Migra!*

13. Speech at January 11, 2019, rally in San Diego, Calif.

14. Detention Resistance, "Our Vision."

15. Pueblo Sin Fronteras, "About Us."

16. For a deeper background on Moraga and Rodriguez's intention and production, see Maese, "Lxs Caravanerxs and Nonsecular Protest."

17. For theorization on *llanto* and the "wail" at this performance protest, see Power-Sotomayor, "Un Llanto Colectivo."

18. Detention Resistance's "Our Vision" statement refers to migrants and asylum seekers as those "criminalized by the state." We credit this organization for this articulation, which we use throughout the chapter.

19. Power-Sotomayor, "Moving Borders and Dancing in Place," 100.
20. El-Tayeb, *European Others*, 30–31.
21. The term *warehousing* is from Childs, *Slaves of the State*.
22. See Migrant and Refugee Solidarity Coalition, event page for "March on DHS, CBP & ICE! In Solidarity with the Migrant Caravan," Facebook, January 11, 2019, https://www.facebook.com/events/342216466632547.
23. Speech at January 11, 2019, rally in San Diego, Calif.
24. Akers-Chacon, *The Border Crossed Us*, 213.
25. Speech at January 11, 2019, rally in San Diego, Calif.
26. Whatcott and Ben-Moshe, "Abolishing the Broom Closets in Omelas," 13.
27 Davis, "Why I Paint Portraits of Adults and Children Who Have Died."
28. Rios, "Standing for Vulnerable Migrants Seeking Refuge."
29. CoreCivic is the private corporation that owns and operates OMDC through an ICE contract.
30. See Pueblo Sin Fronteras, "Inmigrantes Unidos de la Detention de Otay Mesa."
31. Holpuch, "Coronavirus Inevitable in Prison-Like US Immigration Centers."
32. *Alcantara v. Archambeault*, 613 F. Supp. 3d 1337 (S.D. Cal. 2020).
33. Rosa, testimony at May 9, 2020, vigil at OMDC.
34. Speech at May 9, 2020, vigil at OMDC.
35. U.S. Department of Homeland Security, Office of Inspector General, *Violations of ICE Detention Standards at Otay Mesa Detention Center*.
36. Alex Mensing, May 9, 2020, vigil at OMDC.

BIBLIOGRAPHY

AFSC (American Friends Service Committee). *Compounding Suffering During a Pandemic: A Case Study in ICE's Detention Failures*. San Diego, Calif.: AFSC, 2020.

Akers-Chacón, Justin. *The Border Crossed Us: The Case for Opening the US-Mexico Border*. Chicago: Haymarket Books, 2021.

Childs, Dennis. *Slaves of the State: Black Incarceration from the Chain Gang to the Penitentiary*. Minneapolis: University of Minnesota Press, 2015.

Davis, Antonia. "Why I Paint Portraits of Adults and Children Who Have Died in the Custody of U.S. Customs and Border Protection." *San Diego Union-Tribune*, December 8, 2020.

Detention Resistance. "Our Vision." Accessed Feb 11, 2022. https://www .detentionresistance.org/about.

El-Tayeb, Fatima. *European Others: Queering Ethnicity in Postnational Europe*. Minneapolis: University of Minnesota Press, 2011.

Freedom for Immigrants. *Persecuted in U.S. Immigration Detention: A National Report on Abuse Motivated by Hate*. June 2018. https://www.freedomforimmigrants.org/ report-on-hate.

Hernández, Kelly Lytle. *Migra! A History of the U.S. Border Patrol*. Berkeley: University of California Press, 2010.

Hernández, Roberto D. *Coloniality of the US/Mexico Border: Power, Violence, and the Decolonial Imperative*. Tucson: University of Arizona Press, 2018.

Holpuch, Amanda. "Coronavirus Inevitable in Prison-Like US Immigration Centers, Doctors Say." *Guardian*, March 11, 2020.

International Human Rights Clinic. *Neglect and Abuse of Unaccompanied Children by U.S. Customs and Border Protection*. University of Chicago Law School, May 2018. https://chicagounbound.uchicago.edu/ihrc/1/.

Maese, Marcelle. "Lxs Caravanerxs and Nonsecular Protest: Rethinking Migrant Family Separation with Un llanto colectivo." *Feminist Formations* 35, no. 1 (2023): 268–92.

Martinez, Monica Muñoz. *The Injustice Never Leaves You: Anti-Mexican Violence in Texas*. Cambridge, Mass.: Harvard University Press, 2018.

Menjívar, Cecilia, and Leisy J. Abrego. "Legal Violence: Immigration Law and the Lives of Central American Immigrants." *American Journal of Sociology* 117, no. 5 (2012): 1380–1421.

Nixon, Rob. *Slow Violence and the Environmentalism of the Poor*. Cambridge, Mass.: Harvard University Press, 2011.

Power-Sotomayor, Jade. "Moving Borders and Dancing in Place: Son Jarocho's Speaking Bodies at the Fandango Fronterizo." *TDR: The Drama Review* 64, no. 4 (2020): 84–107.

Power-Sotomayor, Jade. "Un Llanto Colectivo: A PerformaProtesta." *Theatre Journal* 75, no. 2 (2023, forthcoming).

Pueblo Sin Fronteras. "About Us." Accessed May 14, 2023. https://www.pueblosinfronteras.org/.

Pueblo Sin Fronteras. "Inmigrantes unidos de la detención de Otay Mesa." Audio recording, 1:25. Posted to Twitter (@PuebloSF), April 17, 2020, 4:45 p.m.

Rios, Pedro. "Standing for Vulnerable Migrants Seeking Refuge." *LA Progressive*, December 18, 2018. https://www.laprogressive.com/vulnerable-migrants-seeking-refuge/.

San Diego Migrant and Refugee Solidarity Coalition. "A Call to Action to Support the Caravan." SocialistWorker.org, November 20, 2018. https://socialistworker.org/2018/11/20/a-call-to-action-to-support-the-caravan.

Schindel, Estela. "Border Matters: Death, Mourning and Materiality at the European Borderlands" *EuropeNow*, no. 33 (April 2020). https://www.europenowjournal.org/2020/04/27/border-matters-death-mourning-and-materiality-at-the-european-borderlands/.

Semple, Kirk. "Inside an Immigrant Caravan: Women and Children, Fleeing Violence." *New York Times*, April 4, 2018.

Southern Border Communities Coalition. "Fatal Encounters with CBP since 2010." Updated April 6, 2023. https://www.southernborder.org/deaths_by_border_patrol.

U.S. Department of Homeland Security, Office of Inspector General. *Violations of ICE Detention Standards at Otay Mesa Detention Center*. OIG-21–61. September 14, 2021.

Whatcott, Jess, and Liat Ben-Moshe. "Abolishing the Broom Closets in Omelas: Feminist Disability Analysis of Crisis and Precarity." *Feminist Formations* 33, no. 3 (2021): 1–25.

8

"AMERICAN" INCARCERATION

Dances That Critique Confinement and Contribute to Prison Abolitionist Possibilities

TRIA BLU WAKPA

IN 2018, ALEXA LOPEZ—A FOURTEEN-YEAR-OLD young woman in full quinceañera attire, including a rhinestone tiara and a beaded, pink dress with a hoop skirt—rhythmically swayed with her mother, Dianeth Mazariegos, outside the West County Detention Center in Richmond, California.[1] Lopez's father—who is originally from Huehuetenango, Guatemala—was imprisoned within the facility as a result of changes in immigration policy made by the Trump administration.[2] The mother and daughter duo danced, encircled by protestors holding signs proclaiming "All families are sacred," and "No human is illegal."

In 2020 at the State Playhouse Theatre at California State University, Los Angeles, four dancers began a production called *La Hielera*.[3] Each person was isolated within a rectangular, black frame, as they slowly stretched and shifted. Their acoustic score came from a detention center, featuring adults speaking in Spanish layered over the cries of distressed children asking for their parents. One child's refrain, "ayyye, Papa," resounded. The performance's title, which translates in English to "The Icebox," is a nickname for a U.S. Customs and Border Protection holding center. These facilities house people of all ages and are notorious for their frigid temperatures.

This chapter begins with snapshots of these two performances to reveal how and where dance as protest intersects with state-sanctioned familial separation, whether directly or indirectly enacted. Whereas *La Hielera* exposes the injustice of policies that separate children from their parents, Lopez's dance reveals the familial loss and trauma resulting from imprisonment. While state-sanctioned abuses targeting children and young people have been core to ongoing colonization in the United States, analyses of dance as protest have often excluded Indigenous peoples who have survived this settler colonial violence and oppression. Among the most insidious sites of familial separation in the past were Indian boarding schools, which originated in the late nineteenth century to educate and rehabilitate Native young people according to Eurocentric norms. In seeking to expand conceptions of dance as protest, I begin by defining "American," then examine the significance of these two performances, and close with possibilities of an abolitionist future. Ultimately, I propose that Native logics and dances—which are inextricably connected to this land called "America"—contribute to prison abolitionist possibilities.

Throughout this chapter, I use scare quotes around "American" because in mainstream U.S. discourses, "American" is often conflated with the United States, U.S. citizenship, and even white and/or European American peoples and practices. From an Indigenous studies perspective, "America" or "the Americas" is Indigenous land, today occupied by thirty-five countries across two continents. And within the United States, this land is disproportionately occupied by prisons, as the Prison Policy Initiative underscores: "with nearly two million people behind bars at any given time, the United States has the highest incarceration rate of any country in the world."[4] In these state and federal carceral facilities, Native adults and youth are overrepresented and receive some of the harshest treatment.[5]

This (mis)treatment is part of a long history of state-sanctioned control of Indigenous bodies and movements. U.S. officials forcibly and coercively removed Native children from their families and communities to aid the assimilation process and frequently prevented them from speaking their Native languages or engaging in their Native cultural and spiritual practices—including dance—in boarding schools. Today, the term "familial separation" is often associated with the Trump administration, which instituted policies that "cruelly and illegally" separated thousands of children from their parents at the U.S.-Mexico border in 2017 and 2018.[6] Many people incarcerated at the U.S.-Mexico border are Indigenous, their incarceration continuing a long-enacted strategy of targeting underrepresented communities to maintain the stability of the settler state.

If "American" exceptionalism envisions the United States as an exemplary nation in which democracy, equality, and freedom are accessible to all, historically and contemporarily, this romantic conception is false. As prison and performance studies scholar Ashley Lucas underscores, freedom for some is at the expense of others.[7] Under the Trump administration, the U.S. immigrant detention system significantly expanded, curbing legal and illegal immigration (authorized and unauthorized). Experts have compared familial separation at the U.S.-Mexico border to "torture" and "child abuse," and studies have identified how children of parents who are incarcerated "face profound and complex threats to their emotional, physical, and financial wellbeing."[8]

At the heart of both *La Hielera* and Lopez's quinceañera are the deployment of dance as potentiality and futurity, combating the repression and confinement of "American" policy. In this way, both sites foreground dance as protest, yet they have remained outside of dance scholars' analysis for reasons included in this chapter. I conduct narrative and visual analysis of the short film *This Young Girl Used Her Quinceañera to Protest the Separation of Families,* complemented by insights from interviews with Raul Lopez and Alexa Lopez, to show how this event challenges and reifies settler colonial oppression. I then turn to *La Hielera,* a pedagogical project that reflects on state-sanctioned separations of families to educate student participants and audiences, weaving together insights from director Seónagh Kummer with my choreographic analysis.

QUINCEAÑERA PROTEST

Lopez's quinceañera protest critiques "American" confinement under the Trump administration by revealing the anguish caused by incarceration, while simultaneously presenting dance as a practice of resistance and resilience. Quinceañeras are diverse and fluid processes that often involve generations of family members coming together to celebrate Latina young women on their fifteenth birthdays. These events can cost as much as twenty or thirty thousand dollars and require "hundreds of hours of preparation undertaken over the course of months or years."[9] Karen Mary Davalos writes, "within the public discourse, the quinceañera is regarded in three ways: as an extension of particular Catholic sacraments, as a rite of passage, and as a practice that has historical continuity or [dynamic] 'tradition.'" Most people attribute the roots of the practice to the "indigenous cultures of Latin America," specifically "Aztec and Mayan cultures." However, others believe that quinceañeras first arose from an "'ancient European social custom' that was later 'adopted in Latin America.'"[10]

In the contemporary U.S. context, quinceañeras can simultaneously communicate Latinx and "American" identity; according to Davalos, the quinceañera "makes a girl into a woman, but more importantly makes her into a Mexican [or Latina] woman." Davalos, however, primarily views quinceañeras as complicit with U.S. assimilation: "the quinceañera borrows from practices and meanings found within dominant culture. The two most obvious dominant narratives are roots and rights, motifs that have developed within 'American' culture. Therefore, mexicanas create and participate in an event that contributes to their own assimilation."[11] A single quinceañera may have multiple and even contradictory meanings. By centering and celebrating a Mexican (or Latina) young woman's coming-of-age, quinceañeras may be understood as challenging a colonial and patriarchal society that subordinates people of color, Indigenous peoples, and women. Yet, as Davalos shows, quinceañeras can also reify patriarchy and heteronormativity, visible in the hyperfeminine clothing and partnering during the dances.

The film *This Young Girl Used Her Quinceañera to Protest the Separation of Families*, produced by the Lens, can similarly be read in multiple ways, and is publicly available on YouTube. It had over 830 views as of July 2023, and several media outlets, such as CBS, have circulated the story. Quinceañeras are complex sites of analysis because of the consumerist and capitalistic pull of a family's expenditures on the ceremony, coupled with the cooperative and communal labor that the event demands. Scholars Azucena Verdín and Jennifer Camacho describe quinceañeras vis-à-vis immigration policies under the Trump administration: "Against the backdrop of an increasingly toxic public discourse on immigrant families, Hispanics who perform the quinceañera ritual construct and enact complex roles as part of normative family identity development. The meanings ascribed to a quinceañera's consumptive activities in the manner of financial investments and resource commitments by multiple family members promote group strength and resilience."[12] Here, the "consumptive activities in the manner of financial investments" signify "normative family identity development" and contribute to capitalism. However, Indigenous ceremonies have long involved "resource commitments by multiple family members," which are integral to solidifying social bonds. This interdependence, which is vital to quinceañeras, departs from "normative family identity development" in European American families, which values individualism and independence. In Indigenous ceremonies, like quinceañeras, a family works together toward a common goal: the realization of a community gathering, and promotion of intergenerational interdependence.

Davalos views it as "ironic" that some Catholic officials condemn and "regulate" the cost of quinceañeras, practices that the author describes as "associated with assimilation."[13] Yet, when quinceañeras are contextualized within histories of U.S. assimilation policies toward Native peoples—in which Catholic and other religious officials played a key role—concerns about the monetary costs of quinceañeras and the ways that these processes supposedly draw people away from other work and church commitments make perfect sense. For example, in the nineteenth century, U.S. colonizers banned Indigenous ceremonial practices that they considered extravagant and counter to Native peoples' assimilation.[14] In other words, quinceañeras can be viewed as at odds with Eurocentric and Protestant values of "hard work, thrift . . . efficiency," and individualism, which are central to U.S. assimilation policies.[15]

Verdín and Camacho position quinceañeras as a critical way to solidify familial bonds in a social environment that is hostile toward immigrants.[16] The film *This Young Girl Used Her Quinceañera to Protest the Separation of Families* depicts Alexa's quinceañera protest as an event that brings together family and community. Yet, the film simultaneously demonstrates how Raul's imprisonment in the detention center hinders the Lopez family's happiness and unity. The aim of Alexa's protest is for the family to be physically unified, for Raul "to be released in time to make it to his daughter's quinceañera."

At the core of quinceañeras is celebration, and this element creates the starkest contrast between the ritual and the film. The pain endured by the Lopez family during Raul's incarceration links their suffering to the Trump administration's immigration and detention policies. The film opens with Alexa and her mother, Dianeth, in tears, discussing how much they miss Raul. The film then cuts to a shot outside of a home during the evening. White words appear against the darkness: "Due to President Trump's changes to immigration policy, there was a 42% increase in ICE arrests over the previous year." In the next shot, a close-up of a house, a small child—who appears to be Latinx—reaches for and plays with a piece of cloth. The ease with which the innocent child moves from one space to the other—indoors to outdoors—contrasts with the confinement and criminalization of immigrants.

Next to the child, in the darkness of the house, white type states: "Raul Lopez has lived in the United States for 29 years. As a part of this new immigration policy, he has been detained by ICE for a year and a half." Because Raul is undocumented, he is isolated and mourns not being able to attend his only daughter's quinceañera. Inside the detention facility, Raul reports having back pain that is so intense he considers self-deporting to Mexico to be treated.

Celebration and sadness are not necessarily incompatible, because both are part of familial and communal collectives, and the process of the quinceañera protest makes these emotions tangible. In the film, Alexa gives a speech to a congregation that contextualizes her forthcoming quinceañera protest:

> I am fourteen years old and unfortunately have been without my father for almost a year and a half, who I adore and miss so much. This has been incredibly difficult because my quinceañera is approaching. This is the time that I am supposed to be in celebration because I am being welcomed into adulthood. And my parents get to recognize the hard work they've put into raising me has finally paid off. At first, I didn't want to celebrate because being happy doesn't feel right knowing that my dad is in pain and forcefully being kept away from us, his family. But then I realized that being kept apart is more of a reason why we should celebrate. It gives us a chance to connect with our communities, so many people have seen our struggle. I will use my quinceañera on June 9 as a protest at the

West County Detention Center to highlight the inhumanity involved in separating immigrant families.

Delivered within a church, this speech amplifies the purpose of quinceañeras as religious ceremonies, rites of passage, and traditions. Alexa also links her quinceañera to social justice, resistance, and resilience.

Choreographies of care in public and private spaces illuminate familial and community solidarity, as well as support for Alexa's quinceañera protest, which is inextricably linked with a call for Raul's freedom. A clergyman addresses the congregation: "I think it is an important time for us to recognize that this is a time when we can come together, to stand side by side, to be in solidarity. To interrupt the balance of power in the ways that we can. And of course, we do that best when we do it together, side by side, together. Amen." The film cuts to a shot of a U.S. flag blowing in the wind as the clergyman speaks, connecting the clergyman's words and Christianity to settler state patriotism. In other words, this moment associates the U.S. flag with unity, democracy, and egalitarianism, not the divisiveness, violence, and injustice attributed to the Trump administration and the settler colonial state.

Women play a prominent role as care providers: female family members gather in the kitchen to make tamales for Alexa's quinceañera protest, and a woman kisses and cradles a baby. The day of the quinceañera protest, two women style Alexa's hair, while three others help her into her dress and fluff its tulle (figure 8.1). One woman holds a bowl of cereal for Alexa while another fastens Alexa's earrings. Dianeth and another woman pin the tiara into Alexa's hair, and then Dianeth and Alexa exit the house beneath the U.S. flag.

Alexa's quinceañera attire, the result of a collective effort, makes her more dependent on others: she holds Dianeth's hand as she carefully walks downstairs in her voluminous dress and high heels. The quinceañera clothing creates conditions for choreographies of care, and the women appear joyful. They smile when they cook, and Dianeth looks happy when she curls Alexa's hair. These moments could be viewed as diminishing the film's critique of confinement, but they are more expressions of resilience than relief. The film opens with the women's tears and concludes with the statement: "Less than a month after Alexa's quinceañera protest, Raul

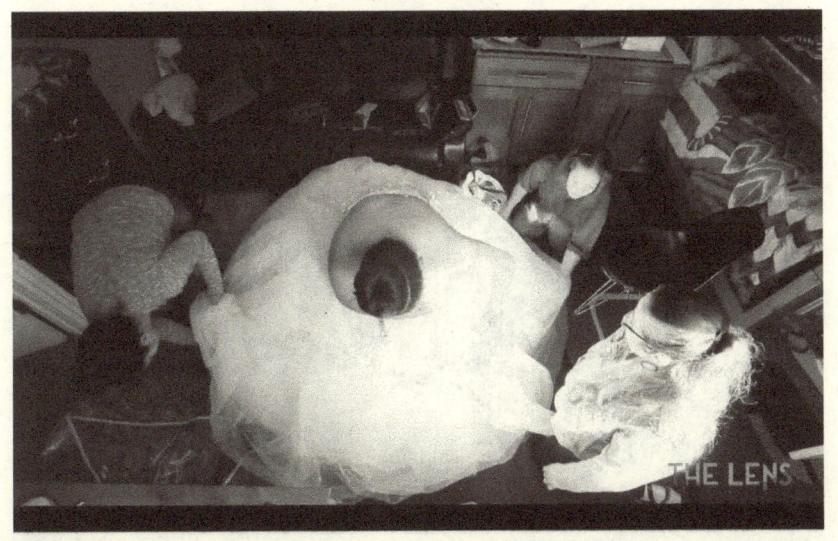

Figure 8.1. Still from *This Young Girl Used Her Quinceañera to Protest the Separation of Families*. 2018. YouTube.

was suddenly moved over 1,000 miles away to a detention facility in Colorado," where his family could "no longer visit him."

The choreography of the quinceañera protest outside of the detention center demonstrates collectivity while powerfully critiquing confinement. Protestors hold handmade signs. A speaker announces: "We're going to actually invite the quinceañera to come and have her traditional dance here and be supported by the community because her father cannot." Accompanied by her male cousin, who is dressed in a dark suit, white dress shirt, and pink bow tie, Alexa enters the circular space created by the protestors. She carries a large, framed photograph of her father. When she dances, Alexa places her hands on her cousin's shoulders while he reaches for her waist. Her right hand is placed on her cousin's shoulder, and her left hand holds his as they sway, somewhat stiffly, to Tercer Cielo's "No crezcas más" (Don't grow anymore). Raul dedicated this song to Alexa.

Lyrics of "No crezcas más" include, "And to think I was carrying you in my arms yesterday. So quickly and already fifteen years old, it cannot be."[17] Her cousin spins her, and as Alexa turns, she smiles, but it appears forced (figure 8.2). Reflecting on the quinceañera protest, Alexa said, "Being in front of so many people got me really scared and nervous. But

(♪ ♪ And to think I was carrying you in my arms yesterday ♪ ♪)

Figure 8.2. Still from. *This Young Girl Used Her Quinceañera to Protest the Separation of Families*. 2018. YouTube.

it was just really exciting, the whole meaning of it. So, I was happy at the time."[18] When I spoke with her, Alexa also told me that the closest experience she'd had to the public spectacle of the quinceañera protest was presenting a "school project" in class. Alexa's words highlight her bravery and commitment to her father.

A little girl watching seems captivated by the dancing. The next scene in the film shows Alexa tightly embracing Dianeth while a handful of protestors, holding up their cell phones, film them. The lyrics continue: "Like a gift I did not deserve." One woman in the audience wipes away tears, and Alexa's cousin, now standing on the sidelines, looks emotional. As the mother and daughter sway together, the lyrics repeat: "Like a gift I did not deserve / As if you would never leave me." Alexa and her mother continue to dance while holding hands, and Alexa's expression shows grief. Dianeth wipes her daughter's tears. The song concludes: "I wish I could ask you already / Please do not grow anymore." Mother and daughter embrace as the audience applauds. Raul's lengthy imprisonment is something that he did not "deserve," reflecting the song's lyric, and he has "left" Alexa through his incarceration, making Alexa's growth more painful since Raul is not present to witness it.

Alexa's bold, brave, and moving quinceañera protest critiques confinement and familial separation, yet the film also reifies mainstream ideas about "American" exceptionalism and the dominance of Christianity. For example, Dianeth narrates, "We are good people. We came to this country to have a better life. Not like in our country [Guatemala], which is a poor country. Sometimes we did not have food to eat." While this information provides important context for why people immigrate to the United States, it also obscures the fact that food insecurity is a huge problem for people in this country. This omission upholds understandings of the United States as "the land of opportunity" without acknowledging the structural and material inequalities that the settler state inflicts. Additionally, the film never specifies that Raul is from Guatemala, instead positioning him as a Latino everyman. This misrepresents Latinx people as a monolith. Furthermore, the ubiquity of the U.S. flag throughout the film eclipses histories of Indigenous peoples and superimposes an image of the settler state as legitimate.

White Christian institutions in the United States have been implicated in immense and enduring structural violence, particularly regarding Native peoples' assimilation. In the nineteenth and twentieth century, many European Americans who participated in Native peoples' assimilation viewed it as a form of "care" and "friendship."[19] The settler state leverages rhetoric around "care" to perpetuate and justify violence. In the film, the clergywoman and man appear to be white, which reifies the racialized histories of assimilation in the United States and adds to the film's contradictions: church officials are presented as champions of social justice, and the church exists as a sanctuary for Alexa and her family.

Simplifying realities of confinement, the film suggests that imprisonment is an individual rather than structural phenomenon, and that Raul's lengthy and unjust sentence is an anomaly. As Alexa states in the film, "My dad is a good man, and I think he deserves a second chance to be reunited with his family." While indeed this may be true, Alexa's words imply that "bad" people should be incarcerated. Additionally, the film associates people of color with tragedy and trauma, which is a stereotype that excludes critical information about lived experiences, structural violence, and "American" exceptionalism.

LA HIELERA

Like Alexa's quinceañera protest and quinceañeras in general, *La Hielera* is best understood as a collective process that aspires both to connect individual stories to larger societal stories, and to raise awareness about the state-sanctioned violence of familial separation and detention. Director Seónagh Kummer created choreography that was inspired by—and, in some cases, directly gleaned from—"body maps" that student performers made that started with their own reflections on experiences of being silenced or empowered. Kummer explained, "they located a certain point on their bodies where they could identify that [feeling] belonged," and then each participant chose "very carefully which shape to put their body in."[20]

The body maps were based on lived experiences and research about child separation and detention. As Kummer described, she opened these workshops to "dancers and nondancers," because "I don't want [concert] dance to be perceived as an elitist practice," which is a mainstream perception in the United States.[21] Kummer shared that neither she nor the students were representative of or directly connected to the communities that they portrayed, namely immigrant children in U.S. detention centers who are separated from their parents.

La Hielera opens with palpable grief that is intensified by audio from a detention center. On a dimly lit stage, four dancers are visible. Two performers move in unison, stretching their hands skyward, as if tracing an arc of the sun or moon, then covering their faces, as if to obscure their identity and individuality. People who are incarcerated are often denied adequate time outdoors, and detention centers frequently operate to hide, silence, and dehumanize those who are confined.

Other dancers, confined to rectangular frames on the stage, squat in a crab-walk position, pressing one foot and then the other into the floor, as if examining their boundaries. Then they crouch with their heads on their knees, arms wrapped around legs. Their movements suggest that they are trapped and vulnerable, but that they have not lost hope. Kummer shared with me: "I think if we're in a horrible, horrible situation, almost the only thing we have to survive is hope."[22] The dancers performing in the frames signified, for Kummer, people's complicity in the Trump administration's immigration and detention policy. Performers' unhurried movements contrast with the desperation, suffering, and urgency of the score's voices: a child's drawn-out cries, a man and woman's rapid speech, a woman pleading.

In a jarring moment during the production, a performer rolls onto stage left from the audience's seating area. Uncurling from a tight ball, she momentarily elongates her prone body, briefly writhing on the floor. In a kneeling position, she backs up, away from the audience, glancing over her shoulders. She stands and runs, with her bare feet making slapping sounds as she darts across the stage and stops suddenly. Under the spotlight, she reveals a pair of white baby shoes, laces tied together. She distorts her face and rolls her shoulders, cringing as she listens to the same audio of a child being separated from their caregiver. Alongside the audio from the detention center and the dancers' movement, *La Hielera* reminds audiences of child imprisonment and familial separation with this poignant prop: baby shoes. Kummer said, "We found several objects . . . from the prop shop . . . a child's shoe or something that makes you think about the vulnerability of these bodies."[23] The baby shoes emphasize that the "children" separated from their parents in detention centers are sometimes infants.

Conveying urgency, the woman sprints across the stage but slows before she reaches the other side, stopping, turning, clasping her hands over her ears, lowering and lifting her head. She crosses the stage again and collapses onto her knees, her head buried in her hands. She pushes the baby shoes away from her; her chest is inches from the floor. Still kneeling, she jolts her upper body upward, head thrown back, neck and heart exposed, palms to the sky. Momentarily, she hugs her abdomen with both arms.

Next, the woman's dancing connotes not dread, but physical violence. The audio shifts to a song titled, "Cucarachas" (Cockroaches). Composer Guillermo Galindo created the music from "the personal belongings of immigrants found along the border between the United States and Mexico."[24] With strong, consistent pressure as if coerced, controlled by someone else, or even pantomiming someone else's hands on her body, the woman continues the solo. She alternates between clenched fists and tense, fully extended fingers, pressing down the length of her thigh, her shin, and back up again in a diagonal motion toward her belly. The audience witnesses her terror and oppression; she does not seem to have control of her own body. The forceful groping of her own body connotes the horrific physical and sexual violence that multiple border patrol officials have committed against people and children—in particular, women and girls.

This performance oscillates between moments of unconscionable violence, and the soothing repetition of actions that convey resistance and resilience. A woman stretches her legs into a deep lunge and repeatedly presses against a heavy object, perhaps a boulder, the wall of a cell, or even racialized social structures that, while fluid, are persistent. In this way, the woman's movements echo those of the dancers in a crab-walk position, pressing their feet against the black frames in which they are confined.

As seen in Alexa's quinceañera, such resistance and resilience can be generated through human solidarity. In *La Hielera* a man joins the woman onstage and, at first, maintains distance. Initially he seems to echo her choreography. Then, he rushes toward her, lifts her upright so she is standing before him, and holds her closely to his body with one of her arms bound behind her back, signifying restraint while in custody. He chucks her toward the floor so forcibly her hands touch the ground and one leg lifts. Then, he shoves her raised leg to the ground, so the momentum lifts her to standing. They each grasp one of the other's forearms and whirl around. Positioned beside each other, both in a deep lunge, they slowly press against an invisible obstacle with all their might. Later, the man carries the woman, curled, like a sleeping child, on his back. During another sequence, he reaches skyward, and she suddenly jumps onto his back, using him as a ladder, her arm stretching beyond his, her gaze following as if searching for an escape. The man seems to be both friend and foe. The duet grapples with the chaos in which they are caught, a sort of chaos they cannot control. The woman shoves the man and sprints away, but not before snatching the baby shoes, the item that connects her to her child.

Sadness and joy are not always at odds, and the characters in *La Hielera* reveal glimmers of happiness and hope through solidarity within confinement. In a duet featuring a male and female dancer—whom Kummer told me represent children—the performers lie on their sides, pulling themselves across the stage with tremendous effort. The movement suggests a perilous journey, such as crossing or attempting to cross the U.S.-Mexico border. They repeat this motion several times before, simultaneously, rolling onto their backs, feet flat on the floor, their hands in a prayer position at their heart centers. Perhaps they have perished and plants have sprouted from their heart, their body, which has become the land.

Their gesture, hands in prayer, is a motif throughout the performance, which can be examined as either evoking and critiquing Christianity or connoting Indigenous spiritualities. Keeping their hands in prayer, the dancers extend them toward the sky, then, with palms still connected, they twist their hands, turning the gesture into blossoming flowers. When the dancers abruptly sit up, they face each other and play a clapping game, symbolizing innocence, joy, and hope. Suddenly, something interrupts the game, as the woman grabs the man by his forearm, pulling him to his feet. She quickly starts in one direction but changes her mind. She clasps the man from behind around his waist; they are both huddled over. With quick feet, they dart backward into the shadows. As their duet concludes, the dancers repeat the gesture of a raised fist, connoting resistance.

When the performers repeat this backing-up motion, they appear in front of a projection of a child's drawing that is being made, line by line. The drawing, made by a child confined in a detention center, illustrates their circumstances. It starts with representations of humans and concludes with horizontal and vertical lines that convey the carceral context: imprisonment (figure 8.3). The two dancers take turns encircling each

Figure 8.3. Still from *La Hielera*. 2020. Photograph by Jaleese Ramos, courtesy of Seónagh Kummer.

other's bodies with their rounded arms, conveying not only child detention, but also human culpability.

During the performance's striking finale, three dancers, leaning
against one another for support, raise a fist and one leg, while another
dancer, lying on his side, lifts his head and arms as if to fend off impend-
ing violence. The dancers momentarily hold their poses. The effort it
takes to balance is visible. On the opposite side of the stage, separated
from the solidarity of the dancers with their raised fists and the man
being attacked, two dancers frantically rub their chests with closed fists,
then draw a closed fist across their mouth like a gag (figure 8.4). The
performance concludes as the dancers make a circular formation, in
seated and kneeling positions. Each of the dancers brings their hands
into prayer at their heart centers and slowly raises their hands skyward.
Simultaneously, they split their hands, with fingers tense and spread, and
then they soften them, and move their hands together, like a wave, like
fire, signaling human and more-than-human interconnections, signaling alternative, abolitionist possibilities to this settler colonial, capitalist,
carceral world.

La Hielera expresses a sense of exigency. Settler colonial discourses
associate people of color and Indigenous people with resistance and

Figure 8.4. Still from *La Hielera*. 2020. Photograph by Jaleese Ramos, courtesy of
Seónagh Kummer.

resilience, but the other side of this coin is tragedy and trauma.[25] Similar to the ending of *This Young Girl Used Her Quinceañera to Protest the Separation of Families*, the family reunion and happy ending are denied. A through line in these performances is the use of dancing as a challenge to imprisonment and confinement, exposing its harsh realities as well as future possibilities.

La Hielera takes a starker view of "American" exceptionalism than the film that centers Alexa's quinceañera. The performance foregrounds horrific audio from the detention center as well as the song "Cucarachas." The song's title is also a derogatory term for immigrants, especially those who are people of color and Indigenous, using anthropocentric logics as an insult. Raul Lopez told me about detention officials: "[They] treat immigrant people really bad. They call them 'cucarachas.' They call them animals. They don't let them go use the bathroom. If someone wants to use the bathroom too many times in a day, they start treating them bad. . . . They tell him, 'Hey bastard. You have to stay in your cell. Don't come out of there until it's free time or dinner or lunch. It's a really big difference how they treat people who are . . . immigrants [and those who are not]."[26] Raul seems to distance himself from being a victim of this violence by using *them* instead of *us*, perhaps as a defense mechanism.

La Hielera directly embodies and shows human rights abuses that occur in U.S. detention centers: when performers rapidly rub their upper arms, they are indicating that the environment is freezing, and when a woman clasps her hand over her mouth, she is silencing herself, or when her entire body shakes, she appears to be tortured, perhaps tasered. Furthermore, religion is not exempt from this critique. A dancer's hands shift from praying to rubbing, using the friction from the movement to warm them. When I spoke with Raul, he told me that when he was being transported in detention it was always "very cold. Everything is concrete and metal there. . . . To stay warm, you have to be doing exercises, because it's very cold."[27] This kind of information is visible in *La Hielera*, but not included in the quinceañera film. Moreover, *La Hielera* implies that social structures and their material consequences can disrupt and complicate people's relationships with one another. Indeed, a child who has endured familial separation might harbor immense anger against their parents.[28] However, neither *La Hielera* nor the quinceañera film—again, both of which seem intended for mainstream audiences—explicitly addresses settler colonialism or the presence of contemporary Indigenous peoples, which can combat "American" exceptionalism and the legitimacy of state-sanctioned violence.

DANCE AND PRISON ABOLITIONIST POSSIBILITIES

This chapter highlights how dance performances and processes—onstage and off, in public and private spaces—operate as powerful modes of protest that challenge unjust assimilation, immigration, and detention policies. These dances display why familial separation causes immense heartache, and how people navigate difficult circumstances through acts of resistance and resilience. Moreover, dance as protest possesses the power to threaten officials and produce material consequences—although not necessarily the ones that protestors desire. I asked Raul why he thought officials transferred him to the detention center in Colorado, far from his family, after Alexa's quinceañera protest: "after the quinceañera protest, there was a lot of protests going on—not just for myself, but other people too. Because when the quinceañera was done [at the detention center], a lot of people saw that. And then whoever had their family in detention, they started to look how to join into the protest and protest for their family now. . . . And I think it was a week and a half later when I got moved to Colorado because I guess [officials] didn't want any more protests outside jail. And I don't know. I think that they wanted to deport me. I'm not sure about what was their plan."[29] Alexa's quinceañera protest inspired other people whose loved ones are imprisoned to protest, demonstrating how choreographies of protest catalyze action for social change by raising awareness of injustices and putting pressure on officials.

Discourses surrounding dance as protest, as well as the Trump administration policies, must be contextualized within the long history of settler colonialism: it is vital to understand incarceration and familial separation as an enduring, structural issue, not an anomaly. On May 8, 2021, the day before Mother's Day, under the Biden administration, Aztec dancers, plus their families, supporters, and immigration campaigners, gathered for a ceremony outside of the Northwest Detention Center on Puyallup land, in what is often referred to as Tacoma, Washington. The Northwest Detention Center is a "private immigration prison run by the

GEO group on the Port of Tacoma." The aim of the gathering was "to pray for and show solidarity with the many mothers locked up there, away from their children and loved ones, some whose children were taken from them at the border."[30]

A film that documents this event, *Prayers for Mothers at Tacoma Immigration Detention Center*, emphasizes the grief surrounding familial separation. One Aztec dancer says, "I can't imagine the pain of those moms in the detention center." This statement challenges dominant discourses surrounding imprisonment by exposing how detention punishes more than an "individual." The film, like Alexa's quinceañera and *La Hielera*, amplifies how human interdependence generates ripple effects, as confinement goes beyond an individual to hurt and wound families and communities. Some Native people have sought to challenge settler colonial rhetoric that labels them "protesters" and instead self-identify as "protectors."[31] By extension, the performances in this chapter could be defined as "dance as protest" and "dance as protection" of family and community.

Unlike *This Young Girl Used Her Quinceañera to Protest the Separation of Families* and *La Hielera*—which eclipse Indigenous peoples and issues—the film *Prayers for Mothers at Tacoma Immigration Detention*

Figure 8.5. Still from *Prayers for Mothers at Tacoma Immigration Detention Center*. Native Daily Network, 2021. Facebook.

Center foregrounds Native peoples' contemporary presence and sovereignty. In the film, one interviewee is a Puyallup representative. He states that the people who organized the event invited him to "give a welcome onto Puyallup territory and to share some of our songs and some of our prayers. And yeah, to work with the Indigenous people of this continent," a statement that highlights intertribal acknowledgment, respect, and solidarity. Then, describing the ceremony that they are conducting at the detention center, an Aztec dancer shares: "It's not a dance. It's more like a prayer, a prayer that we do, that's part of our tradition. The meaning of our prayer was like dancing with our heart, our spirit, you know. So that drum we were hitting is like touching Mother Earth. That energy can go inside of those mothers, inside, so that they can feel that they are not alone. That we are here praying for them." Denying that the ceremony is a "dance," this dancer challenges a Eurocentric definition of dance as secular entertainment.[32] Many Indigenous people view Native dance as a spiritual practice. The dancer states that their prayer is "part of our tradition." Again, scholarly and mainstream narratives likewise conceptualize quinceañeras as "traditions," which many attribute to originating from Aztec and Maya practices. The Aztec ceremony outside the detention center challenges Eurocentric constructs of Cartesian dualism and anthropocentrism, since the dancer relates Mother Earth to the human mothers who are confined. Through prayer, the dancer wants to convey to the women "that they are not alone" and are connected to humans and to more-than-humans, such as Mother Earth. Through enacting relationships with humans and more-than-humans, Indigenous dance is integral to prison abolition.

By tracing long histories of confinement through governmental policy, I suggest, then, that nothing is more "American" than incarceration. The Yellowhead Institute's report *An Indigenous Abolitionist Study Guide* explains, "In settler states . . . the justice system is an integral component of settler colonial warfare against Indigenous peoples. . . . Prisons are colonial impositions on Indigenous lands."[33] Yet, centering Indigenous peoples and practices combats the "Americanness" of incarceration by exposing how Native American peoples and practices, since time immemorial, have supported prison abolition. The report continues: "As Ojibwe Elder Art Solomon explains, 'We are not perfect but we had no jails . . . no old peoples' homes, no children's aid societies, we had no crisis centres. We had a philosophy of life based on The Creator, and we had our humanity.' An abolition future, then, must center the stories of this land as essential to collective flourishing and care."[34] Indigenous dances can do this—"center the stories of this land as essential to collective flourishing and care"—as the Aztec dancer articulates when she connects human mothers to the Earth Mother and prays for an end to incarceration.

NOTES

1. *This Young Girl Used Her Quinceañera to Protest the Separation of Families*, YouTube. All quotations from this film transcribed from the YouTube video.
2. Since imprisonment is a structural phenomenon, I elect not to discuss the crime that Raul, as an individual, committed. However, this information is available in the film on YouTube.
3. *La Hielera* was directed by Seónagh Kummer and performed at State Playhouse, Los Angeles, February 27–29, 2020. Video documentation of the live performance was shared with the author, courtesy of the director.
4. Prison Policy Initiative, "United States Profile."
5. Lakota People's Law Project, *Native Lives Matter*.
6. Buchanan, Wolgin, and Flores, *The Trump Administration's Family Separation Policy Is Over*.
7. Lucas, "Traveling Inside."
8. Martin, "Hidden Consequences."
9. Verdín and Camacho, "Changing Family Identity Through the Quinceañera Ritual," 185, 192–93.
10. Davalos, "La Quinceañera," 108, 112.
11. Davalos, 123.
12. Verdín and Camacho, "Changing Family Identity Through the Quinceañera Ritual," 186.
13. Davalos, "La Quinceañera," 121.
14. Shea Murphy, *The People Have Never Stopped Dancing*, 9, 43–46.
15. *Encyclopedia Britannica*, s.v. "Protestant ethic," accessed February 5, 2020, https://www.britannica.com/topic/Protestant-ethic.
16. Verdín and Camacho, "Changing Family Identity Through the Quinceañera Ritual," 186.
17. Lyrics transcribed from *This Young Girl Used Her Quinceañera to Protest the Separation of Families*, YouTube.
18. Alexa Lopez, interview by author, September 24, 2021.
19. Adams, *Education for Extinction*, 14, 89, 91.

20. Seónagh Kummer, interview by author, September 26, 2021.
21. Kummer.
22. Kummer.
23. Kummer.
24. Galindo, "Border Cantos."
25. Ross, *Inventing the Savage*, 5–6, 11–33, 41, 89, 91.
26. Raul Lopez, interview by author, September 24, 2021.
27. Lopez.
28. Martin, "Hidden Consequences."
29. Raul Lopez, interview by author, September 24, 2021.
30. See *Prayers for Mothers at Tacoma Immigration Detention Center*, Facebook. All quotations from this film transcribed from the Facebook video.
31. Estes, *Our History Is the Future*, 49.
32. My gratitude to Miya Shaffer for this observation.
33. Toronto Abolition Convergence, *An Indigenous Abolitionist Study Guide*, 4. The Yellowhead Institute, which published this guide and is located in Toronto, Ontario, centers the Canadian context; however, these findings are still applicable as the United States is also a settler state in which Native people are significantly overrepresented in the prison system.
34. Toronto Abolition Convergence, *An Indigenous Abolitionist Study Guide*, 4.

BIBLIOGRAPHY

Adams, David Wallace. *Education for Extinction: American Indians and the Boarding School Experience, 1875–1928*. Lawrence: University Press of Kansas, 1995.

Buchanan, Maggie Jo, Philip E. Wolgin, and Claudia Flores. *The Trump Administration's Family Separation Policy Is Over: What Comes Next?* Center for American Progress, April 2021. https://www.americanprogress.org/issues/immigration/reports/2021/04/12/497999/.

Davalos, Karen Mary. "'La Quinceañera': Making Gender and Ethnic Identities." *Frontiers: A Journal of Women Studies* 16, no. 2–3 (1996): 101–27.

Estes, Nick. *Our History Is the Future: Standing Rock versus the Dakota Access Pipeline, and the Long Tradition of Indigenous Resistance*. New York: Verso Books, 2019.

Galindo, Guillermo. "Border Cantos." Accessed September 28, 2021. https://www.galindog.com/wp3/richard-misrach-guillermo-galindo-border-cantos/.

Lakota People's Law Project. *Native Lives Matter*. February 2015. https://lakotalaw.org/resources/native-lives-matter.

Lucas, Ashley. "Traveling Inside." *Plough Quarterly*, no. 25 (Autumn 2020). https://www.plough.com/en/topics/justice/social-justice/criminal-justice/traveling-inside.

Martin, Eric. "Hidden Consequences: The Impact of Incarceration on Dependent Children." *National Institute of Justice Journal*, March 1, 2017. https://nij.ojp.gov/topics/articles/hidden-consequences-impact-incarceration-dependent-children.

Oberg, Charles, Coleen Kivlahan, Ranit Mishori, William Martinez, Juan Raul Gutierrez, Zarin Noor, and Jeffrey Goldhagen. "Treatment of Migrant Children on the US Southern Border Is Consistent with Torture." *Pediatrics* 147, no. 1 (2021). https://doi.org/10.1542/peds.2020-012930.

Prison Policy Initiative. "United States Profile." Accessed October 29, 2022. https://www.prisonpolicy.org/profiles/US.html.

Prayers for Mothers at Tacoma Immigration Detention Center. Facebook, film posted May 9, 2021, by Native Daily Network, 5:42. https://www.facebook.com/watch/?v=287963749396373.

Ross, Luana. *Inventing the Savage: The Social Construction of Native American Criminality.* Austin: University of Texas Press, 1998.

Shea Murphy, Jacqueline. *The People Have Never Stopped Dancing: Native American Modern Dance Histories.* Minneapolis: University of Minnesota Press, 2007.

This Young Girl Used Her Quinceañera to Protest the Separation of Families. YouTube, film posted July 17, 2018, by the Lens, 7:49. https://www.youtube.com/watch?v=ToOOfQ3262c.

Toronto Abolition Convergence. *An Indigenous Abolitionist Study Guide.* Yellowhead Institute, August 2020. https://yellowheadinstitute.org/2020/08/10/an-indigenous-abolitionist-study-group-guide/.

Verdín, Azucena, and Jennifer Camacho. "Changing Family Identity Through the Quinceañera Ritual." *Hispanic Journal of Behavioral Sciences* 41, no. 2 (2019): 185–96.

9

MUSEUM AT THE BORDER

ELISEO ORTIZ

THE BORDER PATROL MUSEUM OPENED in 1985 in El Paso, Texas. Its ten-thousand-square-foot exhibition space is dedicated to the history of the U.S. Border Patrol, which was founded in 1924.[1] The museum archive contains hundreds of photos of border patrol agents posing for the camera and looking vigilant. That repertory of photographs celebrates the heroism of officers apprehending, incarcerating, and deporting undocumented migrants at the southern border while protecting law-abiding Americans. When I first learned about this place I couldn't stop wondering about its purpose. Is there a border patrol gift shop that sells notebooks, T-shirts, baseball caps, and other merchandise? Can visitors dress up in tactical gear to get a picture taken in front of a backcloth? Do they also have K–12 guided tours available for public schools? The answer to all these questions is yes. The Border Patrol Museum offers all that and more.

The gallery space is divided into five permanent exhibitions broadly labeled as Vehicles of the Border Patrol, Weapons, Uniforms of the Border Patrol, Operations, and Special Unit.[2] But who visits the museum? Is this place a popular attraction for tourists visiting El Paso? It is estimated that the museum receives eighteen thousand annual visitors.[3] However, not all of them are there to consume the narrative that the museum has curated. Historians have investigated the archives of the Border Patrol Museum to explore the multiple historical accounts of border patrol agents, or to observe how the crafting of this history plays a leading role in oiling the deportation machinery.[4] My interest here is to draft yet another way to observe and denounce the impact of exhibiting a vast photographic record that portrays border crossings as "illegal" and border crossers as "criminals." In addition to providing an institutional critique of this location, denouncing a discourse that glorifies discrimination against migrants has become a pressing matter, especially in the context of anti-Mexican rhetoric by politicians such as former president Donald Trump.

In exhibiting history, there is a tendency to look at the past as something that has ended. Placing that history behind a glass-framed cabinet or preserving it in a collection, a museum provides a sense of immutability. Such an approach comes with a distance that separates us from a past that is now presented to us in the form of taxidermy—a stuffed animal frozen in time for examination. This is despite the fact that, to echo anthropologist Michel-Rolph Trouillot, history is alive; there is no concrete boundary to cross from past to present.[5] However, the Border Patrol Museum does not provide a critical lens to look at history retrospectively. Instead, it forces visitors to arrive at a narrow interpretation of the history of border enforcement and to think of it as a monolith. In doing that, the museum instrumentalizes the monumentality of history to sustain present violence at the border. Located in El Paso's crossing point with Ciudad Juárez standing on the other side, what is celebrated in the museum is also performed every day at this crossing point. Trouillot asserts that "narratives about the past could expose with utmost clarity positions solidly anchored in the present."[6]

What is narrated through the museum's vast collection is a plot that sustains today's zero tolerance immigration policies directed against migrants heading north. Infused with a renovated suspicion of "foreigners," the Border Patrol Museum is a monument that celebrates discrimination against migrants entering at the U.S.-Mexico border. Archiving, preserving, and showcasing this history is important to U.S. Customs and Border Protection today because it supports this agency's current practices and, more importantly, provides the agency with a symbolic framework to justify itself through what Trouillot has called history's "immutable security of The Past."[7] In view of this claim, who would dare question a past that is so eloquently written in history? And because a museum is synonymous with legitimacy, having a commemorating compound is strategic to today's sophisticated apparatus of border control.

This symbolic framework and convincing passage of the past is represented in a photograph taken in 1958 and archived at the Border Patrol Museum (figure 9.1). Captured in black and white, the photograph shows a row of black, human-shaped targets placed along the border. The background reveals the deserted land of the Southwest. In the foreground, a group of officers appear to be inspecting the row of targets and training to hunt down "intruders." Upon a closer look, I noticed a fabrication with the intention to legitimize border control measures through a staged play—grotesque propaganda of sorts. The officers featured in this photograph are strategically directed to act, to become actors. One can guess the instructions given: don't look at the camera, act naturally. Some of them assess the shooting practice while writing notes on clipboards. Others in lab coats pretend to analyze the effectiveness of the training technologies while the officers on duty continue their training. Who are these experts and doctors? Are they actors employed by the government to perform? In response to photography's visual pantomime, in *Camera*

Figure 9.1. Photograph from the historical collection of the Border Patrol Museum. Attorney General's Inter Service Matches, El Paso, 1958. Holding no. M08339.

Lucida, Roland Barthes describes photographs that are "partially true" as totally false.[8] They are fabrications because they replicate reality. Following Barthes's assessment of photography's accuracy, I can surmise the purpose of portraying and archiving this scene at the Border Patrol Museum. Its function is ideological because it is intended to instill an idea and make us believe it.

In contrast to the photographic charade archived at the Border Patrol Museum is a video of fifteen-year-old Sergio Adrián Hernández Güereca, killed by a border patrol officer across the border in Ciudad Juárez in 2010. The only evidence of the fatal moment is a shaky cellphone video taken by a terrified bystander and made public on YouTube.[9] Angled toward the cement culvert, the pixelated video captures the exact moment when officer Jesus Mesa Jr. opens fire, shooting twice and killing Sergio instantly. He was shot in the face. Although many pictures were taken by Mexican reporters shortly after his killing, this video remains the only evidence that shows how the killing took place. In fact, Officer Mesa had chased after a few kids (one of whom was Sergio) who were playing inside the secondary border fence under the bridge that crosses the Rio Grande into the United States. However, the photographs do not

Figure 9.2. Sergio Adrián Hernández Güereca, gunned down in the culvert of the international crossing point in Ciudad Juárez. Photograph by Luis Hinojos/EFE.

tell this story. One picture, credited to news agency EFE in Mexico and published by several media outlets in the United States, shows the body of Sergio facing up, covered in blood, encircled by a group of Mexican police officers (figure 9.2). This sensationalist picture alienates Sergio's death because we no longer know who killed him and why. All we know is that there is another anonymous body, murdered at the border. And this is precisely the reason why human beings evade photographing: beyond being subjective, cameras are what media artist Hito Steyerl has called "tools of disappearance."[10] With a picture taken, the subject photographed disappears. Sergio's body is no longer Sergio but a corpse, the remains of a person, and the shadow of a human just like the human-shaped dark silhouettes photographed in 1958.

Standing at the doors of the U.S. Supreme Court, Jesus Mesa Jr.'s defense attorney, Randolph Ortega, told reporters that the U.S. Constitution cannot protect Sergio because he died in Mexico, suggesting that his life was less valuable because he was Mexican.[11] But if this is the rationale, then the bullet that caused his death was fired by an American. In response to this, graffiti painted at the border in Ciudad Juárez reads: *A los asesinos gringos, los juzgamos en México* (We judge the gringo murderers in Mexico), alluding to the (never realized) extradition of Officer Mesa to Mexico for trial. In looking at the Border Patrol Museum's photograph of the officers in training in 1958, next to Sergio's death in 2010, one wonders whether the image of Sergio's anonymous and unrecognizable body will also be archived, preserved, showcased, and celebrated at the Border Patrol Museum. Will this and other pictures be part of an exhibition meant to enlarge the bravery of border patrol officers protecting the United States while murdering children? Poet and essayist Saidiya Hartman rightly noted that "to read the archive is to enter a mortuary."[12] Examining and comparing these two images feels like attempting to recognize a swollen body kept at the morgue for a long time while also determining its cause of death.

In Ernst Jünger's writing, photographer Susan Sontag found traces of the violence of representation through the conflicting "identification of the camera and the gun," and in between the acts of "shooting a subject and shooting a human being."[13] Both acts doubled as killing and photographing people. Fatimah Tobing Rony's comprehensive critique of ethnographic cinema's taxidermy resonates with the act of hunting/capturing the body to be fixed in history.[14] Removed from its original context (the events that led to a fifteen-year-old boy being killed at the border by a trained officer), the photograph of a deceased migrant can easily be preserved in history as a token, abused at will by the U.S. Border Patrol. "No doubt it is metaphorically that I derive my existence from the photographer," wrote Barthes.[15] And if the U.S. Border Patrol oversees triggering the camera, then violence is reenacted time and time again in the act of capturing, preserving, archiving, and showcasing a photograph. In doing so, border patrol agents symbolically win the right to a claim of objectivity that sees all migrants as "illegal." About the act of incriminating through photography, Barthes simply asserted that the camera "always turns you into a criminal type, wanted by the police."[16]

THE BORDER ~~PATROL~~ MUSEUM

The Border ~~Patrol~~ Museum is a speculative and imaginative exhibition space that responds to the harmful narrative presented at the Border Patrol Museum in El Paso.

If other museums of history deliberately engender the myth of sovereignty against the invading Other, the Border Patrol Museum is simply situating that myth in a real place with real consequences: Ciudad Juárez–El Paso. In its glorification of a century of detentions, apprehensions, deportations, and killings, the infrastructure at the border starts to look a lot more like a genocidal enterprise, and the Border Patrol Museum a celebratory site of genocidal practices.

In response to the Border Patrol Museum's abusive celebration of genocidal practices at the southern border, what would a Border ~~Patrol~~ Museum look like? Might it, functioning as a liberated space for the dissemination of knowledge about the harmful representations of the border and its crossings, look through the fissures between past and present and denounce the dangers of celebrating past horrors while denying accountability in the present?

EXHIBIT A: STUDY OF A LINE

(Retrieved from the Border ~~Patrol~~ Museum)
Exhibit A: Study of a Line compares two contradictory visual registers of border crossings extracted from YouTube. The first shows the precarious technologies employed by migrants to cross the Rio Goascorán, and the

OCTOBER 19, 2018

Honduran migrants attempting to cross the Goascorán River to enter El Salvador, to join a caravan of several thousand migrants from Guatemala seeking to enter the United States.[17]

16,721 VIEWS.

"Honduran Migrants Attempt to Cross Border River with El Salvador." 2018. YouTube.

PUBLIC COMMENTS:
- This is an invasion. They need to be sent home.
- Lol Pathetic fix your own countries.
- They are headed for the United States, and they don't give a damn about American laws nor Mexico's.
- Are these the so-called peaceful migrants??
- Mexico should build its own wall.
- Soon to be flipping burgers in a fast-food restaurant near you stay tuned.
- Coming to America for free stuff.
- Looks like we'll be needing a lot of 747s to fly them back home, I would fly them to the furthest place I could find let them hike back from that. Wonder how Antarctica would feel about more residents.

NOVEMBER 18, 2018

The United States has sent thousands of military troops to its border with Mexico, a contentious deployment in support of civilian forces that Trump ordered. Troops are installing barbed wire along the Rio Grande in the city of Laredo.[18]

"US Military Place Barbed Wire at the Border with Mexico." 2018. YouTube.

PUBLIC COMMENTS:
- Physical boundaries exist to deter those who have no regard for the law.
- Thank You Soldiers. Thank You Patriots!! God Bless The USA. God Bless Our President!!
- First time I've ever SEEN the government build something I actually want.
- Go get em boys!!!
- I wish I could go and help the troops protect our country. all able-bodied men should feel the same.
- God bless our soldiers. Thanks for protecting our borders.
- This fence should be electric!
- They should use K-9 unit also and land mines too, lasers too.
- Hopefully this will stop the invasion to our beautiful USA. Thanks to our forces.
- Keep them out.

second shows military personnel deployed to the U.S. southern border to secure several crossing points along the Rio Grande.

In the discrepancies between these images, an intention is revealed. Both were made to be consumed by a public that sees in migration an invasion. That public's voice is present in YouTube's public responses to these two videos. The anonymous language of YouTube reveals the deep-rooted xenophobia toward migrants.

NOTES

1. Border Patrol Museum, "A Brief History of the Border Patrol Museum."
2. Border Patrol Museum, "Exhibits."
3. Ross, "Border Patrol Museum Visitors Want to Talk Current Events."
4. Hernández, *Migra!*; Goodman, *The Deportation Machine*.
5. Trouillot, *Silencing the Past*, 20.
6. Trouillot, 152.
7. Trouillot, 146.
8. Barthes, *Camera Lucida*, 66.
9. "Video Shows Border Shooting Scene," YouTube (video no longer available).
10. Steyerl, *The Wretched of the Screen*, 168.
11. Williams, "Supreme Court Appears Headed for a Tie in Cross-Border Shooting Case."
12. Hartman, *Lose Your Mother*, 27.
13. Sontag, *Regarding the Pain of Others*, 80.
14. Rony, *The Third Eye*.
15. Barthes, *Camera Lucida*, 11.
16. Barthes, 12.
17. "Honduran Migrants Attempt to Cross Border River with El Salvador," YouTube.
18. "US Military Place Barbed Wire at the Border with Mexico," YouTube.

BIBLIOGRAPHY

Barthes, Roland. *Camera Lucida: Reflections on Photography*. New York: Hill and Wang, 1981.
Border Patrol Museum. "A Brief History of the Border Patrol Museum." Accessed March 23, 2022. https://www.borderpatrolmuseum.com/nbpm-organization/.
Border Patrol Museum. "Exhibits." Accessed March 23, 2022. https://www.borderpatrolmuseum.com/exhibits/.

Goodman, Adam. *The Deportation Machine: America's Long History of Expelling Immigrants*. Princeton, N.J.: Princeton University Press, 2020.

Hartman, Saidiya. *Lose Your Mother: A Journey Along the Atlantic Slave Route*. London: Serpent's Tail, 2008.

Hernández, Kelly Lytle. *Migra! A History of the U.S. Border Patrol*. Berkeley: University of California Press, 2010.

"Honduran Migrants Attempt to Cross Border River with El Salvador." YouTube, video posted October 19, 2018, by Voice of America, 1:06. https://www.youtube.com/watch?v=x261b1uCjqk.

Rony, Fatimah Tobing. *The Third Eye: Race, Cinema, and Ethnographic Spectacle*. Durham, N.C.: Duke University Press, 1996.

Ross, Robyn. "Border Patrol Museum Visitors Want to Talk Current Events. The Staff Doesn't." *Washington Post*, January 2, 2020.

Sontag, Susan. *Regarding the Pain of Others*. London: Penguin Books, 2005.

Steyerl, Hito. *The Wretched of the Screen*. Berlin: Sternberg Press, 2012.

Trouillot, Michel-Rolph. *Silencing the Past: Power and the Production of History*. Beacon Press, 1997.

"US Military Place Barbed Wire at the Border with Mexico." YouTube, video posted November 18, 2018, by the Nation, 3:08. https://www.youtube.com/watch?v=apBqHMK2ZJo.

"Video Shows Border Shooting Scene." YouTube, video posted June 10, 2010, by grosscrime2, 00:58. https://www.youtube.com/watch?v=0a2LjgL40KE (video no longer available because user account was terminated).

Williams, Pete. "Supreme Court Appears Headed for a Tie in Cross-Border Shooting Case." *NBC News*, February 21, 2017. https://www.nbcnews.com/news/us-news/supreme-court-appears-headed-tie-cross-border-shooting-case-n723656.

10

CANTO Y ORACIÓN IN JUAN GABRIEL'S "AMOR ETERNO"

A Latin@/x Refusal to Forget Lives Lost to State-Sanctioned Violence

KIARA PADILLA

I GREW UP HEARING JUAN Gabriel's "Amor Eterno" in different contexts—funerals, family karaoke, Spanish radio stations. At funerals, either an audio speaker plays the song, or a mariachi band sings the ballad. I tend to feel the song more at family karaoke, when we get together to celebrate the lives of our ancestors who have passed, mostly my Mexican great-grandparents, who raised their nine children in the Sonora borderlands. As our large family comes together and we sing, dance, laugh, and toast to familial bonds, there is always a *tía* or *prima* that sings "Amor Eterno." We all watch and sing along as tears fill up our grieving eyes. This intimate space, usually cultivated by women in the family, brings a sense of togetherness. With rising anti-Mexican and anti-immigrant violences at the forefront of the sociopolitical tensions exacerbated in and by national media attention during Donald Trump's presidential election campaigns as well as during and beyond his presidency, Latin@/x communities came together to grieve the lives of Latin@/xs directly affected by anti-Mexican and anti-immigrant state-sanctioned violence by singing "Amor Eterno" together.[1] "Amor Eterno" offers a broader Latin@/x community the opportunity to participate in a collective voice against state-sanctioned violence steeped in anti-Mexican and anti-immigrant rhetoric.[2]

This essay explores the popular Spanish song "Amor Eterno," composed by Juan Gabriel in 1984, as an *oración*, or collective canto that contests social death, premature death, and broader state-sanctioned violence in Latin@/x communities. While "Amor Eterno" is commonly described as a mariachi ballad that invokes feelings of grief and mourning especially after a loved one's death, it is also a type of Latin@/x sociocultural production that seeks to grasp and memorialize the lives of dead loved ones. By turning to "Amor Eterno" cantos as a community response to the 2019 mass shooting in El Paso and the 2020 death of U.S. Army soldier Vanessa Guillén, I suggest that "Amor Eterno" represents a Latin@/x refusal to forget the lives lost to racialized, gendered, and state-sanctioned violence—a refusal embedded in an avenue of musical expression, a canto, or what Juan Gabriel calls "una oración." I begin and end with Juan Gabriel's live performance in 1990 where he described the song as an "oración de amor" (prayer of love) and use this framing to analyze how Latin@/x resonance with "Amor Eterno" performances at memorials signals a collective resistance.

JUANGA'S "AMOR ETERNO"

In 1990, Juan Gabriel (or Juanga, as he is known) delivered a concert at Mexico's Instituto Nacional de Bellas Artes where one song he performed was "Amor Eterno." A video from this performance was uploaded in 2010 to Gabriel's YouTube channel. The video has since been viewed more than 220 million times, and the YouTube channel has reached 5.95 million people, as of July 2023.[3] The video features Gabriel and the mariachi with whom he is performing. Gabriel is wearing a black fitted suit with beautiful gold sequins that shape elegant patterns, hang from the arms, and line his jacket. What does not have gold sequins on his jacket is filled with black sequins.[4] The mariachi members in the background wear traditional white charro suits with sombreros. Significantly, Gabriel's queer attire contrasts with the mariachi's traditional attire, signaling a disruption of social expectations. Not only does Gabriel disrupt heteronormative societal expectations as a Mexican man here, but the way he initiates the song as a "prayer of love" and invites his audience to sing the lyrics suggests that Gabriel is practicing a collective performance of defiance.

The mariachi begins to play for the large audience, and Juan Gabriel introduces the song with a dedication:

> Claro, Quiero dedicar esta canción con mucho amor y respeto / Mas que canción es una oración de amor que quiero dedicar / Como siempre, con el mismo amor, cariño, y respeto / A todas las mamas que esta noche me han venido a visitor / Sobre todo para aquellas que estén un poquito mas lejos de mi.

> Of course, I want to dedicate this song with much love and respect / More than a song it is a prayer of love that I want to dedicate / As always, with the same love, affection, and respect / For all the moms that have come to visit me tonight / Above all for those who are a little bit further from me.

While Juan Gabriel composed the song in remembrance of his deceased mother, I focus on the description of the song and performance as a "prayer of love" for those who are "further" from him. Expanding the song's resonance of pain, loss, grief, and love to experiences of anti-Mexican violence thus becomes applicable when we examine how the song is collectively sung by families, friends, and community members who show up to perform an *oración* in the form of canto, or prayer through singing, an *oración* that refuses to forget the lives lost to state-sanctioned violence.

Midway through his performance, Juan Gabriel recognizes that the crowd's canto is loudly overpowering. Rather than continuing to sing, he points the microphone toward the audience, closes his eyes, and invites it to participate in singing the "Amor Eterno" prayer of love. The crowd sings in unison:

> Pero como quisiera / Que tu vivieras / Que tus ojitos jamás se hubieran / Cerrado nunca y estar mirándolos / Amor Eterno / Y inolvidable / tarde o temprano estaré contigo / Para seguir, amándonos.

> But how I'd want / For you to live / For your eyes to have never / Closed ever and be seeing them / Eternal Love / and unforgettable / Sooner or later I will be with you / To keep living with one another.

Juan Gabriel slowly walks across the stage with the microphone still pointing at the audience. His gaze moves toward the ceiling or at least upward. The audience finishes singing this section, and he pinches his fingers together, kisses them, pulls his kissed fingers toward his chest, and releases them toward the audience as if blowing a kiss. Away from the microphone, his lips read *bello* (beautiful). The audience applauds as Gabriel finishes the performance.

The video recording of "Amor Eterno" does not show the audience, so we do not see who is present. But we can hear them when they harmoniously sing into Juan Gabriel's microphone. Together in that moment, the audience members literally and figuratively amplify their "Amor Eterno" canto. Literally, their canto is louder than if they were singing as individuals or in smaller groups. Figuratively, their canto demonstrates that singing "Amor Eterno" in unison and into the microphone of a performer who has described the song as a prayer, reflects an act of collective participation in prayer through musical expression. So, while Gabriel's performance at Mexico's Instituto Nacional de Bellas Artes in 1990 initiated a conversation regarding Latin@/x grief and mourning through a musical prayer of love, this practice has extended beyond the concert space and into Latin@/x community gatherings.

"AMOR ETERNO" TAKES OVER U.S. NATIONAL NEWS

EL PASO, TEXAS

On August 3, 2019, a white male named Patrick Crusius arrived at a Walmart in El Paso, Texas, to conduct a mass shooting. He murdered twenty-three people. After he openly turned himself in to Texas Rangers, Crusius was interrogated and admitted to targeting Mexicans. This act was one of the deadliest attacks against Mexicans in U.S. history. It also took place at a time when Trump was publicly calling Mexicans "rapists," "criminals," and "bad hombres," dictating anti-Mexican rhetoric in order to strengthen his base of supporters and fuel xenophobic laws and policies. Mexicanness, as configured by Trump, was to be confronted with U.S. punishment. The shooting in El Paso exemplifies a form of this punishment, where the direct violence resulted in targeted deaths and injuries. While this shooting made national news for just a couple weeks, it is part of a longer history of anti-Mexican violence in the Texas borderlands. The rhetoric pushed by Trump was not new; it was merely rearticulated to sustain systems of power and white supremacy.

While news channels, newspapers, and social media highlighted the shooting as an anti-Latinx and white supremacist event that took place in a Texas border city, very little was published about how the shooting in El Paso reflected a deeper trend in U.S. history to criminalize Mexicans and racialize Latinxs more generally. When anti-Mexican rhetoric in the U.S.-Mexico borderlands is historicized, the mass shooting in El Paso is no longer something that simply resulted from Trump's presidency; rather, it identifies specific markers of anti-Mexican violence in the region (policing, detainment, expulsion, and the deaths of ethnic Mexicans) as acts of violence rooted in the same ideologies administered differently over time.

El Paso briefly became a nationally visible site of death, before it was reduced to an insignificant site in the United States. During these weeks of national attention, vigils in El Paso were highlighted by news outlets and especially on social media, where music was centered as a modality to cope with the pain and disbelief of losing more community members to state-sanctioned violence. Community members gathered to sing "Amor Eterno" for the victims of the massacre. Videos, photos, and testimonials emphasized the Latin@/x cultural value in singing "Amor Eterno" for the victims of the shooting.

For example, figure 10.1 displays a tweet shared by Angélica María Casas, BBC senior videographer and journalist. She attached to the tweet a forty-seven-second video of "Amor Eterno" being sung at a vigil for the massacre victims, explaining that the song "ends with the promise that one day we will reunite." Casas's tweet resonated with so many that it received over fourteen thousand retweets, over a thousand quote tweets, and over thirty thousand likes (as of July 2023). People replied to the tweet in different manners. Some used American nationalist language to denounce the deaths of community loved ones as targeted deaths. One tweet for example contrasted the cultural resonance of "Amor Eterno" for Latin@/x people in the United States with the comment that people who are American and want to be U.S. citizens should want to know "The Star-Spangled Banner," revealing the underlying anti-immigrant rhetoric that sustains the idea that Latin@/xs are second-class citizens

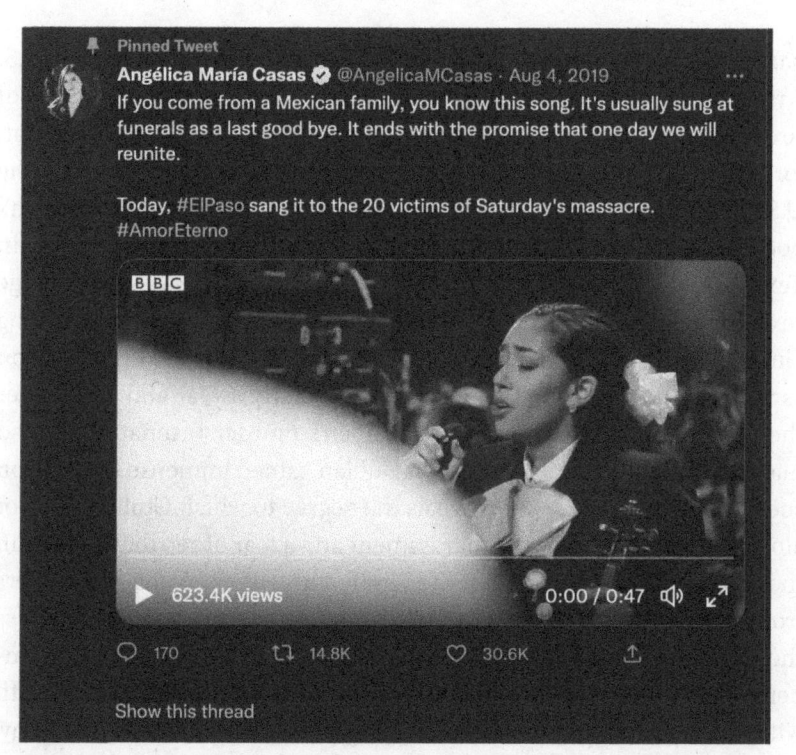

Figure 10.1. A tweet shared by Angélica María Casas (@AngelicaMCasas), BBC senior video journalist, expressing the resonance of "Amor Eterno" in Mexican culture. Twitter, August 4, 2019.

in the United States, never fully American. Most embraced the singing of "Amor Eterno" as the ideal Latin@/x cultural grieving response, sharing how their Latin@/x communities outside of Mexico play and sing this song at funerals, usually bringing people to tears. But the song's resonance with grieving lies beyond Juan Gabriel's performance, Mexico, the U.S.-Mexico borderlands, and even broader Latin@/x ethnic groups. It richly demonstrates what Latin@/x sonic resistance looks like amid the ongoing targeted violence.

FORT HOOD, TEXAS

In April 2020, U.S. Army soldier Vanessa Guillén was murdered at Fort Hood (now Fort Cavazos), a U.S. Army base in Central Texas. She was from Houston, Texas, where she was raised by Spanish-speaking Mexican parents. Her death made national news as her family pressured the U.S. Army to take it seriously, with a proper investigation into instances of sexual harassment that Guillén had shared with her mother but had not, for fear of institutional retaliation, reported to the U.S. Army. It took the U.S. Army Criminal Investigation Division ten weeks to find Guillén's bodily remains located off the military base and near the Leon River in Texas. During those ten weeks, the U.S. Army refused to acknowledge sexual harassment as a central inquiry for investigation, instead listing Guillén as a soldier who had gone absent without leave (AWOL) as soon as she was reported missing by her sister. Nearly a year and a half after the massacre in El Paso, Vanessa Guillén's murder resonated with so many that the hashtag #IamVanessaGuillen gained immense traction on social media networks. This reveals the degree to which Guillén was not alone in experiencing sexual harassment and a fear of retribution within the U.S. military. Additionally, the family's urgent demands for answers from the U.S. Army, especially Fort Hood, prompted Congress to pass the I Am Vanessa Guillén Act (signed into law by Joe Biden in December 2021), intended to protect military service members who come forth with sexual harassment and assault allegations. Significant to this essay, public protests have critiqued the U.S. Army as an institution that both normalizes and disavows its own role in creating gendered violence or violence rooted in heteropatriarchy. Latin@/x communities throughout the United States made this critique at vigils for Vanessa Guillén.

When I heard about Vanessa Guillén's disappearance and murder at Fort Hood, I remember feeling a sense of hopelessness. I knew that the categories of difference that Guillén embodied, specifically her race and gender, made her highly susceptible to violence normalized within an institution built on white supremacy and heteropatriarchal values. As I followed her story, I noted how much of this intersectional analysis was present in Latina-run social media accounts, Latin@/x journalist reports, and local Texas news outlets. They were making connections that national news outlets lacked. Latin@/x communities that held vigils and performed "Amor Eterno" collectively displayed how the song's cultural relevancy translated to those who experience gender-based state-sanctioned violence.

Spanish news outlets like Telemundo broadcast live from vigils held in Texas communities, where community members sang, mourned, and demanded justice. Like figure 10.2 shows, handmade posters held by vigil attendees spoke to the fact that Guillén's identity as a woman was central to understanding her disappearance and murder as part of a larger pattern of feminicide in Latin America.[5] Figure 10.3 encapsulates Latin@/x protest at memorial vigils: women hold lighted candles, attendees wear protective masks due to COVID-19, tall lighted candles adorn the steps of an area dedicated to Guillén, and posters are held high. Some posters read, "They failed you! But your battle is now ours!," "Say Her Name," and "Juntos Venceremos. Divididos Cairemos" (Together We Will Win. Divided We Will Fall). Figure 10.4, in turn, captures a moment during the collective singing of "Amor Eterno" at a Dallas, Texas, memorial vigil for Guillén.[6] The figure shows a poster held by a vigil attendee. It reads, "We won't stop until her chain of command is held *responsible*. Shame on you FT Hood." Coupled with an "Amor Eterno" canto, such posters articulate a Latin@/x contestation of social death, premature death, and broader state-sanctioned violence, revealing a practice at the intersections of Chicana feminism, sonic resistance, and Mexican histories with state violences in Texas.

Figure 10.2. A poster held by someone attending a vigil for Vanessa Guillén in Oak Cliff, Texas, reads "Ni Una Mas" (Not One More). Screenshot from Telemundo39 (Dallas) broadcast, July 7, 2020.

Figure 10.3. Women holding long white lighted candles, shining phone lights in the air, and holding signs demanding justice for Vanessa Guillén. Screenshot from Telemundo39 (Dallas) broadcast, July 7, 2020.

Figure 10.4. A handmade sign demanding that Vanessa Guillén's chain of command is held responsible for her death. Screenshot from "Cantan 'Amor Eterno' en Memoria de Vanessa Guillén (Dallas)." 2020. YouTube.

AN "ORACIÓN DE AMOR"

Understanding the meaning and the practicality of prayer in musical expression captures the decolonial essence that "we pray in a different way now."[7] Juan Gabriel described "Amor Eterno" as a prayer of love. While anthologies like *Fleshing the Spirit* and *Voices from the Ancestors* speak to this claim, I interrogate how this definition translates to and dialogues with scholarship on sonic resistance.[8] In other words, what do scholars who do not focus on spirituality and prayer have to say about sonic modalities of cultural resistance? Chicana feminist Deborah Vargas explores this question by explaining that Chican@/x music creates sonic imaginaries about the social world that are often materially inaccessible due to race, class, gender, and sexuality.[9] So while Vargas does not refer to spirituality, she maintains that music is a gateway through which minoritized communities can imagine what is otherwise deemed socially impossible. "Amor Eterno," examined through Vargas's articulation of Chican@/x sonic imaginaries, exemplifies how culturally distinct music carries messages that reflect the material realities of Chican@/x and Latin@/x experiences in the social world, when we imagine this music as a refusal of state-sanctioned violence.

When a racialized community broadly identified as Latin@/x sings "Amor Eterno" to heal (as described by Chicana feminists who write about spirituality) while also imagining alternative social realities (as discussed by Vargas), we can also think through "Amor Eterno" as a Latin@/x anthem. In a blog post about the shooting in El Paso, Eduardo Cepeda described "Amor Eterno" as "the anthem helping El Pasoans cope with [the] recent shooting."[10] An anthem, as explained by Shana L. Redmond, reflects a political world in which liberation projects emerge through the method of participation. She writes, "Anthems demand something of their listeners. In performance they often occasion hands placed over hearts or standing at attention. Yet more than a physical gesture, anthems require subscription to a system of beliefs that stir and organize the receivers of the music. At its best this system inspires listeners to believe that the circumstances or world around them can change for the better—that the vision of freedom represented in the song's lyrics and/or history are worth fighting for in the contemporary moment."[11] Anthems, therefore, are a sociopolitical relationship between a sociocultural production with a political message and listeners who believe social change toward liberation is necessary. By returning to Juan Gabriel's "Amor Eterno" performance as an invitation for the audience to participate and years later seeing Latin@/x communities further participate in the canto of this song at vigil memorials for communities that have experienced state-sanctioned violence, I suggest that "Amor Eterno" can be considered not only a coping mechanism amid tragedy but also an anthem that demands a collective refusal to forget the lives of people lost or the state's role in these losses.

Geographic specificity plays a crucial role in naming "Amor Eterno" a Latin@/x anthem. The examples I use in this essay reflect two different acts of violence that occurred in Texas, yet the reason I am writing this piece and the reason the Latin@/x community canto was highlighted in the news media is because the song resonates beyond Mexico, beyond the U.S.-Mexico borderlands, and beyond the United States. It resonates beyond Mexicanness. This one song captivates social orders in which people racialized as Latin@/x collectively sing with mutual understanding that any one incident of state-sanctioned violence is not isolated from historical legacies of anti-Mexican, anti-Latin@/x, misogynistic, classist, and xenophobic violence.

"Amor Eterno" is a song that carries multiple meanings and messages. While originally written by Juan Gabriel in remembrance of his mother, who had passed away, the song carries a message of "eternal love" that reverberates far beyond this loss. Just as Gabriel describes the song as a prayer of love, "Amor Eterno" can be viewed as a spiritual calling for Latin@/x audiences to participate in and sonically collaborate on prayer through canto. When Latin@/x communities unite at a memorial for victims of state-sanctioned violence and together sing "Amor Eterno," the voice is literally and figuratively amplified. We can hear the harmonious collective voice on the same note singing a song that reflects a spiritual connection between the living and the dead. Through canto (song/sing) as *oración* (prayer), "Amor Eterno" maintains an approach to seeking justice that is rooted in cultural values that defy the life/death dichotomy. When communities extend an "Amor Eterno" canto to victims of state-sanctioned death, premature death, and social death, the song becomes an anthem that keeps victims alive despite the state's willful forgetting of them. An "Amor Eterno" canto is a contestation or a refusal to forget.

This chapter emerged from a place of not wanting people to forget what happened in El Paso in 2019. I wanted to document how Latin@/xs felt as this targeted violence occurred, and I found myself closing my eyes, tearing up, and being spiritually present as I came across "Amor Eterno" cantos. In 2020, I added the section on Vanessa Guillén as I followed her story and saw community members hold Mexican flags and "Ni una mas" posters at memorial vigils. The immense emotional pain that I physically felt in my body as a Chicana from a working-class background is what led me to question the meaning of "Amor Eterno" as more than a song, to see it as a sonic call to memorialize these violences in connection with one another and to think critically and historically. Latin@/xs urge us to rethink how we understand prayer, solidarity, and resistance through canto, and importantly in an amplified collective voice.

NOTES

1. I follow the use of @/x as an affix that embraces a decolonial approach to opposing gender binaries. The use of @ embraces feminine and masculine energies, while the x affix is inclusive of nonbinary and queer gender and sexual identities. In *Coloniality of the US/Mexico Border* (34), Roberto D. Hernández adds that the use of an affix is reserved for the individual and not an entire community or population. For more on Chicana/o/x/@/e affixes, see Contreras, "Chicana, Chicano, Chica@, Chicanx."

2. Mónica Verea explains how Trump's presidential campaigns promoted anti-immigrant and anti-Mexican violence, contextualizing these displays against his calls for increased funding of a militarized U.S.-Mexico border, racist efforts to reform the U.S. immigration system, and sociolegal orders to punish those who move against these ideologies. See Verea, "Anti-Immigrant and Anti-Mexican Attitudes and Policies."

3. "Juan Gabriel—Amor Eterno (En Vivo [Desde el Instituto Nacional de Bellas Artes])," YouTube. Subsequent quotations from Gabriel are transcribed from this video.

4. Eddy F. Alvarez explains in his article "Finding Sequins in the Rubble" that the oral history interviews of two queer Latinas in Los Angeles inform how he theorizes sequins. He shares, "Dulce and Luna's queer oral histories in particular helped me to understand finding sequins in the rubble not just as a trope, but [as] a means to grasp how queer migrants find beauty, hope, and love in and through the reality of violence and trauma—the rubble" (81).

5. For more on feminicide in Latin America and artivist collectives as resistance, see Herrera, "Ni Una Menos!"
6. "Cantan 'Amor Eterno' en Memoria de Vanessa Guillén (Dallas)," YouTube.
7. Lara Medina and Martha R. Gonzales explain that "spirituality includes the profound understanding that we are not alone, 'that we are spiritual beings in physical bodies,' cocreators of this world, connected to one another and to the Source of all. Our Mesoamerican and Caribbean Indigenous beliefs teach us that death transforms us so that we can (from the spirit world) continue to renew the living. We pray in a different way now." Medina and Gonzales, *Voices from the Ancestors*, 16.
8. Facio and Lara, *Fleshing the Spirit*; Medina and Gonzales, *Voices from the Ancestors*.
9. Vargas, *Dissonant Divas in Chicana Music*.
10. Cepeda, "'Amor Eterno' Is the Anthem Helping El Pasoans Cope with the Recent Shooting."
11. Redmond, *Anthem*, 2.

BIBLIOGRAPHY

Alvarez, Eddy F. "Finding Sequins in the Rubble: The Journeys of Two Latina Migrant Lesbians in Los Angeles." *Journal of Lesbian Studies* 24, no. 2 (2020): 77–93.

"Cantan 'Amor Eterno' en Memoria de Vanessa Guillén (Dallas)." YouTube, video posted July 8, 2020, by HOY Dallas, 4:19. https://www.youtube.com/watch?v= -VQCkpRHJqg.

Cepeda, Eduardo. "'Amor Eterno' Is the Anthem Helping El Pasoans Cope with the Recent Shooting." Remezcla, August 6, 2019. https://remezcla.com/music/amor -eterno-el-paso-catharsis/.

Contreras, Sheila Marie. "Chicana, Chicano, Chica@, Chicanx." In *Keywords for Latina/o Studies*, edited by Deborah R. Vargas, Nancy Raquel Mirabal, and Lawrence La Fountain-Stokes, 32–35. New York: New York University Press, 2017.

Facio, Elisa, and Irene Lara, eds. *Fleshing the Spirit: Spirituality and Activism in Chicana, Latina, and Indigenous Women's Lives*. Tucson: University of Arizona Press, 2014.

Hernández, Roberto D. *Coloniality of the US/Mexico Border: Power, Violence, and the Decolonial Imperative*. Tucson: University of Arizona Press, 2018.

Herrera, Heidi. "¡Ni Una Menos! Feminist Artivism and Collective Resistance Against Feminicide in Latin America." Master's thesis, University of California, Davis, 2020.

"Juan Gabriel—Amor Eterno (En Vivo [Desde el Instituto Nacional de Bellas Artes])." YouTube, video posted June 4, 2010, by Juan Gabriel, 6:57. https://www.youtube .com/watch?v=RgKqxLAhRKE.

Medina, Lara, and Martha R. Gonzales, eds. *Voices from the Ancestors: Xicanx and Latinx Spiritual Expressions and Healing Practices.* Tucson: University of Arizona Press, 2019.

Redmond, Shana L. *Anthem: Social Movements and the Sound of Solidarity in the African Diaspora.* New York: New York University Press, 2014.

Telemundo39. "Realizan vigilia en Dallas en honor a soldado Vanessa Guillén." July 7, 2020. https://www.telemundodallas.com/noticias/local/realizan-vigilia-en-dallas-en-honor-a-soldado-vanessa-guillen/2093603/.

Vargas, Deborah R. *Dissonant Divas in Chicana Music: The Limits of La Onda.* Minneapolis: University of Minnesota Press, 2012.

Verea, Mónica. "Anti-Immigrant and Anti-Mexican Attitudes and Policies During the First 18 Months of the Trump Administration." *Norteamérica* 13, no. 2 (2018): 197–226.

PART III

THE MEDIA AND POPULAR CULTURE

11

AMERICANA WHITE PLIGHT

Bolsotrumpism and the Linear Desire for Westernness

RENATA CARVALHO BARRETO

THIS CHAPTER DISCUSSES THE CULTURAL context and mediascape that helped legitimize the elections of Donald Trump in the United States in 2016 and Jair Bolsonaro in Brazil in 2018. Both of their campaigns and presidencies were supported by nationalist discourses that are entangled with the exclusive celebration of heteronormative families, a meritocracy of white power, and Christian religion. Although important studies have been published comparing the rise to power of these two alt-right politicians, this research aims to contribute further to discussions of the rapid rise of right-wing sentiments (anti-queer, anti-Black, pro-Christian) among the Brazilian and American populations during the 2010s and the beginning of the 2020s.[1]

The liberal ideals classically attached to the American way of life have a lingering historical presence over Latin America. As the basis of a contemporary discourse of freedom and prosperity, liberal and neoliberal ideals still serve imperialist interventions, not only those perpetrated by U.S. corporative power and the U.S. military-industrial complex, but also those enacted through corporate media distributors. I investigate how U.S. imperialism—and specifically cultural colonialism, in the case of the relationship between Trumpism and its Brazilian counterpart, Bolsonarism—is spread through the media.

In the introduction to *Ethnographies of U.S. Empire*, John F. Collins and Carole McGranahan remind us that empire is not an object of study in itself, but rather an "assemblage of shifting conjugations" that need to be taken into consideration when we produce cultural analyses. The present study acknowledges the pervasive presence of empire in every sphere of social and domestic life. Because empire is in the details, this research examines it against and with the grain, acknowledging the pervasiveness of empire's violence, which often works in positive strings of affect across human interaction.[2] In other words, when popular culture is spread through media, imperialism transforms into something desirable. Consumable, the imperial way of life turns into a goal to be attained and consumed. Whiteness and Christian religion, entangled with cisgender family life, become the standard to be copied by everyone. But in order to thrive, the imperial ideals of family, Christian religion, patriotism, and whiteness need enemies, respectively: queerness, Indigenous and African spirituality, multilateral politics, and Blackness, potential vehicles to the institution of an imaginary form of classical communism.[3] Thus, the battle of values and moral references is often cast as a series of Manichaean oppositions by the establishment: hetero and homo, Christian and pagan, freedom and communism, white and Black. Represented, advertised, chanted to exhaustion, and brought to all corners of the world through cultural colonialism, the liberal discourse of family, religion, nation, and whiteness appears to be the real Leviathan: an insurmountable beast to be beaten in the quest(ion) for Black trans feminist futurities.[4]

COMMUNISM IS BLACK, QUEER, AND FEMINIST

Geopolitically, economically, and socioculturally, the 2016 right-wing turn in the United States and the election of Donald Trump had a domino effect over the rest of the world, particularly in regions historically exploited by colonialism. Yet, even before being perceived in the United States in 2016, the conservative wave in politics was first felt throughout Latin America. From Nicaragua to Brazil, sinister networks of capital-based obscure political organizations started to surge through heavy propaganda on web platforms.[5] Their efforts were aimed at reaching institutional power through elected representation and discursive violence.

The massive circulation of gender and racial discourses that secured the rise to power for Trump and Bolsonaro justified violent verbosity against both countries' "leftists." Feeling repressed by the oppressed, communities aligned with right-wing oratory began to react against progressive policies of equity and inclusion.

Latin America is a strategic region in the western hemisphere, and the U.S. government has several agencies that "take care" of Latin American countries, including branches of the CIA as well as the Bureau of Western Hemisphere Affairs, an office of the U.S. Department of State.[6] The South American continent experiences the perennial threat of imperial intervention, whether political, economic, or military. Throughout the twentieth century and well into the twenty-first, U.S. interventionism in Latin America grew in the form of sanctions, neoliberal greed, and the preferred method of imperial intelligence: the breeding of political upheaval and institutional coups. Restricting a number to just 2010–21, I counted at least twenty-one North American interventions on the continent.[7]

In Brazil, the most significant of these historical interventions is the 1964 U.S.-backed coup, which instituted a military dictatorship and deposed of João Goulart, who was aligned with the socially inclusive policies of *trabalhismo* (the Brazilian labor movement). There has been a profound re-memorialization of the 1964 coup in the public rhetoric of Bolsonaro's allies, glorifying the American way of life. This military coup is not a singular event but was accompanied by other interventions in Latin America, like the deposition of Salvador Allende in Chile.[8] The historical processes shaping Brazil's political trajectory before the coup are subject to divergent interpretations, oriented by specific theoretical paradigms and by the historical time of their production. According to Lucilia de Almeida Neves Delgado, there are five dominant currents of thought on the 1964 coup:

1. structuralist and functionalist framing: prevalent in the 1970s, this view privileges an atavistic vision of reality, emphasizing "underdevelopment" discourses

2. emphasis on the preventive character of the coup: this view considers the discontent of conservative sectors of Brazilian politics with the rising autonomy of civil society at the time

3. conspiracy perspective: this view takes the political rupture of 1964 to be due to a concatenated action carried out by international capital, expres-

sive sectors of national business, conservative sectors of the Catholic Church, and anticommunist sectors of the military

4. conjunctural perspective: this view centers historical interpretation of short duration, almost contextual, emphasizing the lack of democratic commitment among both left and right wings

5. new cycle: a new generation of historians having access to unedited documentation, privileging the relationship of history and memory[9]

The collective trauma caused by the military intervention is foundational to any ethnosocial study of contemporary Brazilian society. The sustained attack on personal freedom, along with the persecution, torture, and murder of "communists" across more than twenty years (1964–85), shaped the rise of the Bolsonarism phenomenon.

A revitalization of McCarthyism in tune with U.S. conservatives' view of the Left has been in operation in Brazil, dehumanizing racialized nonwhite people (African Brazilians, Native Brazilians, and all mixed Brown Brazilians, most of the population) and LGBTQIA+ communities. These populations are seen as potential communists/criminals/disruptive outcasts by conservatives, and therefore Brazil figures as the deadliest country in the world to be feminist, queer, or Black.[10] After 2016 it began an open celebration of "communist" persecutors, killers, and torturers, seen in the public shaming of former president Dilma Rousseff.[11] In Bolsonaro's government, the occupation of high official positions by military personnel came together with violent misogynistic and racist speech. In Trump's government, media channels reproduced ideas about conspiracy theories and commended Blue Lives Matter. Additionally, instead of persecuting "communists" per se, neo-McCarthyism in the United States is focused on dehumanizing and caging immigrants of color, particularly those on the Mexican border and, subsequently, all Latin American immigrants. Therefore, in both spaces it is possible to observe a link between anti-leftist discourses and anti-Black, antiqueer, and antifeminist ones.

BULLIES AND "MILICOS"

In the present day, historical elites have control over the media and information, besides sharing land and resources and determining the social division of labor.[12] The plutocratic pact is the glue holding imperial colonialism together. Despite not being part of the historical colonial elite, Donald Trump underwent an upward trajectory that reflects his father's success in real estate since the 1940s. Trump had access to an excellent college education and was heir to his family's wealth. Although he came from a difficult background, grandson of a German immigrant, Trump started his life from a comfortable place. Due to acquired riches, Trump became a celebrity in the 1970s and was slowly permitted to enter the circle of plutocrats, most of them with deeper colonial bourgeois roots.[13]

In contrast, Jair Bolsonaro came from a tiny town in the state of São Paulo. His father was a dentist, and Bolsonaro's early life was difficult. As a child he worked multiple jobs to help the family. Later he joined the military, where his personality was not much appreciated by his superiors. Accused of terrorism (for planning bomb attacks against other military headquarters), indiscipline, and insubordination, he was removed from his position. Moving to Rio, he finally started his political career, an obscure politician aligned with the years of dictatorship and repression.[14]

Both Bolsonaro's and Trump's families are publicly perceived as having suspicious activities—and for good reason. If one looks further into their life story and rise to power, the suspicion is confirmed. Through acts of bullying and association with violent conservative groups, Trump and Bolsonaro made their way to the top. Trump's family-built wealth is based in the real estate business and financial crimes of fraud and tax evasion. But Donald Trump himself has been accused of other transgressions, including sexual crimes.[15] In Brazil, the Bolsonaro family is a top player in the running of a parallel militia government in the city of Rio de Janeiro. Jair Bolsonaro and three of his sons have a long political career as municipal representatives, linked to the military and to illegal and violent paramilitary activities. Following the logic of client webs, retribution, and obligations, the militia organization instituted a reign of terror in the city of Rio. The militia circulates in the liminal space between legal and illegal activities, for example by extorting money from local businesses to allow them to continue functioning.[16] The militia, encompassing police officers, military personnel, and local civilians, is the major force behind the drug trade in the city, currently responsible for almost 60 percent of the illegal drug market in Rio.[17]

While Trump could be a member of the world's plutocracy (even though he is perceived as being outside the traditional elite due to the humble beginnings of his immigrant ancestors), Bolsonaro isn't. Both are seen as puppets for more powerful plutocrats, but a character like Jair Bolsonaro will never be granted real access to decision-making. For a start, despite being recognized as a white person in the Brazilian context, Bolsonaro is not granted a place in the hall of whiteness in the West. Additionally, the crass nature of the Bolsonaro family's activities prevents him from reaching elite status. Nevertheless, Jair Bolsonaro was permitted a peek at the highest level of the plutocrat pact, sharing entitlements and tables with the world's elite.

EVANGELICAL WAVE

Bolsonaro and Trump both received the support of Protestant/neo-Pentecostal denominations dedicated to eloquent religious proselytism and traditional values.[18] In the case of Brazil, the largest neo-Pentecostal denomination, Igreja Universal do Reino de Deus (Universal Church of the Kingdom of God, IURD), acquired a TV channel, Rede Record, in the late 1980s.[19] Rede Record and IURD drummed up support for the rise of Bolsonarism among their enormous audience and devotees.

The recent evangelical empire of neo-Pentecostal denominations in Brazil, like IURD, shares political space with the older and traditional (although smaller) Presbyterian and neo-Calvinist groups. Both latter groups are interested in (or open to) winning the culture war against African Brazilian religions, considered leftists, establishing Christendom as dominant in policymaking. Traditional Presbyterians were the first to benefit from Bolsonaro's rise to the presidency, occupying important offices in justice, education, and culture. Despite pursuing institutional power since the time of the military dictatorship, these Protestant groups had never reached this kind of executive power before.

Nevertheless, the openness of Bolsonaro's genocidal rhetoric made traditional Presbyterians flinch. In the face of his abhorrent declarations, the COVID-19 pandemic, and Brazil's visible decline in quality of life, traditional Protestantism retreated. With the hope of proving moral superiority vis-à-vis neo-Pentecostals, Presbyterians left the Bolsonaro government. But their morals were already stained, and their public façade had already mingled with neo-Pentecostalism.

In the United States, on the other hand, various historical Protestant denominations account for the majority of the country's religious, political, and social formations. In the contemporary era, Trump is not the first Republican candidate to have received support from evangelical sectors—support that, some studies have found, is a matter of business, not Christian morality.[20]

CYNICAL MEDIA PRACTICES

The soft coup engendered by international intelligence in Brazil in 2016–18, culminating in the election of Jair Bolsonaro, is consonant with the mode of action of imperialism in other parts of Latin America.[21] Corporate media serves as the messenger of desirable whiteness, family, country, and morality, often while persecuting "communists" that reach for social inclusion.[22] Since the 2009 coup in Honduras, emergent media technologies, like cell phones and mobile apps, have been widely used to stir public opinion in the region. Corporate social media plays an important role in this scenario. In Brazil, WhatsApp groups served as the main vehicle for the spread of false information attacking the morals of the Partido dos Trabalhadores (Workers' Party, PT), leading to the Brazilian coup.

Similarly, by 2016 the U.S. Republican Party took an aggressive turn in its propaganda strategy. Social media sites like YouTube started to receive a massive amount of material attacking the moral fabric of the Democratic Party, heavily based in conspiracy theories.[23] Like in Brazil, the attacks were rooted in traditional values, those held dear by the conservative audience: elevation of the institution of family, protection of children from nonnormative sexual behavior, celebration of soft femininity and housekeeping abilities for women, violent misogyny as the epitome of masculinity, and exaltation of the positional superiority of whiteness and Westernness in relation to dark-skinned Others. Trump's and Bolsonaro's political campaigns happened through the viral proliferation of hate speech on social media.

Nonetheless, television still holds an important place in both countries' households, and its weight cannot be dismissed. The target audience of both Trump's and Bolsonaro's propaganda excluded so-called (by consumer culture) Millennials, in favor of older populations accustomed to receiving their news over broadcast or cable. Fox News in the United States and Rede Globo in Brazil were the main media outlets supporting, respectively, the reactionary uprising that led the Republicans to power in the United States, and the soft coup in Brazil, which was backed by an important alliance with organized crime as represented by the sinister Bolsonaro family.[24] Rede Globo is a Brazilian media conglomerate that dates to the 1930s. Across newspapers, radio, free-to-air and cable television, cinema, and now the internet, Rede Globo has been a major actor in the political scene since its beginning. A well-known example of its political power relates to the 1989 election in Brazil, the first democratic presidential elections since the 1964 coup.

Representing the PT in the 1989 elections was the leftist union leader Luíz Inácio "Lula" da Silva. Lula was a popular candidate among the people but was disliked by corporate media, specifically Rede Globo, which painted him as a "communist" villain. Despite these attacks, Lula reached the second round of the election, which was a runoff between the two top candidates from the first round. The final presidential debate was broadcast by Rede Globo. Seen as an important event and watched by a significant percentage of the population, it was manipulated to benefit the right-wing candidate, Fernando Collor, son of an aristocratic sugar plantation family in the country's Northeast.[25] Globo was thus allied with Brazil's historical elite, represented by Collor, against Lula, a worker and union leader from a low-income family in the Northeast. So much for Brazil's new "democratic" era.

Nevertheless, the plutocrat pact to deter "communist" policies—like the Left's use of *pré-sal* (pre-salt) profits for public education—worked efficiently.[26] As a result, not only was Jair Bolsonaro elected in 2018, but also a fabricated inquisitorial process that tried to incriminate Lula for crimes of corruption destroyed the Brazilian economy and industry along the way.[27] The *pré-sal* was sold cheaply to international capital. Brazil's low-income population was thrown back to the twentieth century's conditions of famine and lack of basic sanitation.

Radio and editorial conglomerates also contributed to forming the plutocrat pact against "communism" in Brazil.[28] Additionally, throughout the last decade, smaller, free-to-air television channels reproduced anti-leftist propaganda based on disinformation. One such channel based in São Paulo aired a franchised show called *CQC* from 2007 to 2014. The show, a mix of journalism and bad-taste comedy, made Bolsonaro a main feature, giving ample space to his hate speech against women of color, queer people of color, and "leftists" in general.[29] First popular among teenagers for its basic content and high volume of poor jokes, the show gained ground within the extremely conservative bourgeoisie of São Paulo. While still an inexpressive congressman, Bolsonaro gained a regular broadcasting platform from where his name became familiar throughout the mediascape, laying the groundwork for him to become the candidate endorsed by the plutocrat pact in 2018.

From 2015 onward, concomitant to the spread of hate speech in Brazilian broadcasting, Fox News and many right-wing YouTube channels in the United States started to gain visibility in the campaign to elect Donald Trump. Maybe the most notorious of these ventures was the radio and internet program *The Alex Jones Show*. The histrionic host and showman attracted a legion of followers to his daily two-hour live show packed with hate speech and conspiracy theories. Jones's affective performativity and strong stage presence were enough to hold the audience and disseminate his controversial ideas.[30]

The Alex Jones Show and its partner website Infowars became a topic of discussion all over the world. The conspiracy theories advanced by the production were discussed as having factual foundations by a myriad of smaller YouTube channels. In a web of disinformation, these smaller channels appeared to legitimize Jones's discourse. Social networks like 4chan, known for its cultivation of hate speech, aided in the dissemination of stories such as Pizzagate (the primary precursor to the conspiracy theory QAnon), a fantastical account of a pizza place in Washington, D.C., that supposedly held satanic and pedophiliac parties involving Democrats like Hillary Clinton, Trump's opponent in the 2016 election.[31] The show played a pivotal role in Trump's campaign, breeding mistrust and fostering anger at the supposed immorality of the Democrats. The format of the American show was rapidly assimilated in Brazil by representatives of the right wing. Hundreds of YouTube channels appeared in 2016, at the peak of Jones's popularity. The Brazilian counterparts relied, in large measure, on commentary coming from right-wing media conglomerates, but with a more violent disposition. Calls to expose, torture, and kill "communists," queer individuals, and racialized people were normalized, together with a blind devotion to the Bolsonaro family and its politics of exclusion. Absurd conspiracy theories circulated heavily through WhatsApp and Telegram during Bolsonaro's campaign, mirroring the Pizzagate and QAnon episodes: fact-checking organizations found more than seven hundred false or misleading posts being shared on the apps, most of which featured fake statements by candidates, or rumors about legislation, protests, and opinion polls. One of the most absurd examples of the memetic construction and sensationalism of these messages was a viral story that Fernando Haddad, the leftist candidate in 2018, would have handed out "baby bottles with penis-shaped tops at schools to combat homophobia." This story was heavily circulated through images and texts on the apps.[32]

The entanglements of globalized media and conservativism in world politics approximated Brazil and the United States politically, but also subjectively. In 2020, Alex Jones, who had already been removed from social platforms, interviewed Jair Bolsonaro's son Eduardo at the Conservative Political Action Conference (CPAC).[33] Jones opened the interview by declaring how the Bolsonaro family is aligned with the ideals represented by Donald Trump, promoting the triad of nation, God, and family.[34] In response, the visibly nervous Eduardo attempted to reproduce the antiglobalist, anti-leftist speech used in *The Alex Jones Show*. The main theme of the conversation was another fake event: the supposed stabbing suffered by his father while still campaigning in 2018.[35] It is widely assumed in the country that such a stabbing did not actually occur but was instead a fabricated scene, produced with the intent of promoting him as a martyr. The episode was overcapitalized on, and media conglomerates supported the narrative of the murder attempt, blaming leftists. Two months later, Bolsonaro was elected president.

THE LINEAR DESIRE FOR WESTERNNESS

An important question to grapple with concerning both Trump and Bolsonaro is why they have such a big following. Half of the two countries' populations, totaling around 270 million people, openly supported their hate speech. The conditions of possibility for the thriving of conservative discourse on a large scale depend on locality, historical background, and culture. Therefore, the success of the Far Right in the two countries has differentiated causalities. Nonetheless, due to the Brazilian desire for Westernness, the right and left wings in the country keep mirroring the American way of life through the filter of corporate media.

The United States is part of the Western world. The foundation of the American nation produced the foundation of what historians call contemporaneity. Conversely, Latin America is far from this Western world, even having a central role in modern history. The continent seems to imitate the West, as seen repeatedly in the example of Brazil and the United States, but Latin America is not a perfect mirror of the West. On the contrary, it is just a Western-like location, one that strives to achieve the standards prevalent in the imagination of the West, but whose presence does not coincide with the Western position. Latin America's history also runs in a linear form, but it sits in a parallel, subaltern position to the West, according to Western history.

Geographic spaces like Latin America and Africa's ontological contours, assembled by the Western modern imagination, also appear in a subaltern position: in parallel to the linearity of the East-West but physically "below" them. This fact is well reflected in Cartesian cartography. Therefore, as space, time, and being, the entities of Africa and Latin America are simply beyond the horizon, made invisible because they are outside the field of vision for someone included in the West's linearity. The hegemonic verticality within which corporate racial capitalism keeps exploiting these locations is a good measure of the permissibility of violence against those beyond the horizon. Latin American subjects filled with a desire for Westernness are then trapped in perennial inferiority when facing their Western counterparts: invisible, not part of the same linearity, non-concomitant, and not coincident, they are in an inferior parallel reality. In this manner, the Latin American desire to be incorporated into the civilized West becomes an impossible quest. In an irreflective movement, the desireful Latin American tries to imitate the West.[36] Perceived as a parallel, inferior, nonaligned reality to the West, Latin America has struggled to be inserted into the category of civilized location since the first invasion.[37] Latin American elites, mostly white and of European descent, have strived to westernize their way of life since early modernity. From European imported manufactured products to the systematic reproduction of epistemologies and ways of representing the world, the self, and the Other, the continent's elite, albeit identifying as white, have struggled to fit to the Western way of life in a collinear way.

Considering the long duration of the coloniality of power, in the present day, Latin America is a center of interest for racial capitalism.[38] Latin American countries historically served as laboratories of economic, social, political, and behavioral experiments for external political agencies as well as corporate media interests. Focusing on the case of Brazil, I inquire into the permeability of notions of identity, race, class, gender, and political affiliation in the population's support for Jair Bolsonaro, as they seem to be guided by commonsense perceptions of time, culture, and subjectivity drawn from the crystallization of bourgeois ways of knowing as the norm. These notions are reinforced and potentialized by the media every day on a large scale.[39] At the same time, the corporate media empire that dominates broadcasting and digital content utilizes the mechanics of desire to reinforce and reiterate Western perspectives on gender, race, and ethnicity.[40] Brazilian media conglomerates are successful in promoting Westernness in a country where most of the population has African and/or Indigenous roots. The efficacy of media, in all its forms, in maintaining within the population the desire to be part of the "civilized" West, relies on historical constructions of racial identity in the country. These constructions made the West the norm, validating whiteness as the ideal and patriarchal power as a given.

Contributing to the mindset produced by patronage and other historical forms of financing reproducible works of communication and expression, new media and information sciences replicate the long entwining of media practices with local plutocracies having defined symbolic and representational agendas. From the Catholic Church and aristocrats commissioning paintings in the sixteenth century to Big Pharma and corporate businesses financing new media entrepreneurs in the twenty-first, communication practices have long been dominated by elitist discourses, constrained by the high cost of materials and distribution, and reliant on privatized patronage to sustain themselves. In terms of new technologies, their high price also makes their control (and the manufacture of information) accessible only to the elite, learned and taught only at elite schools. This techno-plutocracy reinforces white superiority discourses in many formats. From filmmaking to scripted coding, a desire for Westernness is palpable in the currently available media products.

An example of this process can be seen in the invasion of the U.S. Capitol by Trump supporters and QAnon followers in 2021. It produced an echo of uncertainty over the world, accompanied by ample public commentary on social media. One of the most circulated images of the episode was the Capitol Viking or QAnon Shaman—the American Jacob Chansley, who became an icon of "white superiority" for the American white nationalist movement.

The day after the Capitol invasion, a Brazilian journalist of the leading conservative/neoliberal magazine *Veja* tweeted a commentary that went viral about Chansley's virility and appearance. She asked her Twitter followers whether they would "do" Chansley despite his white supremacy tendencies. The journalist positioned herself as a liberal feminist and justified her desire for Chansley based on the premise that sexual desire cannot be bound by political life. She also responded to the critiques of Black and Indigenous feminists, as well as other sectors of the Left: "That said, (1) The 'desire police' is one of the most bizarre professions born on Twitter in 2021; (2) Some people are acting like puritan gossip girls, like there is no cute 'chernoboy' [a reference to the toxicity of Chansley's political views] or feminine versions of it; (3) Stop misogyny."[41]

Debates about desire for the white supremacism dominated Brazilian Twitter for the next few days. Responding to these debates, Jade Lobo wrote:

> We, black and indigenous women, pointed out the great mockery of our pain, through the symbolic act of advancing white supremacy, and we were quickly thrown into racist stereotypes of quarrelsome and ignorant. The same white people who just a few days ago supported "Black Lives Matter" labeled us "castrators of the desire of others" in defense of their right to desire a supremacist. Now, what kind of person is horny for one racist if not another? Desire is the result of social relations, which in turn are unequal in terms of power-race. In this sense, white women presented their repressed lust in terms of racial purity. . . . During criticism of the desire of white feminists, black and indigenous women had their Twitter profiles denounced and were threatened with prosecution.[42]

Together with commentaries exposing the various layers of intersectionality necessary to analyze questions of identity in Brazil (complicating the prevalent notions of white feminism), Chansley's episode was also appropriated by reactionary white masculinity in the country, with a Brazilian man notably imitating Chansley's performance. In figure 11.1, he appears next to the congressperson Daniel Lucio da Silveira, who promoted hate speech against Marielle Franco, a queer Black woman and municipal representative who was assassinated by Bolsonaro's militia.[43]

The Brazilian "Indigenous Viking" comes in the form of an incongruent caricature, with minor adaptations like the substitution of Brazil's national colors for the U.S. ones and the addition of Native Brazilian Indigenous artifacts. Such appropriation of Indigenous cultures to

Figure 11.1. The Brazilian "Indigenous Viking" with the congressperson Daniel Lucio da Silveira in January 2022. Four years earlier, in 2018, Silveira broke a memorial plaque for the murdered Marielle Franco. Here, he holds a replacement plaque with his own name substituted on it. Photograph by Matheus de Moura/UOL.

legitimize settler colonialism and its values is widespread in the modern Americas. In *Mohawk Interruptus*, for example, Audra Simpson analyzes the Western discourse about the "Iroquois" produced by anthropology, in the figure of Lewis Henry Morgan and his relationship with the Native American Ely S. Parker.[44] Simpson discusses the ways in which desire operates to produce Western knowledge, particularly anthropological knowledge. Members of a "protoscientific society" founded by Morgan drew from "Iroquois" tradition and used signs and symbols to represent themselves, white people, as the new "Iroquois," based on the premise that the Kahnawà:ke people would or should soon be gone.

The banalization and fetishization of Indigenous ways of knowing are also the point of critique in Joanne Barker's introduction to *Critically Sovereign*.[45] Cis-heteronormative appropriations and representations of a homogenized, flat, and general "Indigenous culture" serve as justification for the continuous symbolic and actual violence inflicted against multiple and diverse communities.

In "Decolonization Is Not a Metaphor," Eve Tuck and K. Wayne Yang attest that in settler colonialism, decolonization has mixed results because empire, settlement, and internal colony have no spatial separation.[46] Sentiments of settler nativism, accompanied by claims of the possession of Indigenous blood, are a common theme throughout the settling of Creole populations in Spanish America as well as in Portuguese Brazil. Although discriminated against outside the colonies for not being white enough, Creoles, *fidalgos* (nobles), and *galegos* (Portuguese immigrants) would often be proud of some ancient native blood at their Latin American home.[47]

Moreover, Tuck and Yang write about "settler adoption fantasies," well exemplified by the Brazilian "Indigenous Viking."[48] The mixing of elements of Nordicity, like Viking horns, and North American Indigenous–inspired artifacts, like the stylized headpiece (not characteristic of any Brazilian Indigenous culture), is apparently aleatory. These foreign historical garments are blended with Brazilian national colors and motifs, like feathers of native birds and an animal print of the Brazilian leopard (*onça-pintada*). The "Indigenous Viking" character evokes Tuck and Yang's concept but takes it a step further. According to the authors, when descendants of white colonists claim Indigenous blood through settler adoption fantasies, it constitutes a settler move to innocence. By stating that they desire to be Indigenous, settler colonialists escape the centrality of colonial violence.

The Brazilian "Viking" exposes several operating layers of the coloniality of power. The character violently celebrates the loathing of the Brazilian bourgeoisie for Black and Brown women, reaffirms his whiteness in the commemoration of it (while simultaneously exposing its subalternity to Western whiteness), consecrates the congressman's misogyny, authorizes paramilitary action, legitimizes QAnon and Donald Trump, and glorifies murder of and violence against queer women of color, all while demonstrating his support for Bolsonaro's government and a supposed proprietorship of Indigenous blood.

Against such symbology, the name and image of Marielle Franco, a deputy killed by Bolsonaro's militia, was adopted by the country's Left as an iconic symbol of resistance to fascism, as seen in figure 11.2.

Maria Lugones powerfully asserts that all of us are complicit with the coloniality of power and, therefore, the coloniality of race and gender. Lugones builds this argument based on the assumption that race and

Figure 11.2. Protestors carry Marielle Franco's street plaque, calling for justice. Two flags are visible: one has Franco's face, and the other is a colored Brazilian flag with the inscription "Indians, Blacks . . . ," the country's majority. CC BY 2.0.

gender are complementary and interdependent categories. The author draws from the foundational texts of Aníbal Quijano, a staple in Latin American decolonial studies, to contemplate how the functioning of the capitalist system depends on exploitation of racialized labor and patriarchal systems of dominance. Lugones recognizes that Quijano fails to consider heteronormativity and patriarchalism as essential to comprehending the disempowerment of Latin Americans. Lugones reminds us that, often, the intersectional element of these constructions gets lost among fixed categorical separations. And in the case of the coloniality of power, women that have been racialized by the patriarchal system are the ones who are dismissed and forgotten.[49] Going further, Lugones cites Black and Brown feminists when exposing the patriarchal mechanisms sustaining the gender binary constructions imposed on communities devastated by Eurocentric racial capitalism.

Focusing on the Brazilian case, Denise Ferreira da Silva writes that

> miscegenation, as an eschatological (racial) signifier, already renders the realization of Brazil's racial democracy contingent upon the disappearance of blackness and africanity from Brazilians' bodies and minds. Because the debate is informed by the socio-logic of exclusion, neither position engages Brazil's particular strategy of racial subjection, namely the logic of obliteration. What distinguishes the Brazilian mode of racial subjection is the centrality of miscegenation in the national discourse which has precluded racial difference from becoming a prevailing basis for the constitution of culturally distinct groups, but it has sustained a discourse and practices that constitute racial difference as a social category. That is, in the Brazilian social configuration—its juridical, economic, and symbolic levels—individuals' positions are determined by the degree of blackness in their bodies, and this is expressed by the observable socio-economic disparities that mark black Brazilians['] subaltern social trajectories. Beneath racial equality policies and beyond their limited portrait of the markers of subjection at work in Brazil, the logic of obliteration continues to operate, demarcating for black and brown Brazilians, as has been the case in Brazilian history, a subaltern social position not addressed by the liberal tenets organizing these camps' conceptions of equality.[50]

Thinking about the miscegenation that defines Brazilian nationality, Ferreira da Silva argues that this logic produces the symbolic and physical obliteration of Black and Indigenous people, making whiteness a collective goal to be achieved by the nation. The defining image of the country as mestizo, in patriarchal historiography, serves the purpose of eliminating Black, Indigenous, and Brown people in favor of a desired construction of whiteness in a glorious future where Brazil could finally achieve a place of Westernness.[51]

The lingering effect of cultural colonialism is a collective desire to be part of the current geographic center, the North—that is, a Eurocentrism, or a centering on European values (family, religion, nation, whiteness). "Ec-centric" cultures are dismissed as inferior, their elements suppressed by the local historical elites, all of them made of European invasion roots.

Therefore, we watch similar events play out: the criminalization of Mexican immigrants in the United States and the criminalization of impoverished/exploited "Brown" cultures in Brazil, the mass incarceration of African Americans and African Brazilians in both countries, the institution of anti-abortion laws in Trump's United States and an evangelical Ministry for the Family in Brazil, the American militaristic tradition copied in the Brazilian militarization of basic education, an open call to exterminate non-Christian people of color, and attacks on temples of Indigenous and African Brazilian religions, similar to the erasure of Indigenous and African Americans throughout the last centuries.

The co-opting of Indigenous cultural identities by the Far Right in both countries can only be understood under historical premises. Bolsonarism, running parallel to Trumpism, reflects cultural colonialism spread through imperialist media, producing a collective desire for Westernness. This desire is expressed in the attempt to co-opt local Indigenous identities while violently erasing the owners of these identities. This European historical cultural tradition is systematically sold by racial capitalism as the single goal to be attained by everyone. Family, nation, religion, and whiteness become the norm to be followed, and anyone that deviates from this finality is seen as a threat to society. Therefore, the profound emotional legitimacy attached to the consolidation of the nation-state in Latin America, along with several diverse copies of genocide and discursive violence against Indigenous and African cultures, is subjectively justified by a desire for Westernness.

NOTES

1. For prior studies, see, e.g., Penha-Lopes, *The Presidential Elections of Trump and Bolsonaro*.
2. Collins and McGranahan, "Introduction," 3.
3. See Bey, *Black Trans Feminism*.
4. See Bey. On Leviathan, see Job 40:25–41:3 in the Jerusalem Bible:

   > Leviathan, too! Can you catch him with a fish-hook or run a line round his tongue?
   > Can you put a ring through his nose or pierce his jaw with a hook?
   > Will he plead and plead with you, will he coax you with smooth words?
   > Will he strike a bargain with you to become your slave for life?
   > Will you make a pet of him, like a bird, keep him on a lead to amuse your maids?
   > Is he to be sold by the fishing guild and then retailed by merchants?
   > Riddle his hide with darts? Prod his head with a harpoon?
   > You have only to lay a finger on him never to forget the struggle or risk it again!
   > Any hopes you might have would prove vain, for the mere sight of him would stagger you.
   > When roused, he grows ferocious, no one can face him in a fight.
   > Who can attack him with impunity? No one beneath all heaven.

5. For example, the Movimento Brasil Livre (Free Brazil Movement, MBL) advertises of itself: "The MBL proposes to promote liberalism as the guiding political philosophy of State action in Brazil." MBL, home page.
6. See U.S. Department of State, "Bureau of Western Hemisphere Affairs."
7. These interventions included: Argentina in 2015; Bolivia in 2019 and 2021; Brazil in 2016 and 2018; Cuba in 2021; Ecuador in 2010 and 2015; El Salvador in 2015; Guatemala in 2015; Haiti in 2011 and 2015; Honduras in 2017; Nicaragua in 2018 and 2021; Paraguay in 2012; Peru in 2021; and Venezuela in 2013, 2014, 2017, and 2019. See Smith, "21st Century US Coups and Attempted Coups in Latin America."
8. Delgado, *PTB*.
9. This typology was presented by Delgado in the 2011 seminar "Historiografia, História e Memória" at the Universidade de Brasília. For readings on the listed schools of thought, see, respectively: (1) Ianni, *O colapso do populismo no Brasil*; Cardoso, "Associated-Dependent Development"; (2) Delgado, *PTB*; Gorender, *Combate nas trevas*; (3) Dreiffus, *1964*; Starling, *Os senhores das Gerais*; (4) Figueiredo, *Democracia ou reformas?*; Ferreira, "O governo Goulart e o golpe civil-militar de 1964"; (5) Fico, *Além do golpe*.

10. Mendes and Furtado Passos da Silva, "Homicide of Lesbians, Gays, Bisexuals, Travestis, Transexuals, and Transgender People (LGBT) in Brazil."

11. The case of Dilma Rousseff, Brazil's president (2011–16) after the (first) "Lula Age," being Lula's former minister for Energy Resources, is emblematic of the pervasiveness of U.S. imperialism in Latin America. Rousseff's trajectory is one of defiance of patriarchalism and defense of individual liberties. As a young woman, she was imprisoned and tortured by the military regime instituted after the 1964 coup, the first coup backed by U.S. imperialism in the country. Five decades later, in 2016, another violent coup based in the historical Brazilian patriarchal state, backed by the U.S. government, and enabled by corporate media would deseat Rousseff amid her second term as Brazil's elected president. Attacked daily in all Brazilian licensed media channels, Rousseff endured unprecedented, open attacks on her reputation. Normalized in the media, outrageous misogynistic offenses against her personal honor and integrity were pervasive. There are interesting analyses of Rousseff's impeachment process from a sexist and patriarchal perspective, bringing to light the fixed cultural and historical notions that contributed to her treatment; see, e.g., Palacios, Fleck, and Abbondanza, "Discursos de prejuicio de género en publicaciones."

12. In the section title, *milicos* is a pejorative designation for military men, usually soldiers.

13. See Penha-Lopes, *The Presidential Elections of Trump and Bolsonaro*, chap. 3.

14. See Penha-Lopes, chap. 5.

15. Bartick, "Trump's Criminal History Should Be Front and Center."

16. Martín, "Como a milícia se infiltrou na vida do Rio."

17. Agência O Globo, "Milícias expandem área de atuação e já dominam 57,5% do Rio de Janeiro."

18. See Penha-Lopes, *The Presidential Elections of Trump and Bolsonaro*, chap. 3.

19. IURD reaches Lusophone countries in Africa and some other locations in Latin America as well.

20. Hannah Dick, for example, writes: "There are significant parallels between white evangelical support for Donald Trump, even over more obviously religious candidates during the primaries, and shifting evangelical support for a Southern Baptist presidential candidate in 1976 (Jimmy Carter) to a morally ambiguous, multiple-married celebrity (Ronald Reagan) by 1980." Dick, "Framing Faith During the 2016 Election," 166.

21. It is tacit knowledge in Latin America that the intelligence agencies responsible for raising instability in the region are American, with the acquiescence of the corporate European Union and the support of transnational agencies like the Organization of American States.

22. Among those so targeted was Cristina Fernández de Kirchner in 2015 in Argentina; see Goñi, "Argentina's President May Face Charges over Alleged Terrorist Attack Cover-Up."

23. See, e.g., "What Do Far Left Activists Want?" and "Hillary Must Lose," both posted to YouTube by British far right commentator Carl Benjamin (a.k.a. Sargon of Akkad).

24. That said, in the present day (2022), Bolsonaro's supporters claim that Rede Globo (now known as TV Globo) in fact supports the fictitious "cultural Marxism" and leftist ideals.

25. "A saga do homem que achava que sua vida nao ia terminar," *O Globo de Brasil*.

26. The pre-salt layer is home to significant oil reserves. Off the coast of Brazil between the states of Santa Catarina and Espírito Santo is the approximately 57,500-square-mile Pre-Salt Polygon, "among the most important discoveries of oil and natural gas in recent years." According to the utilities company Pré-sal Petróleo, "reserves are composed of large accumulations of high-quality light oil featuring high commercial value. Pre-salt oilfield production rates are substantial. Daily production rates have increased from 41,000 barrels per day (bpd) in 2010 to 1.41 million bpd in 2018 [and 1.9 million in 2020]. . . . Brazil's pre-salt oilfields are today among the largest producers globally." Pré-sal Petróleo, "Characteristics: The Pre-Salt."

27. See Mészáros, "Caught in an Authoritarian Trap of Its Own Making?" In 2021, Lula's convictions were annulled.

28. The most prominent examples are the magazines *Veja* and *IstoÉ*, the radio station Jovem Pan FM, and the newspapers *Folha de São Paulo* and *Estado de São Paulo*. See Giordano, "Derechas, neoliberalismo y estereotipos de género."

29. See "CQC—Documento Especial com Jair Bolsonaro," YouTube.

30. See Jutel, "American Populism, Glenn Beck and Affective Media Production"; Hyzen and Van den Bulck, "The Most Paranoid Man in America."

31. Bleakley, "Panic, Pizza and Mainstreaming the Alt-Right."

32. Pereira and Bojczuk, "Zap Zap, Who's There?"

33. CPAC was held in the Gaylord National Resort and Convention Center in Fort Washington, Maryland, in February 2020.

34. "Alex Jones entrevista Eduardo Bolsonaro no site Infowars," YouTube.

35. See "Assista ao momento do esfaqueamento de Bolsonaro em 6 de setembro de 2018—3," YouTube.

36. See Bhabha, "Of Mimicry and Man."

37. For *first invasion*, see Estes, *Our History Is the Future*.

38. See Quijano, "Colonialídad del poder, eurocentrismo y América Latina."

39. See hooks, *Black Looks*.

40. See Curtis, *The Century of the Self*.

41. Marina Lang (@marinaLang), "Dito isto . . . ," Twitter, January 7, 2021, 10:44 a.m., https://twitter.com/marinalang/status/1347222488778997760.

42. Lôbo, "Com quantas Sinhás se fez um Brasil?"

43. For the photograph in context, see for Moura, "Esse é branco mesmo."

44. Simpson, *Mohawk Interruptus*, chap. 3.

45. Barker, introduction to *Critically Sovereign*.

46. Tuck and Yang, "Decolonization Is Not a Metaphor."
47. See Anderson, *Imagined Communities*, chap. 4. In Brazil, notably, the term *Creole* was not used; these individuals had specific designations depending on their importance in the imperial scheme.
48. Tuck and Yang, "Decolonization Is Not a Metaphor."
49. Lugones, "The Coloniality of Gender."
50. Ferreira da Silva, "The End of Brazil," 18.
51. Ferreira da Silva, "À brasileira." For an example of patriarchal historiography, see Freyre, *Casa-grande & senzala*.

BIBLIOGRAPHY

Adorno, Theodor W. *The Authoritarian Personality*. New York: Harper and Row, 1950.

Agência O Globo. "Milícias expandem área de atuação e já dominam 57,5% do Rio de Janeiro." *Último Segundo*, October 19, 2020. https://ultimosegundo.ig.com.br/brasil/2020-10-19/milicias-expandem-area-de-atuacao-e-ja-dominam-575-do-rio-de-janeiro.html.

"Alex Jones entrevista Eduardo Bolsonaro no site Infowars." YouTube, video posted March 6, 2020, by Eduardo Bolsonaro, 7:10. https://www.youtube.com/watch?v=LMEBW_4Zisk.

Anderson, Benedict. *Imagined Communities: Reflections on the Origin and Spread of Nationalism*. London: Verso, 2006.

"Assista ao momento do esfaqueamento de Bolsonaro em 6 de setembro de 2018—3." YouTube, video posted September 9, 2018, by Poder360, 0:33. https://www.youtube.com/watch?v=x88RnK1GiUo.

Barker, Joanne. Introduction to *Critically Sovereign: Indigenous Gender, Sexuality, and Feminist Studies*, edited by Joanne Barker, 1–44. Durham, N.C.: Duke University Press, 2017.

Bartick, Melissa. "Trump's Criminal History Should Be Front and Center." *HuffPost*, September 14, 2016. https://www.huffpost.com/entry/trumps-criminal-history-s_b_11983400.

Bey, Marquis. *Black Trans Feminism*. Durham, N.C.: Duke University Press, 2022.

Bhabha, Homi. "Of Mimicry and Man: The Ambivalence of Colonial Discourse." In *Tensions of Empire*, edited by Frederick Cooper and Ann Laura Stoler, 152–60. Berkeley: University of California Press, 2019.

Bleakley, Paul. "Panic, Pizza and Mainstreaming the Alt-Right: A Social Media Analysis of Pizzagate and the Rise of the QAnon Conspiracy." *Current Sociology* 71, no. 3 (2023): 509–23.

Cardoso, Fernando Henrique. "Associated-Dependent Development: Theoretical and Practical Implications." In *Authoritarian Brazil*, edited by Alfred Stepan, 142–76. New Haven, Conn.: Yale University Press, 1973.

Collins, John F., and Carole McGranahan. "Introduction: Ethnography and U.S. Empire." In *Ethnographies of U.S. Empire*, edited by Carole McGranahan and John F. Collins, 1–24. Durham, N.C.: Duke University Press, 2018.

"CQC—Documento Especial com Jair Bolsonaro." YouTube, video posted April 5, 2011, by ProgramaCQC, 13:44. https://www.youtube.com/watch?v=DBEGrNVy4i4.

Curtis, Adam, dir. *The Century of the Self.* 4 episodes. London: BBC, 2002.

Delgado, Lucília de Almeida Neves. *PTB: do getulismo ao reformismo (1945–1964).* São Paulo: Marco Zero, 1989.

Dick, Hannah. "Framing Faith During the 2016 Election: Journalistic Coverage of the Trump Campaign and the Myth of Evangelical Schism." In *Evangelicals and Presidential Politics: From Jimmy Carter to Donald Trump*, edited by Andrew S. Moore, 166–84. Baton Rouge: Louisiana State University Press, 2021.

Dreifuss, René Armand. *1964: a conquista do estado*. Petrópolis, Brazil: Vozes, 1981.

Estes, Nick. *Our History Is the Future: Standing Rock versus the Dakota Access Pipeline, and the Long Tradition of Indigenous Resistance*. London: Verso, 2019.

Ferreira, Jorge. "O governo Goulart e o golpe civil-militar de 1964." In *O Brasil republican: O tempo da experiência democrática, da democratização de 1945 golpe civil-militar de 1964*, edited by Jorge Ferreria and Lucília de Almeida Delgado, 343–404. Rio de Janeiro: Civilização Brasileira, 2003.

Ferreira da Silva, Denise. "À brasileira: racialidade e a escrita de um desejo destrutivo." *Estudos Feministas* 14, no. 1 (2006): 61–83.

Ferreira da Silva, Denise. "The End of Brazil: An Analysis of the Debate on Racial Equity on the Edges of Global Market Capitalism." *National Black Law Journal* 21, no. 3 (2009): 1–18.

Fico, Carlos. *Além do golpe: versões e controvérsias sobre 1964 e a ditadura militar*. Rio de Janeiro: Record, 2004.

Figueiredo, Argelina Cheibub. *Democracia ou reformas? Alternativas democráticas à crise política de 1961–1964*. Rio de Janeiro: Paz e Terra, 1993.

Freyre, Gilberto. *Casa-grande & senzala: formação da família brasileira sob o regime da economia patriarcal*. 5th ed. Rio de Janeiro: J. Olympio, 1946.

Giordano, Verónica. "Derechas, neoliberalismo y estereotipos de género: La revista Veja de Brasil, 1989–1999." *Nuevo Mundo Mundos Nuevos*, October 2, 2017. https://doi.org/10.4000/nuevomundo.71292.

Goñi, Uki. "Argentina's President May Face Charges over Alleged Terrorist Attack Cover-Up." *Guardian*, February 13, 2015.

Gorender, Jacob. *Combate nas trevas. A esquerda brasileira: das ilusões perdidas à luta armada*. São Paulo: Ática, 1987.

Gorski, Philip. "Why Evangelicals Voted for Trump: A Critical Cultural Sociology." *American Journal of Cultural Sociology* 5, no. 3 (2017): 338–54.

"Hillary Must Lose." YouTube, video posted October 12, 2016, by Sargon of Akkad, 27:03. https://www.youtube.com/watch?v=dtRj6x1jHuU.

hooks, bell. *Black Looks: Race and Representation*. 2nd ed. New York: Routledge, 2014.

Hyzen, Aaron, and Hilde Van den Bulck. "'The Most Paranoid Man in America': Alex Jones as Celebrity Populist." *Celebrity Studies* 12, no. 1 (2021): 162–66.

Ianni, Otávio. *O colapso do populismo no Brasil*. Rio de Janeiro: Civilização Brasileira, 1971.

Jutel, Olivier. "American Populism, Glenn Beck and Affective Media Production." *International Journal of Cultural Studies* 21, no. 4 (2018): 375–392.

Lôbo, Jade Alcântara. "Com quantas Sinhás se fez um Brasil?" *Mundo Negro* (blog), January 8, 2021. https://mundonegro.inf.br/com-quantas-sinhas-se-fez-um -brasil/.

Lugones, Maria. "The Coloniality of Gender." In *The Palgrave Handbook of Gender and Development*, edited by Wendy Harcourt, 13–33. London: Palgrave Macmillan, 2016.

Martín, María. "Como a milícia se infiltrou na vida do Rio." *El País Brasil*, July 24, 2016. https://brasil.elpais.com/brasil/2016/07/21/politica/1469054817_355385 .html.

MBL (Movimento Brasil Livre). Home page. Accessed June 5, 2022. https://mbl.org .br.

Mendes, Wallace Góes, and Cosme Marcelo Furtado Passos da Silva. "Homicide of Lesbians, Gays, Bisexuals, Travestis, Transexuals, and Transgender People (LGBT) in Brazil: A Spatial Analysis." *Ciência e Saúde Coletiva* 25, no. 5 (2020): 1709–22.

Mészáros, George. "Caught in an Authoritarian Trap of Its Own Making? Brazil's 'Lava Jato' Anti-Corruption Investigation and the Politics of Prosecutorial Overreach." *Journal of Law and Society* 47, no. S1 (2020): S54–73.

Moura, Matheus de. "'Esse é branco mesmo': Ato pró-Silveira tem sósia de 'viking do Capitólio.'" TAB, May 1, 2022. https://tab.uol.com.br/noticias/redacao/2022/ 05/01/ato-por-daniel-silveira-em-niteroi-reune-em-torno-de-3000-e-maioria -branca.htm.

O Globo de Brasil. "A saga do homem que achava que sua vida nao ia terminar." August 8, 2011.

Palacios, Rosiane Alves, Carolina Freddo Fleck, and Márcia Vanessah Pacheco Abbondanza. "Discursos de prejuicio de género en publicaciones de los medios de comunicación y su relación con la construcción de la imagen de la expresidenta del Brasil Dilma Rousseff." *Contratexto*, no. 35 (2021): 199–224.

Penha-Lopes, Vânia. *The Presidential Elections of Trump and Bolsonaro, Whiteness, and the Nation*. Lanham, Md.: Lexington Books, 2022.

Pereira, Gabriel, and Iago Bojczuk. "Zap Zap, Who's There? WhatsApp and the Spread of Fake News During the 2018 Elections in Brazil." *Global Media Technologies and Cultures Lab* (blog), November 9, 2018. http://globalmedia.mit.edu/ 2018/11/09/zap-zap-whos-there-whatsapp-and-the-spread-of-fake-news-during -the-2018-elections-in-brazil/.

Pré-sal Petróleo. "Characteristics: The Pre-Salt." Accessed August 7, 2023. https:// www.presalpetroleo.gov.br/eng/characteristics/.

Quijano, Anibal. "Colonialidad del poder, eurocentrismo y América Latina." In *La Colonialidad del saber: eurocentrismo y ciencias sociales*, edited by Edgardo Lander, 201–46. Buenos Aires: CLACSO-UNESCO, 2000.

Simpson, Audra. *Mohawk Interruptus*. Durham, N.C.: Duke University Press, 2014.

Smith, Stansfield. "21st Century US Coups and Attempted Coups in Latin America." *Popular Resistance* (blog), January 7, 2022. https://popularresistance.org/21st-century-us-coups-and-attempted-coups-in-latin-america/.

Starling, Heloísa Maria Murgel. *Os senhores das Gerais: os novos inconfidentes e o golpe de 1964*. Petrópolis, Brazil: Vozes, 1986.

Tuck, Eve, and K. Wayne Yang. "Decolonization Is Not a Metaphor." *Decolonization: Indigeneity, Education and Society* 1, no. 1 (2012). https://jps.library.utoronto.ca/index.php/des/article/view/18630.

U.S. Department of State. "Bureau of Western Hemisphere Affairs." Accessed March 19, 2022. https://www.state.gov/bureaus-offices/under-secretary-for-political-affairs/bureau-of-western-hemisphere-affairs/.

"What Do Far Left Activists Want?" YouTube, video posted August 25, 2017, by Sargon of Akkad, 27:29. https://www.youtube.com/watch?v=lqN76kaTLxU.

12

TRUMP'S HERMENEUTICS OF THE ASS

Anal Theory, Gaping Holes, and Backdoor Approaches to
the U.S.-Mexico Border

SERGIO A. MACÍAS

For those of us that have crossed the southern border illegally,
I have something to say; the border hurts.
It will hurt forever, deep within the soul.
No matter what you do;
No matter what you say, admit, repress, enact, obey, believe, become,
or overcome;
The border will forever be part of you,
(In a painful way)
You are the border.
The border created you.
I am (only an inch) of the entire story of the southern border.
S.A.M.

ONE OF THE CENTRAL PROMISES of Donald J. Trump's political career was to build the southern wall: "On day one, we will begin working on an impenetrable, physical, tall, powerful, beautiful southern border wall. We will use the best technology, including above and below ground sensors."[1] The *New York Times* and other outlets reported that "the President had often talked about fortifying a border wall with a water-filled trench, stocked with snakes or alligators," and fantasized that it could be "electrified, with spikes on top that could pierce human flesh."[2] Trump denied the allegations on Twitter, saying, "The press has gone Crazy. Fake News!"[3] Regardless of Trump's campaign promise to not just build the wall but make Mexico pay for it, the United States ended up spending $15 billion on 452 miles of new or replaced border wall. Trump failed to deliver a 2,000-mile wall, just as he failed to force Mexico to finance it. The only wall he managed to build was dogmatic—a wall made of words, symbols, and images of prejudice. Yet, many, including several late-night hosts, poked fun at Trump, his policies, the wall, and the innuendo-laden language surrounding them. For instance, the media's frequent reference to the border as a "gaping hole" lent itself easily to anus jokes by comedians Seth Meyers, Stephen Colbert, and Samantha Bee. The words and images describing the border and wall matter profoundly, each contributing to a collective narrative of the southern border. Among these descriptive aspects, I am interested in the metaphoric erotization of the southern border—most notably, the southern border as an anus. This striking image has entered our pop-cultural lexicon and dialogue, as an intersection of politics, excrement, sex, and race.

Comedy aside, further reflection on Trump's security measures, immigration policies, and foreign relations with Latin America reveals a pattern: a scatological-erotic fixation on Latinxs and Latin America. In my 2020 essay "Trump's Poetics of Caca: Shitty 'Bad Hombres' and 'Shithole' Latin American Countries," I introduce the term *poetics of caca* to capture his colonial mindset, unpack the logic of his love-hate relationship with Latinx masculinities, and interrogate the popularity of his political rhetoric.[4] The essay became a therapeutic channel for my own frustration and anger after years of his racist, sexist, and xenophobic remarks. I began to *curarme del empacho*—heal my Trump-pacho. In borderlands and Mexican folk medicine, *empacho* is a physical, spiritual, or psychological blockage, something stuck in the esophagus or the gut that produces indigestion and overall malaise. Over the years, Trump had become my *empacho*. As José Esteban Muñoz beautifully describes in *Disidentifications*, sometimes the only creative healing for queer Latinxs is through the very mechanisms of oppression—a process of reclaiming a dignity historically denied.[5] In my case, this means repurposing Trump's foul speech. In this essay, I take further steps in healing my Trump-pacho by digesting Trump's narrative of the southern border. Specifically, I delve into Trump's desire to close the southern border with a wall, separating "America" from what Trump considers "shithole" countries. I examine Trump's hermeneutics of the ass—a companion to the poetics of caca—which perceives the southern border as an open orifice, an anal sphincter that allows waste to pour into the United States. He aims to seal it with an impenetrable wall, keeping the United States safe from Mexican drug dealers, "murderers," and "rapists." Further, I offer a theoretical framework that feeds from border studies and anal theory, extending beyond Trump's hermeneutics of the ass.

BORDER THEORY AND METAPHORS

Broadly speaking, border studies is concerned with "geographic border spaces, and notably, ideological, sociological, and identity borders, as unique spaces of exchange, expression, and transformation."[6] Gloria Anzaldúa's insightful reflections on the U.S.-Mexico border and Mexican-American border culture(s) are fundamental to the discipline and continue to inspire scholars today. Anzaldúa established a clear-cut distinction between borders and borderlands, wherein borders "define the places that are safe and unsafe. . . . A border is a dividing line, a narrow strip along a steep edge." A borderland, however, "is a vague and undetermined place created by the emotional residue of an unnatural boundary . . . in a constant state of transition."[7] Hastings Donnan and Thomas M. Wilson rationalize borders based on three fundamental components: "The juridical borderline which simultaneously separates and joins states; the agents and institutions of the state, who demarcate and sustain the border, and who are found most often in border areas but who also often penetrate deeply into the territory of the state; and frontiers, territorial zones [borderlands and contact zones] of varying width which stretch across and away from state borders."[8]

In terms of functionality, Donnan and Wilson highlight ways in which the material aspect of borders is central to the formation and preservation of the political identity of the modern nation-state and national cultures. The authors note that in light of the erosion of nation-states, walls represent desperate attempts by nation-states to perform and display power; essentially, border walls suggest a juxtaposition of strength and weakness.[9] Other scholars acknowledge that borders serve as symbolic "markers of . . . peaceful or hostile relations" among adjacent nation-states and regulate "the movement of people, goods, wealth and information, all of which must be deemed acceptable . . . to cross its borders."[10]

Of course, borders are never neutral. Indeed, modern borders reiterate the asymmetrical global dynamics resulting from centuries of colonial-imperial praxis. Thus, the study of borders matters not only because borders are "meaning-making and meaning-carrying entities," but because "almost all that occurs in the everyday lives of people in the modern world can and does occur in its borderlands."[11]

Study of the U.S.-Mexico border has led several scholars to interrogate the field of border studies. Gillian Roberts and David Stirrup challenged scholars, "to dislodge the primacy of a hegemonic (white, Anglo) Americanness in favor of approaches that address the multiplicities of American identity."[12] Claire F. Fox argues for the need to search for new modes of knowing, writing: "when approached from within the disciplinary boundaries and dominant paradigms of American Studies, [the border] rarely emerges as something that can, could, or should, be crossed but, rather, retains its defensive properties."[13] Consequently, the U.S.-Mexico border has been reduced to "one more othering mechanism . . . that maintains [the inside/outside] binary rather than attempting any meaningful interrogation of the possible conjunction that such a pairing implies."[14] This reductive vision of the U.S.-Mexico border is the norm in some scholarship. Take, for instance, the following citation, which attempts to exemplify the idea of "border conflicts" in which the Global North collides with the South: "The transformations of the post-1989 world have brought with them a rise in the number, type, and intensity of border disputes. These include conflicts between . . . local, regional, and national efforts to support or to curb the cross-border movement of refugees, immigrants, illegal workers, smugglers, and terrorists (perhaps most notably at the US–Mexico border and at the many external borders of the EU)."[15]

When it comes to body politics and border metaphors, Willem van Schendel observes: "[in] the relationship between state borders and the human body . . . the body represents a state system of spatial control, or acts as an outer skin protecting a national social order."[16] This comes as no surprise, says Lois Ann Lorentzen, who notes that undocumented immigrants and queer people are often represented through metaphors of illness, disease, and plagues that present imminent danger.[17] These metaphoric pathologies trigger societal anxiety, as they "weaken, and even kill the nation."[18] Therefore, "for their own protection, national bodies eject foreign intrusions."[19] Gilles Deleuze and Félix Guattari's rhizome theory has been key to understanding and approaching borders through metaphors that depart from the monolithic West. According to Caleb Bailey, the rhizome does "not simply sustain established myths or conform to regional or intranational debates but rather spill[s] . . . over and beyond those boundaries." Bailey examines the southern border through the Deleuzian principle of nomadism, wherefrom a multiplicity of meanings emerge, thus turning a border metaphor into something "mobile, complex, flexible, hybridized."[20] This perspective correlates with Aldama and González's observation that "the proximity of two cultures creates a permeable boundary that allows for movement, contestation, hybridity, and the creation of something new altogether, among other things."[21] Such a methodology allows "for a destratified . . . approach to Border Studies."[22] Nevertheless, some scholars have been cautious to conceive the border through metaphor. For example, Stanislav Shmelev warns: "when the border is condensed to an image, and when this image symbolizes wide-ranging political or theoretical stances, [it] becomes reductive and delocalized."[23] More recently, Victor Konrad and Heather Nicol have claimed that metonymic walls, fences, and gates function as metaphors that "resist American hegemony" and unveil "broader hegemony discourses at play in transnational spaces."[24] This approach resonates with Roberts and Stirrup's project, says Bailey, "in its insistence upon working with extant discursive material but re-articulating it from differentiated ideological and historical positions."[25]

THE SOUTHERN BORDER

Commonly known as the southern border, the U.S.-Mexico border is among the most globally significant series of entry points. It is the tenth largest border in the world, stretching nearly two thousand miles from the Pacific Coast to the Gulf of Mexico. It is the most crossed border in the world, with nearly three hundred million documented crossings per year. In the 2021 fiscal year, Congress budgeted $18.2 billion dollars and more than sixty thousand personnel to border enforcement, making U.S. Customs and Border Protection (CBP) the highest-funded enforcement agency in the world, and the southern border, "the most militarized border zone between two friendly countries."[26] Consequently, it is "one of the most contradictory geopolitical lines in the world."[27] Likewise, the southern border is described as a zone that mirrors "a low-intensity conflict war zone," with several "military-style checkpoints" and "warrantless searches" into U.S. territory.[28] Startling statistics from the CBP confirm that between 1998 and 2020, more than 7,500 people died attempting to cross the border. In 2021 alone, 650 deaths were reported.[29] I somberly and wholeheartedly concur with Aldama and González: "The border allows for legal and illegal crossing, and when the politics of such crossings lead politicians and activists to cite statistics and numbers, it is easy to forget that there are human beings . . . facing very real consequences that shape . . . the nations that lie along either of its sides."[30]

The geopolitical formation of the southern border as we know it today sheds light on the tumultuous history and relationships not only between the United States and Mexico, but between the United States and Latin America as whole. Significantly, from a U.S.-centric historical, political, racial, and ethnolinguistic standpoint, the southern border represents a dividing line that separates us from them. This orientation disregards Latin America's diversity and the unique circumstances of each of the countries therein. As Anzaldúa masterfully describes, "The U.S.-Mexican border *es una herida abierta* [is an open wound] where the Third World grates against the first and bleeds."[31] What are the origins of the southern border, and why is that history key to understanding and unraveling our current cultural and political anxiety (and paranoia) to hermetically seal the southern border?

In the mid-nineteenth century, the United States expanded westward, initially displacing and eliminating Indigenous peoples in violent conflict, and later entering the sparsely populated northern reaches of a newly independent Mexico. The Treaty of Guadalupe Hidalgo ended the Mexican-American War in 1848, with Mexico losing half of its territory but only 10 percent of its population to the United States. The decisive factor that prevented the United States from annexing the entire country was a question of race: the goal was to acquire the greatest amount of territory, but the least number of non-Anglo people. On the Senate floor, John C. Calhoun from South Carolina laid bare the racist underpinnings of this decision: "We have never dreamt to incorporate into the Union any but the Caucasian race—the free white race."[32] Years later, in 1853, the United States purchased a thirty-thousand-square-mile region from Mexico, known as the Gadsden Purchase, which completed and shaped the current southern border. By this point, the United States realized that expansion into and colonization of Latin America did not require further land acquisition. It could be achieved through the economic conquest of American multinationals.

For nearly two centuries, the U.S.-Mexico border has been reinforced through built structures, policy, and ideology. Tracing the trajectory of this buildup allows for an understanding of current rhetoric and policy. Initially, the southern border was demarcated by irregular piles of stones and other rustic markers. In 1891, both countries agreed to define the border more accurately, installing seven-foot-tall stone monuments in border cities, such as El Paso, Texas, and Nogales, Arizona Territory. In 1897, President William McKinley mandated a sixty-foot-wide pathway along the border to better detect trafficking of basic goods (mostly food) that "illegally" circulated without import-export tariffs. In the early 1900s, border fences were erected through open rural areas, beyond border towns, to prevent the free movement of livestock and therefore spread of cattle disease.[33] Later, sharply increased security patrol was precipitated by larger geopolitical developments.

First, the Chinese Exclusion Act of 1882 banned Chinese immigration into the United States. This racist policy was enforced mostly at water ports, but the southern border was perceived as an easy entryway to the United States for non-European immigrants (e.g., Asian, Mexican, and Central American immigrants), so border enforcement increased. Later, during the Mexican Revolution (1910–20), the United States feared that the conflict would spill over into U.S. territory and sent military troops to protect the southern border from so-called violent Mexican rebels and bandits. Additionally, during World War I (1914–19), growing fear and paranoia that the Germans would invade through the southern border prompted the United States to build permanent border walls. Another decisive turn occurred during Prohibition. Alcohol smuggled across the border prompted increased U.S. surveillance to protect, "the regulation of American morality from immoral people."[34] In the 1930s, as the population in border towns grew, fences were reinforced with barbed wire and light posts. During World War II, the United States implemented the Bracero Program to supplement agricultural labor by bringing in

Mexican workers with temporary work visas. At the same time, other Mexican workers crossed the border separately, searching for jobs. This stoked protectionist and nationalist feeling in the United States, and prejudice grew against Mexicans specifically, and Latin Americans in general. Whether immigrants crossed the border legally or without documentation, there were increased restrictions at the border, beginning a cycle of mistrust and paranoia that continues today.

THE SOUTHERN BORDER AND TRUMP'S HERMENEUTICS OF THE ASS

In "Trump's Poetics of Caca," I link the former president's offensive speech to his larger stance on immigration. The poetics of caca refers to a specific type of political rhetoric erected on the mantle of fear. While Trump's words seem improvised, his premeditated and conscious speech acts resurrect obsolete (post)colonial racial, sexual, and ethnic stereotypes about Latinxs and Latin America, which is why I employ the Spanish word *caca*. Not only does this rhetoric draw on foul language and scatological references typically associated with excrement, defecation, and the anus, it also operates through a specific hermeneutics. Caca denotes a xenophobia and disgust toward the Latinx presence in the United States, as a reaction to rapid cultural, linguistic, and racial shifts in the country. Furthermore, Trump's potty mouth—as the locus from which scatological and political rhetoric is discharged—represents a metaphorical inversion of oral and anal cavities. In the present analysis, I draw on Trump's poetics of caca to examine the importance of the southern border for Trump's overall political career. Trump's rhetoric compounds another powerful scatological image through an open/closed dichotomy—that is, a metaphor of the southern border as a dangerous gaping hole, an open anal sphincter that must be closed off to ensure the safety and preservation of the United States. Such rationale is not only racist and paranoid, but also erotic. The eroticism is shameful, tied to racial and bodily impurity—a pleasure and fascination that should not be indulged. Paranoid racism and eroticism are crucial factors that set the foundation of Trump's hermeneutics of the ass. But how did Trump manage to exploit the southern border? And what do I mean by Trump's hermeneutics of the ass?

For sociologist Pierre Bourdieu, the notion of capital expands beyond the material and the economic to encompass the social, cultural, and symbolic. *Symbolic capital* is a blanket term that comprises the "accumulation" of all other forms of capital.[35] Within a given field (e.g., a political party), agents (such as politicians) may acquire symbolic capital, which Bourdieu essentially defines as "a reputation for competence and an image of respectability and honorability." Symbolic capital, explains Bourdieu, may be acquired through a relationship to power and the frameworks of society, and "grasped through categories of perception that recognize its specific logic or, if you prefer, misrecognize the arbitrariness of its possession and accumulation."[36] Beyond Trump's self-presentation and self-promotion as a rich, successful businessperson, the southern border provided Trump with the means to accumulate symbolic capital. Since announcing his candidacy in 2015, throughout his administration (2017–21), and even after his defeat, the southern border has been a staple of Trump's political persona and policies. He promised to secure the southern border from "drug dealers, murderers, and rapists" by means of a "tall, beautiful concrete wall."[37] This became the most emblematic talking point in Trump's quest for the political spotlight, allowing him to transition from reality star into de facto GOP figurehead. He did not hesitate to shift the ideological premise of the GOP, once the party of tradition and family values, into the party of Trump. Along with "Lock her up!," "Build the wall!" became the rallying cry that bonded Trump to his base, and arguably the policy promise that got him elected in 2016. As things stand, Trump's half-finished wall will most likely "be the monument" by which his administration will be remembered.[38]

Trump's hermeneutics of the ass is the epitome of what Eve Kosofsky Sedgwick calls a "hermeneutics of suspicion," in that, "paranoia requires that bad news be always already known" and "every possible meaning is explored for excess meaning."[39] However, excess does not seek to create nuance or explore the symbolic potential of counternarratives; on the contrary, excess exacerbates paranoia, distrust, and fear.[40] The meanings that stem from the hermeneutics of suspicion align with a single dominant narrative that ultimately reiterates a hegemonic view. Certainly, the narrative of the southern border as a dangerous site for illicit crossings (humans, drugs, and crime) precedes Trump's political reign. The racialized southern border is a well-used othering mechanism and vent for national grievances "about difference and division around immigration, international relations, health care, and national security."[41] K. Jill Fleuriet and Mari Castellano note that the southern border "is a concept-metaphor, because . . . the border is less a geopolitical location in the United States than a concept that embeds a metaphor for insecurity and lawlessness."[42] The racist, xenophobic historical grassroots description of the southern border, its militarization, and the security measures set forth to protect our national vulnerability corroborate this concept-metaphor in the American imagination: that is, a reductive, single-sided narrative of prejudice toward Latin America, exploited for excess meaning in Trump's hermeneutics of the ass. The southern border is a specific class of dangerous opening, an anal sphincter though which diseased, undesirable waste is dumped into the United States by Latin America, necessitating hypervigilance or sealing. Furthermore, the southern border, as an open anus, situates the United States in a submissive position, in which the country is receptive, fuckable, a sub, a bottom, contrary to the active penetrator role of the United States as the top world power. It is an inversion of phallocentric power in the imperialistic colonial mindset. In Trump's hermeneutics of the ass, the dynamic of power is a binary—top/bottom, active/passive—and dictated solely by the phallus as an organizing force that structures the world in terms of hierarchies, with itself in the dominant position. As David M. Friedman states, "from the beginning of Western civilization, the penis was more than a body part, [it was] an idea, a conceptual but flesh-and-blood gauge of [a] man's place in the world."[43] It's no wonder that "Macho Man" became a prevailing anthem played during Trump's rallies.

Trump's conception of the southern border echoes obsolete ideas of nationalism in which a nation-state exists if and only if its borders are clearly marked and impenetrable by those perceived as inferior or subordinate to the nation. In one of the many Trump tweets pertaining to this subject, he wrote: "We, as a country, either have borders or we don't. IF WE DON'T HAVE BORDERS, WE DON'T HAVE A COUNTRY!"[44] Hence, a nation-state does not exist under the threat of an Other—in this case (undocumented) immigrants "from shithole countries."[45]

The evolving semantics around the wall further reveals Trump's awareness of its symbolic resonance. Initially, he named it the "Mexican wall," as part of his plan to make Mexico finance construction, and because the wall represented a breakage, a hard barrier separating the United States from Latin America. Once he realized its empowering potential, the "Mexican wall" became the "Trump wall," given how it resonated with his base. As both liberal and conservative media coverage began referring to it as the Trump wall, his message shifted. The wall became an ideal, the embodiment of Trump's political persona: "tall," "strong," "powerful," "impenetrable" (and therefore the penetrator, not submissive). Put simply, from Trump's hermeneutics of the ass, the problem became the openness of the southern border.

In early 2019, after the longest government shutdown in U.S. history, Trump settled for $1.375 billion from Congress to fund his wall, far short of the $5.6 billion he originally requested to tackle what he dubbed a "national security crisis."[46] Speaking at the Rose Garden in February 2019, he opened with a grim image of the southern border—"we're talking about an invasion of our country with drugs, with human traffickers, with all types of criminals and gangs"—and he urged Americans to "confront a problem that we have right here at home." He painted Mexico as violent and dangerous, its problems spilling over the border into the United States: "they have close to 2,000 murders right on the other side of the wall, . . . in Mexico." Congruent to his hermeneutics of the ass, Trump highlighted the penetrable nature of the southern border: "And a big majority of the big drugs—the big drug loads—don't go through ports of entry." Invasion is salient in Trump's rhetoric, and he names two insidious faces of it: undocumented immigrants and immigrant Latinas. The undocumented—who represent chaos, and the flouting of order and policy—are described as a dangerous collective entity that manifests in cyclical manner at the border: "We've broken up two caravans that are on their way. . . . We have another one [coming]." And so, he said over and over, we need a wall.[47] Public statements by Trump on Fox News described undocumented immigrants as carriers of diseases, such as HIV, measles, pertussis, rubella, and rabies. As a prophylactic measure, Trump deployed 5,200 soldiers to the southern border in Tijuana.[48] Furthermore, when Trump discusses the threat of Latina immigrants, he cloaks it in concern for victims of trafficking. Yet, his rhetoric of the preservation of order and purity quickly emerges: "You can't take human traffic—women and girls—you can't take them through ports of entry. . . . They go through areas where you have no wall."[49] Specifically, according to Trump's hermeneutics of the ass, undocumented immigrants are invading not only in large caravans but by way of fertility. For example, when Trump was asked about a migrant caravan from Central America containing nearly seven thousand people of all ages and genders, Trump identified Latino men as the largest threat: "When you look at that caravan, and you look [at] largely, very big percentage of men, young, strong, a lot of bad people, a lot of bad people in there."[50] Ultimately, he articulates a specific fear: the fertility of interracial unions. Once more, Trump verbalizes racial, ethnic, and sexual (post)colonial stereotypes: his fear alludes to an absolute fear that was a subject of debate during the nineteenth century—a fear that found its basis in the alleged degeneration of those of mixed race.[51] This certainly correlates with Nancy Hiemstra's examination of Trump's immigration policies, which fundamentally enact and articulate a series of colonial archetypes of fertile figures. According to Hiemstra, massive deportations, family separations, and the caging of children are a direct response to the idea of Latina women's fertility: "It is a direct assault on the breeder and anchor baby figures, justified by the figure of the bad immigrant parent. . . . We can understand all attacks on immigrant fertility—whether to curtail or compel—as a continuation of racist histories of population control. Immigrants' bodies and reproductive capacities become a mechanism for the exacerbation of hardship and the reinforcement of borders and orders."[52]

ANAL THEORY: RECLAIMING THE SOUTHERN BORDER

Therefore, the wall becomes a symbolic prophylactic strategy to prevent fertility. Under this assumption, the southern border is a specific type of orifice: a cloaca. In birds and reptiles, the cloaca serves as the common opening of the digestive, reproductive, and urinary systems, which opens to the posterior of the animal as the vent. This opened sphincter—both digestive and reproductive—is dangerous per Trump's hermeneutics of the ass, not only because of its ability to spew excrement over the border into the United States, but in terms of fertility and reproduction. Trump invokes the threat of Latina fecundity and its power to alter the demographic and genetic composition of the U.S. population. In June 2021, Trump offered remarks at the southern Texas border in what represented his second public appearance after losing the 2020 presidential election. He used the opportunity to criticize the Biden administration's handling of the border: "Now we have an open, really dangerous border, more dangerous than it's ever been in the history of our country. And we better go back fast."[53] Following his defeat in 2020, the southern border represents a means of political comeback for Trump, as well as a rhetorical strategy to stoke his base and remain current. If we were to apply his criteria for what constitutes a dangerous, diseased thing, a shithole that spews its waste into the vulnerable world, it could be argued that Trump himself is an asshole, a gaping hole, a filthy orifice. In "Trump's Poetics of Caca," I developed the idea of an anal-oral inversion—in Trump's case, an orifice dumping toxic, undesirable waste from the body where a mouth ought to be. I'm not the only theorist to argue the point. Aaron James writes in his book *Assholes: A Theory of Donald Trump*, for example, that an asshole, like Trump, embodies the following definition: "the guy (they are mainly men) who systematically allows himself advantages in social relationships out of an entrenched (and mistaken) sense of entitlement that immunizes him against the complaints of other people."[54] Additionally, he embraces and propagates dangerous, hate- and fear-based sociopolitical views, engaging in what is widely recognized as "shitty" or "asshole" behavior by elevating himself and his followers (privileged white people) above everyone else, whom he depicts as Other, filthy, threatening. The paradigms by which he speaks of power and uses his power depend on a binary model of human relations: dom/sub, top/bottom, powerful/powerless. Trump's hermeneutics of the ass places those unlike him in a position where he both dominates them and fears them. Trump enacts a (post)colonial mindset that possess and appropriates—in this case the southern border—through the oscillation of eroticism and prejudice. Undocumented immigrants who cross the southern border evoke for Trump "an attractive, but dangerous, sexuality, an apparently abundant, limitless, but threatening, fertility. And what does fear suggest if not desire?"[55]

The theoretical backbone and inspiration for this study is Jonathan A. Allan's *Reading from Behind: A Cultural Analysis of the Anus*. Unlike the reductive perspective through which some scholars have approached the anus—that is, in terms of masculinity, an abject symbol, and a ground zero for gayness—Allan's study delves into the critical potential of this organ for reimagining gender, sex, sexuality, body, pleasure, and desire. Indeed, the anus provides surprising creative and theoretical potential for rethinking borders and "the consequences and subsequent theorization of the actual, geographic border between nations and ... other so-called 'soft' borders that arise when examining the confluence and clash of cultures."[56] Thus, like the southern border, the anus is "a remarkably complex organ, sign, and symbol" and "a paradoxical space, which ... makes it so ripe for exploration and theorization."[57] How can the southern border be reimagined through a rectal reading, beyond Trump's paranoid hermeneutics of the ass? What creative, provocative, and surprising meanings may arise?

Unlike other sex organs, "the anus is not exclusive, like the penis or the vagina, to one sex, to one type of body. . . . The anus is a key part of the human body, a remarkably complex organ that has significant symbolic potential, not least because of the numerous ways in which we have tried to keep it repressed."[58] Consequently, "the anus—and discussions of it—continue to remain guarded, closeted, limited. We are still anxious about it. It remains a taboo." But the anus is "a governing symbol that can and does explain a wide range of phenomena," as well as a valuable site of inquiry that can add nuance to "literary and cultural texts in new and exciting ways." Furthermore, the anus, as a way of thinking (call it "anal theory," "methodology of the anus," or "rectal readings"), grants the ability to "turn theory on its head, . . . using other modes of reading, of thinking, and of critiquing."[59]

To rethink Trump's hermeneutics of the ass through anal theory suggests further questions; it invites a reconceptualization of the southern border as an essential player in the functions of the body in potentially productive or illuminating ways. As a critical way of thinking and reading, the anus represents "an opening to the text," an alternative or backdoor approach that enables us "to engage with the other side of textuality" and explore the complexities and the ambiguities.[60] "Reading from behind" feeds from Sedgwick's hermeneutics of suspicion and reparative readings, as the epistemology of the anus is a form of reparative reading that overturns suspicion by welcoming the unknown. Or, as Allan states, "a possible reading, indeed, that does not imagine a potential as even necessary." Reparative reading, thus, comprises a multiplicity of readings and interpretations that occasionally may be predictable, but may also be astonishing, jaw dropping, "and a reader attuned to a given politics or poetics will likely find these meanings in texts."[61] Reparative readings move beyond fearmongering, paranoia, and suspicion, seeking "new environments of sensation for the objects they study by displacing critical attachments once forced by correction, and rejection . . . with those crafted by affection, gratitude, solidarity, and love." As soon as the intentionality in reparative readings is disclaimed, these motives can no longer be a form of paranoia "both because they are about pleasure ('merely aesthetic') and because they are frankly ameliorative ('merely reformist')."[62] Anal theory, as a reparative reading, offers "new expressive grammar" and "works from the part to the whole." As Allan is keen to emphasize, "it is important to remove ourselves from . . . paranoid, sphincter-tightening perspective with respect to the anus, its symbolism, and its effects." Such "flexible circularity" of anal theory is "playful, joyful, salubrious, slippery, (dis)comforting," and distinctive because it vacillates around words and (double) meanings, allowing room for a new way of learning and thinking "that is not depth oriented, but . . . plays on the surface, able to tickle, titillate, tease."[63]

So, what surprises arise by our reading the southern border as an anal sphincter? For starters, the anus cannot be weaponized because it always backfires: *¿Ano? Todos tenemos unos, pero siempre pensamos que el de al lado es el que apesta.* (Anus, everyone has got one, but we always think that the person next to us is the one that stinks.) If, according to Trump's paranoid hermeneutics of the ass, the southern border is a dangerous open anus through which Latin America defecates waste into the United States, what can be said about the United States?

Through the southern border, the United States defecates shitty policies, economic trade deals (e.g., the North American Free Trade Agreement [NAFTA] and now the U.S.-Mexico-Canada Agreement), and (covert) interventions that fuck (over), exploit, and stagnate Latin American countries. These stir and exacerbate violence, and destabilize politics and economies, which results in more migration north—not to mention environmental impact, pollution, and contamination. Trump inspires fear of undocumented immigrants who cross the southern border, while crime statistics demonstrate that undocumented immigrants "are less likely to commit crimes than native-born Americans . . . [and] in counties that have put in place policies to limit cooperation with immigration enforcement and to uphold the Fourth Amendment, there are lower crime rates than in counties without sanctuary policies."[64] Indeed, undocumented immigrants are a significant contributor to the U.S. economy. They are not shit; rather, they are fertilizer. According to a 2011 report by the American Immigration Council, "undocumented immigrants contributed $90 billion in taxes in 2010, while receiving only $5 billion in benefits. On average, an undocumented individual has about 8 percent of their income go to taxes. . . . In 2010, undocumented individuals paid $13 billion into retirement accounts and only received $1 billion in return." In short, undocumented immigrants pay more in taxes than they receive in benefits, as they do not qualify for many benefits and also "tend to keep a low profile and do not seek benefits they . . . could legitimately receive."[65] Undocumented immigrants are an underground economy that benefits the United States, even as they are demonized in conservative political rhetoric. They contribute significantly to the economy yet have extremely limited rights and recourse and live in this country as "impossible subjects."[66] That is to say: immigration restriction produced the illegal alien as a new legal and political subject, whose inclusion within the nation was simultaneously a social reality and a legal impossibility—a subject barred from citizenship and denied rights.

Anal theory helps us consider that the anus requires changing positionalities; to glance at our own asses requires using instruments (e.g., mirrors), as well as bending or even contorting into vulnerable positions. It means opening to the forbidden, seeing what we cannot easily see from our customary upward-looking, front-facing position. This framework facilitates thinking of the southern border as a shared passage between the United States and Latin America, an exchange that occurs in all directions: in, out, in between. Under this assumption, a border is a shared gateway, and the ass (shared gateway) between Latin America and the United States is not pink, Anglo; it is mixed, brown. Furthermore, the anus cannot be sealed permanently. It is practically impossible, unnecessary, and unhealthy. If Trump's paranoid reading of the southern border insists on closing this passage, this closure cannot be permanent: the border, like the anus, resists. Instead, Trump's wall and policies symbolize a butt plug. This discussion leads us to contemplate other functionalities of the anus: not only as a site for defecation, but as a site of pleasure, too. This undermines Trump's open/sealed dichotomy to allow us to embrace other, in-between states of the ass; other positionalities beyond homophobic, colonial, puritanical assumptions in terms of toxic masculinity; and other sexual roles in terms of penetration (top/bottom, dominant/submissive, masculinity/femininity). These colonial ways of thinking are essentially the manifestation of the fear of loss of power, and the moral taboo of anal pleasure. As we see, anal theory as a study of the ass employs the notion of "tunnels, canals, passages" in ambiguous and complex ways to identify a "switch point," which "refers to a point of connection between two things (or rather separate connotative fields) where something from one flows towards (is diverted in the direction of) the other, lending its connotative spread and signifying force to the other."[67] Under this assumption, the anal theory's southern border becomes a shared passage, but also a thing of its own; it produces fear and anxiety, but also surprises and pleasure. It invites us to embrace our own humanity, and to recognize the humanity of others, all as equals—each of us a possessor of a defecating, pleasurable hole.

Without the (exploitation of the) southern border as a rhetorical tactic, Trump's political career would have not had the same resonance. Trump touched on several other issues that rallied his base, but each related to securing the southern border: undocumented immigrants taking American jobs and valuable resources, other countries taking advantage of the United States, and establishment politicians not doing anything about it. As the continuation of his poetics of caca, Trump's hermeneutics of the ass suggests that the southern border is an anal sphincter. The metaphorical implications of this paradigm are many, but the following are theoretically significant:

1. The openness of the border is a site for lawlessness, excrement, and social ills.

2. This orifice is the gateway to Mexico and, by extension, to the entirety of Latin America. The border is not serving its prescribed function, which is to clearly mark and separate "us" and "them." Thus, the border is porous; it has holes.

3. The border is the opening through which other countries (from the Global South) take advantage of the United States (economically). America is fuckable, open, passive, receptive.

4. Through the southern border, Latin America shits into the United States as an open anus—a one-way street. All the shit from Latin America is dumped into the United States.

5. The cloaca is a signifier of the border; it is dangerous in terms of excrement but also fertility and reproduction, which can alter the genetic composition of the United States.

At the beginning of this essay, I invoked the idea of the *empacho*, a physical-spiritual-psychological blockage that prevents the sufferer from properly processing and digesting. I mentioned that the research, conceptualization, and writing of this essay are meant to cure me of a blockage that has been ailing me for some time: my Trump-pacho. By contemplating, recontextualizing, and reclaiming Trump's poetics of caca and, now, Trump's hermeneutics of the ass, I explore my own border experiences in the light of many possible interpretations, and I'm able to begin healing this *empacho*, this blockage.

Certainly, Trump's use of language when he talks about the border is disturbing. It's insulting, but that doesn't stop me from processing and recontextualizing it. If Trump wants to call the border an ass, let's call it an ass. But let's embrace all the possibilities, complexities, and pleasures that come with the ass. Anal theory fits easily into border theory. Anzaldúa's observations were groundbreaking and innovative for their time; however, I would like to reflect on my own experience on the southern border. I have crossed the U.S.-Mexico border many times, beginning with my first unauthorized crossing at the age of seven, up to my current legal crossings as a U.S. citizen, the meaning of which still puzzles me. To me, the southern border is precisely what Anzaldúa pointed out—a border and a borderland—but it is more than that. The southern border resists definitions: it keeps welcoming new possibilities rather than rejecting them. Thus, the border exists in a perpetual state of definition and redefinition, recording the lived experiences and the observations of those who live in, on, or within it. For the Latinxs who have crossed the border, it is time to reclaim our border experiences and identities, whether we buried them ourselves or lost them to cultural appropriation. Whether through anal theory or another framework, the ensuing recontextualization and reclamation are a way to heal collectively and individually, to *curarnos el empacho*.

NOTES

1. "Trump's Wall and Immigration Policies: A Closer Look," YouTube.
2. Shear and Davis, "Shoot Migrants' Legs, Build Alligator Moat."
3. Quoted in Jackson, "Donald Trump Claims He Didn't Want Moat, Snakes, and Gators at the Mexican Border."
4. Macías, "Trump's Poetics of Caca."
5. Muñoz, *Disidentifications*.
6. Aldama and González, *Latinx Studies*, 23.
7. Anzaldúa, *Borderlands/La Frontera*, 3.
8. Donnan and Wilson, *Borders*, 9.
9. Donnan and Wilson, 12–13.
10. Donnan and Wilson, 6.
11. Donnan and Wilson, 15.
12. Roberts and Stirrup, *Parallel Encounters*, quoted in Bailey, "An Alternative Border Metaphor," 767–68.
13. Fox, *The Fence and the River*, quoted in Bailey, "An Alternative Border Metaphor," 768.
14. Bailey, "An Alternative Border Metaphor," 768.
15. Donnan and Wilson, *Borders*, 12.
16. Schendel, *The Bengal Borderland*, quoted in Bailey, "An Alternative Border Metaphor," 769.
17. Lorentzen, "Holy Death on the US/Mexico Border."
18. Chavez, *Covering Immigration*, quoted in Lorentzen, "Holy Death."
19. Donnan and Wilson, *Borders*, 10.
20. Bailey, "An Alternative Border Metaphor," 769.
21. Aldama and González, *Latinx Studies*, 26.
22. Roberts and Stirrup, *Parallel Encounters*, quoted in Bailey, "An Alternative Border Metaphor," 769.
23. Shmelev, "The Mexico–United States Border in Anthropology," quoted in Donnan and Wilson, *Borders*, 13.
24. Konrad and Nikol, *Beyond Walls*, quoted in Donnan and Wilson, *Borders*, 12.
25. Bailey, "An Alternative Border Metaphor," 773.
26. Southern Border Communities Coalition, "Border Facts."
27. Luibhéid and Cantú, *Queer Migrations*, quoted in Lorentzen, "Holy Death on the US/Mexico Border."
28. Lorentzen, "Santa Muerte."
29. Southern Border Communities Coalition, "Border Facts."
30. Aldama and González, *Latinx Studies*, 26.
31. Anzaldúa, *Borderlands/La Frontera*, 3.
32. Quoted in "How the U.S. Stole Mexico," YouTube, 8:32.
33. "How Walls Ended Up Along the U.S.-Mexico Border," YouTube, 1:55 and 3:22.
34. "How Walls Ended Up Along the U.S.-Mexico Border," 5:26.
35. Bourdieu, "The Forms of Capital," 280–81.

36. Bourdieu, 283.
37. "Trump's Wall and Immigration Policies: A Closer Look," YouTube, 3:44.
38. "Trump's Wall and Immigration Policies: A Closer Look," 0:23.
39. Sedgwick, *Touching Feeling*, quoted in Allan, *Reading from Behind*, 33.
40. Allan, *Reading from Behind*, 32.
41. Fleuriet and Castellano, "Media, Place-Making, and Concept-Metaphors," 882.
42. Fleuriet and Castellano, 883.
43. Friedman, *A Mind of Its Own*, quoted in Allan, *Reading from Behind*, 5.
44. Donald J. Trump (@realDonaldTrump), "We, as a country, either have borders or we don't . . . ," Twitter, November 12, 2015, 6:50 a.m., https://twitter.com/realdonaldtrump/status/664787273184108545.
45. Trump, quoted in Macías, "Trump's Poetics of Caca," 38.
46. White House, "Remarks by President Trump on the National Security and Humanitarian Crisis."
47. White House.
48. Macías, "Trump's Poetics of Caca," 47.
49. White House, "Remarks by President Trump on the National Security and Humanitarian Crisis."
50. Trump, quoted in Macías, "Trump's Poetics of Caca," 47.
51. Macías, 47.
52. Hiemstra, "Mothers, Babies, and Abortion at the Border," 1707.
53. "Former President Trump and Governor Abbott Hold Border Wall Briefing," C-SPAN, 36:30.
54. James, *Assholes*, 3.
55. Young, *Colonial Desire*, quoted in Macías, "Trump's Poetics of Caca," 42.
56. Aldama and González, *Latinx Studies*, 24.
57. Allan, *Reading from Behind*, 5; Aldama and González, *Latinx Studies*, 24.
58. Allan, *Reading from Behind*, 5.
59. Allan, 5–6.
60. Allan, 6.
61. Sedgwick, quoted in Allan, 37.
62. Sedgwick, quoted in Allan, 37.
63. Allan, 38.
64. Unidos, "7 Ways Immigrants Enrich Our Economy and Society."
65. Abrego et al., "Making Immigrants into Criminals," 700–701.
66. Ngai, *Impossible Subjects*, quoted in Lorentzen, "*Santa Muerte.*"
67. Allan, *Reading from Behind*, 39.

BIBLIOGRAPHY

Abrego, Leisy, Mat Coleman, Daniel E. Martínez, Cecilia Menjívar, and Jeremy Slack. "Making Immigrants into Criminals: Legal Processes of Criminalization in the Post-IIRIRA Era." *Journal on Migration and Human Security* 5, no. 3 (2017): 694–715.

Aldama, Frederick Luis, and Christopher González. *Latinx Studies: The Key Concepts.* New York: Routledge, 2019.

Allan, Jonathan A. *Reading from Behind: A Cultural Analysis of the Anus.* London: Zed Books, 2016.

Anzaldúa, Gloria. *Borderlands/La Frontera: The New Mestiza.* San Francisco: Aunt Lute Books, 2007.

Bailey, Caleb. "An Alternative Border Metaphor: On Rhizomes and Disciplinary Boundaries." *Journal of Borderlands Studies* 34, no. 5 (2018): 767–81.

Bourdieu, Pierre. "The Forms of Capital." In *Readings in Economic Sociology,* edited by Nicole Woolsey Biggart, 280–91. Malden, Mass.: Blackwell, 2002.

Chavez, Leo R. *Covering Immigration: Popular Images and the Politics of the Nation.* Berkeley: University of California Press, 2001.

Donnan, Hastings, and Thomas M. Wilson. *Borders: Frontiers of Identity, Nation and State.* Oxford: Berg, 2001.

Fleuriet, K. Jill, and Mari Castellano. "Media, Place-Making, and Concept-Metaphors: The US-Mexico Border During the Rise of Donald Trump." *Media, Culture & Society* 42, no. 6 (2020): 880–97.

"Former President Trump and Governor Abbott Hold Border Wall Briefing." C-SPAN, video uploaded June 30, 2021, 39:20. https://www.c-span.org/video/?513085-1/.

Fox, Claire F. *The Fence and the River: Culture and Politics at the U.S.-Mexico Border.* Minneapolis: University of Minnesota Press, 1999.

Friedman, David M. *A Mind of Its Own: A Cultural History of the Penis.* London: Free Press, 2009.

Hiemstra, Nancy. "Mothers, Babies, and Abortion at the Border: Contradictory U.S. Policies, or Targeting Fertility?" *Environment and Planning C: Politics and Space* 39, no. 8 (2021): 1692–710.

"How the U.S. Stole Mexico." YouTube, video uploaded July 27, 2020, by Johnny Harris, 13:14. https://www.youtube.com/watch?v=3OMmxKiG4LE.

"How Walls Ended Up Along the U.S.-Mexico Border | NYT News." YouTube, video uploaded July 25, 2019, by the New York Times, 7:12. https://www.youtube.com/watch?v=FxbXhSAia_o.

Jackson, David. "Donald Trump Claims He Didn't Want Moat, Snakes, and Gators at the Mexican Border." *USA Today,* October 2, 2019.

James, Aaron. *Assholes: A Theory of Donald Trump.* New York: Doubleday, 2016.

Konrad, Victor, and Heather Nicol. *Beyond Walls: Re-Inventing the Canada–United States Borderlands.* London: Routledge, 2016.

Lorentzen, Lois Ann. "Holy Death on the US/Mexico Border." University of Chicago Divinity School, May 28, 2009. https://divinity.uchicago.edu/sightings/articles/holy-death-usmexico-border-lois-ann-lorentzen.

Lorentzen, Lois Ann. "*Santa Muerte*: Saint of the Dispossessed, Enemy of Church and State." *Emisférica* 13, no. 1 (2016). https://hemisphericinstitute.org/en/emisferica-13-1-states-of-devotion/.

Luibhéid, Eithne, and Lionel Cantú Jr., eds. *Queer Migrations: Sexuality, U.S. Citizenship, and Border Crossings*. Minneapolis: University of Minnesota Press, 2007.

Macías, Sergio. "Trump's Poetics of Caca: Shitty 'Bad Hombres' and 'Shithole' Latin American Countries." In *Decolonizing Latinx Masculinities*, edited by Arturo J. Aldama and Frederick Luis Aldama, 38–50. Tucson: University of Arizona Press, 2020.

Muñoz, José Esteban. *Disidentifications: Queers of Color and the Performance of Politics*. Minneapolis: University of Minnesota Press, 2015.

Ngai, Mae M. *Impossible Subjects: Illegal Aliens and the Making of Modern America*. Princeton, N.J.: Princeton University Press, 2014.

Roberts, Gillian, and David Stirrup. *Parallel Encounters: Culture at the Canada-US Border*. Waterloo, Ont.: Wilfrid Laurier University Press, 2014.

Schendel, Willem van. *The Bengal Borderland: Beyond State and Nation in South Asia*. London: Anthem, 2005.

Sedgwick, Eve Kosofsky. *Touching Feeling: Affect, Pedagogy, Performativity*. Durham, N.C.: Duke University Press, 2006.

Shear, Michael D., and Julie Hirschfeld Davis. "Shoot Migrants' Legs, Build Alligator Moat: Behind Trump's Ideas for Border." *New York Times*, October 1, 2019.

Shmelev, Stanislav. "The Mexico–United States Border in Anthropology: A Critique and Reformulation." *Journal of Political Ecology* 1, no. 1 (1994): 43–66.

Southern Border Communities Coalition. "Border Facts." Accessed March 27, 2022. https://www.southernborder.org/border-facts.

"Trump's Wall and Immigration Policies: A Closer Look." YouTube, video posted February 22, 2017, by Late Night with Seth Meyers, 8:55. https://www.youtube.com/watch?v=wh1v74YFpSs.

Unidos. "7 Ways Immigrants Enrich Our Economy and Society." *Culture-Pop* (blog). Accessed May 14, 2023. https://culturepop.com/hrblog/gt12to9znravtz9j7kjpxkbg99inap-g8h2k.

White House (archived website). "Remarks by President Trump on the National Security and Humanitarian Crisis on Our Southern Border." Press release, February 15, 2019. https://trumpwhitehouse.archives.gov/briefings-statements/remarks-president-trump-national-security-humanitarian-crisis-southern-border/.

Young, Robert J. C. *Colonial Desire: Hybridity in Theory, Culture and Race*. London: Routledge, 1995.

13

THE DEHUMANIZING FRAMING OF CENTRAL AMERICAN AND MEXICAN CHILDREN AND YOUTH SEEKING REFUGE IN THE UNITED STATES

MARIA VARGAS AND HEIDY SARABIA

JOHN MOORE, A PHOTOGRAPHER FOR Getty and a Pulitzer Prize winner, captured a horrendous yet captivating moment on the U.S.-Mexico border in 2018: a two-year-old Honduran child crying as her guardian was apprehended.[1] That year, explicit photographs such as Moore's, exposing the pain and suffering of Central American women, men, and children, filled the front pages of the news media. Throughout 2018 and the rest of the Trump administration, American audiences witnessed the unimaginable violence occurring at the border as children were separated from their families. However, there was an imbalance between the sheer terror seen on the faces of the children and the mainstream narrative accompanying the photographs: mainstream media often referred to the children as "illegal." These media representations were voyeuristic among an already misinformed readership.

In this chapter, we use the theoretical framework of coloniality of power to analyze how the media covered and framed the trauma of Central American children, compared to the framings of Mexican and white children. We argue that the ways particular bodies incite outrage and prompt a call for justice are categorized within a hierarchy of victimhood that renders racialized and gendered bodies socially and politically invisible. Additionally, we argue that state violence along the border highlights the coloniality of power that renders certain migrants visible and deserving while other migrants are invisible and undeserving; nevertheless, both visibility and invisibility lead to empty outrage that ultimately limits radical social change.

THEORETICAL FRAMEWORK

Coloniality of power is a theoretical framework that posits colonialism as based on the intersecting racial and economic projects of white supremacy and capitalism—the main systems of oppression that produced modernity—with long-lasting consequences to this day. Colonization became a "model of power," in which race, as decolonial theorist Aníbal Quijano argues, "became the fundamental criterion for the distribution of the world population into ranks, places, and roles."[2] Using this theoretical framework of coloniality illuminates how and why the cruelty afforded to children at the border has been so vicious yet ignored. This is because one effect of coloniality is, according to Nelson Maldonado-Torres, "the naturalization of extermination, expropriation, domination, exploitation, early death, and conditions that are worse than death such as torture and rape."[3] At the border, where the United States must deal with the influx of mostly Latin American migration, a project of bordering emerges in the cruelest manner through not just neglect, but also the conscious enactment of cruel and unimaginable violence on children—as well as unauthorized adults framed as "illegal."[4]

This chapter examines the photographs selected by human rights organizations to illuminate storylines on the humanitarian crisis along the border during the Trump administration. Our main source of analysis is photography, which we frame as a truth-telling technology because it is used by news media and journalists to invoke a particular reality of the struggle that immigrants experience. Despite viewers' ability to see migrants in pain while attempting to cross the U.S.-Mexico border, these visuals did not translate to critical and radical responses from the mainstream. We situate photography as a truth-telling genre to expose the colonial function of recordkeeping methods entangled with racialized and gendered bodies. Wendy S. Hesford defines truth-telling genres as the contexts, technologies, and disciplinary knowledge that demand the telling of true experiences and form the site from which human rights subjects emerge.[5] Truth-telling genres are produced through cultural and institutional knowledge that imputes truth value and empirical evidence to visual constructs, solidifying the "seeing is believing" logic. Examples of truth-telling genres also include the field of archival science, human rights law, and documentary film, all of which have been used to archive trauma and violence in humanitarian efforts. However, such recordkeeping methods used as textual and visual documentation tend to be constructed under a Western epistemology to benefit the colonizer and his colonial project and as a result invalidate or racialize experiences and violence that lack such evidentiary value. In the case of Central American migrants, despite their experiences having evidentiary support such as photography, firsthand testimony, or witnesses, truth-telling genres are still not enough for American audiences to empathize with Indigenous and poor children and demand radical change to immigration reform. This contrast demonstrates the clash between colonial recordkeeping and truth-telling, with racialized bodies and genocidal violence that continues to be negated in mainstream news media and politics.

It is critical to understand how truth-telling genres interlock with a hierarchy of victimhood that consists of competing racist, sexist, homophobic, transphobic, and nationalist agendas.[6] This chapter discusses the agendas embodied in competing efforts by human rights organizations and news media channels to determine which migrants are more deserving of refuge, even if it means discarding other populations that are more vulnerable to state terror. Under the coloniality of power framework, "human" is reserved for white, civilized, heterosexual, bourgeois, Christian colonizers, who symbolize "a being gifted with reason."[7] Hence, the category of human used to birth modern human rights discourse is rooted in racist, capitalist, and heteronormative power differentials that render racialized and gendered bodies as nonhuman and nonman.[8] Therefore, it is imperative to understand how the coloniality of power has historically affected human rights rhetoric that prioritizes human bodies over nonhuman bodies. Human rights discourse and advocacy lack a critical reckoning with their racist and heteronormative history because human rights rhetoric perpetuates neocolonial humanity. The ideal human rights victim is a white, heterosexual, capitalist male, and it is his suffering that has the power to incite public outrage and change. However, the focus on contemporary human rights issues tends to be concentrated in the Global South, explaining why most people seen in photographs of war and other forms of violence are colonized and racialized peoples.

METHODS

In order to contextualize patterns of migration from Central America and Mexico, we drew data from multiple sources, including: statistics from the U.S. Department of Homeland Security (DHS); fact sheets from the Migration Policy Institute; documents issued publicly during the Trump administration; government records obtained through Freedom of Information Act (FOIA) requests filed by the American Immigration Council, Florence Immigrant and Refugee Rights Project, National Immigrant Justice Center, Kids in Need of Defense, and Women's Refugee Commission; and photographs published by the Associated Press.[9] Grounded theory facilitated inductive analysis of the data. In addition, we conduct an in-depth visual analysis of photographs that show the way coloniality of power produces visibility and invisibility among migrants. Ultimately, we argue, different processes of dehumanization brand Central American and Mexican children as neoliberal Others in the United States. This is the result of coloniality of power, which uses the ideology of illegality to mute outrage. We situate photographs as technologies of truth telling rooted in colonial methods of recordkeeping such as textual and visual documentation that function in service of the colonial project, never meant to benefit colonized groups, whose humanity has already been denied. We also analyze the ways that these photographs invoke affective responses resulting in divided public opinion as to the ethical responsibility of the United States.

Using Sara Ahmed's politics of recognition, we apply an affective analysis focused not on the children but on the way they are recognized within racist and anti-immigrant rhetoric. Ahmed's work situates the "stranger" as the mobile, racialized, classed, and gendered Other, distinguishable from the "native" (i.e., the ideal white citizen). Hence, the politics of recognition interlocks with truth-telling genres because these genres are colonial technologies that construct a visual economy for subjects to be seen. Both the stranger and the native are seen under the politics of recognition. Ahmed calls this dynamic "seeing in difference." She states, "I complicate recognition as 'seeing the difference' by considering the implications of the structural possibility that the difference might not be seeable as the subject may be passing."[10] Such difference resonates with Walter Mignolo's conception of "the colonial difference," defined as "the space where coloniality of power is enacted."[11] The coloniality of difference is the space where the human and the nonhuman struggle for survival within varying power differentials. For example, through the eyes of the American subject, the stranger, such as the Central American migrant child, is recognized as not belonging within the nation's borders. Ahmed explains, "the enforcement of boundaries requires that somebody—here locatable in the dirty figure of the stranger—has already crossed the line, has already come too close."[12] Ahmed's words are timely and relevant to Central American children, who are seen, labeled, and treated as "strangers" because their social exclusion renders their visible bodies not only out of place but less valuable than those of native citizens. The seeing of difference is an essential method for understanding the hierarchy of victimhood, where multiple groups of strangers, such as Central American and Mexican migrant children and transgender migrants, are forced to compete to be seen for their survival.

This chapter traces the way that the Trump administration (from the beginning of its term in 2017) designed family separation as a deterrent strategy, and the way that this strategy remained in place despite the horrendous, viral images of children in cages. We also chart the practice of family separation alongside colonial practices that have historically dehumanized families of color, to argue that today's caged children can be understood in the context of the brutality of coloniality, and that the visibility and invisibility of certain children produce hierarchies that obscure the cruelty of border enforcement. Finally, we contrast the treatment of white and nonwhite children to showcase the extent to which coloniality shapes the treatment of minors in the United States.

PRODUCING A CRISIS: ZERO TOLERANCE AND THE DEHUMANIZATION OF BROWN CHILDREN

On January 20, 2017, Donald Trump took office as president, and his administration immediately began to make plans to separate families as a deterrent strategy to prevent migration to the United States.[13] According to a *Washington Post* article, two weeks after Trump's inauguration, John Lafferty, the chief of asylum at U.S. Citizenship and Immigration Services, "raised the idea of using family separation as a deterrent in a town hall meeting for Citizenship and Immigration Services officials."[14]

Just over a year later, on April 6, 2018, Attorney General Jeff Sessions announced the Zero Tolerance policy, which meant that all people entering the United States without authorization would be prosecuted and subject to imprisonment. Given that children cannot be detained with adults, they were separated as minors/children. The policy, which was in place for about six weeks, from May 5 to June 20, resulted in the separation of 3,014 children, according to DHS.[15] (The American Civil Liberties Union places this number much higher, with more than 5,400 children separated from their families.)[16] Such cruelty can only be contextualized using a coloniality perspective: poor Brown children were traumatized to prevent them from entering the United States. From the beginning, the Trump administration framed its practice of family separation as a deterrent strategy.

The atrocities committed by the U.S. government were documented in the government records obtained through FOIA requests filed by the American Immigration Council, Florence Immigrant and Refugee Rights Project, National Immigrant Justice Center, Kids in Need of Defense, and Women's Refugee Commission.[17] They found that separation from parents was so traumatizing that clinicians recommended therapy for a twelve-year-old boy who had been separated from his mom. In addition, a form was found that stated that a nine-year-old female child had experienced "Abuse in DHS custody," without any other description or explanations. While in custody, children reported various forms of abuse. For example, several children reported physical assault, and one even reported being suicidal.[18] This abuse is systemic and so prevalent in DHS custody—even before the time of the Zero Tolerance policy—that more than 4,556 reports of sexual abuse or sexual harassment were filed between October 2014 and July 2018 with the Office of Refugee Resettlement (in the U.S. Department of Health and Human Services), which is charged with caring for unaccompanied minors.[19] In addition, reports by doctors and the media documented the gross neglect and inhumane conditions under which children were kept in detention. For example, Dr. Scott Allen and Dr. Pamela McPherson, experts for the DHS Office for Civil Rights and Civil Liberties, wrote a letter to Congress about atrocities witnessed:

In our time monitoring the existing family residential centers, we have uncovered significant weight loss in children that went largely unnoticed by the facility medical staff, including the case of a sixteen-month-old baby boy who lost 31.8% of his body weight over ten days during a diarrheal disease yet was never given IV fluids or sent out to an Emergency Room. In another case, we identified a 27-day-old infant who had been born in the field during the mother's journey. Having never been examined by a physician before, this infant was at extremely high risk for medical problems but was not seen by a pediatrician until the child had a seizure in the facility five days after arrival. He was subsequently diagnosed at an outside hospital with an intracranial bleed likely present since birth and missed by the facility on arrival due to inadequately trained staff. Another facility accidentally vaccinated numerous children with adult doses of vaccine as a result of poor interagency coordination and the unfamiliarity of the providers with pediatric dosing. We found numerous severe child finger injuries (including lacerations and fractures) due to the spring-loaded closure of heavy medical doors (the facility is a converted medium-security prison), and even when the problem was identified, mitigation efforts were slow and additional injuries occurred. In another case, we discovered that a facility was using the medical housing unit for punitive segregation of families and children, a violation of medical autonomy and a violation of standards of medical practice.[20]

These atrocities were further emphasized when Melania Trump, the First Lady of the United States, visited a detention center in June 2018. She wore a jacket that read, "I really don't care. Do U?," a statement that cynically and cruelly summarized the administration's response to the violence and suffering enacted on these children.[21] Given such cruelty, we examine how the media represented this violence and suffering.

THE HIERARCHIES OF CHILDHOOD SUFFERING

The arrival of immigrant children in the United States is not an entirely new phenomenon. In fact, the very first immigrant to arrive at the Ellis Island port of entry in 1892 was fifteen-year-old Annie Moore from Ireland.[22] The U.S. government sponsored the mass migration of children from Cuba (known as Operation Peter Pan) in 1960–1962, and from Vietnam (known as Operation Babylift) in 1975.[23] But from 2008 to 2014, the UN High Commissioner for Refugees reported a 1,185 percent increase in the number of asylum applications from citizens of El Salvador, Honduras, and Guatemala to Mexico, Panama, Nicaragua, Costa Rica, and Belize, signaling a mass migration of people being forced to move.[24] Yet, most of the attention in the news was on the "surge" of migrants from Central American countries, ignoring the fact that the largest group of children was from Mexico. From 2009 to 2014, the largest number of unaccompanied children detained by the U.S. Border Patrol were Mexican children, and in 2020, they were, again, the largest group of those detained (figure 13.1). But very little has been covered about Mexican children, in part because U.S. laws do not allow Mexican children to automatically seek asylum in the United States. Unaccompanied minors arriving to the United States have the right to seek relief from removal (and thus apply for asylum), unless they are from contiguous countries to the United States (i.e., Canada and Mexico), as children from these countries are not eligible.[25] Hence, the largest share of unaccompanied minors (those from Mexico) are excluded from these protections, erasing a more nuanced conversation about unaccompanied minors at the border in mainstream media.

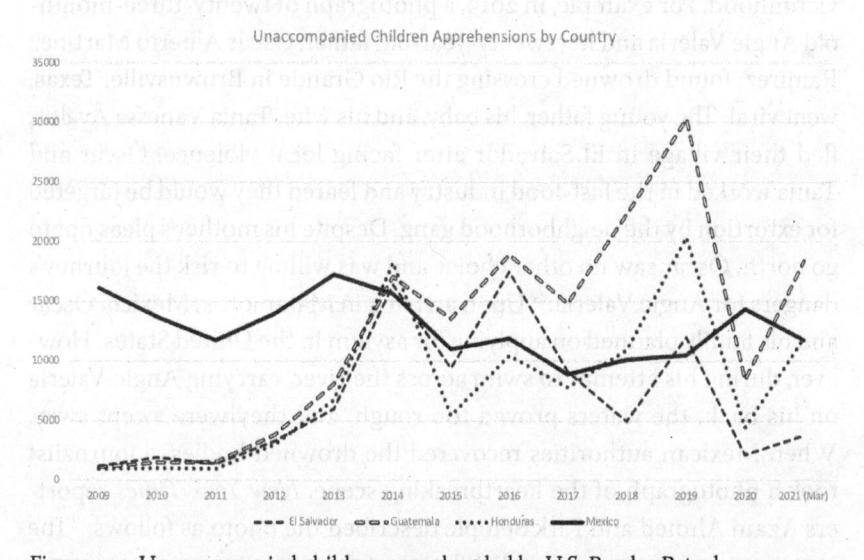

Figure 13.1. Unaccompanied children apprehended by U.S. Border Patrol, 2009–2021.

Under the Zero Tolerance policy, most children separated from their parents were from Guatemala (55.8 percent) and Honduras (33.2 percent).[26] These demographics are striking, given that previous research has denounced the fact that children are often labeled "Hispanic" despite the linguistic differences of Indigenous people.[27] Guatemalan children, for example, are likely to be disproportionately Indigenous, with unique linguistic needs. In the United States, race has decisively shaped family separation—from slavery to boarding schools, to the current foster care system, to the separation of families at the border.[28]

Under both the Obama and Trump administrations, the visibility of Central American immigrants increased substantially through photography. However, Mexican children did not experience the same visibility, despite facing similar genocidal threats in their home country. Photojournalism produces a spectacle framed within a nationalist divide that makes hypervisible unaccompanied children, caravans, and detention among Central Americans, while also rendering Mexican children invisible. In other words, hypervisibility enables a hierarchy of victimhood in which Central American migrants are placed above Mexican immigrants in terms of garnering media attention that speaks to their individual journeys and histories.

Mainstream photographs of migrants engender these hierarchies of victimhood. For example, in 2019, a photograph of twenty-three-month-old Angie Valeria and her twenty-year-old father, Óscar Alberto Martínez Ramírez, found drowned crossing the Rio Grande in Brownsville, Texas, went viral. The young father, his baby, and his wife, Tania Vanessa Ávalos, fled their village in El Salvador after facing local violence. Óscar and Tania worked in the fast-food industry and feared they would be targeted for extortion by the neighborhood gang. Despite his mother's pleas not to go north, Óscar saw no other choice and was willing to risk the journey's dangers for Angie Valeria.[29] Upon arriving in Matamoros, Mexico, Óscar and his family planned on applying for asylum in the United States. However, during his attempt to swim across the river, carrying Angie Valeria on his back, the waters proved too rough, and they were swept away. When Mexican authorities recovered the drowned bodies, a journalist took a photograph of the heartbreaking scene. *New York Times* reporters Azam Ahmed and Kirk Semple described the photo as follows: "The image represents a poignant distillation of the perilous journey migrants face on their passage north to the United States, and the tragic consequences that often go unseen in the loud and caustic debate over border policy."[30] This statement captures the suffering of a father and his baby girl. Their remark on the often "unseen" consequences of border policy poses a pressing question. Does *seeing* the pain and death of migrants such as Angie Valeria and Óscar make a difference among lawmakers and the broader American public?

Given the number of deaths at the border that seem to go "unseen" by the U.S. public (figure 13.2), it is imperative to understand how the innocence of children varies and is entrenched in white supremacist and neoliberal rhetoric. Millions of Americans read heartbreaking stories of terror and pain and witnessed images of children's faces in cages, yet few people called for mass mobilization or radical change regarding the policing of borders and the treatment of children.

In 2018, about half the U.S. population (51 percent) supported letting Central American refugees into the United States, while 54 percent of the U.S. public also reported that the level of immigration to the United States was already too high.[31] In this context of contradictory public opinion, the Trump administration enacted more than four hundred immigration policies rooted in racist and xenophobic nationalism.[32]

The asylum system suffered historical setbacks under the Trump administration, demonstrating how little change has taken place. Photos

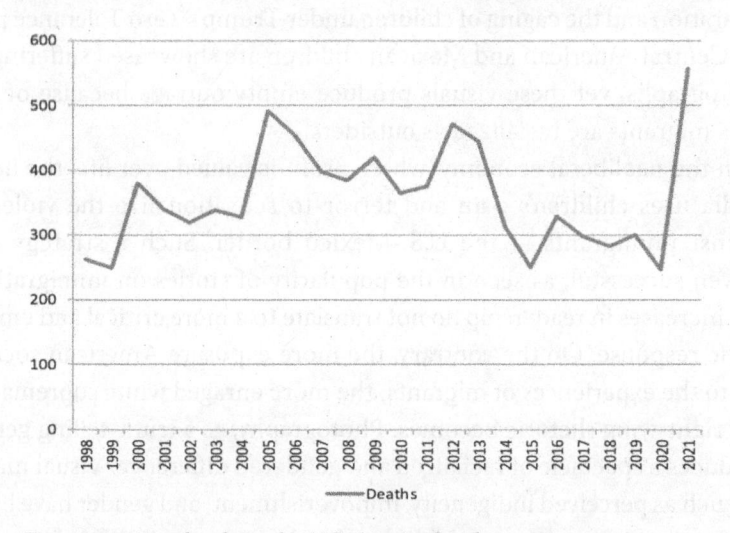

Figure 13.2. Deaths along the U.S.-Mexico border, 1998–2021.

of Central American children's fear, desperation, and death are not enough "evidence of suffering" to generate radical social change or abolition. The fact that terror expressed by children was "announced" from the beginning of the Trump administration further normalizes such dehumanization in the U.S. imaginary. In fact, placing children in cages continues to be practiced under the Biden administration.[33]

The acceptance of such horrendous acts on the bodies of children is justified by the ideology of illegality linked to law and order. Scholars have pointed out that policing and enforcement of the border are unjustifiable, but these practices have only escalated since the 1990s.[34] While Mexican mothers and children have been fleeing Mexico as long as Central Americans have been fleeing their home countries, at this moment in history they are invisible because they are ineligible to seek asylum. Yet, the visibility of Central American children is part of the media spectacle attached to stories of injustice and perseverance. Journalists focus on Central American data pertaining to the small number of children and mothers granted asylum. Few networks situate Central American migrants within a critical analysis of the unforgiving U.S. foreign policies responsible for pushing them out of their native countries, along with the immigration enforcement policies that have imposed cruel suffering on them and their families. The absence of newspaper articles regarding Mexican immigrant children erased them from the narrative of family separation and the caging of children under Trump's Zero Tolerance policy. Central American and Mexican children are showcased suffering in photographs, yet these visuals produce empty outrage because of the ways migrants are racialized as outsiders.

In the neoliberal economy, where profit is valued over life, the news media uses children's pain and terror to sensationalize the violence against immigrants at the U.S.-Mexico border. Such a strategy has proven successful, as seen in the popularity of stories on immigration. Yet, increases in readership do not translate to a more critical and empathetic response. On the contrary, the more exposure American society has to the experiences of migrants, the more enraged white supremacist and right-wing rhetoric becomes. Photography, as a truth-telling genre, produces a spectacle of racialized and gendered difference. Visual markers such as perceived indigeneity, impoverishment, and gender have been read as cues of "foreignness," "threats," and "economic burdens."

WHITE CHILDREN

The portrayal of Trump's family is also telling about the dehumanization of Brown and Black children in the United States. In the following analysis, we focus on a photograph of a white child to delineate the racialized experiences of Brown children and question the universality of childhood innocence. In this analysis, we juxtapose an image of the Trump family against the images of Central American and Mexican migrant families that the American readership has seen throughout news outlets and social media to highlight the different emotional responses that affective economies invoke for white, normative bodies and for those of Brown and Black immigrant children.

The photograph was published by the *Huffington Post* under the title, "Tristan, Donald Trump's Grandson, Is Desperately over This Whole Presidency Thing." The article poked fun at the first family by using the innocence of one of its youngest members, five-year-old Tristan Trump. In the picture, Tristan, one of Donald Trump Jr.'s five children, appears uninterested in what many Americans called "a historic day in American history": Trump's inauguration day, and the signing of his first executive orders. Tristan stood alongside his grandfather hours before the inaugural parade as the president signed his first executive order on January 20, 2017. The article stated, "Tristan wasn't the only kid wishing to be home playing Minecraft. His cousin and Ivanka Trump's daughter, Arabella Kushner, was also desperately bored."[35] In addition to the first family and the other children in the photograph—Tristan's siblings, cousins, and eleven-year-old uncle Barron Trump—vice president Mike Pence, wife Karen Pence, and Speaker of the House Paul Ryan were also present, among other influential politicians. The photographer expressed amusement over Tristan's innocence. Tristan's "Americanness" and whiteness are accentuated through phenotypic features such as his blond hair, blue eyes, and kinship within the presidential family. Donald Trump's family and political allies embody a campaign built on promises to protect white values and white life.

The picture focuses on the boredom of the children, symbolizing the essence of ideological and economic constructions of American family values. The whiteness and heteronormativity seen in the American political family spill out of the photo, and a haunting absence reminds us how unnatural the image is. Missing from the photograph are the racialized and gendered bodies that would very likely be affected by these signatures. This first signature event captured the enactment of executive order 13765, "Minimizing the Economic Burden of the Patient Protection and Affordable Care Act Pending Repeal," aimed to dismantle Obamacare, a policy designed to redistribute wealth in the United States.[36] The photo of the bored white child highlights the racial politics behind white anxiety and the demographic shifts in the United States; it is a symbolic signature with dire consequences for children of color, who tend to be disproportionately poor.

The second executive order signed by Trump was titled, "Expediting Environmental Reviews and Approvals for High Priority Infrastructure Projects," aimed at dismantling environmental protections; and his third executive order, "Border Security and Immigration Enforcement Improvements," aimed to "plan, design, and construct a physical wall along the southern border." Both of these orders would disproportionately affect people of color in the United States, with the latter being the basis for subsequent policies aimed at using any means necessary to stop adults and children from coming to the country.[37] This assemblage shows how the white childhood innocence afforded to Tristan is possible through the expulsion of the immigrant child. The Brown and Black child is constructed as a racial threat and robbed of their innocence because American family values are recognized effectively through white heteronormativity.

Not only are Tristan and the other Trump children granted the personhood to be bored and to have the desire to play, but their perceived innocence amid a significant political moment produces a particular affective identification. American audiences appeared to be entertained and even charmed at Tristan's behavior, expressing emotions of lightheartedness and enjoyment at the situation. For example, Trump Jr's tweet sharing the photo received thousands of retweets, and countless other users quote-tweeted it with comments such as "keeping it real," "I wanna go home," and "when their plans are boring, and you just wanna do your own thing."[38] In contrast, when American audiences see photographs of unaccompanied Central American immigrant children, they respond with hateful and racist-nativist emotions. Such reactions dehumanize BIPOC children and negate their innocence. The purity recognized in Trump's grandchildren humanizes them and gives them the privilege of being named, while many Central American children we see in photographs remain anonymous. The power of affective identification is one way the Trump family was politically and socially legitimized as representing the nation-state. Even though the massive media spectacle that had accompanied the migrant surge of 2014 was several years in the past at the time of the inauguration, images of migrant children remained ingrained in the memory of the American audience. Therefore, the Trump family acts as a proxy for the heart of neoliberal governmentality. In sum, the January 20 photograph provided a site of identification for American citizens at a moment of anxiety about who is acceptable within U.S. national borders.

Despite the thousands of photographs that circulated with children in cages, separated from their families, the bodies of Brown and Black immigrant children were read through colonial, racist, and xenophobic logics that imagined them as "illegal." These haunting photographic reminders of the suffering and unimaginable violence inflicted on vulnerable populations were not enough to incite a critical and radical social movement from the U.S. public to demand action.

NOTES

1. Moore, Park, and Almond, "This 2-Year-Old Has Become the Face of 'Zero Tolerance.'"
2. Maldonado-Torres, "On the Coloniality of Being," 244; Quijano, "Coloniality of Power, Eurocentrism, and Latin America," 535.
3. Maldonado-Torres, "Outline of Ten Theses on Coloniality and Decoloniality," 16.
4. For *bordering*, see Mignolo, *Local Histories/Global Designs*, 50–89.
5. Hesford, *Spectacular Rhetorics*.
6. Vargas, Maria Elena. "Forensic Injustice."
7. Quijano, "Coloniality of Power, Eurocentrism, and Latin America," 555.
8. Lugones, "The Coloniality of Gender."
9. See American Immigration Council, "Family Separation FOIA Request."
10. Ahmed, *Strange Encounters*, 31, 33.
11. Mignolo, *Local Histories/Global Designs*, ix.
12. Ahmed, *Strange Encounters*, 31.
13. Ainsley, "Trump Administration Considering Separating Women, Children."
14. Bump, "Here Are the Administration Officials."

15. The Zero Tolerance policy applied to offenses under 8 U.S.C. § 1325(a) (1994), which penalizes improper entry by unauthorized immigrants; see also U.S. Department of Homeland Security, Office of Inspector General, *DHS Lacked Technology Needed to Successfully Account for Separated Migrant Families.*

16. Spagat, "Tally of Children Split at Border Tops 5,400 in New Count."

17. American Immigration Council, "Family Separation FOIA Request."

18. American Immigration Council, "Government Documents on Family Separation."

19. Haag, "Thousands of Immigrant Children Said They Were Sexually Abused in US Detention Centers."

20. Allen and McPherson, letter to Charles E. Grassley and Ron Wyden, 3.

21. Rogers, "Melania Trump Wore a Jacket Saying 'I Really Don't Care.'"

22. Library of Congress, "Huddled Masses Yearning to Breathe Free."

23. On Operation Peter Pan, which brought more than fourteen thousand Cuban children to the United States, see Operation Pedro Pan, home page. On Operation Babylift, which lasted about sixteen days and brought thousands of Vietnamese babies to the United States, see Martin, "Remembering the Doomed First Flight of Operation Babylift."

24. UNHCR, "Children on the Run."

25. Lee et al., "Update on Legal Relief Options for Unaccompanied Alien Children."

26. ACLU, "Family Separation."

27. Gentry, *Exclusion of Indigenous Language Speaking Immigrants.*

28. Minoff, *Entangled Roots.*

29. Ahmed and Semple, "Photo of Drowned Migrants Captures Pathos."

30. Ahmed and Semple.

31. McCarthy, "U.S. Support for Central American Refugees Exceeds Norm."

32. Migration Policy Institute, "New MPI Report Catalogs the 400-Plus Immigration Executive Actions."

33. Sheehy, "White House Releases Heartbreaking Photos from Inside Child Detention Sites."

34. Nevins, "Thinking Out of Bounds."

35. Abedi, "Tristan, Donald Trump's Grandson, Is Desperately Over This Whole Presidency Thing."

36. Trump, "Minimizing the Economic Burden of the Patient Protection and Affordable Care Act Pending Repeal"; and see Mindo, "Obamacare and the Fight Against Income Inequality."

37. Trump, "Expediting Environmental Reviews and Approvals for High Priority Infrastructure Projects"; Trump, "Border Security and Immigration Enforcement Improvements."

38. Donald Trump Jr. (@DonaldJTrumpJr), "Surrounded by family @realDonaldTrump signs his first orders yesterday. I think Tristan just wanted to go play," Twitter, January 21, 2017, 5:05 p.m., https://twitter.com/DonaldJTrumpJr/status/822943177900486656.

BIBLIOGRAPHY

Abedi, Maham. "Tristan, Donald Trump's Grandson, Is Desperately Over This Whole Presidency Thing." *HuffPost*, January 21, 2017. https://www.huffpost.com/archive/ca/entry/14291666.

ACLU (American Civil Rights Union). "Family Separation: By the Numbers." October 2, 2018. https://www.aclu.org/issues/family-separation.

Ahmed, Azam, and Kirk Semple. "Photo of Drowned Migrants Captures Pathos of Those Who Risk It All." *New York Times*, June 25, 2019.

Ahmed, Sara. *Strange Encounters: Embodied Others in Post-Coloniality*. London: Routledge, 2013.

Ainsley, Julia Edwards. "Trump Administration Considering Separating Women, Children at Mexico Border." Reuters, March 3, 2017.

Allen, Scott, and Pamela McPherson. Letter to Charles E. Grassley and Ron Wyden of the Senate Whistleblowing Caucus, July 17, 2018. https://www.wyden.senate.gov/imo/media/doc/Doctors%20Congressional%20Disclosure%20SWC.pdf.

American Immigration Council. "Family Separation FOIA Request." April 3, 2018. https://www.americanimmigrationcouncil.org/foia/family-separation-foia-request.

American Immigration Council. "Government Documents on Family Separation: Tracking the Policy's Evolution, Implementation, and Harm." Last modified March 17, 2020. https://www.americanimmigrationcouncil.org/FOIA/government-documents-family-separation-tracking-policys-evolution-implementation-and-harm.

Bump, Philip. "Here Are the Administration Officials Who Have Said That Family Separation Is Meant as a Deterrent." *Washington Post*, June 19, 2018.

Gentry, Blake. *Exclusion of Indigenous Language Speaking Immigrants in the US Immigration System, a Technical Review*. Ama Consultants, May 2015. http://www.amaconsultants.org/uploads/Exclusion_of_Indigenous%20Languages_in_US_Immigration_System_19_June2015version_i.pdf.

Haag, Matthew. "Thousands of Immigrant Children Said They Were Sexually Abused in US Detention Centers, Report Says." *New York Times*, February 27, 2019.

Hesford, Wendy S. *Spectacular Rhetorics: Human Rights Visions, Recognitions, Feminisms*. Durham, N.C.: Duke University Press, 2011.

Lee, Deborah, Manoj Govindaiah, Angela D. Morrison, and David Thronson. "Update on Legal Relief Options for Unaccompanied Alien Children Following the Enactment of the William Wilberforce Trafficking Victims Protection." Texas A&M Law Scholarship, February 19, 2009. https://scholarship.law.tamu.edu/facscholar/820/.

Library of Congress. "Huddled Masses Yearning to Breathe Free." Today in History for January 1. Accessed May 15, 2023. https://www.loc.gov/item/today-in-history/january-01/.

Lugones, Maria. "The Coloniality of Gender." In *The Palgrave Handbook of Gender and Development*, edited by Wendy Harcourt, 13–33. London: Palgrave Macmillan, 2016.

Maldonado-Torres, Nelson. "On the Coloniality of Power: Contributions to the Development of a Concept." *Cultural Studies* 21, no. 2–3 (2007): 240–70.

Maldonado-Torres, Nelson. "Outline of Ten Theses on Coloniality and Decoloniality." Fondation Frantz Fanon, October 2016. http://fondation-frantzfanon.com/wp -content/uploads/2018/10/maldonado-torres_outline_of_ten_theses-10.23.16.pdf.

Martin, Rachel. "Remembering the Doomed First Flight of Operation Babylift." *Weekend Edition Sunday.* NPR, April 26, 2015. https://www.npr.org/2015/04/26/ 402208267/.

McCarthy, Justin. "U.S. Support for Central American Refugees Exceeds Norm." Gallup, December 20, 2018. https://news.gallup.com/poll/245624/support-central -american-refugees-exceeds-norm.aspx.

Mignolo, Walter D. *Local Histories/Global Designs: Coloniality, Subaltern Knowledges and Border Thinking.* Princeton, N.J.: Princeton University Press, 2000.

Migration Policy Institute. "New MPI Report Catalogs the 400-Plus Immigration Executive Actions That Have Occurred During the Trump Presidency." Press release, July 31, 2020. https://www.migrationpolicy.org/news/mpi-report-catalogs -immigration-executive-actions-trump-presidency.

Mindo, Perry T., Jr. "Obamacare and the Fight Against Income Inequality." *Undergraduate Economic Review* 13, no. 1 (2016): article 19. https://digitalcommons.iwu .edu/uer/vol13/iss1/19.

Minoff, Elisa. *Entangled Roots: The Role of Race in Policies That Separate Families.* Center for the Study of Social Policy, October 2018. https://cssp.org/wp-content/ uploads/2018/11/CSSP-Entangled-Roots.pdf.

Moore, John, Madison Park, and Kyle Almond. "This 2-Year-Old Has Become the Face of 'Zero Tolerance.'" *CNN*, June 12, 2018. https://www.cnn.com/interactive/ 2018/06/us/crying-girl-john-moore-immigration-cnnphotos/.

Nevins, Joseph. "Thinking Out of Bounds: A Critical Analysis of Academic and Human Rights Writings on Migrant Deaths in the U.S.-Mexico Border Region." *Migraciones internacionales* 2, no. 2 (2003): 171–90.

Operation Pedro Pan. Home page. Accessed May 15, 2023. https://www.pedropan .org/.

Quijano, Aníbal. "Coloniality of Power, Eurocentrism, and Latin America." Translated by Michael Ennis. *Nepantla: Views from South* 1, no. 3 (2000): 533–80.

Rogers, Katie. "Melania Trump Wore a Jacket Saying 'I Really Don't Care' on Her Way to Texas Shelters." *New York Times*, June 21, 2018.

Sheehy, Kate. "White House Releases Heartbreaking Photos from Inside Child Detention Sites." *New York Post*, March 23, 2021.

Spagat, Elliot. "Tally of Children Split at Border Tops 5,400 in New Count." *PBS NewsHour*, October 25, 2019. https://www.pbs.org/newshour/nation/tally-of-children -split-at-border-tops-5400-in-new-count.

Trump, Donald J. "Border Security and Immigration Enforcement Improvements." Exec. order 13767, January 25, 2017. American Presidency Project. https://www .presidency.ucsb.edu/node/322155.

Trump, Donald J. "Expediting Environmental Reviews and Approvals for High Priority Infrastructure Projects." Exec. order 13766, January 24, 2017. https://www.presidency.ucsb.edu/node/322146.

Trump, Donald J. "Minimizing the Economic Burden of the Patient Protection and Affordable Care Act Pending Repeal." Exec. order 13765, January 20, 2017. American Presidency Project. https://www.presidency.ucsb.edu/node/322095.

UNHRC (UN Refugee Agency). "Children on the Run." Accessed May 15, 2023. https://www.unhcr.org/us/children-run.

U.S. Department of Homeland Security, Office of Inspector General. *DHS Lacked Technology Needed to Successfully Account for Separated Migrant Families*. OIG-20–06. November 25, 2019.

Vargas, Maria Elena. "Forensic Injustice: Human Rights, Archival Science and Racialized Feminicide in Guatemala." PhD diss., University of Maryland, 2016.

14

MIGRANT CHILDREN AND THE CARCERAL STATE IN THE COMIC BOOK *HOME*

JOSÉ ENRIQUE NAVARRO

THE CULTURAL EXPRESSION OF A given society often constitutes a commentary on its way of life, its political system, and its ghosts. A case in point could be *Home*, a monthly comic book miniseries published in the United States in 2021, shortly after the end of the presidential term of Donald Trump (2017–21). This comic book was produced by a multinational team: the script was written by Latinx author Julio Anta, the art was by Polish cartoonist Anna Wieszczyk, the coloring was overseen by Bryan Valenza from Indonesia, and the lettering was the work of Algerian British graphic designer Hassan Otsmane-Elhaou. While standard practice with comic books is for the cover to showcase merely the work of the writer and artist, *Home* featured the colorist and letterer as well, perhaps indicating an awareness that when so many individuals contribute to the configuration of a cultural product, their sensibilities inevitably permeate the final work. Having such a diverse artistic team is of great relevance in a comic that delves into the meaning of otherness.

Home follows the story of Juan, a young Guatemalan boy who seeks asylum with his mother, Mercedes, at the U.S. border in Texas. It is a contemporary story that takes place after the Zero Tolerance policy toward immigrants was implemented in 2018. This policy called for the criminal prosecution of all individuals who entered the United States without authorization, and it led to the separation of families at the border. Hence, the comic portrays the incarceration of the mother and her son, their subsequent forced separation, and the deportation of Mercedes. The final two chapters focus on the persecution of Juan by U.S. Immigration and Customs Enforcement (ICE) agents in Houston, after he manages to escape the detention center thanks to his recently manifested superhuman abilities.

This chapter examines how the comic book, through the joint effort of the team behind it, succeeds in portraying the transformation of the border region between the United States and Mexico into a carceral state, that is, one in which "the powers to police and punish drive the boundaries and borders of everyday life."[1] In this sense, *Home* constitutes one of those "potent new imaginaries" that, according to Gilberto Rosas, have emerged in conjunction with the intensified state of exception lived in the borderlands.[2] The miniseries portrays diverse forms of state-sanctioned violence that dehumanize migrants and show how white supremacy and toxic masculinity go hand in hand with migrant criminalization. Both physical and symbolic violence permeate the relationships between migrants and their captors (in "iceboxes" and detention centers) or persecutors (ICE agents).

THE CARCERAL STATE

The hardening of the border comes as the result of a series of U.S. federal regulations that in recent decades have normalized both the construction of border walls and the expedition of deportation proceedings. These policies have also increased the number of migrant deaths, incarcerations, and removals at the southern border. It is worth noting that apprehensions happen not only in the frontier region itself but also in the "100-mile border zone," or the land within one hundred miles of a U.S. land or coastal border—an area that encompasses almost 200 million people, two-thirds of the U.S. population.[3] This explains why the protagonist of *Home* is persecuted by ICE agents (an interior enforcement mission) after he arrives in Houston. This set of regulations has allowed agencies such as the U.S. Department of Homeland Security (DHS) to bypass diverse pieces of federal legislation, including environmental laws and even protections on Indigenous access to sacred sites, to erect barriers. Such actions exemplify a recent recurring practice at the border, in which "the sacralized discourse of public safety desacralizes people, places, and landscapes."[4]

Several scholars have associated this process with sovereignty, conceptualized as the power to institute states of exception.[5] The legal concept of "exception" was first developed in the 1920s by German thinker Carl Schmitt and later reexamined by two contemporary philosophers, Giorgio Agamben and Achille Mbembe. Schmitt defines the state of exception as the sovereign's power to suspend the rule of law as a means of safeguarding the common good. This arises from what he describes as the sovereign's "monopoly of the final decision."[6] Schmitt's formulation has led to the articulation of two complementary, yet subtly divergent, concepts. On the one hand, Agamben, much in line with Michel Foucault's definition of biopolitics as a complex form of state power that focuses on its population, considers the state of exception to be an expression of how political power may decide on the value of human life.[7] Meanwhile, Mbembe goes further than Agamben and underscores the sovereign's necropower, or "right to kill."[8] Two programs implemented in the last three decades at the border, the "deterrence strategy" and the "consequence approach," could be considered as examples of states of exception. The former, which stems from the mid-1990s, created and expanded surveillance and physical barriers in certain sections of the border. The aim was to force migrants to opt for alternative, more dangerous migratory routes. Since crossing a desert entails extreme temperatures, the presence of venomous animals, and longer distances to reach the border, these alternative routes resulted in a significant increase in the number of migrants who died on their journey to the United States. The second program, the "consequence approach," which was put into practice in the early 2010s, encourages, among other measures, the deportation and incarceration of undocumented immigrants, whether they are detained at the border or inside the United States. Another outcome of this program is the naturalization of practices such as speedy and collective trials, the separation of families, and the internment of minors in prisons. *Home* deals precisely with the aftermath of the "consequence approach" and the U.S. criminalization of irregular migration.

Economic pressures are important forces in this legal framework. The intensification of boundary policing in the last decades has gone hand in hand with a shift to neoliberal forms of government. As a result, the tightening of U.S. immigration and refugee law has benefited certain economic sectors, such as the prison-industrial complex. As Gregory L. Cuéllar notes, immigrant family detention has created a booming market, with significant benefits for private prison companies. In fact, in addition to the government revenue they receive from the state in exchange for their services (transportation and imprisonment), these corporations frequently exploit border crossers as a cheap source of forced labor, for salaries as low as a dollar a day.[9] These families are then deported and replaced by others, following a scheme that creates a constant flow of wealth for the prison-industrial complex. This has led Daniel E. Martínez and Jeremy Slack to state that in detention facilities the commodification of the imprisoned body goes beyond simply the surplus value of labor.[10] Likewise, the increasing privatization of war, with countries turning over their warfare operations to private contractors, has led, in the context of the war on terror, to significant employment of private military and security firms at the border. The militarization of the border, which entails "the use of military rhetoric and ideology, as well as military tactics, strategy, technology, equipment, and forces," would represent a further step in the reconfiguration of the U.S.-Mexico transborder region into what Arturo J. Aldama describes as a "free zone of violence."[11]

BARBED WIRES AND THE LONGING FOR A HOME

Several elements in *Home*, in addition to the plot, are worth examining. Wieszczyk's drawing style and the page layouts she presents, along with Valenza's color palette and Otsmane-Elhaou's lettering, help convey more than what meets the eye. The work of these and other individuals, including cover artists Lisa Sterle and Jacoby Salcedo as well as logo designer Dylan Todd, converges not only in the interior pages of the comic book but also on its cover. Both logo and cover are elements that could fit within Gérard Genette's concept of the paratext, that is, a textual or nontextual element that accompanies, reinforces, and presents the main text. As an accompaniment to the main text, the paratext serves as a framework for the work, providing the text with a setting while also advancing its intention.

In Genette's words, paratexts sometimes provide the text with "a commentary."[12] This is precisely what Todd's logo for *Home* does. Placed on the left side of the cover, this large logo strictly follows the rule of thirds, occupying a third of the cover's length. With its four large letters crossed with barbed wire, the title communicates the sense of homelessness that undocumented migrants ordinarily suffer. Home, wherever it may be, is a place too risky and hazardous to approach, full of thorns, with entry barred by a wired fence. In the case of Juan and his mother, Mercedes, who left their home country fleeing violence from the street gangs that have plagued Guatemala and other Central American countries, this feeling of homelessness endures even after they reach a point of entry in McAllen, Texas.[13] As we learn later in the story through a flashback, their decision to migrate came after Juan's father, Armando, was killed for refusing to join a local gang.[14] Yet when they turn themselves in as asylum seekers at the border, they are incarcerated, separated, and persecuted.

These circumstances force the protagonists to recalibrate what home means to them. In the opening pages of the comic, as they are approaching the border, Mercedes explains to her son that their trip is about to end and that they will soon be reunited with his Aunt Gladys, Armando's sister. After a panel that depicts them hugging and Juan smiling, a splash page, or full-page panel, shows a long shot with the mother and her son, hand in hand, approaching the pedestrian access to the McAllen-Hidalgo-Reynosa International Bridge. For the first time in the comic, the sun makes its appearance, crowning a slightly cloudy, pastel green sky. Mercedes tells Juan (with colored lettering to denote that they are speaking in Spanish), "Let's go home."[15] For Mercedes, home lies on the other side of the border, in U.S. territory, where some of their relatives live. However, as the story unfolds, Juan seems to reject identifying the United States as a home. After being separated from his mother, he escapes the detention center on the outskirts of San Antonio, and as he runs into the forest in the middle of the night, he tearfully laments, "I just want to go *home*."[16] This stated desire to go home is ambiguous; he does not say which place he means. In fact, the next morning Juan has two conflicting memories while walking in the forest. After he says to himself that he wishes he "could just go back to Guatemala," he remembers the morning his mother woke him up and told him lovingly that it was time to get dressed because they were leaving the country. But immediately afterward, as he sights a clearing in the woods, he remembers their arrival at the U.S. point of entry and his mother's telling him that, with the help of his Aunt Gladys, they were "going to start a whole new life" in America, and that it was "going to be great." Those are Juan's only two memories in the comic book of Guatemala and the grueling journey to Texas.

Interestingly, *Home*'s protagonists do not show any nostalgia for Guatemala. Juan does not seem to have left behind any cherished people or places. The only other character who has memories of Central America is Gladys. Through two flashbacks, the reader learns how her brother, Armando, discovered his superhuman abilities in his childhood and how he was killed much later, when Juan was a child.[17] The first memory is evoked with a certain fondness. This flashback happens shortly after Mercedes is deported and Juan manages to find Gladys. The two sisters-in-law talk on the phone, and when Gladys tells Mercedes about Juan's newfound powers, Mercedes rekindles the support Armando found in his sister, who helped him control his abilities when they were children. Gladys now promises Mercedes she will do the same again, this time with her nephew. The final panel of this first, brief, half-page flashback is composed of two images: the one on the left shows the siblings hugging, and the one on the right, Mercedes talking on the phone. The memory of her dead husband brings tears to her eyes. In sum, in the comic, memories from Guatemala end up always being painful and traumatic. For that reason, it could be argued that in the end both Mercedes, who is repatriated, and her son realize that no matter how much they are longing for it, they have no home—thus, the appropriateness of the title of the comic book as it delves into what this seemingly simple word and concept mean for undocumented migrants in our present time. The barbed wire that runs through it is a visual representation of the myriad obstacles (legal, economic, and physical, to name only a few) that the protagonists, a broken family, must overcome.

RENDERING VIOLENCE FROM COVER TO COVER

It could also be argued that the wire that, in a sense, rips across the letters of the logo typifies the border and its effects. The title or logo usually appears on the cover of a publication in conjunction with other elements, such as the name of its author or authors and an illustration. Following a marketing strategy that started in comic books in the mid-1980s for the collectible market, *Home* was published in different editions, with the same content but varying covers. Each issue of the comic book was printed with two different covers, featuring cover art by two different artists: Sterle did the regular shipping covers, or the A covers, and Salcedo did the alternative covers, also known as the B covers. Sterle's cover for the first issue of *Home* depicts a youngster and a woman walking along some old railroad tracks. They carry a backpack and a travel bag, and they are not alone: the background features a man and a woman, as well as some greenery. The woman and child seem to have paused for a minute and are standing, looking back at the reader with a serious expression, as if wanting to assert their presence. In the context of this cover, the barbed wire operates as an obvious symbol of the border and exclusion. But a closer look may point to the idea that the wire functions here as a metonymy for the structures and practices inherent in the fortified U.S. border with Mexico. This means that it is possible to establish a connotative relationship between the two terms and associate the barbed wire with the hardening of the border, which in turn is plausibly related to violence. The metonymy unfolds in at least two different but related ways. On the one hand, the wire is an object that does not belong to nature, but rather was created by humans. And although these humans are not displayed, the reader could associate the one with the other, with those who installed it. The barbed wire is hence a tool or instrument that represents a job or those who perform it. On the other hand, the wire is also the final product of the process of fencing off one population from another and is just one means of preventing people such as Juan and Mercedes from entering. In this vein, the wire stands for an activity. In both cases, a relationship of contiguity between two objects or ideas can be established.

This association of ideas is even clearer in cover B, by Mexican American artist Salcedo.[18] It depicts Juan with a grim expression, standing in front of a chain-link fence. In the background, on the right, the American flag waves in a dark sky. He is in U.S. territory, and his glowing hands, indicative of his superpower, are grabbing the fence. The cover art employs a low-angle perspective, also known as worm's-eye view. The portrayed subjects are viewed from below, causing the effect of magnifying the depicted object or character.[19] The use of this perspective on *Home*'s cover produces the opposite effect, given that Juan looks anything but dominant, powerful, or confident. Whereas the low-angle perspective should portray Juan as a hero, what the reader perceives instead is a helpless, anxiety-ridden, incarcerated child. This paradoxical, yet dramatical and effective, usage of the low-angle perspective not only undermines the conventions of the superhero genre—which will be discussed later in this chapter—but also reinforces the sense of homelessness.

For all these reasons it can be argued that Salcedo's cover is more straightforward in its representation of the themes and issues that *Home* tackles. It would be possible to speculate that its standing as an alternative or variant cover may be a consequence of the highly—and increasingly—polarized political atmosphere in the United States. In this sense, in a note that closes the first issue of the comic book, author Julio Anta explains that the idea of the comic book arose as a reaction to the separation of families at the border, but also to the "lack of Latinx heroes in American comics."[20] The language in this one-page text is profoundly emotional and demonstrates a deep concern on Anta's side. He states that he is "horrified" and defines the situation as "enraging," and its consequences as "real horrors." The last paragraph, though, aims to share with readers a sense of hope and optimism. As Anta puts it, "it's not all sad and desperate." Perhaps this brief note epitomizes at its best the subtle balance that this comic book had to strike when it hit the shelves. Curiously enough, in a second note, printed in the next issue of the comic book, Anta recalls how the project was repeatedly rejected by indie comic book publishers: "Some publishers told me they thought it was 'important work' but 'too political' for them, others kindly passed, and of course, some ignored the pitch completely."[21] These unsettling experiences may also help explain the contrast between the overall action-packed but uncritical approach of the covers and the cruelty that the story reveals as it unfolds inside the comic book.[22] For instance, the first issue narrates the incarceration and separation of several families, including a nursing infant and her mother, and the reclusion of Juan in a solitary cell after he is discovered, in the cell he shares with others, eating an orange he was served for dinner.

Still, the set of covers drawn by Sterle and Salcedo communicate to the reader the suffering experienced by both Juan and his U.S.-based extended family. For example, the cover art points recurrently to the threat of a faceless armed DHS agent (issue 2, both versions) that leaves the protagonists with only two options: either escape (Juan is always on the run in this comic, as shown on cover A of issue 4) or fend off ICE agents' attacks, most frequently with the help of extended family members (his Aunt Gladys on both covers for issue 3, and his cousins Camila and Andres on cover B of issue 5). The number of covers that depict the protagonists being fired on and using their powers to protect themselves is remarkable. In this regard, *Home*'s covers illustrate another recurrent motive that the story explores as well: the persecution undocumented immigrants are subject to in the hundred-mile border zone and the emotional toll it takes. Characters in the comic book adopt invisibility as their strategy to avoid detection. The next section of this chapter analyzes how *Home* makes visible what desires to go unnoticed: on the one hand, the reality of migrant prisons disguised as—in Ordaz's words—"non-punitive holding centers" and, on the other, the invisibility migrants seek to achieve.[23]

VISIBILIZING VIOLENCE

The story of *Home* takes place at the time the Zero Tolerance policy was announced and implemented. In fact, the comic book opens with a sequence of panels that in three pages outline Juan and Mercedes's journey from the moment they leave Guatemala City until their arrival at the border. These initial pages depict mother and son taking a bus, sleeping under open skies with others, riding atop one of the freight trains that cross Mexico and are known as La Bestia, and getting into the box of a crowded truck that they later step out of. In lieu of dialogue, the only text that accompanies these images is a series of captions reproducing a memorandum that the comic attributes to the attorney general of the United States, with information on the implementation of the Zero Tolerance policy. The memorandum quotes "the President"—with no further indication of his identity—asserting that "when Mexico sends its people, they're not sending their best," and accusing those newcomers of being drug dealers, criminals, and rapists. This statement obviously replicates the words Donald J. Trump spoke in the speech that launched his electoral campaign in summer 2017.[24] Frederick Luis Aldama notes that "comics do engage and elicit a response."[25] At times that response might not be the one the author was expecting. Probably because of the inclusion of the alleged memorandum, some branded *Home* as an "anti-Trump comic" or "open borders propaganda."[26] This reductionist view overshadows one of the main merits of this graphic narrative, namely, that it makes visible what has attempted to remain unseen: the methods and strategies employed to enforce immigration restrictions and their effects.

Half a century ago, in 1972, Reinhold Reitberger and Wolfgang Fuchs stated that comics, like any mass media, can mirror both "changes in public taste and ideological conflicts."[27] Consequently, when a comic tackles a given theme or topic, it is plausible to consider that this correlates or responds to a growing social concern. While the imprisonment of immigrant children started as a practice in 1981 under Ronald Reagan, the leaking of images and sound recordings in 2018 that showed the separation of families and the incarceration of minors at the U.S.-Mexico border sparked exceptional outrage and numerous protests.[28] Nevertheless, those images and sound recordings offered only a fragmentary account of what was happening in migrant detention facilities. As such, they could be considered as snippets of reality. Julio Anta uses these unconnected pieces to build a plausible narrative that contextualizes the imprisonment, separation, deportation, and persecution that Central American families have suffered at the border as well as in the U.S. interior. Michelle Brown explains that, in their depictions, conventional carceral images reduce carceral subjects to perpetrators or victims. Counterimages—or, in the present case, counternarratives—ought to "show people as having a history of belonging, now caught in life and death distinctions of law and citizenship, often in direct relation with state violence."[29] *Home* does so by chronicling the vicissitudes that led Mercedes and Juan to seek asylum in the United States.

In addition, the comic sketches the lives that their relatives Gladys, Andres, and Camila have in Houston. Gladys is portrayed as a nurse, a recent immigrant niche for Central Americans due to the expansion of the health-care sector and the labor shortages it has produced, and her children as college students.[30] Gladys is the tie that connects Mercedes to the United States. In Mercedes's first interview with DHS officials, she claims: "We didn't sneak across the border. We have family here that's ready to take us in, help me get work, and send my son Juan to school."[31] From a narrative point of view, Gladys needs to exist for various reasons. First, from the beginning of the story she represents the future. Gladys and Houston are the future for Mercedes, the reason she embarked with her son on their journey. Second, she is a sympathetic figure, an industrious single mother who serves as a felicitous counterpart to the heteronormative hard-working family men that, according to Jeremy Slack, Daniel E. Martínez, and Scott Whiteford, populate pro-immigrant discourses and accounts.[32]

Their helplessness, too, makes Mercedes and Juan sympathetic figures, counterbalancing the hegemonic representation of migrants as criminals. In sum, these characters and circumstances help create a context that pushes Mercedes and Juan beyond the prototypical image of carceral subjects. In the specific case of Juan, he becomes a sympathetic figure not only because of his vulnerability as a child, but also because he demonstrates that he is a hero. In the first three issues of the comic, he uses his superpowers—such as his energy blasts and his superspeed—only to defend himself or to escape from his persecutors. However, in issue 4 Juan is playing soccer with other children in Gladys's neighborhood and saves one of them when the boy is about to be run over by a car. All the children are stunned by Juan's speed and wonder how he could run so fast. On a corner, a white, blonde female in sunglasses and a gray jacket calls 911 to report that "something is not right with one of the Spanish kids in my neighborhood."[33] This almost faceless citizen informant puts ICE on the track of Juan's whereabouts. Juan's rescue of his peer makes him fit some parameters of the superhero genre, defined as having a mission of "act[ing] selflessly to aid others in times of need" when using his extraordinary powers.[34] Even so, Juan has neither a code name nor an iconic costume, which means that he is missing one of the triad of core conventions present in the superhero genre: mission, powers, and identity.[35] That Juan is not entirely defined as a superhero also corresponds to Image Comics' editorial line in the last decade, which has prioritized the publication of fantasy, sci-fi, horror, and crime series over superhero stories. Still, and following Peter Coogan's terminology, Juan the superhero could be defined as "a hero that has powers" rather than "a superhero genre protagonist."[36]

Juan's superhuman abilities have several implications, beyond the fact that he becomes in some sense a hero. They also alienate him further: not only is he a foreigner and a migrant, but he is also someone with abilities that place him, and several family members, above other humans. As a result, Juan, his aunt, and his cousins are viewed as different, which causes fear and rejection. When Juan escapes from the child detention center in San Antonio, he flees upon encountering a young African American guard. "He just ran—faster than I've ever seen anyone run," recounts the guard. The next panel is a close-up shot, which is usually employed to focus on the facial expression of a character to help communicate their emotions. In this case, it depicts the guard, apparently in some distress. "It was *scary*," he adds.[37] A similar feeling impels a middle-aged white man to call 911 when he sees Gladys helping Juan control his powers in the forest.[38] The man, in a similar fashion to the other citizen informant in the comic book, is hidden behind a tree, wearing a green jacket and bucket hat that shadows his face. While Juan is by no means an extraterrestrial alien, his abilities may resemble one. In any event, Juan (like any other sci-fi outer space Other, either destructive or sympathetic) will be perceived as a threat and will need to "be eliminated—either lovingly, by returning them to their native environs . . . or violently, by destroying them."[39] This is precisely what happens after Gladys and Juan confront the police in the forest and get away after stunning the officers momentarily. Once this information is reported to ICE, a decision is made to consider Juan "a serious threat to the security" of the United States. "We need to find this kid and *terminate* him," the nameless white, blond, male chief of the ICE Houston Field Office angrily asserts in his morning briefing.[40] The rhetoric used by this character ("menace," "terminate") belongs to the realm of the military. Likewise, the identification of Juan as a national threat defines him as a counterinsurgent, a military mantra that, according to Nicholas Mirzoeff, "means to remove insurgents from a locality using lethal force, then to sustain that expulsion by physical means such as walls, and finally to build neoliberal governance in the resulting space of circulation."[41] From a narrative point of view, Juan's superhuman abilities help advance the plot. Otherwise, *Home* would probably have revolved around Mercedes and Juan's imprisonment and later repatriation, and Juan would never have had an encounter with ICE agents. In other words, if the protagonist hadn't had superpowers, the reader would have witnessed a lesser amount of violence.

One possible analysis of the various instances of violence to which the protagonists are subjected is to make use of the taxonomy developed by Norwegian sociologist Johan Galtung. He distinguishes between direct or personal violence, indirect or structural violence, and cultural violence. Direct or personal violence may be defined as violence that is visible and carried out by an identifiable perpetrator. Meanwhile, structural or indirect violence is of a collective nature, and cannot be attributed to an identifiable individual. It originates within the political and economic system and manifests itself in the form of social imbalances or inequalities. Finally, cultural violence is defined as any aspect of a culture that can be used to give rise to the previous two.[42]

Home includes several actual instances of personal violence, along with attempts at violence that are repulsed by the superpowered characters that populate this narrative. Most episodes of personal violence take place at the beginning of the story, at the icebox or the child detention center. This aligns with Foucault's conceptualization of the prison as a "primary tool of normalizing violence in the contemporary era."[43] In these carceral spaces, violence permeates not only the relationships between the migrants and the guards, but also those among the guards themselves. Most of the guards are white men, and only those of color show some leniency or compassion toward the migrants. Such is the case, for example, of the African American female prison employee who unsuccessfully asks her white male colleague whether they can allow a mother to breastfeed her child before they are separated. The man responds harshly: "What do you mean? Grab the damn kid . . . *now!*"[44] This same guard reads the next name on the list, "Juan Gomez," and when Mercedes tries to block his way to protect Juan, she is simply shoved aside. The other Brown icebox guard depicted in the comic is Humberto, a mestizo whose main role is to serve as a Spanish interpreter for migrants who do not speak English. The reader sees Humberto interact only with Mercedes, and he does so respectfully, addressing her by her first name and sometimes accompanying his requests with the word "please." He seems to try to be as empathetic as possible. On several occasions, he is portrayed looking down, as if he were concerned. For example, thanks to another Spanish-speaking migrant, Felipe, Mercedes learns about the Zero Tolerance policy, which was implemented while she was on the road. Mercedes then asks a dejected Humberto about this, but he cannot provide much information and simply states: "Listen, things have changed recently. . . ." This attitude contrasts with the coldness of his superior, a white man who seems tired of dealing with migrants.[45] For instance, when they are interviewing Mercedes, she asks in anger where her son is, and the higher-ranking agent orders Humberto, pointing a finger at him, to tell Mercedes to simply answer the questions. Later, again pointing the finger at Humberto, he commands him to "get her out of here."[46] These examples suggest the existence of a race-based hierarchy inside the icebox, which, in turn, would constitute a legacy of colonialism.

The racial divide depicted in the icebox replicates and is intensified both at the children's detention center and in all subsequent interactions between Juan, the white people he encounters, and the ICE workforce. There is, however, one exception that keeps *Home* from being accused of having a Manichaean narrative that reinforces an us/them dialectic. After Juan escapes the detention center in the night, he falls asleep. The next morning, he is awakened by a hand that softly touches his shoulder. The first two panels in this sequence depict Juan resting close to a tree trunk when a white hand approaches and touches Juan's shoulder. The corresponding speech balloons point to the person that is trying to wake him up. The voice mutters in English: "Hey, wake up . . ." and ". . . Are you okay?" The third panel shows a white youngster on his knees, touching Juan's arm. Behind the young boy stands an adult, also white, who carries a rifle that is pointing to the ground. The lad affirms: "My dad and I saw you from across the way. . . . We were worried you might be lost."[47] Due to the language barrier, Juan does not understand, becomes frightened, and loses control of himself. As a result, he starts glowing and scares the father and his son away. This is the only instance in the story that portrays a friendly—even if ultimately unfavorable—interaction between Juan and a white person.

As discussed above, both citizen informants and ICE agents are racially white, and their faces are invariably shadowed, whether by sunglasses and hats or helmets and face shields. It could be argued that precisely because of this shared commonality (and irrespective of their membership in ICE) these faceless individuals act as a collective, and therefore their actions (either informing or enforcing border policy) can be classified as examples of structural violence. As a reminder, the head of this workforce is an unnamed but identifiable individual—the angry, racially white, blond man in charge of the ICE Houston Field Office—but his orders are always executed by a crew of faceless agents. Regarding cultural violence, that is, the cultural substratum that underlies the other two forms of violence, its clearest example in the story can be found on the last pages of the first episode. Right before Juan's energy blasts go out of control and blow out a wall of the isolation cell where he is being kept, he has an encounter with a tattooed white male guard equipped with a rubber baton. Although Juan is crying, the guardian growls that he is not going to be fooled. "I'm onto you *people*," he says, sneering. The next panel is a close-up with the faces of both the tearful young boy and the censorious guard. The latter adds: "This isn't the same country you saw on TV back in whatever shithole country you come from. We're taking it *back* from you people. . . ."[48] The reference to the "shithole country" replicates the words President Trump pronounced during a meeting with a bipartisan group of senators at the White House in early 2018.[49] But here the metatextuality in the first sentence matters less than the deep roots of the content of the second utterance. This idea of the migrant as an invader allows aggressors to justify and exonerate their acts of violence against those whom they conceive as intruders. According to Charles Ramírez Berg, what is at stake in the minds of these characters is no longer the alleged "loss of jobs or the drain on social services," but rather "the ideal of a unified, national 'self.'"[50] According to this line of thought, the migrant becomes a threat to national security and, indeed, to the nation itself. This explains why border enforcement has been linked in recent decades to terrorism. Not surprisingly, both U.S. Customs and Border Protection and ICE describe their mission, defined post-9/11, as protecting America itself.[51]

The comic book *Home* seeks to make visible and to illustrate how exceptionality permeates the border region and beyond. This attempt is in consonance with Mirzoeff's claim for "the right to look," or what he defines as "a right to the real": "not simply a matter of assembled visual images but the grounds on which such assemblages can register as meaningful renditions of a given event."[52] *Home* integrates images and texts into a narrative that contextualizes a given event, namely the current state of exceptionality at the U.S.-Mexico border, as well as its manifold renditions or derivatives: on the one hand, militarization as an exceptionality, along with the exceptional violence it engenders; and on the other, exceptionality as a way of life for migrants, asylum seekers, and refugees, and exceptional superhuman abilities as a desirable survival kit. If, as Rosas proposes, exceptionality "marks the formation or actually the forging of 'immigrant' subjectivity," it is this process and no other that *Home*'s artistic team strives to address.[53]

NOTES

I would like to thank the editors of this volume for their careful reading. Also, many thanks to Julie Henderson for helping me edit this article.

1. Brown, "Visual Criminology and Carceral Studies," 179.
2. Rosas, "The Thickening Borderlands," 336.
3. Plascencia, "Where Is the Border?," 252.
4. Cuéllar, *Decrasalizing the Other at the US-Mexico Border*, 82.
5. Dorsey and Díaz-Barriga, "Exceptional States and Insipid Border Walls," 68.
6. Schmitt, *Politische Theologie*, 19.
7. Agamben, *Homo Sacer*, 28.
8. Mbembe, *Necropolis*, 78.
9. Cuéllar, *Decrasalizing the Other at the US-Mexico Border*, 87, 94.
10. Martínez and Slack, "What Part of 'Illegal' Don't You Understand?," 125.
11. Dunn, *The Militarization of the U.S.-Mexico Border*, 3; A. Aldama, "Millennial Anxieties," 15.
12. Genette, *Palimpsests*, 3.
13. It is curious that a combative comic like *Home* does not allude to the relationship between prison gangs in the United States, the forced repatriation of many of these gang members at the beginning of this century, and the subsequent expansion of street gangs through Central America.
14. Anta and Wieszczyk, *Home*, no. 4. Neither the original comic book series nor the trade paperback edition has pagination.
15. Anta and Wieszczyk, *Home*, no. 1.
16. Anta and Wieszczyk, *Home*, no. 2 (bold emphasis in the original).
17. Frederick Luis Aldama and Christopher González identify flashbacks as one resource authors may employ to either accelerate or decelerate the tempo of the telling. In *Home*, flashbacks help slow down the at times frenetic tempo of the story, whose protagonists are constantly on the run. The effect of this resource is especially visible in issues 3 and 4 of the series: flashbacks on their first pages set a slow tempo that contrasts with the action-packed second half of each of

these comic books. Aldama and González, "Latino Comic Books Past, Present, and Future," 16.

18. Anta had worked with Salcedo on previous projects. Letterer Hassan Otsmane-Elhaou is another longtime collaborator with Anta. These previous works are short comics that can be found at Julio Anta's website.

19. Casetti and Di Chio, *Cómo analizar un film*, 89.

20. Anta, author's note, in Anta and Wieszczyk, *Home*, no. 1.

21. Anta, author's note, in Anta and Wieszczyk, *Home*, no. 2.

22. The analysis of other paratexts could support the idea that Image Comics used *Home* and other comics published around the same time to showcase its commitment to diversity. Perhaps it is not by coincidence that most comic book series announced in the final pages of all the issues of *Home* either have Latinx or Asian American authors or have nonwhite leading characters. In fact, issue 2 includes a five-page preview of Latinx comic author J. Gonzo's *La Mano del Destino* (2021), about a Mexican luchador. Likewise, Anta devotes much of the author's note in that same issue and in issue 5 to recommending comics created by Latinx creators, both those published by Image and by its competitors. The publication of *Home* could then have demonstrated Image's support for certain causes, such as denouncing family separation at the border. In fact, the trade paperback edition includes a bonus educator guide on migration. But *Home* also served Image as an endorsement of diversity. Unfortunately, such an analysis would exceed the scope of this chapter.

23. Ordaz, "Migrant Detention Archives," 253.

24. Anta and Wieszczyk, *Home*, no. 1. For a transcription of the campaign's launch speech, see Phillips, "They're Rapists."

25. F. Aldama, "Multicultural Comics," 18.

26. Anta, author's note, in Anta and Wieszczyk, *Home*, no. 5.

27. Reitberger and Fuchs, *Comics*, 151.

28. On the Reagan-era history, see Cisneros, "Resisting 'Massive Elimination,'" 242.

29. Brown, "Visual Criminology and Carceral Studies," 180.

30. Eckstein and Peri, "Immigrant Niches and Immigrant Networks," 8.

31. Anta and Wieszczyk, *Home*, no. 1.

32. Slack, Martínez, and Whiteford, introduction to *The Shadow of the Wall*, 12.

33. Anta and Wieszczyk, *Home*, no. 4.

34. Coogan, "The Hero Defines the Genre," 4.

35. Coogan, 10.

36. Coogan, 7.

37. Anta and Wieszczyk, *Home*, no. 2 (bold emphasis in the original).

38. Anta and Wieszczyk, *Home*, no. 3.

39. Berg, *Latino Images in Film*, 158.

40. Anta and Wieszczyk, *Home*, no. 4 (bold emphasis in the original).

41. Mirzoeff, "The Right to Look," 487.

42. Galtung, "Violence, Peace, and Peace Research," 170–71; Galtung, "Cultural Violence," 291. Very much in line with Galtung, Slavoj Žižek classifies violence as either subjective, systemic, or symbolic. See Žižek, *Violence*, 1–2.

43. Quoted in Cisneros, "Resisting 'Massive Elimination,'" 251.

44. Anta and Wieszczyk, *Home*, no. 1 (bold emphasis in the original).

45. Anta and Wieszczyk. It would not be a stretch to state that the African American guard and Humberto have internalized the hegemonic structures of domination, or even that their attitude can be representative of a generalized resistance among minority members of border enforcement workforces. As a matter of fact, in issue 4, an ICE agent named Sanchez receives the order from his unmasked boss, with the finger pointing at him, to knock down Gladys's door, and he does so apparently without compunction.

46. Anta and Wieszczyk, *Home*, no. 1.

47. Anta and Wieszczyk, *Home*, no. 2.

48. Anta and Wieszczyk, *Home*, no. 1 (bold emphasis in the original).

49. See Vitali, Hunt, and Thorp, "Trump Referred to Haiti and African Nations as 'Shithole' Countries."

50. Berg, *Latino Images in Film*, 164.

51. Silva, "On the Militarization of Borders and the Juridical Right to Exclude," 221.

52. Mirzoeff, "The Right to Look," 473, 477.

53. Rosas, "The Thickening Borderlands," 340.

BIBLIOGRAPHY

Agamben, Giorgio. *Homo Sacer: Sovereign Power and Bare Life*. Translated by Daniel Heller-Roazen. Stanford, Calif.: Stanford University Press, 1998.

Aldama, Arturo J. "Millennial Anxieties: Borders, Violence, and the Struggle for Chicana and Chicano Subjectivity." In *Decolonial Voices: Chicana and Chicano Cultural Studies in the 21st Century*, edited by Arturo J. Aldama and Naomi H. Quiñonez, 11–29. Bloomington: Indiana University Press, 2002.

Aldama, Frederick Luis. "Multicultural Comics: A Brief Introduction." In *Multicultural Comics: From Zap to Blue Beetle*, edited by Frederick Luis Aldama, 1–25. Austin: University of Texas Press, 2010.

Aldama, Frederick Luis, and Christopher González. "Latino Comic Books Past, Present, and Future—A Primer." In *Graphic Borders: Latino Comic Books Past, Present, and Future*, edited by Frederick Luis Aldama and Christopher González, 1–21. Austin: University of Texas Press, 2016.

Anta, Julio. Website. Accessed May 15, 2023. https://www.julioanta.com/.

Anta, Julio, and Anna Wieszczyk. *Home*. 5 issues. Portland, Ore.: Image Comics, 2021.

Berg, Charles Ramírez. *Latino Images in Film: Stereotypes, Subversion, Resistance*. Austin: University of Texas Press, 2002.

Brown, Michelle. "Visual Criminology and Carceral Studies: Counter Images in the Carceral Age." *Theoretical Criminology* 18, no. 2 (2014): 176–97.

Casetti, Francesco, and Federico Di Chio. *Cómo analizar un film*. Translated by Carlos Losilla. Barcelona: Paidós, 1991.

Cisneros, Natalie. "Resisting 'Massive Elimination': Foucault, Immigration, and the GIP." In *Active Intolerance: Michel Foucault, the Prisons Information Group, and the Future of Abolition*, edited by Perry Zurn and Andrew Dilts, 241–57. New York: Palgrave Macmillan, 2016.

Coogan, Peter. "The Hero Defines the Genre, the Genre Defines the Hero." In *What is a Superhero?*, edited by Robin S. Rosenberg and Peter Coogan, 3–10. Oxford: Oxford University Press, 2003.

Cuéllar, Gregory L. *Desacralizing the Other at the US-Mexico Border*. New York: Routledge, 2020.

Dorsey, Margaret E., and Miguel Díaz-Barriga. "Exceptional States and Insipid Border Walls." In *The U.S.-Mexico Transborder Region: Cultural Dynamics and Historical Interactions*, edited by Carlos G. Vélez-Ibáñez and Josiah Heyman, 65–80. Tucson: University of Arizona Press, 2017.

Dunn, Timothy J. *The Militarization of the U.S.-Mexico Border, 1978–1992: Low-Intensity Conflict Doctrine Comes Home*. Austin, Tex.: Center for Mexican American Studies Books, 1996.

Eckstein, Susan, and Giovanni Peri. "Immigrant Niches and Immigrant Networks in the U.S. Labor Market." *RSF: The Russell Sage Foundation Journal of the Social Sciences* 4, no. 1 (2018): 1–17.

Galtung, Johan. "Cultural Violence." *Journal of Peace Research* 27, no. 3 (1990): 291–305.

Galtung, Johan. "Violence, Peace, and Peace Research." *Journal of Peace Research* 6, no. 3 (1969): 167–91.

Genette, Gérard. *Palimpsests: Literature in the Second Degree*. Translated by Channa Newman and Claude Doubinsky. Lincoln: University of Nebraska Press, 1997.

Martínez, Daniel E., and Jeremy Slack. "What Part of 'Illegal' Don't You Understand? The Social Consequences of Criminalizing Unauthorized Mexican Migrants in the United States." In *The Shadow of the Wall: Violence and Migration on the U.S.-Mexico Border*, edited by Jeremy Slack, Daniel E. Martínez, and Scott Whiteford, 120–40. Tucson: University of Arizona Press, 2018.

Mbembe, Achille. *Necropolitics*. Translated by Steven Corcoran. Durham, N.C.: Duke University Press, 2019.

Mirzoeff, Nicholas. "The Right to Look." *Critical Inquiry* 37, no. 3 (2011): 473–96.

Ordaz, Jessica. "Migrant Detention Archives: Histories of Pain and Solidarity." *Southern California Quarterly* 102, no. 3 (2020): 250–73.

Phillips, Amber. "'They're Rapists': President Trump's Campaign Launch Speech Two Years Later, Annotated." *Washington Post*, June 16, 2017.

Plascencia, Luis F. B. "Where Is the Border? The Fourth Amendment, Boundary Enforcement, and the Making of an Inherently Suspect Class." In *The U.S.-Mexico*

Transborder Region: Cultural Dynamics and Historical Interactions, edited by Carlos G. Vélez-Ibáñez and Josiah Heyman, 244–80. Tucson: University of Arizona Press, 2017.

Reitberger, Reinhold, and Wolfgang Fuchs. *Comics: Anatomy of a Mass Medium.* London: Studio Vista, 1972.

Rosas, Gilberto. "The Thickening Borderlands: Diffused Exceptionality and 'Immigrant' Social Struggles During the 'War on Terror.'" *Cultural Dynamics* 18, no. 3 (2006): 335–49.

Schmitt, Carl. *Politische Theologie: Vier Kapitel zur Lehre von der Souveränität.* 1922. Reprint, Berlin: Duncker and Humblot, 2015.

Silva, Grant J. "On the Militarization of Borders and the Juridical Right to Exclude." *Public Affairs Quarterly* 29, no. 2 (2015): 217–34.

Slack, Jeremy, Daniel E. Martínez, and Scott Whiteford. Introduction to *The Shadow of the Wall: Violence and Migration on the U.S.-Mexico Border*, edited by Jeremy Slack, Daniel E. Martínez, and Scott Whiteford, 3–17. Tucson: University of Arizona Press, 2018.

Vitali, Ali, Kasie Hunt, and Frank Thorp V. "Trump Referred to Haiti and African Nations as 'Shithole' Countries." *NBC News*, January 11, 2018. http://www.nbcnews.com/politics/white-house/trump-referred-haiti-african-countries-shithole-nations-n836946.

Žižek, Slavoj. *Violence: Six Sideways Reflections.* New York: Picador, 2008.

15

I'M THE SHOOTER

J-M RIVERA

Tho living leaves recoil before our fires.
Baring to us war-charred and broken branches,
And seeing theirs, we for our own destruction weep.
—KATHLEEN RAINE

SEVENTY THOUSAND LATINXS DEAD. I recoil like an overcharged gun at data about Latinx gun violence. During the Bush, Obama, and Trump administrations, guns killed nearly seventy thousand Latinxs between 1999 and 2019, and male "Hispanics," the term the Violence Policy Center uses, are twice as likely as white non-Hispanics to die from gunfire. The statistics are staggering: 44,614 gun murders, 21,466 suicides, 3,920 accidental. Young male Latinxs are taking the brunt of this violence. Gun homicide is the third leading cause of death for male Hispanics ages fifteen to twenty-four. And from the time that Trump took office until 2019—the same year twenty-three Latinxs were murdered during the El Paso mass shooting in August—the Violence Policy Center indicates that the numbers accelerated tremendously. Male Hispanic homicide rates rose overall from the first years of the Obama administration to Donald Trump's first years. In 2022, CDC researcher Thomas Simon and colleagues noted that although they do not know the exact reasons for the rise in male Hispanic gun deaths, "systemic inequities (e.g., in economic, educational, housing, and employment opportunities) and structural racism have contributed to disparities in outcomes, and the COVID-19 pandemic could have worsened these conditions, especially in some racial and ethnic communities." Here is what we know: when Trump took office, gun deaths jumped 12 percent in the first year, and in the last two years of Trump's term, Hispanic murders and suicide rates rose dramatically. In total, during Trump's term in office, guns killed over a hundred thousand Americans. Gun smoke enveloped Trump's administration.

Seventy thousand. I recoil in quarantine while awaiting the statistics for the last two years of Trump's reign of terror, hoping that my recently purchased gun will protect me from the coming populist apocalypse that Trump conjures dangerously like the child playing with a hair-trigger gun. I did not, nor did most of the 330 million people in the United States, hear one of the seventy thousand shots. Instead, I learn about this tragedy unfolding by reading the Violence Policy Center report in the backdrop of the now-solidified populist rhetoric of Trump, language aimed at immigrants on the border that enables insurrectionists to call for "the second American Revolution." I recoil from my own apathy; I negate this negativity, and what emerges is melancholy. While shots are fired around the world, I speak the number in silence, I cannot hear the seventy thousand screams. . . . I can only whisper. . . . Hispanic males twice as likely to die, and seventy thousand pieces of data reverberate through my body like mortar hitting the Gulf of Mexico. The ripples echo long enough to make me bookmark the report, and later, when it hits the networks, I change the channel when it becomes an anecdotal headline that will infect Americans' understanding of Latinxs as violent people.

"Shoot them!" they scream at Trump populist anti-immigrant spectacles. And those who are not so bold as to yell out this populist rage privately state, "must be cartel violence," or insist from their homes a thousand miles from the border, "Trump's gotta' build that wall," and they hope Trump's people, the silent majority, "will rise and take back America from the immigrant animals who Trump has identified as murders and rapists." Americans tell themselves stories to solidify their populist image of the people, created by concealing and carrying their racism on their lips. No one hears seventy thousand shots fired toward Latinxs around the United States. Though the eyes and ears of the body politic neither see nor hear, I follow and go about my daily routine.

Seventy thousand. I have grown tired from the recoil of guns. I am numb from the human tragedy created from seventy thousand projectiles piercing bodies and its reactive resonance destroying the eardrums of the world. This is our condition, this mortal recoil that rips through Latinx communities; it dismembers, mushrooms, damages, murders, mutilates, devoices, voices, embodies, disembodies, heals, tears flesh from bone, unites and tears family from family, turns people into strangers, destroys communities, screams, whispers, cries, turns friends to enemies, tears state from nation and country from union, creates and destroys borders, facilitates genocide, creates genocide, ends genocide, fractures neighbors, freezes and speeds up time, imbues entropy, ends and begins civilizations, begins and ends world wars; and at the same time that it has become the force of humanity, recoil numbs America's mind, my mind, dulls its senses and creates a permanent anaphia on every inch of our body politic. We have lost touch with the force of pain, the sound of death, now hidden in the black boxes, explained in pure math and algorithms presented to us in perfectly pixelated graphs.

Seventy thousand. The data fail to define the true nature of recoil; we are left with the memorialization of the gun, and we celebrate its recoil in schools between mass shootings and poetry lessons about the American Revolution, which gave birth to "the people," who are constituted by "the shot heard round the world," a shot that, as Ralph Waldo Emerson poetically reminds us, created the United States of America. We are all the apathetic officers in Uvalde who watched and listened to mass tragedy unfold from afar; we all ignore the recoil that ended America's history. And yet, "the people" forge on, deafly, and continue to cock the gun that unwittingly fires a path leading to our future destruction. Paolo Gerbaudo calls this the "Great Recoil," the moment when societies turn backward and inward and retreat into themselves. The effect is numbness, apathy, and pain.

$$GunVelocity = \frac{BulletWt*MuzzleVelocity + \frac{PowderWt*MuzzleVelocity}{2} + PowderWt*GasExitVelocity*(1-MuzzleBrakeEfficiency))^{1/Ne}}{GunWt}$$

—ISAAC NEWTON, THIRD LAW

The reflective movement is to be taken as an absolute recoil upon itself.
—GEORG WILHELM FRIEDRICH HEGEL

There is omnipotence of recoil.
—RALPH WALDO EMERSON

The absolute power of recoil haunted the minds of the past, for the desire to come to terms with force, movement, and reaction became not only the central tenet of motion, but the logic of culture. After Newton set the theoretical foundations of movement, Hegel and Emerson extended Newton's third law by positing recoil as absolute and omnipotent, as a dialectical and metaphysical historical force that sees conscious embodiment emerging from being and nothingness and from fate and free will. Emerson in particular looked to the recoil as the poetic force of peoplehood, extending it to U.S. history and nation-building in his poem "Concord Hymn," wherein "the shot heard round the world" commemorates the revolutionary emergence of a populist America. Ironically, though, this sonic emergence perforates eardrums and mutilates bodies at the same time that it builds the Shining City on the Hill. Recoil is the absolute dynamism of the American nation's rise as a populist utopia, a country where Emerson's "embattled" white yeoman farmer, standing with gun in hand, becomes the symbol of "the people" during this first American revolution. As Emerson prophetically hints in the lines of "Concord Hymn," recoil continues to reverberate in the soul of America, where, as the poem marks, "the conqueror silent sleeps." He leaves me asking two questions: What happens when the shot of a gun and its recoil are the constituting force of the American people's rise? What happens when the gun marks the race toward our oblivion?

Recoil emerges from our hands as an absolute originary force of world making and of world ending. Recoil is the moment of immanent dynamism of both our ontological and epistemological imaginations; it is the terror of being unaware of the repercussions of our actions as we make our way through time. Absolute recoil is the condition whose force creates a democracy that fosters both chaos and apathy, and a president that loads the gun with every hate-filled speech. Absolute recoil frames the temporal chaos of Trump's administration. Absolute recoil is a historical force and condition that leads to the idolization of a man who says he "could shoot somebody and wouldn't lose any voters." Trump's rhetoric exists on the chaos of recoil. He fires out destructive shots about elections, race, masculinity, and sexuality, knowing that they will reverberate through our social media and turn Americans against one another. His is a reign based on the manipulation of absolute recoil, a strategy that keeps the American people bound together by hate of one another.

They're bringing crime. They're rapists. And some, I assume, are good people.
—DONALD TRUMP

Living in the Borderlands means you fight hard to / resist . . . /
the pull of the gun barrel.
—GLORIA ANZALDÚA

Hundreds of years before Trump would scope Latinx immigrants in his crosshairs, the conquered of the Americas would feel the recoil of guns tearing their civilization apart. Written in the early modern era of Shakespeare, Bernardino de Sahagún's *Florentine Codex* was the first document to mark the moments when Spanish guns and their recoil destroyed the Indigenous civilizations of the Americas. In the last book, "The Conquest," where my book *Undocuments* ends, Sahagún recounts that the recoil of harquebuses (HAR-QUE-boos-es), "exploded, sputtered, discharged, thundered, and disgorged. Smoke spread, it grew dark with smoke, everyplace filled with smoke. The fetid smell made people dizzy and faint." He continues, "they especially made them faint when they heard how the guns went off at [the Spaniards'] command, sounding like thunder, causing people actually to swoon, blocking the ears. And when it went off, something like a ball came out from inside, and fire went showering and spitting out. And the smoke that came from it had a very foul stench, striking one in the face. And if they shot at a hill, it seemed to crumble and come apart. And it turned a tree to dust; it seemed to make it vanish, as though someone had conjured it away."

This conjuring recoil of the harquebus would haunt the Indigenous and Latinx peoples of the Americas and continues to reveal itself in the lives behind the data of the seventy thousand dead. The fetid smoke created four hundred years ago by harquebuses continues to engulf Latinxs living in a borderland formed not on maps, but from the reverberation of a colonizer's gun, a weapon that helped destroy the Americas and break it into carceral borders now patrolled by U.S. Border Patrol and men of the Minuteman Project carrying Beretta 96Ds and AK-47s. Today, Anzaldúa reminds us that for those in the borderlands, recoil reverberates for centuries and gives birth to the colonized consciousness, for to live in the *fronteras* is to be in the crosshairs of a gun barrel with a hairpin trigger, whose pull began to recoil when Spaniards fired their harquebus hundreds of years prior.

My Life had stood—a Loaded Gun
—EMILY DICKINSON

August 1987, Antelope Valley, California. Twelve years before the study would collect the first gun datum, my recoil began in memories carried by the Santa Ana winds that emanated from aircraft sonic booms, and shotgun muzzles that mutilated four desert cats. Two distant brothers, connected only by blood, choreographed this mass killing for me under the sun of the Mojave Desert. The teens' names do not escape me, but I bury them in the sands, and I will tell you that the younger twin had a limp and slouched from an accident that was strangely unspoken in a town where everyone knew every detail of their past. Their father was the sheriff of a small desert town, mostly keeping secrets of the military and aerospace industries, which fed its inhabitants with the government dollars Reagan would funnel to our tables. We grew up between the large square metal Lockheed hangars and the vastness of Edwards Air Force Base, where daily they tested weapons of mass destruction. Boom, boom,

boom, boom. Every day over our heads we heard the sonic booms of military planes. As bombs exploded on dry lake beds, we became desensitized while we learned how to read, write, and do arithmetic.

The brothers had a ranch in Lake Los Angeles, roughly twenty-three miles from where I grew up in Lancaster, California. Their audience today were all children of Reagan's Cold War—our parents worked on the elusive Skunk Works project, wherein they created a stealth plane that could elude radar and drop laser-targeted bombs thousands of miles away, leaving only the recoil of hundred-pound munitions that mutilated bodies. This violence, this recoil on the other side of the world, penetrated us slowly, surreptitiously marking our relationship to objects of war, objects of pain.

The brothers created their own theater of war for the local boys—I watched as they herded cats with tuna cans. One, two, three, four, five cats strung up on a tree with wire. The cats crying, screaming, violently shifting, and contorting trying to escape. One is able to free their leg, falls to the ground, and limps off; the brother with his own limp points the gun at the fleeing cat but stops short of shooting. "We don't need that one," he says. The others are now more quiet, tired, and exhausted from the trauma of being hung by their hind legs. I am about ten feet behind the audience. Quiet. We are all so quiet, waiting for the performance to begin. "Why are we doing this? Why are you doing this?" one of the boys asks. The older brother says his dad wants them to kill the feral and rabid cats who have taken over the property, and he pays them for each cat they kill. "They are wild and diseased and kill the chickens." At the time, this relieved me. The detective said we should do this—the law wants us to kill rabid cats and free our city from disease. I begin to walk closer to the audience; and at the first step the first shot goes off, boom, boom, boom, and the first cat is hit, his body torn into two parts. Blood pours onto the desert earth, flesh scattered yards away, carried by the Santa Ana winds. The cat did not turn to dust; it did not vanish, as though someone had conjured it away. Its mutilated body, barely hanging, looms louder than the shot. The other three cats begin to wail above the winds again, and the brothers ask whether any of us wants to "take a shot." Boom, boom. Two volunteers. My best friend and I respond, "we are good." We are good, a phrase that both condoned and questioned the act I was witnessing. The older brother looked at me as if he knew my motivations. "Rivera is scared of guns. . . . His momma didn't teach him how to shoot," a dig by the brother, pointing out that I was the only one being raised by a single mother. "Fuck you, shoot your daddy's gun and get this over with so we can go to Noggles with that fucking cat money. I am fucking hungry," I yell back. "It's my gun," he exclaims. "Just load the gun," I tell him. He hands the gun to his younger brother to reload. Boom, boom, boom, boom, boom, boom; the multiple muzzle blasts create shock waves in front and behind that engulf us all. The force from the pellets disintegrates the remaining cats behind the smoke of the recoil. After the last scream, everyone stares at the remains hanging on the wires. "The crows and coyotes will pick the parts up. We can just leave them there, but I have to gather the paws to show dad what we killed," the older brother tells us as he ends his performance. We walk back to the car to get food, not in silence, but amid chatter about the power of the gun, not of the dead cats or the mass killing we partook in and the mutilations and death we had created; we act as if nothing that just took place mattered. "That gun is insane. I felt it everywhere." "I told you, it's cool, huh? It's not so heavy." We were under the spell of the recoil, captivated by the technology and vibrancy of the force of the shotgun. The cats were our final baptism; we were no longer children of Reagan's Cold War, but young men complicit in our culture of mass violence. We were, after all, born under the shadows of warplanes and raised by sonic booms that perforated our childhood. This mortal recoil framed our manliness, our history, our humanity long before our shots would mutilate four defenseless desert cats in 1987.

I did not ask it then, but I question it now: am I the recoil of a gun?

❦

July 28, 2019, 5:45 p.m.:

. . . How is the garlic festival? Did you try any ice cream?

. . .

. . .

You didn't hear?

Hear what? I've never had it before. . . .

There was a shooting as we left the parking lot. We left five minutes before.

. . .

Are you ok?

. . .

. . .

I tried the ice cream.

. . .

Was it any good?

The mass shooting of cats in the summer of 1987 reverberates for decades. I am fascinated with mass shootings and the shooters. I recoil from their destruction, but lunge toward their spectacle. This inward and outward pull frames my eye as I search for information about the August 3, 2019, El Paso shooting, which, today, stands as the largest hate crime against Latinxs in the United States. Perhaps it is due to the temporal proximity of the Gilroy shooting, which my friend attended with his family and would text me after, as he drove away from the devastation, or perhaps it was those four dead cats, which are still imprinted on my psyche. After each shooting, I read every article and watch every news feed. I follow the trials and the reactions. Shock and horror lead to the call for gun legislation, which leads to a quiet, until the next shot, then the recoil, over and over.

I search YouTube and Instagram for video feeds of the El Paso shooting. I find one that captures two minutes of the chaos, the carnage, the screams, the cries, the smoke; the recoil covers the entire frame. I watch from a distance, and like with an action movie I am fixated on each boom, boom, boom. I watch the mass shooting from the safety of my home; a thousand miles away from El Paso, I hear the recoil of shots penetrating bodies, emanating through the speakers into my ears. I stare in silence, an apathetic spectator who sees but cannot truly feel the recoil of the pixelated gun.

Videos give way to the reality of me living in a metropolis that has the third highest mass shooting rate of any city in the United States. Having lived in Colorado for over twenty years, I have grown desensitized to the shots of guns, to the headlines of school and mass shootings. The year Trump announced his run for president, I recoiled into myself, despite living through the recoil of a foiled mass school shooting at my daughter's middle school. A student at her school brought a gun and smoke bombs and had planned to shoot up the school in the late afternoon. Though the student was detained and the gun was confiscated an hour before the shootings were planned to start, the threat was real, and was close. With no real details to this day, we only know that there was a gun, a smoke bomb, ammunition, and a threat; the parents still search for answers but mostly bury it deep, knowing that the shot was imagined by a twelve-year-old shooter but never realized.

With the other parents, I stand outside the school, waiting for my daughter to get escorted out the back. She walks out with a group of friends, smiling and laughing, as if the day was like any other. She gets in the car, and I suggest we go get ice cream. "Sure," she says. "Dairy Queen?" "That works." We drive away, and I begin to ask her questions: How do you feel? Were you scared? She looks up from her phone: "I wasn't there today, Dad. Our grade had a field trip." I forgot that she was gone during the incident. I am relieved that even if it did not occur, if it did, she would have been spared. I do not think of the other children. My only concern is that she was not in the gun's crosshairs. I am apathetic about the lives of other children. But how do you feel, I ask. I wasn't there, Dad, how am I supposed to feel anything?

"There goes another one, boom, boom, boom," Castro said, gesturing as if he was holding a large rifle, firing off rounds.
Adria Gonzalez, joined in, adding her own recreation of the sounds of the shooting. "Boom, and then boom, and boom."
—ANGELA KOCHERGA

August 3, 2019, 11:03 a.m., 69,999 Latinxs dead. El Paso, Texas.

The tragedy unfolds with a self-declaration inscribed by the recoil of a gun: "I'm the shooter." The officer recounts that the shooter calmly stated his identity with an action of an AK-47, "I'm the shooter," in what first sounded like a muttered whisper to him as he was turning off his motorcycle. "I'm the shooter," this time the shooter is yelling as he raises his hands, exiting the dark gray Honda Civic that he drove for eleven hours from Allen, Texas, to El Paso. There was a calm confidence the second time he yelled at the officer, "I'm the shooter." He felt prouder of himself than at any other time in his angry, hate-filled life. A self-fashioned loner, he began turning away from the world and his peers at the first high school he attended, Liberty High School, in a predominantly white suburb of Frisco, Texas; by the time he transferred to the affluent Dallas suburb of Allen, where he attended Plano High School, he ate alone at lunch tables and rarely interacted with his middle-class peers. His former neighbor Leigh Ann Locascio said that he rode the bus or walked alone, and that he spoke poorly of his classmates, especially athletes, who tended to bully him. An acquaintance in high school, Jacob Wilson, said that his only real friends were his snakes, and he was bullied and shunned because of a speech impediment that framed his "irritable and short-tempered" manner toward his white classmates. Before this mass killer would perpetuate the largest hate crime against Mexicans in the history of the United States, most of his peers thought he had no aspirations, as he himself stated that he was "not really motivated to do anything more than what's necessary to get by."

August 3, 2019, 10:15 a.m., 69,977 Latinxs dead.

At twenty-one, he already felt as if the entire world were conspiring to replace him, writing in his manifesto: "My whole life I have been preparing for a future that currently doesn't exist. The job of my dreams will likely be automated. Hispanics will take control of the local and state government of my beloved Texas, changing policy to better suit their needs. They will turn Texas into an instrument of a political coup which will hasten the destruction of our country."

As he planned out the shooting, he did so knowing he had nothing to lose; in his paranoid mind, he was already expendable and insignificant. In deep screams in his mind, he thinks constantly about what it means to be replaceable. He can see it over the horizon of the 104-degree desert. He quiets his unsettled thoughts, knowing that his gun will speak for him. His gun and its recoil will memorialize his life and counter his self-perceived insignificance. The gun will be the final stroke of his 2,356-word hate-filled manifesto, "The Inconvenient Truth," which he posts on 8chan while he eats lunch, fifteen minutes before he starts his rampage. But before he would take a shot, he first walked into the Walmart at 710 Gateway Road, five miles from the U.S.-Mexico border, to study the layout of the store, to see where security was standing, to pick out his targets. His eyes were like the crosshairs of a gun, scanning the thousands of Latinxs believed to be in the store that midmorning. He pensively smiled, thinking that the recoil of his gun would strike such fear in Latinxs that they would return to Mexico and their "invasion" would cease. He slowly walks back to his car, reciting words from his manifesto, each syllable, like a mantra, "stop the invasion," helps him stay calm. He returns to his car, sits in the passenger seat, opens the glove compartment to grab his tactical leather heat-resistant shooting gloves, the ones with the rubber palms, so he can withstand the heat of the gun after shooting it more than a hundred times, his clear shooting glasses, and his protective earmuffs. There is a handgun in the glove compartment as well, but he decides he wants to use a larger caliber rifle, whose recoil will inflict the most damage. He gets out of the car and walks toward the trunk, where he unwraps the blanket that concealed his semiautomatic AK-47-style assault rifle, which he earlier loaded with 8M3 bullets, the ones that fragment and break up in the body and have less recoil. He grabs two extended magazines and puts them in his right cargo pants pocket. No one recalls a man walking across the parking lot in tactical gear and with a rifle. His pace was hurried, but not frenetic. He had made this walk and performed this action hundreds of times in his mind. As he walks toward the parking lot, he begins shooting. Boom, boom, boom. One witness, Alden Hall, recalls, "As he entered, he was very calm and relaxed, he did not look like someone who just shot up a parking lot." The calmness did not grow entirely from preparation, but mostly emerged from a manifesto and a racist mind that were filled with a hate so deep that he felt he was right in his actions. This time the hate returns to a muted silence as he walks through the doors where the produce is located, luckily farther away from the back-to-school section . . . and without a word, he turns to his right, his twenty-three shots heard around the world as each victim of the borderlands succumbs to the recoil caused by yet another "pull of the gun barrel."

Boom, boom. . . . Jordan Anchondo; Andre Anchondo; David Johnson; Javier Amir Rodriguez; Angie Silva Englisbee; Arturo Benavides; Elsa Mendoza Márquez; Leonardo Campos; Maribel Loya; Juan Velazquez; Gloria Irma Marquez; Maria Eugenia Legarreta Rothe; Sara Esther Regalado; Adolfo Cerros Hernandez; Margie Reckard; Ivan Filiberto Manzano; Jorge Calvillo Garcia; Maria Flores; Raul Flores; Alexander Gerhard Hoffman; Teresa Sanchez; Luis Alfonzo Juarez. . . .

May 10, 2018.

Guillermo "Memo" Garcia succumbs to his injuries and is the last person to die from gunshots sustained at the El Paso shooting. Seventy thousand Latinxs dead. The gun violence report data is complete, and twenty-three Italian cypress trees are planted.

This attack is a response to the Hispanic invasion of Texas. They are the instigators, not me. I am simply defending my country from cultural and ethnic replacement brought on by an invasion.

—"THE INCONVENIENT TRUTH"

June 3, 2018, Allen, Texas.

No one knows the exact date when he started writing his manifesto, "The Inconvenient Truth," but we do know from his words that his "ideology has not changed for several years," and that the manifesto's composition would be preparing a document of his rampage. What some do think is while writing he was living with his grandparents in a two-story home in a subdivision called Star Creek. It is a predominantly white neighborhood in a county that voted overwhelmingly for Trump in 2016. Some think he began researching the Great Replacement theory, the motivating theory of his manifesto, in the summer of 2017. For the shooter, the ill-begotten theory loaded the gun, as he would write, "the Hispanic community was not my target before I read The Great Replacement." The theory espouses that welcoming immigration policies and people is a larger plot to undermine white culture, and, in time, immigrants will replace white Americans in the Southwest and eventually the entirety of the United States. This white paranoia is coupled with the Reconquista narrative, wherein Mexico and Mexicans are going to invade and reconquer the Southwest and expel white Americans from what was once Mexican land. With 80 percent of its population Latinx, El Paso was ground zero.

Did he find his "Hispanic hate" from reading French author Jean Raspail, whose dystopian apocalyptic novel *The Camp of Saints* depicts an "invasion of immigrants" who replace the white electorate, leading to the demise of Western society? Did this book create his recoil of Mexicans? The book was panned by the *New York Times*, which stated in its 1975 review that "the narrative is sluggish, the symbolism banal, the scolding tone an affront to the reader. The characters have no independent existence; they exist as mouthpieces for the author. There must be a lofty purpose to this exercise; but after wading through the torrent of windy rhetoric, the reader is simply too numb to find it." The review of an elitist eastern newspaper means nothing to the populist Far Right, however; its adherents feed off this disdain, take pride in the rejection. Thirty years later the white supremacists and the alt-right, Trump's political allies and cabinet, and Trump himself would look to the subject and language of this book in order to turn its xenophobic plot into a mainstream rallying cry that would help foment Trump's hate-filled populist rise as the savior of the "unheard people" who were being replaced.

None other than Trump's immigration czar, Stephen Miller, who was responsible for the administration's anti-immigrant xenophobic policies and wrote many of Trump's speeches, referenced *The Camp of Saints* in emails, where he stated that the book gives clarity to the United States' current historical moment, and criticized Pope Francis's desire for a more humane refugee policy. Trump's other main adviser, Steve Bannon, also recommended the book, and in veiled language taken from the novel, he used its xenophobic polices and rhetoric of "invasion" in Trump's campaign speeches of 2016. Senator Steve King (R-Iowa) went as far as telling his constituents that *The Camp of Saints* "should be imprinted into everybody's brain."

It is not surprising, then, that the El Paso shooter would use similar language from the novel *The Camp of Saints* in his own apocalyptic, populist manifesto, which ultimately concludes that gun violence is the only answer to the Great Replacement. It is not a difficult proposition to see that the shooter walked into Walmart with the book's hate-filled rhetoric "imprinted on his brain." And yet, he spends a paragraph explaining that he did not learn these ideas from the president and was not motivated by Trump: "My opinions on automation, immigration, and the rest predate Trump and his campaign for president. I am putting this here because some people will blame the President or certain presidential candidates for the attack. This is not the case. I know that the media will probably call me a white supremacist anyway and blame Trump's rhetoric." Despite the author's desire to exonerate Trump in his actions, Trump is the only named person in the entire manifesto. The author does not even sign the manifesto, but he still finds it necessary to name and defend Trump, a past act of protecting his president. Trump stands starkly as the lone identifying subject of the manifesto, a specter of hate who may not have written the text or walked into Walmart, but whose hate-filled campaign and rhetoric helped load the guns with populist hate. In speeches and in his campaign fundraisers, Trump referenced "shithole countries," talked about the immigrant "invasion" at the border, and called immigrants "rapists and murderers." The year before the El Paso shooting, Trump ran 2,200 Facebook ads that referenced the "invasion." And at a rally in Macon, Georgia, in November 2019, Trump screamed: "You look at what is marching up, that is an invasion! That is an invasion!"

Crusius the killer, Trump the accomplice.
—EL PASO RALLY AGAINST GUN VIOLENCE AND ANTI-
IMMIGRANT HATE SPEECH, AUGUST 5, 2019

Trump was the shooter's prosthetic, or perhaps he was Trump's prosthetic. Hyperbolic. Perhaps. But let us not forget that for Trump, like for the El Paso shooter, the solution to this invasion was to take up arms. To him and his followers, only through force can America stop the invading Mexican hordes. In a rally in Panama City Beach, Florida, two months before the El Paso shooting, Trump asked a roaring crowd, "How do we stop these people?" In an act of call-and-response to Trump and Miller's "invasion," a supporter in the crowd yelled, "Shoot them!" Trump smiled and responded, "only in the panhandle can you get away with that." This rhetorical flint was not new to Trump. In 2018, he would tell his patriot minutemen on the border that "perhaps" they should be allowed to use weapons to protect the border from the invasion. Countless other moments frame the first term of Trump. Year after year, he pointed his bilious rhetoric toward Latinxs while a hundred thousand Americans died during his term from gun violence. He reminds his followers that he is tough on crime while he stokes fear of immigrants and calls for their removal by any means necessary. His followers and others in the United States bought more guns in four years than were purchased in any other period in U.S. history. We are all armed watching the fictitious invasion on the border that is scripted for us every four years on the screen. All the while, we grow too numb to do anything about the mass shooting episodes that occur two blocks away at our neighborhood schools. "This is crazy," "What a world we live in," "I can't believe this, again"; we recoil into our screens and text our horror, hoping that each textual character will counter the bullets flying all around us and not hit their target.

It feels like being hunted.
—KARLA CORNEJO VILLAVICENCIO

As the pandemic closes the borders, I recoil in my house in the fall of 2021. I watch Lara Trump, Trump's daughter-in-law, campaign for Trump's second term on Fox News, saying that Trump's followers should "arm up" and "get guns" if they live near the border. I am not sure whether this was the imprinting factor that led to my decision to buy a gun. Maybe I had already ordered the gun in the summer of 1987, when I unwittingly watched the killing of four desert cats. Or was it when I read that despite the overwhelming gun violence against Latinxs, or perhaps due to the violence, more Latino males are buying guns than in any other period in history. Many want to protect themselves against the alt-right and white supremacists and fear the populist rhetoric of Trump; some fear the police; and some have bought into Trump's populist fearmongering rhetoric of arming up. After months of searching, I find a gun, a Dan Wesson 9mm with a heartwood grip. It is a beautiful black semi-automatic. I order it, register it, and have it in my possession in three days. This is longer than usual in Colorado, but the demand for all guns and ammunition has made the system slower than usual. I join a Latino gun club and sign up for shooting lessons. The increased lockdown makes it impossible to make an appointment at a range. I am left staring at the gun in a gun safe during the pandemic. I unwrap the celluloid wrapper and pull the trigger once a week to ensure that the workings remain greased and actioned. I read gun safety books and study recoil for hours on the internet. When the pandemic restriction ends, I think I am finally going to learn to shoot. But by the spring of 2022, I have lost interest; Biden is in office, the vaccine is out and I am fully vaccinated, and mass shootings have lost their appeal in the media, so it is hard to follow them, despite knowing that they continue to devastate America. I don't plan on selling it though. I will wait and see what 2024 looks like. Better safe than sorry in case another January 6 spills into the cities, and the alt-right's prognosticated civil war erupts in the United States. Until then I will wrap and unwrap it, pulling the trigger of an empty clip weekly, never really knowing what the recoil of the gunshot feels like.

BIBLIOGRAPHY

Aguilar, Julian. "'Forgiveness Isn't Given Lightly': El Pasoans Balance Healing with Anger a Year After Walmart Massacre." *Texas Tribune*, August 3, 2020.

Arluke, Arnold. "How Reliably Does Animal Torture Predict a Future School Shooter?" *Washington Post*, February 21, 2018.

Baek, Grace. "For Black and Latino Gun Owners, Being Armed 'Evens the Playing Field.'" CBS Reports, October 28, 2021. https://www.cbsnews.com/news/black-latino-gun-owners-armed-cbsn-originals/.

Baker, Peter, and Michael D. Shear. "El Paso Shooting Suspect's Manifesto Echoes Trump's Language." *New York Times*, August 4, 2019.

Bethea, Charles. "'Trump the Accomplice': El Paso Residents Blame the President for a Hate-Fuelled Mass Shooting." *New Yorker*, August 5, 2019.

Carlson, Jennifer. *Policing the Second Amendment: Guns, Law Enforcement, and the Politics of Race*. Princeton, N.J.: Princeton University Press, 2020.

Charlton, Lauretta. "What Is the Great Replacement?" *New York Times*, August 6, 2019.

Choiniere, Alyssa. "Patrick Crusius: 5 Fast Facts You Need to Know." *Heavy*, August 6, 2019. https://heavy.com/news/2019/08/patrick-crusius/.

Chute, Nate. "El Paso Shooter Timeline." *El Paso Times*, August 9, 2019.

Crusius, Patrick. "The Inconvenient Truth." 8Chan (site shut down), August 3, 2019.

Daly, Michael. "Suspected El Paso Shooter's Dad Once Sought to Help Gun Violence Victim." *Daily Beast*, August 4, 2019.

Danner, Chas. "Everything We Know About the El Paso Walmart Massacre." *Intelligencer*, August 7, 2019.

Elmahrek, Adam. "Suspect in El Paso Massacre 'Didn't Hold Anything Back' in Police Interrogation." *Los Angeles Times*, August 4, 2019.

Emerson, Ralph Waldo. *The Concord Hymn and Other Poems*. New York: Dover, 1996.

Fernández Campbell, Alexia. "Trump Described an Imaginary 'Invasion' at the Border 2 Dozen Times in the Past Year." *Vox*, August 7, 2019. https://www.vox.com/identities/2019/8/7/20756775/.

Garcia-Navarro, Lulu. "Stephen Miller and 'The Camp of the Saints': A White Nationalist Reference." NPR, November 19, 2019. https://www.npr.org/2019/11/19/780552636/.

Gerbaudo, Paolo. *The Great Recoil: Politics after Populism and Pandemic*. New York: Verso Press, 2021.

Hasan, Mehdi. "After El Paso, We Can No Longer Ignore Trump's Role in Inspiring Mass Shootings." *Intercept*, August 4, 2019.

Hayes, Mills. "Man Who Recorded Video Inside Walmart During Shooting Recounts What Happened." KFOX 14, August 5, 2019. https://kfoxtv.com/news/local/man-who-recorded-video-inside-walmart-during-shooting-recounts-what-happened.

Helling, Steve. "2 Years Later, Remembering 23 Fatal Victims of El Paso Mass Shooting." *People*, August 3, 2021.

Huber, Craig. "El Paso Marks 2 Years Since Deadly Mass Shooting." Spectrum News 1, August 3, 2021.

Hutchinson, Bill, Aaron Katersky, and Josh Margolin. "Alleged Shooter Cased El Paso Walmart Before Rampage That Killed 22: Law Enforcement Officials." *ABC News*, August 5, 2019.

Jackson, Amanda. "Police Believe the El Paso Shooter Targeted Latinos. These Are the Victims' Stories." *CNN*, August 7, 2019. https://www.cnn.com/2019/08/04/us/el-paso-shooting-victims/index.html.

Kocherga, Angela. "El Paso Remembered." *Texas Observer*, August 3, 2020.

Laclau, Ernesto. *On Populist Reason*. New York: Verso Press, 2005.

Langley, Marty, and Josh Sugarmann. *Hispanic Victims of Lethal Firearms Violence in the United States: 2021 Edition*. Violence Policy Center, July 2021.

Litton, Andra. "Victims of the El Paso Walmart Shooting." KTSM, August 4, 2019. https://www.ktsm.com/news/el-paso-strong/list-victims-of-the-el-paso-walmart-shooting/.

Minor, Nathaniel. "Colorado Has More Mass Shootings Than Other Places." *CPR News*, March 23, 2021. https://www.cpr.org/2021/03/23/colorado-mass-shootings-survivors-trauma-boulder-king-soopers/.

New York Times. Review of *The Camp of the Saints*, by Jean Raspail. October 5, 1975.

Ngangura, Tarisai. "'White Supremacy Is Not Just for White People': Trumpism, the Proud Boys, and the Extremist Allure for People of Color." *Vanity Fair*, February 2, 2021.

Porter, Tom. "The El Paso Shooter Seemed to Try to Distance Himself from Trump—but the Similarities with Trump's Rhetoric Are Obvious." *Insider*, August 5, 2019. https://www.insider.com/el-paso-suspects-trump-inspiration-denials-dont-convince-experts-2019-8.

Rivera, John-Michael. *Undocuments*. Tucson: University of Arizona Press, 2021.

Romero, Simon, Caitlin Dickinson, Miriam Jordon, and Patricia Mazzei. "'It Feels Like Being Hunted': Latinos Across the U.S. in Fear After El Paso Massacre." *New York Times*, August 6, 2019.

Schaefer, Jim. "Inside the El Paso Shooting." *El Paso Times*, August 10, 2019.

Simon, Thomas R., Scott R. Kegler, Marissa L. Zwald, May S. Chen, James A. Mercy, Christopher M. Jones, Melissa C. Mercado-Crespo, Janet M. Blair, and Deborah M. Stone. "Increases in Firearm Homicide and Suicide Rates—United States, 2020–2021." *Morbidity and Mortality Weekly Report* 71, no. 40 (October 7, 2022): 1286–87.

Stieber, Chelsea. "Camp of the Saints." *Africa Is a Country*, March 17, 2019. https://africasacountry.com/2019/03/camp-of-the-saints.

Villas-Boas, Antonio. "A Video of Trump Laughing at a Proposal to 'Shoot' Migrants Is Resurfacing After Shootings in Texas and Ohio." *Insider*, August 4, 2019. https://www.businessinsider.com/trump-shoot-them-video-resurfacing-after-texas-ohio-mass-shooting-2019-8.

Žižek, Slavoj. *Absolute Recoil: Towards a New Foundation of Dialectical Materialism*. New York, Verso Press, 2014.

PART IV

RESISTANCE AND ABOLITIONIST DREAMS

16

SEXUAL TERROR AND THE PRISON/BORDER ARCHIVE

Theorizing a Feminist Abolition Praxis of Migrant Detention

CINTHYA MARTINEZ

IN 2014 ALMA, AN UNDOCUMENTED *woman who had been detained in Texas's Karnes ICE detention center for four months, confided in local community organizers that she had been subjected to sexual assault inside the facility by ICE guards and staff members. Adding more devastation to her declaration, Alma shared that she was not the only woman inside the facility who had been sexually abused. She declared that she had witnessed a multitude of other incidents occurring inside the facility's walls. This was a rampant phenomenon in the Karnes detention facility. Her words provide a glimpse of the gravity of the horrors that occur inside other migrant detention centers across the nation. Alma recounted the haunting memories of terror when she would hear a cell door opening in the middle of a quiet night. Sometimes she'd hear the screeching doors in the early morning hours. She would shut her eyes tight and pray into the night, hoping they weren't there for her. It wasn't just the fear of being deported; Alma and the other women feared the ICE guards who had been visiting women during these hours, removing them from their cells to take them to secluded parts of the facility to sexually abuse them. This daily ritual, the sexual violence, had become so widespread that the ICE guards and staff had assigned themselves "novias" or "girlfriends." Alma and the women were promised by ICE guards that if they cooperated, which meant not reporting the sexual abuse, they would receive support to advance their legal case and acquire financial support after their release. After being in the Karnes ICE facility for almost two years, Alma wanted to be free, more than anything. But she also wanted justice for what was happening inside the facility to her and the other women. Therefore, Alma decided to embark on the journey for justice, despite the risks she had been warned of, and reported the incidents to the facility's sergeant. When the sergeant heard what Alma had to say, he asked her, what was her proof of these accusations? Alma hesitated and asked, "proof?" He looked at her in a mocking manner, smiled, and whispered to her as he leaned in: "If I were you, I wouldn't bring this up again . . . you don't want to be deported, do you?"*

Stories like Alma's were at the center of controversy in 2017 when the U.S. National Archives and Records Administration (NARA) approved the U.S. Immigration and Customs Enforcement (ICE) request to dispose of thousands of records detailing reports on sexual violence and death inside its migrant detention facilities.[1] This prompted the American Civil Liberties Union to file a petition to overturn the motion, stating that "ICE shouldn't be allowed to purge important records and keep its operations out of the public eye."[2] In its response, NARA expanded the retention of these records from a period of twenty years to twenty-five years but restated its approval, arguing that NARA prioritizes "historically valuable records requiring permanent preservation" and authorizes agencies to "dispose of all other records."[3] Further, in cases of sexual assault, it stated that the "information is highly sensitive and does not warrant retention." This motion by NARA leads to the following questions: How is the official state archive constructed? How do these records of sexual violence threaten, inform, or destabilize the state's identity and its prison/border formations? How has the state's archiving practice itself become a form of gendered, sexual, and carceral violence? Finally, how does a feminist abolitionist analytic, rooted in Black feminist methodology, of state sexual violence destabilize and bring into crisis the official historical record?

In this chapter I analyze the prison/border state archives produced by the United States and its agencies to uphold and rationalize carcerality in a liberal modernity, most notably the archives regarding sexual violence produced by the U.S. Department of Homeland Security (DHS). The archives I discuss include statistics generated through DHS reports, DHS polices and U.S. federal law regarding gender-based and sexual violence (such as the 1994 Violence Against Women Act and the 2003 Prison Rape Elimination Act), data collected through a Freedom of Information Act (FOIA) request, and allegation statements of sexual assault and abuse filed with the DHS Office of Inspector General. These statistics, reports, and policies are part of the prison/border archive, which is an archive of violence that quantifies humanity, agency, rape, and sexual assault, aligning them with legible liberal concepts that facilitate sexual violence in migrant detention rather than eliminating it.[4]

I posit that the prison/border state archives document sexual violence in migrant detention not to end sexual violence in ICE facilities but rather to instrumentalize sexual violence and create an illusion of justice and state accountability. This illusion is critical for two reasons: sexual violence is a tool of dominance exerted to manage racialized populations in the state's prison/borders; and U.S. liberal modernity demands that its carceral institutions adapt the language of liberal feminism to rationalize captivity and removal. Rather than relying on the state archives (such as those approved for disposal by the NARA) to portray the severity of sexual violence in carceral spaces such as migrant detention, I dislodge the validity of the official historical record, bring it into crisis, and propose a feminist abolitionist approach toward understanding sexual violence. Therefore, in this chapter, I engage with the work of Black feminist radical scholars to employ a method of critical speculative writing rooted in feminist abolition theorization, which allows for possibilities of relationality, speculation, and questioning that counter the state record.

SEXUAL TERROR IN PRISON/BORDERS

ICE detention centers are prison/borders.[5] *Prison/border* is a term I conceptualize to highlight the ways in which migrant detention is a site of collision between prisons and borders, informed by both carceral and bordering logics. Migrant detention facilities and criminal prisons share identical staff and guard training protocols, a similar public and private for-profit model, and the same criminalizing discourses to rationalize their existence. Additionally, both prisons and migrant detention centers are host to rampant cases of sexual violence against their incarcerated populations. Therefore, to elucidate the formation of the prison/border I position sexual violence in ICE facilities as a form of both gendered prison violence and gendered border violence.

Sexual violence is applied here in a manner that reaches beyond the legal definitions established by the liberal state, referring to the bodily violation of people through sexual assault, sexual abuse, sexual harassment, and medical violence such as coerced sterilizations. In the Violence Against Women Reauthorization Act (VAWA), signed into law by President Barack Obama in March 2013 (reauthorizing the 1994 act), the legal definition of rape was changed for the first time since 1927, when it was defined as "the carnal knowledge of a female, forcibly and against her will."[6] The legal definition of rape is now, "the penetration, no matter how slight, of the vagina or anus with any body part or object, or oral penetration by a sex organ of another person, without the consent of the victim." This definition, according to policy, is intended to be inclusive, encompassing "either male or female victims or offenders, . . . instances in which the victim is incapable of giving consent because of temporary or permanent mental or physical incapacity, and . . . the various forms of sexual penetration understood to be rape."[7] The objective to be inclusive reflects a shift toward liberal modernity in policy rather than a holistic approach toward understanding sexual violence. That is, the legal definition of rape does not capture sexual violence as a phenomenon that is foundational to carceral spaces and migrant control. Most critically, this legal definition fails to recognize the complexities of coercion and consent in carceral spaces such as prisons, borders, and migrant detention. I thus employ an understanding of sexual violence beyond this definition in order to interrogate methods of control that rely on the weaponization of the body, sexuality, and reproduction.

Crucially, in May 2012, the year before VAWA, President Obama issued a presidential memorandum implementing the 2003 Prison Rape Elimination Act (PREA) in all federal confinement facilities, not just those under the U.S. Department of Justice.[8] This memorandum, which applied as well to DHS migrant detention facilities, prompted DHS to establish its own PREA regulation, "Standards to Prevent, Detect, and

Respond to Sexual Abuse and Assault in Confinement Facilities," in 2014. This new regulation builds on previous DHS policies that addressed sexual abuse and assault in ICE holding facilities and integrates standards previously established by the U.S. Department of Justice. The adoption of this policy, which is part of the prison/border archive, highlights another instance in which the infrastructure of migrant detention mirrors that of criminal prisons: its approach to sexual violence against its captive population is managed through the implementation of liberal reforms.

The 2012–13 adjustments to PREA and VAWA, both policies purportedly centered on women's rights, came at a time when ideas of progress and social equality had entered mainstream sociopolitical discourse under the Obama administration. Not only did this moment become a quintessential indicator of progress for victims/survivors of sexual violence, but in the immigrant rights community it also meant new protections for undocumented communities through the 2012 Deferred Action for Childhood Arrivals (DACA) program, as well as the expanded U visa access that VAWA granted to undocumented victims/survivors of gendered violence. However, despite this show of justice for marginalized communities, Obama soon became known as the "deporter in-chief" for the record number of migrants he deported. Similarly, both PREA and VAWA have been critiqued as failing to protect criminalized women of color and other vulnerable populations targeted for sexual violence.

To further demonstrate the shift to and shortcomings of liberal modernity in policy, it is useful to examine a monumental concept in mainstream feminist political discourse: consent. As feminism gains traction in mainstream culture, consent has become a key term in introductory conversations regarding gender, justice, and politics. In liberal feminist reforms—as embodied in PREA and VAWA—the notion of consent is highlighted as a metric to identify whether sexual assault has taken place. In migrant detention, allegations of sexual violence are often dismissed as lacking "evidence" to make this determination of consent. However, following interventions by antiviolence scholars who have critiqued mainstream feminism, I argue that the notion of consent in ICE detention is instrumentalized to protect ICE. That is, detained migrants do not have constitutional rights (they cannot consent), and so policies such as PREA that seemingly grant consent protect the facilities, not the detained migrants.[9]

Despite these liberal policies, allegations of abuse and sexual assault have continued to grow.[10] A 2017 FOIA report attained by the *Intercept* and CIVIC (now Freedom for Immigrants) demonstrated that since 2014, sexual assault and abuse complaints had outnumbered most other types of allegations made inside ICE facilities. Further troubling, despite the increase in reports from 2010 to 2016, only 0.4 percent of complaints pertaining to abuse had been turned into investigations.[11] In 2018, ICE responded to the *Intercept* by claiming that between 2012 and 2017 all allegations were investigated and that about 160, or 12 percent, of allegations were found to be "substantiated." The *Intercept*'s report demonstrates contradictions and inconsistencies with the number of investigations as provided by ICE, raising questions as to how this determination is made.[12]

THE PRODUCTION OF THE ARCHIVE AS GENDERED VIOLENCE

Angelique had just lived through a nightmare. She prayed it was a nightmare . . . but found herself unable to wake up from it. When she came back to herself, she heard the screaming demands of the ICE staff, ordering her to shower. She stood still in horror, and again he yelled at her. She must shower. He instructed her that she must "get rid of the evidence" on her body.

When I began this study, I was searching for data to prove that sexual violence is a prevalent technology of dominance in migrant detention facilities. The motivation was to inform the public of the sexually violent nature of migrant detention, in hopes that migrant detention will one day come to an end. However, the revelation of the 2017 FOIA report, which contained a spreadsheet detailing more than thirty thousand sexual violence allegations and over sixty pages of narratives reported by detained migrants, made it imperative that a study on sexual violation of detained migrants be done with care so as to not reproduce violence on the immigrant communities through the spectacle of abuse.[13] Saidiya V. Hartman's study of the Black subject in the Reconstruction era, *Scenes of Subjection: Terror, Slavery, and Self-Making in Nineteenth-Century America*, posits that instead of focusing on the scene of terror and Black suffering, it is more productive to study and intervene in "the savage encroachments of power that take place through notions of reform, consent, and protection."[14] Therefore, rather than displaying the violent cases of rape and sexual assault buried within the prison/border archive (in this case the narratives of sexual violence attained through FOIA), which would reproduce the spectacle of violated migrant bodies (an image already hypervisible in mainstream media), I build on a Black feminist abolitionist approach that centers the archive as the subject of analysis to reveal its role in a liberal carceral state.

In centering the state archive as a subject of study, I demonstrate that the omission of information in allegations, the discarding of reports, and even the progressive policies that otherwise seem to be holding the state accountable all uphold and legitimize U.S. state violence and its carceral regime. I consider these documents part of the prison/border archive as they are the voice of the nation-state that narrates its own history through records, intakes, and public statements. One major area of importance in the prison/border encompasses DHS policies and statistics on sexual violence. Through the archives regarding sexual violence of migrants, DHS demonstrates its effectiveness in eliminating foreign threats and proves its validity as a logical and humanist institution.

In her analysis of colonial archives, Lisa Lowe states, "I do not treat the colonial archive as a stable, transparent collection of facts." Rather, she approaches archives as "rooms of the imperial state" that house the colonial instruments of colonial governance and ways of knowing and disciplining populations.[15] Lowe derives her argument from Ann Laura Stoler, who argues that archives are not places of knowledge retrieval, but instead sites of state ethnography. She coins the term *colonial archive* to signify the way in which colonial, racial, and gendered power is inscribed in the historical record.[16] Similarly, in "Venus in Two Acts," Hartman describes the official archive of the slave trade as "a death sentence, a tomb, a display of the violated body."[17] Like Stoler, Hartman, and Lowe, I identify the prison/border archive as an archive of violence that erases the violation of migrants and legitimizes state and migrant detention via liberal language on sexual assault.

The prison/border archive's liberal rhetoric in its polices and reports on sexual violence is not in contradiction to decisions like NARA's motion to eliminate records; rather, they are all part of an archive of violence that secures migrant detention in a liberal modernity. For instance, the 2014 DHS regulation relating to PREA states, "sexual violence, against any victim, is an assault on human dignity and an affront to American values."[18] This statement brings into question what can be considered "American values," given that sexual violence against racialized and criminalized populations is a historical condition of the U.S. nation-state. Further, it masks the trend of state-sanctioned sexual violence in migrant detention. Hartman argues that during Reconstruction, the legal recognition of "slave humanity" intensified rather than ameliorated the "brutal exercise of power" against Black people.[19] Similarly, other scholars have critiqued humanist rhetoric in reform discourse after the postwar period to demonstrate how the current antiracist liberal modernity secures white supremacy and its institutions of violence and exclusion. The reiteration of certain humanist phrases in the DHS PREA policy—"human dignity" is mentioned twenty-two times—supports a liberal illusion of migrant detention as a fair bureaucratic process.

MODERN LIBERALISM AND MIGRANT DETENTION

Statistical reports on sexual assault in migrant detention solidify and rationalize migrant detention as a transparent and legitimate institution by neutralizing violence in a modern liberal fashion. The social and political philosophy of modern liberalism derives from the theory of liberalism, which centers ideas of the free man, inalienable rights, citizenship, and social equality as indicators of social progress.[20]

However, as Lisa Lowe contends, modern liberalism's ideas of freedom and equality are dependent on the very same conditions it presumably seeks to absolve: the subjection of racially gendered populations in the Global South and in U.S. racial social strata.[21] Lowe critically formulates the "archive of liberalism" as "narratives of progress and individual freedom that perform the important work of mediating and resolving liberalism's contradictions."[22] These narratives are written in the language of humanism and human rights. In the prison/border archive, sexual violence in migrant detention is redressed and made legible along modern liberal principles through the state's language of enumeration and consent.

The prison/border archive is part of the liberal archive and the construction of the modern liberal state. It documents the narratives and statistics of people who have been in captivity and who are considered ineligible to receive "citizenship rights," and it is tasked with mediating the perceived contradictions of liberalism, which espouses the value of rights and the notion of the free man while demanding the deportation and incarceration of people for state sovereignty and national security. In other words, as Michel Foucault argues in his theory of biopolitics, citizenship rights and freedom for some are maintained by negating the very same concepts for others, to the point of civil death.[23] The prison/border archive is thus integral to the project of modern liberalism, helping construct a secure state founded on rights through the detention of perceived threats, or racialized migrants. Specifically, the records on sexual violence in the prison/border archive demonstrate the state's conflict and anxieties as feminism enters mainstream discourse and as testimonies of sexual violence by survivors are made public. Furthermore, the humanist language in sexual violence policies in the prison/border archive secures the incarceration of migrants and their violation via the use of enumeration and rhetoric of consent.

Lowe argues that humanism works through a regime of "desiring freedom" by way of an economy of affirmation and forgetting: "the affirmation of desire for freedom is so inhabited by forgetting of its conditions of possibility, that every narrative articulation of freedom is haunted by its burial, by the violence of forgetting."[24] Lowe reads liberal state archives against the grain to reveal how national history both mediates and absorbs Western liberalism, progressive rights, and reforms as a condition of possibility for the sovereign state. Lowe's economy of affirmation and forgetting in modern liberalism is productive to an understanding of how the prison/border archive's reports, policies, and statistics utilize language on humanity, rights, and consent to create a liberal discursive fantasy of the free state. However, the prison/border archive also needs to forget state violence, as demonstrated by the motion approved by NARA to dispose of files on sexual violence. That is because the archive of the prison/border state is tasked with securing the state in two major ways: it secures the state against perceived crises such as racialized migrants, and it secures the state as a benevolent modern liberal democracy. Therefore, the prison/border archive reveals the state's aspirations as a carceral liberal democracy that must constantly affirm itself as liberator and simultaneously "forget" its own violence.

QUANTIFYING SEXUAL VIOLENCE OF MIGRANTS

For Stoler, the colonial archive's written accountability documents—its reports, summaries, and recommendations, which are produced through coding systems—are the foundations of colonial statecraft. Likewise, Lowe states that modern liberal state governance is assembled through logistics:

> As a material bureaucracy of rule, *and* the historical trace of imperial activities, the colonial archive portrays colonial governance as a strategic, permeable, and improvisational process: the tireless collection of tables, statistics, measurements, and numbers; the unending volumes of records and reports; the copied and recopied correspondence between offices; the production of legal classifications, cases, and typologies— these actively document *and* produce the risks, problems, and uncertainties that were the conditions of imperial rule.[25]

In a similar manner, the prison/border archive of sexual assault in migrant detention utilizes the same method of governing through a labyrinth of statistics, tables, charts, reports, and manuals. Through these documents, the DHS quantifies sexual violence and concepts of "human dignity," assigning violations to categories that are managed and measurable. For instance, the 2014 DHS PREA regulation states that "with respect to benefits," DHS conducts what is known as a "break even analysis" to reduce sexual abuse in its facilities by "first estimating the monetary value of preventing various types of sexual abuse (incidents involving violence, inappropriate touching, or a range of other behaviors) and then, using those values, calculating the reduction in the annual number of victims that would need to occur for the benefits of the rule to equal the cost of compliance."[26] This calculation is further expanded by DHS in a table describing the "cost and benefits" of the proposed PREA regulation in migrant detention facilities (figure 16.1). In this table, DHS calculates the necessary thresholds for reduction in sexual abuse to "break even with monetized costs" associated with implementing PREA

SUMMARY TABLE—ESTIMATED COSTS AND BENEFITS OF FINAL RULE
[$Millions]

	Immigration detention facilities	Holding facilities	Total DHS PREA rulemaking
10-Year Cost Annualized at 7% Discount Rate	$4.9	$3.3	$8.2
% Reduction of Sexual Abuse Victims to Break Even With Monetized Costs	N/A	N/A	*147%
Non-monetized Benefits	An increase in the general wellbeing and morale of detainees and staff, the value of equity, human dignity, and fairness for detainees in DHS custody.		
Net Benefits	As explained above, we did not estimate the number of incidents or victims of sexual abuse this rule would prevent. Instead, we conducted a breakeven analysis. Therefore, we did not estimate the net benefits of this rule.		

* For ICE confinement facilities.

Figure 16.1. DHS-produced table detailing the estimated costs and benefits of the PREA regulation. Published in the 2014 Standards to Prevent, Detect, and Respond to Sexual Abuse and Assault in Confinement Facilities.

standards and protocols. According to this table, the nonmonetized benefits of reducing sexual abuse in migrant detention are an "increase in the general wellbeing and morale of [detained migrants] and staff, the value of equity, human dignity, and fairness for [detained migrants] in DHS custody."[27]

Thus, the dignity and well-being of migrant people in DHS facilities become a line in a chart for the purpose of portraying migrant detention, and the U.S. carceral regime, as calculable, rational, and "fair." Indeed, the classification of human dignity and morale of detained migrants as one of the utmost valuable categories in this cost-benefit calculation is necessary to position migrant detention as fundamental to the modern liberal state.

In twentieth- and twenty-first-century U.S. immigration policy, numerical technologies have been central in constructing the "illegal immigrant" as a "crisis." Crimmigration scholar Jonathan Xavier Inda argues that the practices of enumeration through statistics construct "facts" as truth to portray an immigrant crisis to the public.[28] Further, immigration historian Mae M. Ngai asserts that immigration quotas produce a numerical threshold of authorized migrants, which in turn marks anyone above the threshold as "illegal."[29] Alongside their use in constructing crises, statistics are also utilized to conceal violence in marginalized populations. For instance, in the case of sexual violence against racialized communities such as Native women, Sarah Deer argues that statistics individualize state violence and generalize violence into data.[30] In these examples, statistics and enumeration produced by the state either rationalize violence in response to perceived crises or reduce the human impact and harm of state violence.

According to the *National ICE Detainee Handbook*, sexual violence allegations are commonly validated through "sexual assault forensic medical exam" (rape kit) and investigative interviews.[31] Moreover, the ICE directive titled Sexual Abuse and Assault Prevention and Intervention (issued in 2012, revised in 2014) states that the training for staff to investigate allegations of sexual assault and abuse "should cover, at a minimum, interviewing sexual abuse and assault victims, sexual abuse and assault evidence collection in confinement settings, [and] the criteria and evidence required for administrative action or prosecutorial referral."[32] According to this protocol, interviews and other "evidence" must be collected and must corroborate an allegation for it to be fully investigated. Most critically, in the allegations filed with the DHS Office of Inspector General, migrants testify that the evidence, or the lack thereof, is a recurring determinant as to why their allegation was rendered "unfounded." As discussed earlier, most allegations of sexual violence are found to be unsubstantiated and thus are not subject to investigation.

The systems to measure sexual violence in migrant detention implemented through PREA have thus effectively obscured the culture of sexual violence in ICE detention and have allowed for the further perpetration of sexual assault with impunity inside these carceral spaces. The stories of detained migrants such as Angelique's demonstrate how the allegations submitted to authorities (and even elements of the assaults themselves) revolved around the tracing of "evidence."

In some instances, detained migrants have testified that the form of sexual assault inflicted by ICE staff was meant to prevent traces of biological evidence. The logistical technologies employed by the prison/border archiving methods to measure sexual violence in ICE detention do not capture the reality of sexual violence in carceral facilities or protect people who are rendered criminal (i.e., detained migrants) from sexual violence. Instead, the act of governing through enumeration in modern liberalism enables the quantifying of sexual violence as a method to neutralize violence and to position state captivity as calculable and rational. This use of empirical data strategically secures migrant detention as an expanding regime and allows for the continuation of sexual violation of migrants as a form of border control.

THE IMPOSSIBILITY OF CONSENT IN ICE DETENTION

The 2014 revision of the Sexual Abuse and Assault Prevention and Intervention directive distinguishes between sexual abuse by another detained migrant and sexual abuse by an ICE staff member, contractor, or volunteer. In the case of the former, it is determined to occur when the "victim did not consent or was unable to consent or refuse, engages in or attempts to engage in" sexual acts. However, in the case of the latter, the definition changes to sexual acts "with or without the consent of the [detained migrant]."[33]

In this revised policy, DHS establishes sexual abuse and sexual assault as any sexual act between detained migrant and staff member, whether consensual or not, acknowledging the impossibility for incarcerated people to give consent to staff due to the imbalance of power. The DHS PREA regulation likewise notes that existing federal and state laws acknowledge the impossibility of consent by a detained migrant to sexual relations with a staff member while in custody, and moreover provide that any such sexual acts be criminalized, regardless of the age of the detained migrant. These clauses in the revised directive and the DHS PREA regulation signal a progressive understanding of consent in incarceration. However, despite this legal recognition, sexual assault allegations in ICE facilities by staff members still increased after 2014. Further, many of the "unsubstantiated" allegations were dropped due to an inability to establish whether sexual relationships were "nonconsensual."

Consent is also a major point of contention in the cases of coerced hysterectomies in ICE detention and prison facilities. However, unlike consent in sexual acts, "informed consent" in medical procedures is described as something that detained migrants can provide. A 2020 complaint detailing coerced hysterectomies of migrant women at the Irwin County Detention Center in Ocilla, Georgia, echoes the testimony of women formerly incarcerated in California prisons that a lack of proper informed consent during abdominal surgery led to their forced sterilizations.[34] In the 2020 film *Belly of the Beast*, Kelli Dillon testifies that at the age of twenty-four, while incarcerated in California, she was told that she needed surgery to treat ovarian cysts; she agreed to a hysterectomy in the case that cancer was detected. However, the doctors conducted a hysterectomy despite Dillon not having cancer—and she was not informed of this procedure until after her release. Mirroring this testimony, in the Irwin County complaint filed to the DHS Office of Inspector General by Project South, one unnamed immigrant woman in ICE custody reported that a hysterectomy procedure was never fully explained to her and that she was given three different explanations by different correctional and medical staff.[35] In another testimony, Pauline Binam, a Cameroonian migrant, attested that while awaiting deportation she underwent surgery for ovarian cysts. When she woke up, she was told that she had been given a hysterectomy, although she had only consented to removing the cysts.[36]

The mirroring of coerced hysterectomies in U.S. prisons and ICE detention reveals that in both carceral spaces, consent is utilized as a contested and floating term to justify medical abuse. The use of consent in migrant detention is applied differently for rape than it is for medical procedures such as hysterectomies. In analyses of coerced hysterectomies among incarcerated women, scholars argue that the practice of informed consent is a "reformist reform" that enforces the practice of forced sterilization. That is, by providing doctors with an avenue to argue that they had been granted consent, it affords them and the state freedom from liability.[37] However, feminist scholars writing on reproductive justice contend that incarcerated people are incapable of giving informed consent since their imprisoned condition subjects them to "stress, undue pressure, duress, or undue influence," making consent fundamentally coercive.[38] These are the same conditions that prevent people in captivity from consenting to sex.

Black feminist historian Sarah Haley grapples with the political concept of consent to argue that Black incarcerated women in the Jim Crow era did not have access to consent in the violent racial patriarchal system of convict labor. She demonstrates how John Locke, Thomas Hobbes, and Jean-Jacques Rousseau conceived the concept of consent as fundamental to a free democratic society, where free individuals must voluntarily enter into a relationship with the state and its institutions for protection of their rights and "freedom."[39] In other words, a "free man" must consent to be governed for the construction of a free society. Haley builds on the work of feminist political theorist Carole Pateman to demonstrate the paradox at play: "the problem for theories in which consent produces freedom is that 'individual freedom and democracy is also a precondition for the practice of consent.'" Therefore, Haley concludes that imprisoned women's engagement in sex in captivity and under "conditions of force" is nonconsensual, a method of acquiring protection from those in power who "would otherwise terrorize or kill you."[40]

In the prison/border archive, detained migrants are granted consent and human dignity in policy documents that correlate with contemporary liberal feminist political discourse. However, detained migrants are not granted citizenship rights such as the right to habeas corpus (which protects against indefinite and unlawful imprisonment) and are considered inherently criminal through the notion of illegality. Moreover, the conditions of ICE detention as a prison/border mark the impossibility for noncitizens in captivity to consent in a myriad of ways. One way that consent is not afforded to migrants is that they are displaced populations, pushed by the global political economy to migrate from the Global South, their migration a manifestation of coercive power.[41] Even more, the status of "illegality" and the captivity of people in ICE detention are forced conditions. Therefore, the "consent" that is granted to migrants in ICE detention is not granted to them as free, willing subjects; it is instrumentalized, laying the groundwork for the dismissal of allegations of sexual violence and helping secure ICE detention by concealing sexual violence within its walls.

The weaponizing of consent in PREA and VAWA to reinforce sexual violence against migrant women demonstrates how liberal reform policies further criminalize and violate communities of color. Feminist scholars have critiqued VAWA on the grounds that it works under a legal rubric that has historically criminalized immigrants and women of color in the United States. Lee Ann S. Wang argues that VAWA's racial logics perpetually position Blackness as criminal and white woman victimhood as a "universalizing humanitarian discourse."[42] For migrant women, Obama's reauthorization of VAWA expanded the U visa program, which grants legal status to undocumented survivors and victims of crimes. Wang argues, however, that the U visa's expansion revictimizes undocumented immigrant survivors through concepts of innocence, while affording citizenship status only to victims who agree to cooperate with police and participate in the deportation regime by aiding in the detainment of their abuser. In this transaction, the U.S. legal system is absolved from accountability in creating the legal status that makes migrants vulnerable and viable. This also remains true in the DHS PREA regulations, where the state is positioned as innocent and neutral via the use of humanist and consent-based rhetoric, while sexual violence is individualized into managed and measured events that are done by individuals rather than structural systems. Far more than granting consent to detained migrants, PREA and VAWA instead provide institutions with a pretext to avoid accountability and to conceal sexual violence facilitated by the state.

ICE detention centers and the reform policies implemented to address sexual violence demonstrate how the notion of consent under liberal feminism and humanism is invested in reinforcing the prison/border state. The concept of consent is developed to protect white womanhood. It is rooted in the concept of the free white citizen with access to rights. Therefore, the assignment of consent in carceral settings presents a paradox, where detained migrants have no rights protected under the Constitution but are given consent when allegations of sexual abuse are raised. Sexual violence in ICE detention centers continues despite liberal feminist policies, and is even strengthened by these policies, demonstrating the need for an abolitionist framework toward ending migrant detention and sexual violence. The liberal policies that grant conditional rights such as consent do not make migrant detention safe; on the contrary, carcerality is maintained by sexual violence. Liberal policies and humanist language strengthen carcerality and sexual violence and, therefore, are ultimately incompatible with justice. Thus, a feminist abolitionist lens is critical if we are to challenge and end the violence in ICE detention centers.

DEPORTATION OR DEATH

When Jaali had a medical visit to the Adelanto ICE facility's doctor, he asked to use the restroom before his appointment. He was escorted by a tall Latino guard who had previously made uncomfortable remarks about his body in front of other detained migrants to humiliate him. The guard followed him past the restroom and asked him to leave the stall door open while he used it. After realizing what was happening, Jaali felt his heart stop and nervously told the guard that he no longer had to use the restroom. Jaali then walked toward the sink to splash water on his face in the hope that he could wash away the shame and that the cold droplets of water could bring back strength to his body. The guard walked up behind him and grabbed his waist. The guard told Jaali that he was a longtime friend of an immigration judge and that he could work out a deal with Jaali in exchange for citizenship.

While there are important connections between prisons and immigration detention centers, the latter also reproduce violence all their own. Many scholars have raised concerns over noncitizens in ICE detention having an added layer of criminalization and dehumanization, as well as a fundamental lack of constitutional rights such as habeas corpus.[43] Moreover, migrants in ICE detention are marked as both noncitizens and people in captivity, making them hypersusceptible to removal and deportation. This hyper-deportability is what makes sexual violence in migrant detention different than cases of sexual violence in U.S. prisons and anywhere else within the U.S. nation-state. The status of deportability follows undocumented migrants, whether in detention or after release.[44] But because migrants in ICE detention have open and pending cases for removal, the reality that they can be deported at any time is increased exponentially. This heightened threat of deportability, coupled with the historical sexualization of migrants, is how sexual violence of detained migrants has become routine in ICE facilities.

Unlike U.S. prisons, ICE detention centers weaponize deportation as both a punishment and a pretext to sexual violence and death. Amid the 2020 outbreak of the COVID-19 pandemic, there were numerous reports of ICE deporting detained migrants who had tested positive rather than providing them with medical treatment.[45] This practice of instrumentalizing deportation is not new. Before the pandemic, sick detainees inside ICE detention facilities were subject to medical abuse and medical neglect.

Similarly, in the reports of the coerced mass hysterectomies at the Irwin County Detention Center, an advocate testified that at least one woman requested to be deported due to a fear of being forcefully sterilized: "she was worried that she would 'lose her reproductive system' if her only choices were to see the doctor or remain untreated. The woman was subsequently deported."[46] Mass coerced hysterectomies in migrant detention thus also function as a migration deterrent. A similar logic underpins the separation of families along the U.S.-Mexico border.[47] The violence of separating families is instrumentalized as a warning to future migrants to not attempt to cross the border. In 2018, Donald Trump proclaimed his support for policies that separate families at the border, stating, "if they feel there will be separation, they don't come."[48] Like these separations, coerced sterilizations target migrant parenthood and reproduction. Therefore, the mass coerced hysterectomies in ICE facilities are also a method of border control in two major ways: either people ask for self-deportation, via "voluntary departure," or they risk losing their reproductive organs, a practice that reduces the migrant population and its futurity.

Similarly, in the FOIA report already discussed, many sexual assault allegation narratives refer to deportation as a primary factor in the assault they endured. According to the testimonies, deportation is instrumentalized in a couple of ways: detained migrants must comply with the assault because they fear they will be deported if they do not (or, in some cases, are promised protection from deportation if they engage in sexual acts), and migrants have been deported by ICE agents who feared that a complaint would be lodged against them. For example, an intake form included in the FOIA report attests that over seven victims/survivors of sexual assault by a sheriff's deputy were deported by ICE before they were able to testify: "prosecutors had planned to call a dozen men" who had claimed to have been sexually abused, but when it came time to call the victims to testify, "most of those victims had since been removed." In another allegation narrative, an unnamed detained migrant and survivor of sexual abuse retells the events that led him to "ask" to be deported. He testifies that after the continuous sexual abuse, detention became unbearable: "Every day there was name calling and tension which led me to ask for voluntary departure on my first court date on April 2, 2014."[49]

These examples demonstrate how ICE weaponizes sexual violence in migrant detention facilities to coerce detained migrants into choosing between voluntary deportation or exposure to coerced sterilization and sexual assault. The mass coerced hysterectomies of migrant women in ICE detention are a form of death at a wide scale; historically, the sterilization of racialized women has been instrumental in preventing the continuation of undesired populations, what some describe as a form of genocide. Similarly, sexual assault is also a form of death. Feminist theorists like Hortense Spillers and Sarah Deer argue that what allows the violation of Black and Indigenous women is their corresponding reduction to flesh or to sexualized objects.[50] The sexual assault and sexual abuse of migrants in ICE detention reinforce their dehumanization and legitimize their exclusion from the state. The "choice" between deportation and violence is a limited choice between different forms of death. For migrants escaping social, state, and economic violence, deportation is a death sentence. On the other hand, sexual violence, coerced sterilizations, rape, and sexual assault are also forms of civil, social, and biological death.

SPECULATIVE WRITING AS A FEMINIST ABOLITIONIST PRAXIS

What happened to the thousands of people who made these reports across ICE detention centers from 2010 until 2016?

Did they have hope after they hung up the phone with the DHS staff recording their assault incident? Were they able to breathe just a little after dropping off their testimony letter in the facility's mailroom? Or did it bring more fear of retaliation?

Did they get deported? Were they coerced to sign voluntary removal, or rather, forced displacement by another name?

Do they have the care they need as survivors of sexual violence?

Is there ever enough care that can nourish the wounds?

Do they have nightmares of the violence that occurred?

Are they alive to still have nightmares or dreams?

What happened when they didn't hear back?

Or when they heard back and were told that there was "no proof" of the horrors they had endured inside ICE's prison walls?

What did they feel? Did they feel alone?

What happened when Power told them that the violence inflicted on their body and soul was not real . . . but their haunting memories do not let them forget.

The prison/border archive is made up of public statements, policy documents, and statistics reports that maintain the continuity of migrant detention in the present and crystallize state power into history. The questions I contemplate here are questions that cannot be answered via the official archive. When researching sexual violence in ICE detention, I found inconsistent statistics of allegations, thousands of incomplete narratives of complaints, and DHS policy documents aimed at reducing sexual assault in its facilities. However, I knew that I could never really understand the severity of sexual violence in these prison/borders. That is because we can never truly know the stories of the detained migrants who were subject to sexual violence. Many have been deported, and others have been threatened into silence with their legal cases on the line. Further, the limited data discussed in this chapter, retrieved from the state through an FOIA request, cannot narrate sexual violence as state violence. Thus, when I uncovered the horrific testimonies of violence and torment inflicted onto people's bodies and spirits, I knew that these gruesome details also reduce migrant suffering into quantified categories fixed into boxes.

Therefore, throughout this chapter I have utilized a form of speculative writing rooted in Black feminist praxis, narrating in opposition to the prison/border archive and dislodging the power of DHS. Here, I am indebted to Hartman, who utilizes what she calls *critical fabulation* to make a speculative intervention into the archive. Hartman posits: "Is it possible to exceed or negotiate the constitutive limits of the archive? By advancing a series of speculative arguments and exploiting the capacities of the subjunctive (a grammatical mood that expresses doubts, wishes, and possibilities), in fashioning a narrative, which is based upon archival research, and by that, I mean a critical reading of the archive that mimes the figurative dimensions of history, I intended both to tell an impossible story and to amplify the impossibility of its telling."[51]

I wrote these stories as an act of critical speculative writing: a combination, intertwining, and rearranging of testimony along with speculative fiction. The stories are semifictionalized narratives built from the allegations found within the thousands of buried DHS reports and drawn from my own relationships with people I have visited and supported inside the Adelanto ICE Processing Center in San Bernardino County, California. For instance, Alma's story draws from a complaint filed by the Mexican American Legal Defense Educational Fund and partnering organizations that alleged that numerous women had been sexually abused at the Karnes County ICE Residential Center in Karnes City, Texas. Other elements of stories I discussed here draw from thematic patterns I identified in other allegations, such as a complaint where an ICE officer asked, "you don't want to get deported, do you?" after sexually assaulting a male migrant in detention. Jaali's story also contains elements from an allegation where an ICE officer offered to provide citizenship to an incarcerated migrant if he engaged in sexual acts with the officer. In this collection of statements, I found hundreds of accounts detailing the fear of deportation and retaliation that accompany sexual assault and abuse in ICE detention.

Moreover, the questions I raised were critically gathered after I read the thousands of allegation statements, recollected the stories of people in detention I have met, and reflected on my own life. My aspiration to reach beyond the archive is also informed by my own positionality in a mixed-status family and my witnessing of the desperation, hope, and resilience of my migrant community.

Thus, the forms of speculative writing I conduct in this chapter allow me to read against the grain of the prison/border archive and to reach beyond the state narrative that commits to securing the state. The practice of reaching beyond the numerical data, partial statements, and policy procedures of the prison/border archive pushes us to also look beyond the liberal policies that have failed to protect migrants in ICE detention. The critical speculative writing I employ here results in critical narration that resists absorption by the prison/border archive and refuses weaponization.

We can never truly know the number of people who have been subjected to sexual violence in migrant detention, or the severity of what happens in these carceral spaces. We also can never know how many people could not file a complaint for the allegation to ever become part of the archive labeled "historically invaluable" and set for disposal by NARA. We do not know how many people were deported before or after filing a complaint. We can only speculate. The critical speculative writing method I employ is an invitation toward a feminist abolitionist praxis that refuses to solidify the prison/border archive as history and truth. This speculation is also a refusal of the liberal humanist language produced by DHS, which utilizes narrative to legitimize sexual violence against migrants as quantified and controlled events. When we look beyond the blacked-out boxes of redacted information, case numbers, and data tables, we can imagine the names, faces, and emotions of people who have migrated and survived violence. We can push through the silencing, omission, and denial created by the archive of violence and instead move toward an alternative mode of relationality, imagining forms of creating justice and freedom that do not depend on state-centered policies.

NOTES

1. NARA, "ICE Detainee Records Schedule Nears Completion."
2. Lopez, "ICE Plans to Start Destroying Records of Immigrant Abuse."
3. NARA, "Consolidated Reply: DAA-0567-2015-0013."
4. See Ann Stoler's theory of the colonial archive, in "Colonial Archives and the Arts of Governance."
5. This concept is inspired by theories that identify migrant detention as an extension of the U.S.-Mexico border. See, e.g., Loyd and Mountz, *Boats, Borders, and Bases*; Macías-Rojas, *From Deportation to Prison*; Wilsher, *Immigration Detention*; Wong, *Rights, Deportation, and Detention in the Age of Immigration Control*.
6. Congressional Research Service, "The Violence Against Women Act (VAWA)," 7.
7. Congressional Research Service, 7–8.
8. White House, "Presidential Memorandum."
9. Wang, "Unsettling Innocence." Scholars such as Lee Ann S. Wang and Jess Whatcott have argued that reform policies such as the VAWA operate under a carceral approach to "safety" for survivors, which has resulted in the revictimization and criminalization of women of color survivors.
10. Standards to Prevent, Detect, and Respond to Sexual Abuse and Assault in Confinement Facilities, 79 Fed. Reg. 13,100 (March 7, 2014).

11. U.S. Department of Homeland Security, "OIG Freedom of Information Act Request No. 2016–126," FOIA report, 2017.

12. Speri, "Detained, Then Violated."

13. U.S. Department of Homeland Security, "OIG Freedom of Information Act Request No. 2016–126," FOIA report, 2017.

14. Hartman, *Scenes of Subjection*, 283.

15. Lowe, *The Intimacies of Four Continents*, 4.

16. Stoler, *Along the Archival Grain*, 12.

17. Hartman, "Venus in Two Acts," 2.

18. Standards to Prevent, Detect, and Respond to Sexual Abuse and Assault in Confinement Facilities, 79 Fed. Reg. 13,100, at 13,103 (March 7, 2014).

19. Hartman, *Scenes of Subjection*, 10.

20. Lowe, *The Intimacies of Four Continents*. Lisa Lowe argues that liberal modernity is founded on notions of the free man (or free citizen), who has the right to own property. She emphasizes the need for citizenship, and rights, to maintain a liberal modern nation-state that promotes ideas of progress and humanism.

21. Lowe, 3.

22. Lowe, 4.

23. Foucault, *The History of Sexuality*.

24. Lowe, "The Intimacies of Four Continents," in *Haunted by Empire*, 206.

25. Lowe, *The Intimacies of Four Continents*, 4 (emphasis in original).

26. Standards to Prevent, Detect, and Respond to Sexual Abuse and Assault in Confinement Facilities, 79 Fed. Reg. 13,100, at 13,154 (March 7, 2014).

27. Standards, at 13,155.

28. Inda, *Targeting Immigrants*.

29. Ngai, *Impossible Subjects*.

30. Deer, *The Beginning and End of Rape*.

31. U.S. Immigration and Customs Enforcement, *National ICE Detainee Handbook*, 34–35.

32. See ICE directive 11062.2, Sexual Abuse and Assault Prevention and Intervention (May 22, 2014), 9.

33. ICE directive 11062.2, at 9; Standards to Prevent, Detect, and Respond to Sexual Abuse and Assault in Confinement Facilities, 79 Fed. Reg. 13,100, at 13,167 (March 7, 2014).

34. Jindia, "Belly of the Beast."

35. Project South, "Lack of Medical Care, Unsafe Work Practices, and Absence of Adequate Protection."

36. Chapin, "ICE Tried to Deport a Woman Who Says She Was Sterilized in Custody."

37. Whatcott, "No Selves to Consent."

38. Whatcott, 143.

39. Haley, *No Mercy Here*, 62.

40. Haley, 63, 107.

41. Whatcott, "No Selves to Consent," 149.
42. Wang, "Unsettling Innocence."
43. Menjívar and Kanstroom, *Constructing Immigrant "Illegality."*
44. De Genova, "Migrant 'Illegality' and Deportability in Everyday Life."
45. Kassie and Marcolini, "It Was Like a Time Bomb."
46. Olivares and Washington, "He Just Empties You All Out."
47. Roth, Grace, and Seay, "Mechanisms of Deterrence."
48. Shepardson, "Trump Says Family Separations Deter Illegal Immigration."
49. U.S. Department of Homeland Security, "OIG Freedom of Information Act Request No. 2016–126," FOIA report, 2016.
50. Spillers, "Mama's Baby, Papa's Maybe"; Deer, *The Beginning and End of Rape.*
51. Hartman, "Venus in Two Acts," 11.

BIBLIOGRAPHY

Chapin, Angelina. "ICE Tried to Deport a Woman Who Says She Was Sterilized in Custody." *The Cut*, September 17, 2020. https://www.thecut.com/2020/09/auline-binam-says-she-was-sterilized-under-ice-custody.html.

Congressional Research Service. "The Violence Against Women Act (VAWA): Historical Overview, Funding, and Reauthorization." Report R45410, April 23, 2019.

Deer, Sarah. *The Beginning and End of Rape: Confronting Sexual Violence in Native America.* Minneapolis: University of Minnesota Press, 2015.

De Genova, Nicholas P. "Migrant 'Illegality' and Deportability in Everyday Life." *Annual Review of Anthropology* 31 (2002): 419–47.

Foucault, Michel. *The History of Sexuality: An Introduction.* New York: Vintage Books, 1990.

Haley, Sarah. *No Mercy Here: Gender, Punishment, and the Making of Jim Crow Modernity.* Charlotte: University of North Carolina Press, 2016.

Hartman, Saidiya V. *Scenes of Subjection: Terror, Slavery, and Self-Making in Nineteenth-Century America.* New York: Oxford University Press, 2010.

Hartman, Saidiya V. "Venus in Two Acts." *Small Axe: A Caribbean Journal of Criticism* 12, no. 2 (2008): 1–14.

Inda, Jonathan Xavier. *Targeting Immigrants: Government, Technology, and Ethics.* Hoboken, N.J.: John Wiley, 2008.

Jindia, Shilpa. "Belly of the Beast: California's Dark History of Forced Sterilizations." *Guardian*, June 30, 2020.

Kassie, Emily, and Barbara Marcolini. "It Was Like a Time Bomb: How ICE Helped Spread the Coronavirus." *New York Times*, July 10, 2020.

Lopez, Victoria. "ICE Plans to Start Destroying Records of Immigrant Abuse, Including Sexual Assault and Deaths in Custody." American Civil Liberties Union,

August 28, 2017. https://www.aclu.org/news/immigrants-rights/ice-plans-start-destroying-records-immigrant.

Lowe, Lisa. *The Intimacies of Four Continents*. Durham, N.C.: Duke University Press, 2015.

Lowe, Lisa. "The Intimacies of Four Continents." In *Haunted by Empire: Geographies of Intimacy in North American History*, edited by Ann Laura Stoler, 191–212. Durham, N.C.: Duke University Press, 2006.

Loyd, Jenna M., and Alison Mountz. *Boats, Borders, and Bases: Race, the Cold War, and the Rise of Migration Detention in the United States*. Berkeley: University of California Press, 2018.

Macías-Rojas, Patrisia. *From Deportation to Prison: The Politics of Immigration Enforcement in Post-Civil Rights America*. New York: New York University Press, 2016.

Menjívar, Cecilia, and Daniel Kanstroom. *Constructing Immigrant "Illegality": Critiques, Experiences, and Responses*. Cambridge: Cambridge University Press, 2014.

NARA (National Archives and Records Administration). "Consolidated Reply: DAA-0567-2015-0013, Immigration and Customs Enforcement, Detainee Records." December 12, 2019.

NARA (National Archives and Records Administration). "ICE Detainee Records Schedule Nears Completion." Press release, June 21, 2019. https://www.archives.gov/press/press-releases-2.

Ngai, Mae M. *Impossible Subjects: Illegal Aliens and the Making of Modern America*. Princeton, N.J.: Princeton University Press, 2014.

Olivares, José, and John Washington. "He Just Empties You All Out: Whistleblower Reports High Number of Hysterectomies at ICE Detention Facility." *Intercept*, September 15, 2020. https://theintercept.com/2020/09/15/hysterectomies-ice-irwin-whistleblower/.

Project South. "Lack of Medical Care, Unsafe Work Practices, and Absence of Adequate Protection Against COVID-19 for Detained Immigrants and Employees Alike at the Irwin County Detention Center." Letter to Joseph V. Cuffari, Cameron Quinn, Thomas P. Giles, and David Paulk, September 14, 2020. https://projectsouth.org/wp-content/uploads/2020/09/OIG-ICDC-Complaint-1.pdf.

Roth, Benjamin J., Breanne L. Grace, and Kristen D. Seay. "Mechanisms of Deterrence: Federal Immigration Policies and the Erosion of Immigrant Children's Rights." *American Journal of Public Health*, 110, no. 1 (January 2020): 84–86.

Shepardson, David. "Trump Says Family Separations Deter Illegal Immigration." Reuters, October 13, 2018.

Speri, Alice. "Detained, Then Violated." *Intercept*, April 11, 2018.

Spillers, Hortense J. "Mama's Baby, Papa's Maybe: An American Grammar Book." *Diacritics* 17, no. 2 (1987): 65–81.

Stoler, Ann Laura. *Along the Archival Grain: Epistemic Anxieties and Colonial Common Sense*. Princeton, N.J.: Princeton University Press, 2009.

Stoler, Ann Laura. "Colonial Archives and the Arts of Governance." *Archival Science* 2, no. 1–2 (2002): 87–109.

U.S. Immigration and Customs Enforcement. *National ICE Detainee Handbook.* 2023 edition. https://www.ice.gov/doclib/detention/ndHandbook/ndhEnglish.pdf.

Wang, Lee Ann S. "Unsettling Innocence: Rewriting the Law's Invention of Immigrant Woman as Cooperator and Criminal Enforcer." *Scholar and Feminist Online* 13, no. 2 (2016). https://sfonline.barnard.edu/navigating-neoliberalism-in-the -academy-nonprofits-and-beyond/.

Whatcott, Jess. "No Selves to Consent: Women's Prisons, Sterilization, and the Biopolitics of Informed Consent." *Signs: Journal of Women in Culture and Society* 44, no. 1 (2018): 131–53.

White House (archived website). "Presidential Memorandum: Implementing the Prison Rape Elimination Act." Press release, May 12, 2012. https:// obamawhitehouse.archives.gov/the-press-office/2012/05/17/presidential -memorandum-implementing-prison-rape-elimination-act.

Wilsher, Daniel. *Immigration Detention: Law, History, Politics.* Cambridge: Cambridge University Press, 2011.

Wong, Tom. *Rights, Deportation, and Detention in the Age of Immigration Control.* Palo Alto, Calif.: Stanford University Press, 2015.

17

TRUMP'S BELLICOSE BORDER WALL AND THE HATEFUL RHETORIC AND VIOLENCE IT INSPIRES IN THE PASO DEL NORTE REGION

CYNTHIA BEJARANO AND DIANA J. LÓPEZ

DURING THE TRUMP ADMINISTRATION, XENOPHOBIA incited hate and heightened border security in the U.S. border region. Although conservative arguments for more border security infrastructure predate the Trump administration, Donald Trump's presidency perpetuated a relentless narrative of lawlessness, crime, and illegality to justify a new and more fortified multimillion-dollar border wall. Trump's arguments exacerbated images of violent landscapes and perpetuated negative narratives of transborder residents living in the Paso del Norte region of the U.S.-Mexico border.

Outside of the U.S.-Mexico border region, it is challenging to explain what living at, near, or in proximity to a border wall physically, emotionally, and materially represents. The U.S. border wall signifies an unnatural, foreign, and alien materiality that interrupts natural, fluid environments and familial and cultural relations between the United States and Mexico. The building of border fences and walls—which involves dismantling and rebuilding them with new, reinforced materials, wasting resources needed by local, disenfranchised border communities—serves as a distraction to the vitriolic targeting of local transborder residents. Key to this chapter is our description of the constant disruptions to the natural environment by the border wall, and to people's relationality to the land and with one another, as they are forced to precariously cross walls and borders, or are forced to live within bordered, carceral settings unable to cross these reinforced and man-made walls.[1]

Lipan Apache scholar, poet, and activist Margo Tamez, someone directly affected by the occupation of the border wall in her family's ancestral South Texas lands, recognizes the hype that the border wall discourse creates, and its diversion from the serious problems affecting border communities. One of Tamez's poetic prose pieces exclaims, "||||the wall is not a wall||||there are holes in the wall||||the wall is a reference to U.S. institutions, systems, and structures||||and emulates each||||that is, the wall||||is a prison."[2] Tamez's prose is poignant here, since the border wall, Trump's bellicose border wall, is a distraction from the underlying politics of empire building and the racial, colonial, and intersectional violence that we witness and experience across border communities.[3] The Trump administration's wastefulness in building new iterations of the already existing border wall and the security apparatus backing it remain diversions from the violence and neglect that communities endure.

This chapter focuses broadly on the impact and implications of the border wall in the Paso del Norte region, but specifically on two New Mexico cities, Sunland Park and Santa Teresa, that intersect with El Paso, Texas, and Ciudad Juárez, Chihuahua, Mexico. As a state wedged between Texas and Arizona (and the border politics surrounding them), our home state of New Mexico is often absent from larger conversations regarding the U.S.-Mexico border. But the cities of Sunland Park and Santa Teresa are central to security debates in the U.S. Border Patrol's El Paso sector, and were often framed as security narratives during the Trump era.

Sunland Park, a city incorporated in 1983, is home to the venerated Mount Cristo Rey, a sacred site known for its annual religious pilgrimages. The Union Pacific Railroad, which moves parallel to the never-ending construction of a swath of the U.S. border wall, cuts across the mountain's base here. The most populous city in New Mexico's border region, Sunland Park is commonly known for its eponymous Racetrack and Casino and the Western Playland Amusement Park. The two local entertainment conglomerates have long monopolized the city's location near the large urban communities of El Paso and Ciudad Juárez. Neighboring Santa Teresa is its affluent sibling, known for its port of entry, growing industry and railroad development, and a once-gated community with a popular country club. On the other side of the border wall from Sunland Park is Lomas de Poleo, an outlier community of Ciudad Juárez. Opposite to Santa Teresa is San Jerónimo, an isolated yet significant international port of entry into Mexico, popular for trade routes and passageways that bypass the city metropolis of Ciudad Juárez. This beautifully complex landscape is an overlooked yet important component of the greater Paso del Norte region. Together, these communities have experienced new border wall construction in areas where a border wall already existed, or where the U.S. Border Patrol already had technological surveillance. Much of this costly earth-moving, earth-altering construction took place during the Trump era, which magnified numerous injuries in border communities, including racialized, social, political, and environmental violence.[4]

Often absent from border wall discussions are the on-the-ground experiences of locals, particularly in Sunland Park, where residents live as close to the border wall as one can, some as close as several hundred feet, as border patrol agents and surveillance systems saturate the area. In nearby Santa Teresa, on the other hand, the new wall perimeter appears useless, cutting into the desert and beginning as quickly as it ends, revealing open land between the United States and Mexico. Both sections of the newly constructed border wall cost millions of dollars, a symbol of power and empire, all too familiar in this geopolitical zone.

Our chapter discusses the impact and implications of the border wall in the Paso del Norte region, while focusing on (1) the need to center feminist research and praxis in scholarship on the border wall and the securitization of the border; (2) the historical, colonial, and legal proliferation of border security propaganda at the U.S.-Mexico border; (3) Trump's border wall rhetoric, the border wall construction at New Mexico's border with Texas and Chihuahua, intersectional violence, and border wall's negative implications on local communities; and finally, (4) the use of social protests as interventions to obstruct the Trump regime's border wall and the aftermath of his administration.[5]

FRONTERIZA FEMINISTAS UP AGAINST THE BORDER WALL

A significant body of literature concerning the border wall existed prior to Trump's reign of terror, but research grew exponentially during his administration, as policies and practices emanating from his administration were often cruel and inhumane, especially as they pertained to migration, deportation, and national and border security. Often missing from these analyses, though, are the gendered and embodied experiences of Latinx border residents. This chapter is written from our critical observations and analysis as two *fronteriza* women that have worked together in different capacities for seven years, and as women born and raised in this borderland region. Written from the perspectives of *feminista* teachings and border discourse, this chapter centers on our lived experiences, as well as what we have witnessed as resilience narratives with other border residents. It juxtaposes *feminista fronteriza* thought and logic with current research on the border-industrial complex. We offer resilience narratives as counterhegemonic narratives, as gendered and embodied work that speaks to existing research on the border-industrial complex. We argue that feminist analysis is often lacking in analysis and critique of the hypermasculine and toxic masculinities represented in the border context.[6]

In this writing, we acknowledge the privilege and responsibilities that we carry as borderlands scholars. We draw from Kimberlé Crenshaw's conceptualization of intersectionality to acknowledge how interconnectedness and intersectional *transfronteriza* identities allow us to understand and contextualize the meaning and representation of a border wall from firsthand perspectives.[7] Growing up, Diana could see the border wall from her family's home in Sunland Park, and during her frequent trips across the border to visit family in Ciudad Juárez. Cynthia grew up fifteen miles north of the border wall in a colonia, where she witnessed the earlier iterations of the reinforced chain link fence and its metamorphosis into the monstrosity of steel and technology that it is today. Living in proximity to the U.S.-Mexico border has shaped our careers as activists, scholars, and *fronteriza* women. As we highlight here, our purpose is to create a reflexive *feminista* interpretation of the current securitization of the border. Notwithstanding the securitization, privatization of this region is part of the colonial legacies that remain in this country. We highlight the border wall protests that take place in this region as interventions to these colonial legacies, which are pivotal to our analysis of the borderlands. Border people do not acquiesce to this violence, but rather choose to resist the heightened securitization along the border wall through activism and through their resilience narratives.

We are interested in articulating a broader picture of the border wall's symbolism and its reverberating effects on local Latinx border residents.[8] Although the current migration crisis and ongoing mass deportations are necessary to discuss, a concentrated analysis of these calamities is beyond the scope of this work.[9] Instead, we would like to draw attention to the often forgotten local, disenfranchised Latinx communities, who, according to current U.S. Census data, account for 97 percent of Sunland Park residents and 82.4 percent of Santa Teresa residents. Both communities confront chronic surveillance as they live "in the shadow of the wall."[10] We arrive at the spectacle of the wall through the increasing rise of the carceral industry and the carceral state, and the xenophobia and nativist sentiments that grew during the Trump era.

THE HISTORICAL AND COLONIAL CONTEXT OF WHITE SUPREMACY UNDERGIRDING BORDER VIOLENCE

The United States has a long and violent legacy of historical, colonial, and legal frameworks, which set the foundation for the border security propaganda that we now experience. The settler states we are interrogating in this chapter wrested lands from Indigenous people living in the region for millennia. The Lipan Apache, Mescalero Apache, Piro, Manso, Suma, Jumano, Ysleta del Sur Pueblo, Tortugas Pueblo, and Piro/Manso/Tiwa were dispossessed of their lands and displaced for colonizing and empire-building purposes. A flagrant and contemporary example is *Tamez et al. v. Chertoff* (2008), an internationally recognized fight by border communities against Bush-era border militarization.[11] Despite a multiyear battle against the U.S. Department of Homeland Security (DHS), a Lipan Apache family from South Texas had its land taken by the U.S. government's eminent domain mandate. Elder and matriarch Eloisa García Tamez, who sued DHS secretary Michael Chertoff, once said as she walked along her land, now divided by the border wall, "I know what this wall is: It's a prison."[12] This is a poignant sentiment for many of us.

The presence of the physical border wall, and the further militarization of the region through high-tech surveillance and national guard soldiers, heavily affects the communities and Latinx people living there, exemplifying a history of colonial violence that ultimately derives from a white supremacist settler colonial agenda. As Roberto Hernández puts it, anti-immigrant sentiment and violence toward Mexicanos is directly associated with their Indigenous roots.[13] While Sunland Park was incorporated in 1983, the border policies that surround its neighboring cities of Ciudad Juárez and El Paso have a direct impact on the border militarization that exists in the community today.[14]

Settler colonialism and the advancement of white supremacist ideologies cannot be separated from the history of the United States or, for that matter, from the history of borders. People of color are directly targeted through policies that are used as tools of reinforcement for contemporary whiteness.[15] Individuals that fail to fit into the imagery of whiteness become enemies of the nation. Citizenship and belonging are directly affected by an individual's willingness to be "American," and willingness to comply with whiteness.[16] Therefore, the embodiment of taming, controlling, shaming, ridiculing, intimidating, and imposing violence on Indigenous peoples and Brown people at the border is an exercise established long before the Trump administration.[17] From 2017 to 2021, however, and on the campaign trail, Trump perpetuated earlier colonial tactics of violence, particularly framing the U.S.-Mexico border as the battleground against the Mexican "invasion," which, therefore, warranted further militarization, securitization, and surveillance. He incited a narrative of the border as lawless, corruptible, and violent, and border residents as "the enemy"—demonstrating that his concern was never for protecting border residents, but for stopping more Brown people from entering the United States. His warmongering language of "invasion" and "building a big, beautiful wall" influenced people across the nation, who, although unfamiliar with border regions, regurgitated and opined Trump's words.

The border wall is a reminder of the tangible efforts to separate nation-states through enforced border policing, used as a tool that advances settler colonialism in the United States. Kelly Lytle Hernández recalls how, "settler colonial projects seek land. On the land, colonists envision building a new, permanent, reproductive, and settler society."[18] There are extensive events that we will later describe that have occurred in the Ciudad Juárez–El Paso area, just minutes from Sunland Park, that depict the historical violence that immigrants have faced. Advancing a colonial agenda that centered whiteness was important for settlers in El Paso in the early twentieth century. The physical abuses suffered by Mexican migrants derived from eugenic perspectives, often centered on public health matters. As historian Heather Sinclair describes in her work on perceptions of tuberculosis at the El Paso border in the early twentieth century, "racializing and gendered discourses in medicine and public health were critical to the Anglo American colonial project in the region."[19]

Also, in the early twentieth century, the delousing of Mexican migrants at the Santa Fe Bridge between Ciudad Juárez and El Paso marked a point in history that is often remembered through Carmelita Torres's protest, popularly known as the Bath Riots of 1917, where seventeen-year-old Carmelita protested the use of toxic chemicals on Mexican border crossers. At the time, government officials held a strong belief that Mexican people would spread typhus into the United States. Delousing continued during the Bracero Program (1942–65), where thousands of Mexican men were subjected to body inspections due to the country's racist perceptions of Mexicans as nonhygienic.[20] The use of the chemical substance DDT and gasoline on Mexican bodies reinforced racially charged stereotypes.

In 1942, Margaret Sanger, the founder of the birth control movement in the United States and a staunch eugenicist, held campaigns across the country arguing for the necessity of contraception by focusing on the rise of immigrant families. Sanger was a constant visitor to places like El Paso, where she saw an increase in Mexican mothers and children.[21] These earlier colonial, racialized, and politicized forms of violence remind us of the U.S. Title 42 policy, which cited public health policies to forbid migrants from entering the United States during the COVID-19 pandemic. The "anchor babies" arguments popular during the Trump administration also undergirded racialized and gendered violence, arguing that Brown women were crossing the border in droves to give birth to their children in the United States. Such false rhetoric resurrects hateful historical gendered and xenophobic discourse.[22]

We return to the distraction of the wall, where historical accounts of exploitation, extraction, displacement, occupation, and colonialism are overlooked and intentionally minimized. The displacement of Native peoples from the area to make room for the railroad paved the way for boundary making and empire building, which led to the border wall.[23] The neoliberal colonial project of the Bracero Program also promulgated cheap, exploitative labor, and racial capitalism spread further through the creation of the Border Industrialization Program (later the Programa Nacional Fronterizo) in 1965. Subsequent policies like the North American Free Trade Agreement (NAFTA, established in 1994) furthered the neocolonial project of racialized and gendered violence in the area.[24] A look at the intertwined stories of labor's supply and demand and migration flows for "global capitalism" reveals a ritualistic justification for securitizing the border to facilitate the flow of goods in market economies while obstructing the movement of undesirable people.[25]

A remapping of the United States through arguments to further secure and divide people has been well underway since the 1920s. Each decade marks a watershed moment in the carceral state's encroachment on rights. The following list of historical legislation helps us contextualize current crises taking shape: the Page Act of 1875, the Chinese Exclusion Act of 1882, the Geary Act of 1892, and the Immigration Acts of 1903, 1910, and 1917, the last of which implemented literacy tests at the U.S.-Mexico border. The litany of laws enacted across these four decades fostered exclusionary practices toward Mexicans and led to their further racialization. Mae M. Ngai's salient work asserts: "The regime of immigration restriction remapped the nation in two important ways. First, it drew a new ethnic and racial map based on new categories and hierarchies of difference. Second, and in a different register, it articulated a new sense of territoriality, which was marked by unprecedented awareness and state surveillance of the nation's contiguous borders."[26] The politicized violence created by these restrictive laws gave birth in 1924 to the U.S. Border Patrol, which facilitated the mass deportations of Mexicans from the United States in the 1930s. These deportations spurred labor shortages in the United States during World War II. Realizing the mistake it had made, the United States recruited Mexicans as cheap, exploitable, and racialized labor through the Bracero Program. Ngai's analysis captures the racialized practices of the United States to further assign undesirable work to undesirable people as a racialized project that promoted the ideological exercise of us versus them. Mass deportations took place once more as the 1950s Operation Wetback was executed to expel people back to Mexico, once their labor was extracted and Mexicans were no longer necessary for "global capitalism."[27]

The U.S.-Mexico border is a place for global capitalist experimentation and the creation of national hierarchies through labor. The colonial, political, and ideological violence exerted for empire building led to the proliferation and growth of industry through the earlier mentioned Border Industrialization Program in 1965. This industry growth was also used to further securitize the border by amplifying migration and immigration as national and border security threats.[28] The Immigration Reform and Control Act of 1986, the Immigration Act of 1990, and the Illegal Immigration Reform and Immigrant Responsibility Act of 1996 laid the groundwork for additional policies and laws controlling labor and the desirability of Mexicans as laborers. The U.S. project of perpetuating racialized violence was built on exclusion and selectivity. When Mexican laborers were desired, the border magically opened. When U.S. empire building and labor needs were satiated, then, expulsion began again, as we see occur with each new wave of laws and policies that build on iterations of nineteenth- and twentieth-century laws and propaganda. NAFTA and border control strategies in El Paso like Operation Hold the Line in 1993 helped bolster more border wall construction.[29]

In recent history, the initiation of post-9/11 punitive policies and legislation with the Secure Fence Act of 2006, and language underscored in subsection 287(g) of the earlier 1996 immigration law, aided in creating more oppressive measures of exclusion and carceral environments that our border communities and others across the United States experience. The data-sharing program Secure Communities, created by the DHS and FBI in 2008, used biometric information to identify deportable in-custody individuals based on whether they had criminal records or outstanding warrants or were were found within immigration databases. It led to thousands of deportations between 2008 and 2014 and again throughout fiscal year 2017. Although Secure Communities was revoked by the Biden administration in 2021, biometric information continues to be shared between DHS agencies and other federal agencies through the Automated Biometric Identification System (IDENT).[30] And facilitating these combined efforts is the long-standing federal grant program Operation Stonegarden, which provides funding to law enforcement agencies to "support joint [law enforcement] efforts to secure the United States' borders." Several critics argue that this program "undermines trust between immigrant communities and law enforcement, while draining resources from more urgent public safety priorities."[31] Although the timeline of government initiatives outlined above is not exhaustive, it historicizes the multiple sorts of violence experienced by migrants, immigrants, and border residents on both sides of the U.S. border wall. Border residents are hence forced to deal on a large scale with politics and violence not of their doing. We are caught in the exploitative and racialized experiment that empire building has created at the border.

TRUMP'S RHETORIC OF HATE AND THE GRAND NARRATIVE OF THE WALL

In recent times, the border wall narrative has taken on a life of its own. In southern New Mexico, we see the fragmentation that takes place across both sides of the border, with separated families, traumatized and stressed conditions, exhausted local and state expenditures, and on and on. It is analogous to prison settings, where families are separated and scrutinized, and walls and surveillance obstruct people's relationality. In 2016, the rhetoric of hate was materially articulated with Trump's fixation on "building a big, beautiful wall," a slogan he used often during his campaigning. While in office, Trump appropriated millions of dollars in taxpayer monies for new wall construction along the U.S.-Mexico border. Part of the border wall machinery includes stadium lighting, cameras, infrared sensor devices, and the human machinery of the wall: border patrol agents. From 2017 to 2021, the U.S. government replaced existing walls and barriers with new, reinforced fencing in the outskirts of El Paso, Sunland Park, and Santa Teresa. Historically, the U.S. government has rallied for a border wall as a necessary tactic to curb drug smuggling and migrants, leaving out its history of controlling labor's supply and demand this way. Instead, the wall created dangerous corridors across desert and water landscapes that claimed thousands of migrant lives, while contributing to deadly encounters with traffickers.[32] Hateful rhetoric led to increased carceral logics justifying deportations, detentions, and exclusions—all taking place through the U.S. border wall.

Trump's references to "building a big, beautiful wall" as his rallying cry during his presidential election and thereafter led to reverberating chants across the country. We recall an El Paso school bus that was heckled by rivals in West Texas as opponents yelled to students on the bus, "build the wall, build the wall!" Cynthia recalls passing a group of students at a kiosk at her university's student activity center and hearing them casually saying to one another, "What part of 'build the wall' don't they understand?" as they laughed.

Trump's words had hateful reverberations across the world. Those who suffered the consequences were transborder residents viscerally affected by his actions. Trump's ideas of Mexican "rapists" and "bad hombres" continue to feed the narrative of an untamed, insufficiently surveilled border, which is argued as justification to hire more border patrol agents, to build additional concrete vehicle barriers, and to use steel cables and fencing, stadium lighting, mile markers, infrared systems, electronic sensor alarms, air drones, video monitors, night vision scopes, ATVs, horses, bicycles, boats, foot and city patrols, and transportation checks at airports and border highways. Despite this investment in securitizing the border, Trump and his allies claimed this was still insufficient to secure the border. A repeated practice for members of U.S. Congress was to visit the border wall region, claiming that they had visited the border and had seen with their own eyes the "invasion" of migrants, or the drug control problem, or the myriad negative depictions engineered to solicit more funding for national or border security and to generate tough-on-crime speeches and legislation for reelection. Visits were less than a day, escorted by DHS agents and an army of Secret Service. Never did members of Congress visit border residents affected by construction to see the wasteful spending of the wall, or other measures that would never directly benefit U.S. border residents by way of infrastructure needs, health care, education, or family reunification. Supporting the wall is contrived as synonymous with supporting America, where the wall is emblematic of a seductive narrative of safety, patriotism, and nationalism. The framing and reframing of the wall narrative comes to symbolize the us-versus-them grand narrative of the United States.

THE U.S. BORDER WALL

During Trump's reign, messages of a pathological and deviant border region fraught with danger and illegality, and the need for taming this region through a taller and better reinforced wall, were ubiquitous. New and replacement construction of the U.S.-Mexico border wall continued along the 1,954-mile-long border, despite the COVID-19 pandemic, devastating poverty in border communities, and constant deportation of countless people to their home or transit countries, which oftentimes led to further violence. For those of us living at the U.S.-Mexico border, some iteration of the wall has existed in urban and rural areas since the early twentieth century. More visible and entrenched fencing began in the 1990s and continued to evolve into combinations of primary, secondary, and tertiary barriers, fences, and walls. While in office, Trump appropriated millions of dollars in taxpayer monies for new wall construction along the U.S.-Mexico border.[33] During his campaign, Trump initially said he would build a wall for $4 billion, which grew to $10 billion by 2017, but the Senate Committee on Homeland Security and Governmental Affairs claimed that costs could reach $70 billion, not including the costs of and legal resources required for land acquisition.[34]

The U.S. government busies itself replacing previously existing walls and barriers to justify new, reinforced fencing like that erected on the outskirts of El Paso, Sunland Park, and Santa Teresa between 2017 and 2020 during the Trump administration. The construction of the new wall and the replacement of the existing border wall—in essence, the raping of the land—took place due to the Trump administration's requests for proposals to build the wall.[35] More than 350 companies across the United States submitted proposals for the wall construction, responding to a 2017 DHS request for a prototype of a "physically imposing" and "aesthetically pleasing" border wall that would build on Trump's references to "building a big, beautiful wall."[36]

THE SANTA TERESA GROUNDBREAKING CEREMONY

A private contractor from outside the area was given $73 million to construct twenty miles of fencing. Vehicle barriers were also replaced near the Santa Teresa port of entry with taller barriers under the contract awarded to Barnard Construction, a company whose base was in Montana.[37] The construction took place as local communities struggled with food insecurity and access to other resources. A groundbreaking ceremony took place on April 9, 2018, in Santa Teresa, with El Paso sector border patrol chief Aaron Hull stating, "the president has started his project." Standing near the newly constructed wall, Hull added, "this is the beginning, in this sector, of the president's border wall—very much so." The construction was mandated under Trump's executive order 13767. The wall would be a bollard wall (steel poles), and Chief Hull described the wall as an effective tool for agents and their technology. He spoke about security, drug trafficking, and environmental hazards and alluded to the future presence of National Guard units.[38] He failed to mention anything about the twenty environmental laws that were waived to build the wall (laws outlined in the Secure Fence Act of 2006), and how waiving these protections jeopardized ecosystems like wildlife corridors and desert vegetation (figure 17.1).[39]

During that same period, local television footage showed National Guard troops in full fatigues, wearing their helmets and riding DHS

Figure 17.1. New construction of the border wall in the desert, Santa Teresa, New Mexico. 2018. Photo by Cynthia Bejarano.

vehicles as if they were going into battle. In September 2018, an estimated four thousand troops were sent to the wall. National Guard troops were sent all along the border, as they have been throughout recent history, to form what Trump called a "virtual wall" until Congress passed legislation for border funding. Trump argued for sending National Guard troops to aid border patrol officers in "keep[ing] the American people safe." The presence of the National Guard contributed to the growing militarization of the border and fears of civil rights violations. The pomp and circumstance of government entities on display in the Paso del Norte region reinforced the toxic masculinities associated with the wall, a phallic symbol jutting out of the land, a modern symbol of might and power, of colonial violence and empire building.[40]

TWENTY-FIRST-CENTURY WHITE SUPREMACY AT THE U.S. BORDER

While the Trump administration stirred xenophobia and moral outcry over "invasions" by "Mexicans" and other migrants across the U.S.-Mexico border, Trump promulgated public acts of white supremacy across the country. His antimigrant, anti-immigrant rhetoric fueled vigilantism by supporters, who acted as self-deputized border wall builders and enforcers. Trump fanned the embers of hate and xenophobia as his followers funded private construction of the border wall on a parcel of land located just a few miles from the new fence construction in Santa Teresa and less than half a mile from the federal border wall construction in Sunland Park, New Mexico.[41] The nonprofit organization We Build the Wall fundraised to build segments of the wall on private property cutting into the side of the sacred Mount Cristo Rey. The We Build the Wall GoFundMe initiative raised $23 million in five months for these private construction efforts, fanning the hatred that prompted ever more heinous acts. In August 2019, barely two months after the three-day building of this small segment of wall in Sunland Park, a white supremacist killed nearly two dozen people at a Walmart in El Paso.[42] This construction smacked in the face of false promises by the Trump administration that the wall would not be built in natural barriers like mountain ranges or the Rio Grande. Linda McDowell's words resonate here, where "images of the land . . . are bound up with representations of nationality," which relay messages of nativism and xenophobia.[43] The Trump administration not only expanded the border wall, wasting millions in federal dollars, but proliferated and encouraged the privatization and securitization of the wall by private citizens. Trump's rhetoric of "build the wall" resulted in the border wall construction on private property, and alleged collusion by private citizens with border patrol, instigating vigilantism in the name of national and border security.

Throughout the nation, right-wing extremism decreased between 2007 and 2011, with five or fewer incidents per year, but this number increased to thirty-one incidents in 2017.[44] In April 2019, the United Constitutional Patriots from Flora Vista, New Mexico, led by Larry Hopkins, descended on Sunland Park. The United Constitutional Patriots share their mission with two other antigovernment militia groups whose goal is to secure the border against Central American migrants.[45] Sunland Park police chief Javier Guerra was aware that the border militia group had been policing the city for nearly two months but stated that its members presented no official threat to the community. The United Constitutional Patriots set up camp on the Union Pacific Railroad's private land. There, on April 16, 2019, they detained three hundred migrants at gunpoint. Videos of the illegal apprehension and detention flooded the internet, and the city gained national attention, attracting additional armed people from across the United States to Sunland Park with the purpose of detaining as many migrants as possible. A few days later, Hopkins was arrested by the FBI on a federal warrant, and members of the group left the city.[46] Why were the United Constitutional Patriots drawn to Sunland Park? Why were they able to camp out at the border with no repercussions for several weeks? What does this tell us about white supremacy and the role of the United States in contributing to social and racialized violence against migrant bodies falling from the border wall, or lost in the border's massive desert landscapes?

The threat of border militia groups in the city angered border residents, whose tendency was to provide aid to migrants in need.[47] The constant exposure to a militarized border, border militia groups, and border patrol agents creates fear for residents, especially Latinx women. At border crossing checkpoints and within the city of Sunland Park, Latinx women navigate encounters of sexism and patriarchy with U.S. Border Patrol and U.S. Customs and Border Protection agents.[48] McDowell claims, "for feminists the important issue to address is the extent to which these institutions act in the interests of men and masculinist powers."[49] Our own analysis contemplates the masculine notions of power, protection, and control in relation to the border wall and the border-industrial complex. This includes how women experience the masculine gaze of the border wall, its invisible technologies of surveillance, and the overwhelmingly male border patrol agents, watching, observing, and surveilling. Drones are common during peaceful protests as we have witnessed and experienced. These hyper- and toxic masculinities personify the militarization and securitization that blanket the area.

PROTESTS AS INTERVENTIONS AT THE U.S. BORDER WALL

At the borderlands, we ask ourselves: what kinds of societies are forged when governments encourage frameworks of violence? As the Trump era's proposition for more border walls emerged, and the absurdity of tearing families apart seemed unending, the need for relational resistance and transborder solidarities grew more imperative.[50] Community mobilizing and antiwall and antiviolence work took place across myriad organizations and everyday people, thus articulating what *feminista fronterizas* personify. Dana Collins and colleagues argue, "a radically progressive human rights project can emerge when marginalized communities from around the world demand that the state be accountable to them. These constituencies are not asking the state to legitimize their citizenship; rather, they, along with their allies, are demanding that the state respond to their needs."[51] Where there are spaces of conflict and contention, there is always resistance. Community mobilizing against the wall engendered multimodalities across legal offices, migrant advocacy groups, religious organizations, and everyday people. Groups working on the ground like the American Civil Liberties Union (ACLU), Comunidades en Acción y de Fé, Hope Border Institute, Border Network for Human Rights, and New Mexico Dream Team mobilized numerous activities and events. Members of these groups, including academics, artists, and others, came together to work in solidarity on border wall interventions. During these border wall interventions, people used the language of resistance, reciprocity, and dignity against settler colonial practices.

For years, an isolated segment of the U.S. border wall in Sunland Park was the site of protests concerning family separation, the greater violence taking place in Ciudad Juárez due to the drug trade, and U.S. drug consumption and feminicides. It is also the site of an annual nondenominational binational religious service, a gathering where people from all sides of the border wall convene. Figure 17.2 captures a protest against violence when the border wall was not a bollard wall but a fence, where people could see each other and even touch fingertips through the wall. *Feminista fronterizas* from New Mexico hold hands as they face Juarenses in transborder solidarity to protest border patrol shootings, like that of fifteen-year-old Sergio Adrián Hernández Güereca, whose photograph they hold. Figure 17.3 captures a protest two years later, the 2018 All Against the Wall rally, as the federal government began building a new segment of the border wall on Santa Teresa's outskirts. Everyday people, environmentalists, and members of the groups came together to protest the wall. Together, these forms of resilience capture the sentiments of thousands of border residents at the U.S. borderlands.

"Resistance is encoded in the practices of remembering, and of writing. . . . The very practice of remembering against the grain of

Figure 17.2. ACLU Revitalize not Militarize protest at Sunland Park border wall. 2016. Photo by Cynthia Bejarano.

Figure 17.3. All Against the Wall rally in Santa Teresa. 2018. Photo by Cynthia Bejarano.

'public' or hegemonic history, of locating the silences and the struggle to assert knowledge that is outside the parameters of the dominant, suggests a rethinking of sociality itself."[52] Although the U.S. border wall is guarded by border patrol agents and surveillance technologies, the other side of that same wall speaks freely and openly, offering a canvas for political protest (figure 17.4). Painted on the Mexico side of the wall are demands to Mexico and the U.S. government, and an image of the U.S. president, number forty-five, with the number crossed out in red. Trump is shown wearing a white Ku Klux Klan (KKK) robe painted on the blue canvas of the U.S. flag. We wonder whether the image of the KKK was painted intentionally here, as a secret code questioning the U.S. notion of justice, since this is what blue represents on the U.S. flag. The words in Old English lettering seem to be a direct message to President Trump: "Ni delincuentes ni ilegales somos trabajadores internacionales" (not delinquent or illegal, we are international workers). This imagery is adjacent to a father's demand to know what happened to his missing daughter, Esmeralda Castillo, followed by the statement "Nos Faltan 43" (We are missing 43), referencing the forty-three missing students from Iguala, Guerrero, Mexico, and additional images of feminicides.

Figure 17.4. View of border wall from Ciudad Juárez. This portion of the wall is shared with Sunland Park. 2019. Photo by Cynthia Bejarano.

The border wall cannot be represented as the sole problem that we confront, nor its destruction as the single solution. The border wall and its rhetoric are a project to fracture people's relationality with their environment, their culture, and one another, yet millions of borderlanders live their lives daily despite the wall.

"REVITALIZE NOT MILITARIZE" LOCAL COMMUNITIES

Looking beyond the wall reveals a historical, spatial, and temporal analysis of the border wall as a distraction to the costly and constantly moving parts of DHS. Analogies to spectacles of war and fearmongering are ubiquitous, used to foster the further securitization and militarization of the region. Borderlands communities have not been asked about public safety concerns, the encroachment of more surveillance and policing in their neighborhoods, or their fears and perceptions of the border wall travesty. Border residents, specifically Mexican American women, share tools of resistance against the policing of their communities through the spread of underground knowledge, engaging in their own countersurveillance to combat intersectional violence.[53]

What does further militarizing the U.S.-Mexico border mean for local communities? The language of resistance, reciprocity, and dignity forms part of the resilience narratives enacted against the vestiges of Trump-era policies. If we look beyond the spectacle of the wall, we see a police state forming, building on the racialized, colonial violence our border region has experienced. This also includes the decades-long militarization of the border and the perpetual isolation and cutting off of families and communities from each other. The borderlands, its people, and the environment are on lockdown. The border wall and its intersecting parts are a broader project of taming and controlling bodies, of forging "work your fingers to the bone" bodies through factories, railroads, agricultural fields, and, yes, construction of the wall. The wall, like detention centers, is a physical barrier that reproduces marginalization and invisibility for border communities.[54] The expansion and construction of the border wall in cities like Sunland Park and Santa Teresa, New Mexico, are not coincidental. The visual representation of the border wall is a violent display of the obsession with prohibiting mobility across geopoliticized spaces and creating carceral environments.

We focus here on the mantra of the local ACLU branch, which created a yearlong campaign in 2015 titled Revitalize not Militarize, where local people engaged in interventions at the border wall, at border highway checkpoints, and in other ways, to raise an alarm against the wasteful spending on the border wall when local communities have crumbling infrastructures. What could the border communities of Sunland Park and Santa Teresa do with the $73 million that was spent to build or rebuild this fraction of the border wall? People live in poverty at the border, especially in places like Doña Ana County, where Sunland Park and Santa Teresa are located. Poverty rates here are higher than the national average.[55] Despite the billions of dollars spent militarizing, securitizing, and weaponizing the border area, little to nothing is done to revitalize border colonias to address problems such as the lack of health care and environmental pollution.

Prior to the Trump administration, the ACLU campaign Revitalize not Militarize asked the U.S. federal government to invest in rural and urban infrastructure and education for borderland communities, rather than containing us with even higher border walls and surveillance mechanisms. The cruelty of the Trump era's border wall construction and the

Trump era itself has left its indelible mark on this miles-long section of the New Mexico border.

NOTES

We would like to thank Fatima Oliveros for her assistance with this manuscript.

1.   Bejarano and Hernández Sánchez, "The Mantling and Dismantling of a Tent City."

2.   Tamez, *Father Genocide*, 224.

3.   Stephen and Speed, *Indigenous Women and Violence*.

4.   In 2021, for instance, a number of migrants (five to ten per week) desperate to enter the United States attempted to climb the border wall through Sunland Park and Santa Teresa, New Mexico, only to plunge several feet and break or even lose limbs in their falls; see Resendiz, "Treating Injured Migrants Who Fall over Border Wall."

5.   On intersectional violence, see Stephen and Speed, *Indigenous Women and Violence*.

6.   Aldama and Aldama, *Decolonizing Latinx Masculinities*.

7.   On intersectionality, see Crenshaw, "Mapping the Margins."

8.   It is important for us to acknowledge here that many residents identify themselves as Mexicano, Mexican immigrant, Mexican American, Chicana/o, or *fronterizo/as*. For this analysis, however, we use the term *Latinx*.

9.   See Bejarano and Hernández Sánchez, "The Mantling and Dismantling of a Tent City," as well as other chapters in the same volume.

10. Tamez, "Our Way of Life Is Our Resistance"; Slack et al., "The Geography of Border Militarization." We acknowledge that not all border residents are critical toward the border wall and other securitization measures at the U.S. border. We recognize that many local Latinx residents have profited from or are employed by the border security industrial complex, a local phenomenon that is imbued by internal colonization (see Fanon, *Black Skin, White Masks*) and that we see prominently in our region, where El Paso Border Patrol sector employees are overwhelmingly Latinx. We also recognize that many border residents are directly in favor of the border wall and other proposed security. These statements reveal the complexities of life at the U.S. border, where federal securitization employment is bountiful—with hearty wages, quality health insurance, retirement benefits, and other perks that people gravitate to—and has few educational requirements. Low-skill, low-wage jobs are the bleak alternative for many border residents, who find employment in retail, caregiving work, construction, and agriculture.

11. *Eloisa García Tamez et al. v. Michael Chertoff*, civil action no. B-08–044 (S.D. Tex. 2008).

12. Tamez, "Place and Perspective in the Shadow of the Wall," 184.

13. R. Hernández, *Coloniality of the US/Mexico Border*; see also Aldama, *Violence and the Body*.
14. Dunn, *The Militarization of the U.S.-Mexico Border*.
15. Lipsitz, *The Possessive Investment in Whiteness*.
16. Benton-Cohen, *Borderline Americans*.
17. Castellanos, Gutiérrez Nájera, and Aldama, *Comparative Indigeneities of the Américas*; Tamez, "Place and Perspective in the Shadow of the Wall"; R. Hernández, *Coloniality of the US/Mexico Border*.
18. K. Hernández, *City of Inmates*, 7.
19. Sinclair, "White Plague, Mexican Menace," 504.
20. Romo, *Ringside Seat to a Revolution*.
21. Murillo, "Birth Control, Border Control."
22. Chavez, *Anchor Babies and the Challenge of Birthright Citizenship*.
23. Tamez, *Father Genocide*; Karuka, *Empire's Tracks*; Montelongo, "Illicit Inhabitants."
24. Romo, *Ringside Seat to a Revolution*; Morales and Bejarano, "Transnational Sexual and Gendered Violence."
25. Sassen, *Expulsions*.
26. Ngai, *Impossible Subjects*, 3.
27. Sassen, *Expulsions*.
28. Andreas, *Border Games*; Dunn, *The Militarization of the U.S.-Mexico Border*.
29. Like Operation Gatekeeper (San Diego, California), Operation Safeguard (Nogales, Arizona), and Operation Rio Grande (McAllen, Texas), Operation Hold the Line also placed border patrol agents in vehicles to "keep watch" over the border line—despite El Paso being separated from Mexico by a menacing border wall, a dried-up concrete riverbed, and (on the opposite side of the wall) a marginalized colonia. See Madsen, "Local Impacts of the Balloon Effect of Border Law Enforcement."
30. See U.S. Immigration and Customs Enforcement, "Secure Communities"; U.S. Department of Homeland Security, "DHS/OBIM/PIA–001 Automated Biometric Identification System."
31. National Immigration Forum, "Fact Sheet."
32. Madsen, "Local Impacts of the Balloon Effect of Border Law Enforcement."
33. Miroff and Blanco, "Trump Ramps Up Border-Wall Construction."
34. Nichols, "The Estimated Price of President Trump's Border Wall."
35. By July 2017, engineers had already started drilling and soil testing in El Paso, as well as in Santa Teresa, New Mexico; Calexico, California; and the Rio Grande Valley. Nixon, "Engineers Begin Preparatory Work for Border Wall Construction."
36. Rodriguez, "Trump's Partially Built 'Big, Beautiful Wall.'"
37. Bryan, "Montana Company Gets $73M Contract for Border Fence Work."
38. Quoted from Aguilar, "El Paso Border Patrol Sector Kicks Off Construction."
39. Borunda, "Environmental Laws Waived."

40.   Aldama and Aldama, *Decolonizing Latinx Masculinities*.
41.   Da Silva, "Boy, 7, Who Raised $22,000 for Donald Trump's Border Wall."
42.   Silva, "White Supremacy, Racism."
43.   McDowell, *Gender, Identity and Place*, 170.
44.   Jones, "The Rise of Far-Right Extremism in the United States."
45.   Southern Poverty Law Center, "United Constitutional Patriots."
46.   Borunda, "After Weeks-Long Presence."
47.   Romero, "Militia Defiant in New Mexico."
48.   López, "Identity Building in Militarized U.S.-Mexico Border Colonias."
49.   McDowell, *Gender, Identity and Place*, 173.
50.   Bejarano and Hernández Sánchez, "The Mantling and Dismantling of a Tent City."
51.   Collins et al., "New Directions in Feminism and Human Rights," 305.
52.   Mohanty, *Feminism Without Borders*, 83.
53.   López, "Identity Building in Militarized U.S.-Mexico Border Colonias."
54.   Ordaz, *The Shadow of El Centro*.
55.   Doña Ana County, New Mexico, is home to approximately thirty-seven colonias, or rural communities lacking critical infrastructure such as sewer services and paved roads. The $73 million wasted in border wall construction could instead, say, be put toward the total county infrastructure needs for colonias, which amount to $606 million and include, for example, $81 million in county roads, $34 million for a wastewater system, $29 million for professional services, and $113 million for public facilities. See Esquinca and Jaramillo, "Colonias on the Border Struggle with Decades-Old Water Issues."

BIBLIOGRAPHY

Aguilar, Julián. "El Paso Border Patrol Sector Kicks Off Construction of Trump's Wall on Border." *Texas Tribune*, April 9, 2018.

Aldama, Arturo J. *Violence and the Body: Race, Gender, and the State*. Bloomington: Indiana University Press, 2003.

Aldama, Arturo J., and Frederick Luis Aldama, eds. *Decolonizing Latinx Masculinities*. Tucson: University of Arizona Press, 2020.

Andreas, Peter. *Border Games: Policing the U.S.-Mexico Divide*. Ithaca, N.Y.: Cornell University Press, 2000.

Bejarano, Cynthia, and Ma. Eugenia Hernández Sánchez. "The Mantling and Dismantling of a Tent City at the U.S.-Mexico Border." In *Handbook on Human Security, Borders and Migration*, edited by Natalia Ribas-Mateos and Timothy J. Dunn, 71–89. Cheltenham, UK: Edward Elgar, 2021.

Benton-Cohen, Katherine. *Borderline Americans: Racial Division and Labor War in the Arizona Borderlands*. Cambridge, Mass.: Harvard University Press, 2009.

Borunda, Daniel. "After Weeks-Long Presence, Militia in Sunland Park, NM, Told to Leave Encampment." *Las Cruces Sun News*, April 22, 2019.

Borunda, Daniel. "Environmental Laws Waived for New Mexico Border Wall West of Santa Teresa." *El Paso Times*, January 22, 2018.

Bryan, Susan Montoya. "Montana Company Gets $73M Contract for Border Fence Work near Santa Teresa." *Las Cruces Sun News*, February 28, 2018.

Castellanos, M. Bianet, Lourdes Gutiérrez Nájera, and Arturo J. Aldama. *Comparative Indigeneities of the Américas: Toward a Hemispheric Approach*. Tucson: University of Arizona Press, 2012.

Chavez, Leo R. *Anchor Babies and the Challenge of Birthright Citizenship*. Stanford, Calif.: Stanford University Press, 2020.

Collins, Dana, Sylvanna Falcón, Sharmila Lodhia, and Molly Talcott. "New Directions in Feminism and Human Rights: An Introduction." *International Feminist Journal of Politics* 12, no. 3–4 (2010): 298–318.

Crenshaw, Kimberlé. "Mapping the Margins: Intersectionality, Identity Politics, and Violence Against Women of Color." *Stanford Law Review* 43, no. 6 (1991): 1241–99.

Da Silva, Chantal. "Boy, 7, Who Raised $22,000 for Donald Trump's Border Wall Leads Ribbon Cutting at Newly Built Section." *Newsweek*, June 3, 2019.

Dunn, Timothy J. *The Militarization of the U.S.-Mexico Border, 1978–1992: Low-Intensity Conflict Doctrine Comes Home*. Austin: University of Texas Press, 1996.

Esquinca, Maria, and Andrea Jaramillo. "Colonias on the Border Struggle with Decades-Old Water Issues." *Texas Tribune*, August 22, 2017.

Fanon, Frantz. *Black Skin, White Masks*. New York: Grove Press, 2008.

Hernández, Kelly Lytle. *City of Inmates: Conquest, Rebellion, and the Rise of Human Caging in Los Angeles, 1771–1965*. Chapel Hill: University of North Carolina Press, 2017.

Hernández, Roberto D. *Coloniality of the US/Mexico Border: Power, Violence, and the Decolonial Imperative*. Tucson: University of Arizona Press, 2018.

Jones, Seth G. "The Rise of Far-Right Extremism in the United States." Center for Strategic and International Studies, November 7, 2018. https://www.csis.org/analysis/rise-far-right-extremism-united-states.

Karuka, Manu. *Empire's Tracks: Indigenous Nations, Chinese Workers, and the Transcontinental Railroad*. Oakland: University of California Press, 2019.

Lipsitz, George. *The Possessive Investment in Whiteness: How White People Profit from Identity Politics*. 20th anniversary ed. Philadelphia: Temple University Press, 2018.

López, Diana J. "Identity Building in Militarized U.S.-Mexico Border Colonias: Testimonios of Women of Color Resisting Militarization." Master's thesis, University of Arizona, 2020.

Madsen, Kenneth D. "Local Impacts of the Balloon Effect of Border Law Enforcement." *Geopolitics* 12, no. 2 (2007): 280–98.

McDowell, Linda. *Gender, Identity and Place: Understanding Feminist Geographies*. Minneapolis: University of Minnesota Press, 1999.

Miroff, Nick, and Adrian Blanco. "Trump Ramps Up Border-Wall Construction Ahead of 2020 Vote." *Washington Post*, February 6, 2020.

Mohanty, Chandra Talpade. *Feminism Without Borders: Decolonizing Theory, Practicing Solidarity*. Durham, N.C.: Duke University Press.

Montelongo, Irma Victoria. "Illicit Inhabitants: Empire, Immigration, Race, and Sexuality on the U.S.-Mexico Border, 1891–1924." PhD diss., University of Texas at El Paso, 2014.

Morales, Maria Cristina, and Cynthia Bejarano. "Transnational Sexual and Gendered Violence: An Application of Border Sexual Conquest at a Mexico-US Border." *Global Networks* 9, no. 3 (2009): 420–39.

Murillo, Lina. "Birth Control, Border Control: The Movement for Contraception in El Paso, Texas, 1936–1940." *Pacific Historical Review* 3, no. 90 (2021): 314–44.

National Immigration Forum. "Fact Sheet: Operation Stonegarden." April 27, 2020. https://immigrationforum.org/article/fact-sheet-operation-stonegarden/.

Ngai, Mae M. *Impossible Subjects: Illegal Aliens and the Making of Modern America*. Princeton, N.J.: Princeton University Press, 2014.

Nichols, Chris. "The Estimated Price of President Trump's Border Wall Is the Same as the Cost of 'One and a Half Aircraft Carriers.'" Fact-checking of statement made April 24, 2017, by Scott Peters. Politifact, April 28, 2017. https://www.politifact.com/factchecks/2017/apr/28/scott-peters/would-trumps-border-wall-cost-same-one-and-half-us/.

Nixon, Ron. "Engineers Begin Preparatory Work for Border Wall Construction." *New York Times*, July 18, 2017.

Ordaz, Jessica. *The Shadow of El Centro: A History of Migrant Incarceration and Solidarity*. Chapel Hill: University of North Carolina Press, 2021.

Resendiz, Julian. "Treating Injured Migrants Who Fall over Border Wall Becomes New Normal in Small New Mexico Town." *Border Report*, May 20, 2021. https://www.borderreport.com/hot-topics/the-border-wall/treating-injured-migrants-who-fall-over-border-wall-becomes-new-normal-in-small-new-mexico-town/.

Rodriguez, Sabrina. "Trump's Partially Built 'Big, Beautiful Wall.'" *Politico*, January 1, 2021. https://www.politico.com/news/2021/01/12/trump-border-wall-partially-built-458255.

Romero, Simon. "Militia Defiant in New Mexico: 'It's My God-Given Right to Be Here.'" *New York Times*, April 23, 2019.

Romo, David. *Ringside Seat to a Revolution: An Underground Cultural History of El Paso and Juarez, 1893–1923*. El Paso, Tex.: Cinco Puntos Press, 2005.

Sassen, Saskia. *Expulsions: Brutality and Complexity in the Global Economy*. Cambridge, Mass.: Harvard University Press, 2014.

Silva, Cynthia. "'White Supremacy, Racism': Remembering the El Paso Massacre That Targeted Latinos." *NBC News*, August 3, 2021. https://www.nbcnews.com/news/latino/white-supremacy-racism-remembering-el-paso-massacre-targeted-latinos-rcna1580.

Sinclair, Heather. "White Plague, Mexican Menace: Migration, Race, Class, and Gendered Contagion in El Paso, Texas, 1880–1930." *Pacific Historical Review* 85, no. 4 (2016): 475–505.

Slack, Jeremy, Daniel E. Martínez, Alison Elizabeth Lee, and Scott Whiteford. "The Geography of Border Militarization: Violence, Death, and Health in Mexico and the United States." In *The Shadow of the Wall: Violence and Migration on the U.S.-Mexico Border*, edited by Jeremy Slack, Daniel E. Martínez, and Scott Whiteford, 94–119. Tucson: University of Arizona Press, 2018.

Southern Poverty Law Center. "United Constitutional Patriots." Accessed March 25, 2022. https://www.splcenter.org/fighting-hate/extremist-files/group/united-constitutional-patriots.

Stephen, Lynn, and Shannon Speed, eds. *Indigenous Women and Violence: Feminist Activist Research in Heightened States of Injustice*. Tucson: University of Arizona Press, 2021.

Tamez, Margo. *Father Genocide*. New York: Turtle Point Press, 2021.

Tamez, Margo. "'Our Way of Life Is Our Resistance': Indigenous Women and Anti-Imperialist Challenges to Militarization Along the U.S.-Mexico Border." *Works and Days* 28 (2011): 281–318.

Tamez, Margo. "Place and Perspective in the Shadow of the Wall: Recovering Nde Knowledge and Self, Determination in Texas." *Aztlán: A Journal of Chicano Studies* 38, no. 1 (2013): 165–88.

U.S. Department of Homeland Security. "DHS/OBIM/PIA–001 Automated Biometric Identification System." Last updated March 31, 2023. https://www.dhs.gov/publication/dhsnppdpia-002-automated-biometric-identification-system.

U.S. Immigration and Customs Enforcement. "Secure Communities." Content archived February 9, 2021. https://www.ice.gov/secure-communities.

18

WHITE SUPREMACY AND MIGRANT ADVOCACY AT THE U.S.-MEXICO BORDER

ALLISON GLOVER

THIS CHAPTER CENTERS THREE EXAMPLES of white supremacy in discourse, policy, and practice toward Latinx migrants during the Trump administration (2017–21). They are: (1) political assaults on migrants who entered the United States via the nation's southern land border; (2) conditions in detention centers; and (3) attacks on migrants who pursued their asylum claims after being released from detention. I frame these attacks within the context of unbridled racism and xenophobia, further fueled by Donald Trump's mission to dismantle asylum programs and criminalize asylum seekers.

My analysis is also grounded in my experiences as a white ally. For reasons I explain below, in 2019, I worked for the Dilley Pro Bono Project in Dilley, Texas, in a U.S. Immigration and Customs Enforcement (ICE) detention center, about ninety miles north of the U.S.-Mexico border. For nine weeks I was part of a team of lawyers, paralegals, students, community members, bilingual professionals, and English-speaking support staff that worked together to get migrant women and children out of jail. When I worked for the Center for Human Rights and Constitutional Law, in 2019, I collaborated with teammates from across the United States to interview migrant children held in U.S. Customs and Border Protection (CBP) camps in El Paso and Clint, Texas, and Santa Teresa, New Mexico (figures 18.1 and 18.2). Currently, I am at the Colorado Hosting Asylum Network, where I help asylum seekers in Colorado find health care, apply for work permits, connect with food and clothing banks, enroll in English classes, secure housing, and find lawyers. These experiences inform my analysis of Trump's racism and xenophobia toward migrant communities.

I am white. I recognize that as a white person born and raised in a white-dominated social system, such as the one in the United States, I have always been and continue to be a beneficiary of white supremacy. I recognize that as a white person with U.S. citizenship I have always benefited from and continue to reap the rewards of white settler colonialism. The lands where I live today are within the territories of the Cheyenne, Arapaho, and Ute peoples. About 80 percent of the current population of the state of Colorado, however, is white. Like my house, the University of Colorado Boulder, where, in 2018, I earned a PhD, is built on the ancestral lands of Native peoples. At my alma mater, 65 percent of full-time undergraduate and graduate students and 85 percent of full-time faculty members are white. Native people of many Indigenous nations live in Colorado today, but the fact is that their ancestral lands are dominated and controlled by the descendants of western Europeans such as me. In addition to being white, I am also a homeowner and a career professional. Class privilege is the most obvious reason why I went to the border in 2019. I could afford to work for free for a while.

Due to my interest in white supremacy, I examine the white supremacist ideology that drove the Trump administration's efforts to: (1) frame asylum-seeking Latinx migrants as undesirables and criminals; (2) prevent them from entering the United States; (3) force migrants into cold rooms or cages by separating families (CBP) or by imprisoning them for months or years (ICE); and (4) set them up for failure if they pursue their asylum claim in immigration court. I underscore a constellation of tactics the Trump administration used in 2018 and 2019: the Zero Tolerance policy, metering, the Migrant Protection Protocols, the third-country transit bar, asylum cooperative agreements (ACAs), the Prompt Asylum Claim Review (PACR) program, and the Humanitarian Asylum Review Process (HARP) program.

This chapter also builds a bridge between the present and the past. I anchor my discussion of white supremacy in contemporary U.S. politics

Figure 18.1. Drawing by a detained child. South Texas Family Residential Center.

Figure 18.2. Drawing by a detained child. South Texas Family Residential Center.

by exposing Trump's attacks on asylum law and asylum seekers. At the same time, the thread of the story this chapter tells runs through a longer past. As many leading scholars have pointed out, the roots of white supremacy can be traced back to the invasion of Abya Yala, renamed the Americas, by white, European explorers, conquistadores, and colonizers.[1] Socially constructed notions of race and white superiority buttressed this racialized hierarchy of a new social order and enabled widespread violence against Native populations. The destruction and death that U.S. interventionism caused Indigenous peoples in the Americas are undeniable. The United States' overt and covert support of ultraconservative right-wing politicians and the repressive regimes they commanded is indisputable.

Nonetheless, politicians rarely acknowledge the wars the U.S. government has waged on democratically elected leaders and the popular movements that swept them into power. This chapter posits that the scores of asylum-seeking Latinx migrants arriving at the nation's southern border render visible the devastating and long-lasting impact of U.S. proxy wars and interventionist policies in the Americas. It suggests that the oral testimony each asylum seeker gives during their credible fear interview can be viewed as a radical act of enunciation, an indictment, and a call for accountability from responsible agents.

I focus on Latinx migrants including women and children because I worked in the South Texas Family Residential Center in Dilley, Texas. The Dilley Pro Bono Project staff referred to this ICE detention center as "Baby Jail" because children of all ages were incarcerated there alongside their mothers. In July 2019, the vast majority (88 percent) of asylum seekers imprisoned in Dilley had fled El Salvador, Guatemala, and Honduras. Therefore, this chapter centers the state violence that migrants from these countries suffer in U.S. border camps and detention centers.

Examples of Donald Trump's xenophobic rhetoric abound. In her book *Demagogue for President: The Rhetorical Genius of Donald Trump*, Jennifer Mercieca provides a thorough analysis of the discursive strategies he used to fan the flames of racism against migrants of color. What the businessman and reality TV star lacked in knowledge and experience he more than made up for in weaponized rhetoric. Ever the dangerous demagogue, contends Mercieca, Trump sought and secured his followers' compliance by appealing to their "passions and prejudices." She explains six of his key rhetorical strategies: (1) argumentum ad populum (appeal to the crowd); (2) American exceptionalism; (3) paralipsis (Greek for "I'm not saying, I'm just saying"); (4) argument ad hominem (attacking the person instead of their argument); (5) argument ad baculum (threats of intimidation or force); and (6) reification (treating humans as objects).[2] By soaking these discursive tactics in the bloody waters of racism and xenophobia before airing them out to dry in his speeches and tweets, explains Mercieca, Trump simultaneously unified his followers and cordoned off his opponents.

Trump's rhetoric inspired his supporters to come together and carry the banners of white supremacy, nativism, and U.S. exceptionalism, and he responded by calling on his followers to attack his opponents, convincing them that anyone who was not with him was "their mortal enemy."[3] Trump used reification to convince his followers that Latinx migrants arriving at the nation's southern border were less than human and thus undeserving of fair treatment. Adept at using "exterminationist or infestation rhetoric to position people as objects of disgust or as animals," the former president homogenized Black and Brown migrants and cast them as a deadly threat to U.S. immigration laws and the homeland's long-established white supremacist social and economic order.[4]

During his campaign announcement speech at Trump Tower in New York on June 16, 2015, Trump at once vilified Mexicans and praised his followers. "When Mexico sends its people, they're not sending their best. They're not sending you," he said. "They're sending people that have lots of problems. . . . They're bringing drugs. They're bringing crime. They're rapists."[5] Less than two weeks later, he amplified and further homogenized the targets of his vitriolic rhetoric, saying this on CNN: "You have people coming in and I'm not just saying Mexicans, I'm talking about people that are from all over that are killers and rapists and they're coming into this country."[6] And at the end of July, he told reporters: "There's great danger with the illegals. . . . We have a tremendous danger on the border with the illegals coming in."[7] It took Trump less than six weeks to master what Arturo Aldama calls the "violent practices of representation that reify" Chicanas/os, Mexicanas/os, and Native Americans as "barbarians, illegal aliens, addicts, primitives, criminals, and sexual deviants."[8]

Trump's use of ad populum appeals to extol his supporters was matched by his use of reification to cast Latinx immigrants crossing the southern land border as a threat to the nation's sanctity and security. At the same time, Suketu Mehta points out that Trump and his political allies were unconcerned about the ninety-three thousand Canadians who overstayed their U.S. visas in 2015. Despite the fact that this was double the number of Mexicans who overstayed their visas that same year, explains Mehta, there were no armed civilians "zealously guarding the northern border, standing watch for Canadians coming in through the snowy wastes of the Dakotas." Unlike Central Americans, the one hundred thousand Canadians who reside without authorization in the United States did not flee a failed state marked by "chaos and lawlessness" for which the U.S. government bears significant responsibility.[9] Furthermore, the federal government projects onto nonwhite migrant bodies the social and political disorder that forced them to flee. They come from lawlessness; therefore, they are lawless. They come from a violent region; therefore, they are inherently violent. Even though the U.S. government contributed to the conditions that caused Central American nation-states to fail, it forces migrants fleeing that region to "bear the burden of their failed state."[10]

Professor of law at the University of Denver and immigration attorney César Cuauhtémoc García Hernández centers the stark contrast between the U.S. government's response to noncitizens crossing the northern border and its response to those doing so via the southern border. He quotes Asa Hutchinson (George W. Bush–appointed director of the U.S. Drug Enforcement Administration and later undersecretary in the newly created U.S. Department of Homeland Security [DHS]), who said in 2007: "Historically we have evidence of more terrorists coming across our northern Canadian border than our southern border."[11] Nonetheless, speaking to the press and CBP officials in Nogales, Arizona, U.S. attorney general Jeff Sessions fanned the flames of racialized fears. "It is . . . here, along this border," he said, "that transnational gangs like MS-13 and international cartels flood our country with drugs and leave death and violence in their wake. And it is here that criminal aliens and the coyotes and the document-forgers seek to overthrow our system of lawful immigration. . . . It is here . . . where we first take our stand against this filth."[12] Sessions, who boasted more than ten years as a federal prosecutor and state attorney general as well as two decades in the Senate (R-Ala.), fervently believed that all immigrants constituted a threat to the nation by "depressing wages, committing crimes, and competing for welfare benefits."[13]

The president and his attorney general were not, however, the only politicians degrading migrants. John Kelly, Trump's chief of staff, used racist tropes to debase Spanish-speaking migrants crossing into the United States via the country's southern land border. "They're . . . not people that would easily assimilate into the United States into our modern society," he said. "They don't speak English. They don't integrate well, they don't have skills."[14] In the speech he wrote for Trump's first address to Congress, Stephen Miller, the president's senior policy adviser—and, as Mehta writes, the most "notorious immigrant hater in the Trump administration"—alerted the public to the "drug dealers" and "criminals" who were transforming the nation's border into "an environment of lawless chaos" to "prey on our very innocent citizens." The new president, Miller wrote, would not allow terrorism to gain a foothold in the homeland. Most people found guilty of "terrorism and terrorism-related offenses" in the wake of 9/11, the speechwriter continued, "came here from outside the country."[15]

Although top officials in the U.S. Department of Justice had insisted that their data "showed just the opposite," Miller's lie was not omitted from the address.[16] The truth would have sounded something like this: "between 2008 and 2017, white supremacists accounted for 71% of deaths in terror attacks in the United States."[17] Donald Trump, Jeff Sessions, John Kelly, and Stephen Miller are contemporary iterations of the white people with power who began reifying and pathologizing nonwhite populations in Abya Yala more than five hundred years ago. Their racist rhetorical attacks against migrants underscore what Aldama calls the "legacy of colonialism and violence in the Americas" and Anibal Quijano calls the coloniality of power.[18] As both scholars point out in their work, when the white European conquistadores demanded reverence from all Native peoples, they staked their claim in the notion of white supremacy. They weaved their imagined notion of racial superiority into the very fabric of their discourse and used it to legitimize the unconscionable acts of genocide they committed against the nonwhite populations they conquered, populations whose identities they racialized across time and space. Aldama and Quijano make plain that during the sixteenth and seventeenth centuries colonizers elaborated the notion of racial superiority and used it to justify the killing, enslaving, exploiting, maiming, raping, and disappearing of Native populations.

Quijano's notion of the coloniality of power is rooted in the capitalist structure of colonization, which was based on race and racial hierarchies. The notion of the fierce savage racializes the Indigenous or Black man as a threat. The only way to mitigate and eradicate the danger that men of color posed to society—as the colonial invaders constructed it in Abya Yala—was to subjugate or kill the fierce savage. Walter Mignolo explains that the original colonial articulation of difference and the concomitant relations of domination and subordination enabled white Europeans to impose their perceived racial and cultural superiority onto Native populations.[19] Aldama, Quijano, and Mignolo interrogate how nations, places, and societies operate within these hyperembedded ideals that were imposed during colonialism and that continue to be reiterated in our contemporary moment. Occupying the White House, Trump produced and distributed racialized and xenophobic knowledge about Latinx migrants.

In the spring of 2005, members of the Minuteman Project flocked to the Southwest to prevent immigrants from crossing the Arizona-Mexico border. These "illegal aliens," the minutemen claimed, were "creating an imminent danger to all Americans" and "destroying America."[20] Conservative media championed these armed civilians as patriots who were serving the nation by doing what the government would not do on its own: beat back the Brown and Black bodies that were invading the homeland. Both the minutemen and the media used rhetoric that dehumanized migrants to condone violence against them.

In 2005, like in the Trump era, conservative news outlets narrativized the inherently savage nature of immigrants by objectifying them, producing false knowledge about them, and displaying manipulated imagery of them. These tactics illustrated their status as nonpersons, objects, and animals, none of which "qualify for the rights and benefits of citizenship." As Leo R. Chavez points out, however, illegality is a social, cultural, and political construction that aims to serve the interests and objectives of the dominant group in the nation-state.[21]

In November 2018, as a caravan of migrants, journeying together on foot, approached the southwest border of the United States, members of the Minuteman Project joined other armed, unregulated citizen patrols to prevent the migrants from entering the country. "We believe our nation is under attack by foreigners," Howie Morgan, the project's national political director, said. Weapons were necessary to keep volunteers safe, he explained, because the border is dangerous. Armed civilians, Morgan claimed, would help CBP agents defend U.S. "sovereignty and its heralded stature as a nation of laws." Only Trump, he added, was fighting for better border security.[22]

The minutemen, like Trump, employed dominant discursive strategies that represent Latinx women as abnormally fertile. Their unbridled sexuality, coupled with their "pathologically high fertility levels," would decrease the "demographic presence of white Americans" while simultaneously increasing the demographic of Brown and "illegitimate" Americans.[23] Trump used this racist trope when he threatened to abolish the Fourteenth Amendment of the U.S. Constitution, which protects birthright citizenship. He employed it again when he accused pregnant Latinx migrant women of entering the United States "illegally" to give birth to anchor babies.[24]

The Trump administration's white supremacist discourse propelled its xenophobic response to the humanitarian "crisis" at the U.S.-Mexico border. A clandestine pilot program that CBP carried out in El Paso, Texas, from July to November 2017 separated upward of 280 families. Agents working in the field reported that the records management system at CBP did not allow them to keep track of separated children and their parents. Turning a blind eye to these reports, Jeff Sessions—bolstered by his deputy, Rod Rosenstein; by John Kelly, who at the time was DHS secretary; and by the president himself—issued his infamous Zero Tolerance memo in April 2018. Reframing asylum-seeking parents with children as smugglers and human traffickers, Sessions vowed to fully prosecute them under the law. The combination of negligence and indifference at the federal level makes exact numbers impossible to come by. While some sources report that the U.S. government separated at least 2,800 children from their parents, others suggest the number to be over 5,000.[25]

Metering was another unprecedented and illegal tactic the Trump administration used to turn back asylum seekers who presented themselves and their families at ports of entry. Beginning in April 2018, instead of processing asylum seekers in accordance with U.S. law, CBP officers met them on the bridges to the United States, waitlisted them, and told them to return weeks or months later. Once again, accurate numbers are nonexistent. Data released by two research centers in the United States, however, suggests that in August 2018 up to 26,000 names appeared on the waitlists. Six months later, at least 15,000 asylum seekers were still in Mexico, struggling to stay alive in cities just south of the border.[26]

Conditions in these locations would be exacerbated in early 2019, when the Trump administration ordered CBP to return migrants, excluding Mexicans, to Mexico to await their U.S. immigration court hearings and final adjudication. The Migrant Protection Protocols, more commonly known as Remain in Mexico, changed the trajectory of more than 65,000 lives. Strong-arming the Mexican government into the agreement by threatening U.S. tariffs enabled the Trump administration to force migrants back to Mexico, subjecting them to homelessness, violence, illness, and fear as they waited for their immigration hearings. Human Rights First documented more than 1,000 cases of assault, extortion, kidnapping, and rape by November 2019.[27]

Put into effect on July 16, 2019, the third-country transit bar prohibited migrants from applying for asylum if they entered or tried to enter the United States at the southern border on or after that date and had failed to apply for protection from persecution or torture in at least one of the countries they passed through while en route to the United States. This bar, the Trump administration argued, would reduce human smuggling, improve diplomatic relations, and expose fake and meritless asylum claims. For the first time in U.S. history, applicants were expected to articulate why they and their children did not apply for asylum in other countries. The third-country transit bar was both unprecedented and blatantly illegal. In the words of senior supervising attorney at the Southern Poverty Law Center's Immigrant Justice Project, Melissa Crow, it was nothing more than "another volley in the ongoing war against asylum seekers."[28] It wouldn't be the last.

Because threatening Mexico with tariffs had proven to be a useful tactic, the Trump administration used it again to bend the will of the Guatemalan, Honduran, and Salvadoran governments, forcing all three into asylum cooperative agreements. Scores of asylum seekers were already fleeing the Northern Triangle, but the ACAs, in principle, could empower the Trump administration to deport Guatemalans to Honduras or El Salvador, and Hondurans and Salvadorans to Guatemala. Although the Guatemala ACA was the only one to be fully implemented, it enabled the U.S. government to do plenty of damage to the 950 Honduran and Salvadoran children and adults forced into Guatemala. "U.S. officials put the asylum seekers on planes to Guatemala without telling them where they were going; they landed without knowing what country they were in. There they waited on the tarmac for hours, sometimes with small children, with no food, water, or medical attention."[29] Questioned about the lack of morality and the illegality of both the Migrant Protection Protocols and the Guatemala ACA, Trump, unsurprisingly, doubled down on his racist rhetoric, casting all migrants as threats to the security of the nation. Speaking in the Rose Garden in February 2019, he said: "We're going to confront the national security crisis on our southern border. And we're going to do it one way or the other. . . . It's an invasion."[30] Meanwhile, migrant children began dying in CBP custody.

The Prompt Asylum Claim Review and the Humanitarian Asylum Review Process enabled the Trump administration to deport people from the United States without providing them with an immigration hearing. No previous administration—Democratic or Republican—had held asylum seekers in CBP custody during their credible fear interview without access to legal counsel. This interview is a high-stakes moment, and the outcome determines whether a person can remain in the United States to pursue their claim for asylum in immigration court. It is the first step in a long and complex legal process. If an asylee who is placed in PACR or HARP receives a negative determination, they are sent back to the country from which they fled. While PACR targets all single adults and families who are subject to the third-country transit bar, HARP goes after Mexican families. DHS began implementing both programs in December 2019, in El Paso, Texas.[31]

Created by Congress in the aftermath of September 11, 2001, DHS enforces immigration laws. CBP and ICE, the strong arms of DHS, have the power to catch, arrest, and deport noncitizens from the United States. U.S. Citizenship and Immigration Services (USCIS), the third unit within DHS that executes immigration law, is charged with approving or denying applications for benefits and humanitarian relief such as citizenship or asylum. The statute that grants CBP, ICE, and USCIS the power to enforce immigration laws against noncitizens is the Immigration and Nationality Act, which was enacted by Congress in 1952.[32]

To be eligible for asylum, an applicant must meet the definition of refugee. The 1952 act defines *refugee* as: "Any person who is outside any country of such person's nationality or, in the case of a person having no nationality, is outside any country in which such person habitually resided, and who is unable or unwilling to avail himself or herself of the protection of that country because of persecution or a well-founded fear of persecution on account of race, religion, nationality, membership in a particular social group, or political opinion."[33] Moreover, the USCIS website states the following: "You may apply for asylum regardless of your immigration status."[34]

In the wake of World War II, national and international policy was developed to address the refugee "crisis." This policy included but was not limited to the Displaced Persons Act (1948), the UN Convention Relating to the Status of Refugees (1951), the Cuban Adjustment Act (1966), the UN Protocol Relating to the Status of Refugees (1968), the Orderly Departure Program (1979), and the Refugee Act (1980). The 1980 act became the basis for the contemporary asylum system in the United States. That same year, 3.5 percent of all asylum applications filed came from refugees fleeing El Salvador, Guatemala, and Honduras. The percentage more than tripled by 2000. By 2006, 26.4 percent of all asylum applications filed in the United States came from Salvadoran, Guatemalan, and Honduran refugees. In 2015, this figure soared to 33.8 percent.[35]

The contracts that ICE began offering to Corrections Corporation of America (later CoreCivic) and Geo Group, the two largest and most known private prison companies in the United States, became so profitable that they "rescued" both companies from financial devastation. Geo Group receives about $200 per day per adult, and ICE will pay a private prison company approximately $300 per day per family. The immigrant detention network in the United States comprises more than two hundred facilities.[36] As García Hernández writes, "Migrants are turned into commodities—their bodies valued for the revenue stream they promise."[37]

The conditions inside CBP facilities are notoriously inhumane. The *perreras* (dog pounds) and *hieleras* (iceboxes) are overcrowded and dirty, and the people held there, including children, are "virtually incommunicado, forced to sleep on the floor, and not provided enough food." In the words of Andre Segura, legal director for the American Civil Liberties

Union of Texas, "immigrants deserve due process, and yet CBP jails are effectively legal black holes, where no attorney, and in fact no outsider at all, can enter."[38] Interviews I conducted with parents and children detained in CBP stations in the El Paso sector in August 2019 revealed, for example, that a family of three spent seven days and seven nights in *la hielera*. CBP officials did not provide the family with medical treatment or dry clothing. At the time of the interview, the child, age four, was sick with diarrhea and vomiting. When the family was released from *la hielera*, the three of them were taken to large rooms that housed up to forty or fifty people, all of whom slept on mats on the floor because beds were not provided. It was virtually impossible to sleep because bright lights were always left on. Several people who had been in these rooms for more than one week reported having access to a shower on only one occasion. Two siblings, both minors, showed me the dried mud that was still on their ankles and feet.

Although some people I spoke to had provided CBP officials with names, phone numbers, and addresses of sponsors who were willing and able to receive them, as far as they knew, the officials had not contacted these friends or family members. None of the migrants I interviewed were given a notice of their rights (I-770 form). No one was provided with a list of free legal services or attorneys. Border patrol officers had not spoken to anyone about the Flores Settlement Agreement (1997), which grants minors the right to be released to a parent or relative living in the United States. Two sets of parents had been told that they and their children would be sent to Ciudad Juárez, where they would remain until their court appointment in February 2020. These migrants were from El Salvador, Guatemala, and Honduras.

In 2019, if migrants seeking asylum in the United States were released from CBP camps, they were transported directly to an ICE facility. Women with children under the age of eighteen were sent to the South Texas Family Residential Center (figure 18.3). The most immediate impact that the Trump policies and protocols had on people seeking refuge in the United States was the increase in negative determinations after the credible fear interview. This means that the rate at which people in danger were denied the right to pursue their claim for asylum began to skyrocket in the latter half of July 2019. All the testimonies from women and children in Dilley were horrifying and heartbreaking.

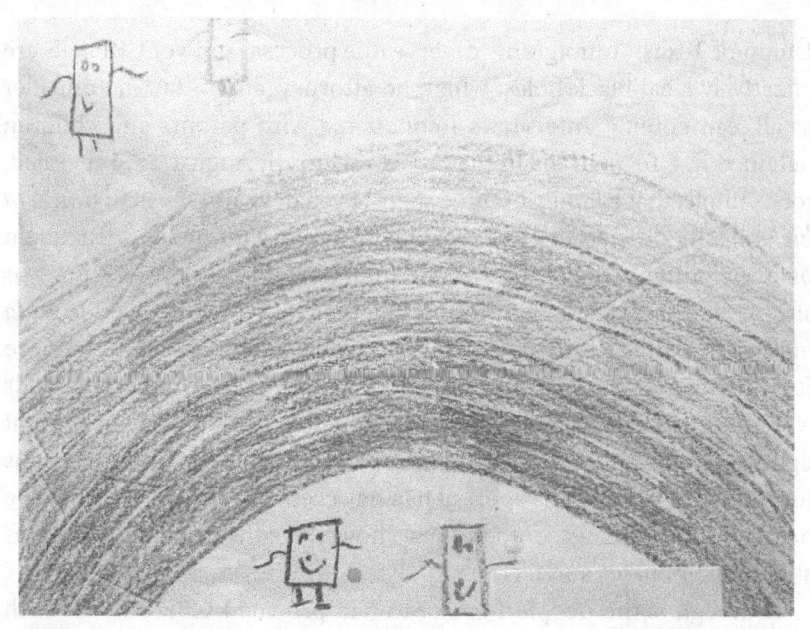

Figure 18.3. Drawing by a detained child. South Texas Family Residential Center.

Currently, thousands of Central American asylum seekers are being held in border camps and detention centers throughout the United States. These facilities are under the jurisdiction of either CBP or ICE. CBP faced intense scrutiny in the spring of 2018, when ProPublica made public a haunting recording of traumatized children sobbing after CBP agents took them away from their parents.[39] CBP remains under fire for keeping detained asylum seekers of all ages, including babies and toddlers, in *hieleras* for prolonged periods. ICE continues to be criticized for holding migrants for more than thirty consecutive days in overcrowded cages. Let us recall that requesting asylum is legal. All people have the right to ask a foreign country to protect them from the persecution they suffer in their home country due to their race, religion, nationality, political opinion, or membership in a particular social group.

NOTES

1. Aldama, *Disrupting Savagism*; Quijano, "Coloniality of Power, Eurocentrism, and Latin America; Rodríguez, *Sexual Futures, Queer Gestures, and Other Latina Longings.*
2. Mercieca, *Demagogue for President*, 13, 15–19.

3. Mercieca, 72.
4. Mercieca, 20.
5. Trump, "Remarks Announcing Candidacy for President."
6. Trump, "Donald Trump on CNN's State of the Union."
7. Quoted in Burnett, "Donald Trump Visits the Border."
8. Aldama, *Disrupting Savagism*, 3.
9. Mehta, *This Land Is Our Land*, 132.
10. Mehta, 162.
11. Quoted in García Hernández, *Migrating to Prison*, 12.
12. Sessions, "Attorney General Jeff Sessions Delivers Remarks."
13. Davis and Shear, *Border Wars*, 15.
14. Kelly, "Transcript."
15. Mehta, *This Land Is Our Land*, 146; speech quoted from Davis and Shear, *Border Wars*, 97–99.
16. Davis and Shear, *Border Wars*, 98.
17. Mehta, *This Land Is Our Land*, 151.
18. Aldama, *Disrupting Savagism*, 4; Quijano, "Coloniality of Power, Eurocentrism, and Latin America."
19. Mignolo, *Local Histories/Global Designs*.
20. Chavez, *The Latino Threat*, 134, 138.
21. Chavez, 10.
22. Quoted in LaPorta and Da Silva, "Migrant Caravan."
23. Chavez, *The Latino Threat*, 177–78.
24. Mercieca, *Demogogue for President*, 110–12.
25. Schoenholtz, Ramji-Nogales, and Schrag, *The End of Asylum*, 53–54.
26. Schoenholtz, Ramji-Nogales, and Schrag, 58–59.
27. Schoenholtz, Ramji-Nogales, and Schrag, 62.
28. Quoted in Helmore, "Trump Administration's Bid to Limit Asylum Seekers."
29. Schoenholtz, Ramji-Nogales, and Schrag, *The End of Asylum*, 73, and see 71–72.
30. Trump, "Remarks on Declaring a National Emergency Concerning the Southern Border."
31. K. Shepherd, "DHS Reveals New Details of Secretive Asylum Programs PACR and HARP."
32. Wadhia, *Banned*, 1–2, 49–50.
33. Immigration and Nationality Act of 1952, 8 U.S.C. § 1101(a)(42) (1952).
34. U.S. Citizenship and Immigration Services, "Questions and Answers."
35. Mehta, *This Land Is Our Land*, 25.
36. Schoenholtz, Ramji-Nogales, and Schrag, *The End of Asylum*, 143; Walia, *Undoing Border Imperialism*, 55.
37. García Hernández, *Migrating to Prison*, 16.
38. American Civil Liberties Union, "ACLU Calls on President Biden to End PACR/HARP Protocols."
39. Thomas, "Listen to Children Who've Just Been Separated from Their Parents at the Border."

BIBLIOGRAPHY

Aldama, Arturo J. *Disrupting Savagism: Intersecting Chicana/o, Mexican Immigrant, and Native American Struggles for Self-Representation*. Durham, N.C.: Duke University Press, 2001.

American Civil Liberties Union. "ACLU Calls on President Biden to End PACR/ HARP Protocols." Press release, January 27, 2021. https://www.aclu.org/press -releases/aclu-calls-president-biden-end-pacrharp-protocols.

Burnett, John. "Donald Trump Visits the Border and Calls for Tougher Enforcement." *Morning Edition*. NPR, July 25, 2015. https://www.npr.org/2015/07/24/425834225/.

Chavez, Leo R. *The Latino Threat: Constructing Immigrants, Citizens, and the Nation*. Stanford, Calif.: Stanford University Press, 2013.

Davis, Julie Hirschfeld, and Michael D. Shear. *Border Wars: Inside Trump's Assault on Immigration*. New York: Simon and Schuster, 2019.

García Hernández, César Cuauhtémoc. *Migrating to Prison: America's Obsession with Locking Up Immigrants*. New York: New Press, 2019.

Helmore, Edward. "Trump Administration's Bid to Limit Asylum Seekers Blocked by US Judge." *Guardian*, July 24, 2019.

Kelly, John. "Transcript: White House Chief of Staff John Kelly's Interview with NPR." NPR, May 11, 2018. https://www.npr.org/2018/05/11/610116389/.

LaPorta, James, and Chantal Da Silva. "Migrant Caravan: Border Troops Preparing for Threat of Armed, Unregulated Militias, Leaked Documents Show." *Newsweek*, November 1, 2018. https://www.newsweek.com/1196855.

Mehta, Suketu. *This Land Is Our Land: An Immigrant's Manifesto*. New York: Farrar, Straus and Giroux, 2019.

Mercieca, Jennifer. *Demagogue for President: The Rhetorical Genius of Donald Trump*. College Station: Texas A&M University Press, 2020.

Mignolo, Walter. *Local Histories/Global Designs: Coloniality, Subaltern Knowledges, and Border Thinking*. Princeton, N.J.: Princeton University Press, 2000.

Quijano, Aníbal. "Coloniality of Power, Eurocentrism, and Latin America." *Nepanlta: Views from South* 1, no. 3 (2000): 553–80.

Rodríguez, Juana María. *Sexual Futures, Queer Gestures, and Other Latina Longings*. New York: New York University Press, 2014.

Schoenholtz, Andrew I., Jaya Ramji-Nogales, and Philip G. Schrag. *The End of Asylum*. Washington, D.C.: Georgetown University Press, 2021.

Sessions, Jeff. "Attorney General Jeff Sessions Delivers Remarks Announcing the Department of Justice's Renewed Commitment to Criminal Immigration Enforcement." April 11, 2017. U.S. Department of Justice. https://www.justice.gov/opa/ speech/attorney-general-jeff-sessions-delivers-remarks-announcing-department -justice-s-renewed.

Shepherd, Katie. "DHS Reveals New Details of Secretive Asylum Programs PACR and HARP." Immigration Impact, March 11, 2020. https://immigrationimpact.com/ 2020/03/11/dhs-asylum-programs-pacr-harp/.

Thomas, Ginger. "Listen to Children Who've Just Been Separated from Their Parents at the Border." *ProPublica*, June 18, 2018. https://www.propublica.org/article/children-separated-from-parents-border-patrol-cbp-trump-immigration-policy.

Trump, Donald J. "Donald Trump on CNN's State of the Union: 'I'm in It to Win It . . . I will Make Our Country Great Again." CNN Press Room, June 28, 2015. https://cnnpressroom.blogs.cnn.com/2015/06/28/donald-trump.

Trump, Donald J. "Remarks Announcing Candidacy for President in New York City." June 16, 2015. American Presidency Project. https://www.presidency.ucsb.edu/node/310310.

Trump, Donald J. "Remarks on Declaring a National Emergency Concerning the Southern Border of the United States and an Exchange with Reporters." February 15, 2019. American Presidency Project. https://www.presidency.ucsb.edu/node/332900.

U.S. Citizenship and Immigration Services. "Questions and Answers: Affirmative Asylum Eligibility and Applications." Last reviewed August 7, 2023. https://www.uscis.gov/humanitarian/refugees-and-asylum/asylum/affirmative-asylum-frequently-asked-questions/.

Wadhia, Shoba Sivaprasad. *Banned: Immigration Enforcement in the Time of Trump.* New York: New York University Press, 2019.

Walia, Harsha. *Undoing Border Imperialism.* Oakland, Calif.: AK Press, 2013.

19

"FREE THEM ALL"

A Conversation on Trans Abolitionist Visions
with Jordan Garcia

NISHANT UPADHYAY

JORDAN T. GARCIA IS THE IMMIGRANT ally organizing director for Colorado for Immigrant Rights. Jordan has been working on queer and trans migrant justice issues locally and nationally for over a decade. Since 2020, Jordan has coordinated a mutual aid network to support trans migrants incarcerated at the U.S. Immigration and Customs Enforcement (ICE) detention center in Aurora, Colorado. Jordan believes that community organizing for systemic change can and will lead to liberation. He uses theater of the oppressed, popular education, and an anti-oppression lens to do leadership development in movements for justice.

NISHANT: Tell us about your journey to activism and organizing.

JORDAN: I got really involved with organizing on my college campus, which was largely a white-dominated campus. I went to Colorado College in Colorado Springs. I had dealt with whiteness before, but there I really needed community. So, I got closer to other students of color and started making connections. We started to work together on things. I also came out as trans when I was in college, and it was a challenging environment for sure. But I learned a lot.

I did a program through the Associated Colleges of the Midwest called the Urban Studies Program. During my junior year I went to Chicago for a semester and studied community organizing, like Saul Alinsky–style community organizing and critiques of the Alinsky style.

I was in a group, Queer to the Left, and we did a lot of housing advocacy and tenant rights around gentrification. We did a bunch of different actions. There was a particular slumlord in Chicago who was not turning the heat on in the wintertime. That's a deadly situation. We did this action where we would go to his house in the suburbs and play volleyball and soccer in his front yard until he consented to meet with the tenant rights committee. We basically embarrassed him in front of his community as much as we could.

I liked building community in my early twenties because that was fun, and it was awesome to be with friends. I thought activism is awesome, so I just stayed with it when I came back to Denver. I started with unpaid stuff or would do actions around queer liberation stuff. I became a street medic in Denver. I also did a lot of work with the Colorado Coalition Against Sexual Assault. I worked with young people who are mostly homeless and queer. I was an education and employment counselor with them. It was more nonprofit direct service provider work, instead of organizing or activism. But I worked with young people who are homeless, mostly because of their queer identity, and I was helping them get housing and jobs.

After that, I came to the American Friends Service Committee (AFSC), it was sixteen years ago this week!

NISHANT: Wow! Sixteen years, that's a long time.

JORDAN: Yeah, I've been doing immigrant rights organizing through AFSC for sixteen years now.

NISHANT: How did you get into immigrant rights work?

JORDAN: A couple of things. I've a couple of grandparents who were part of the Bracero Program and were migrant workers from Mexico. They settled in San Antonio. On my dad's side I'm second-generation Mexican, and on my mom's side I'm third-generation Mexican, as well as one-eighth Native American. So, I'm definitely not a child of immigrants. In addition to that, when I lived in Chicago my girlfriend at the time was a Hmong refugee born in a refugee camp in Thailand. I learned about her immigrant experience, and how different it was from my parents'. I realized why we need to do better by people, and immigrant rights became something I could throw my heart and soul into.

NISHANT: Thanks for sharing this. Can you share what kind of work you do with AFSC?

JORDAN: At the AFSC I run a group called Colorado for Immigrant Rights. It's actually a group of allies who are trying to use their privilege for good and not evil. We work hand in hand and step by step with the immigrant lead organizing committee, from working against deportations, working for congressional meetings, collecting testimony, etc. It is a little bit interesting that I actually work a lot with allies. It's been an interesting journey. It's really important to me that we clean people up before we send them out into the movement. I actually do believe it's important to work with these allies who are wanting to make change in the world. We talk about what actually being an accomplice looks like, how it's going to be uncomfortable sometimes, and how you're going to make mistakes, and why it's important to stay in anyway. I think it's really important for people with resources, whether it's a privilege or financial resources or sociopolitical capital, to use that for good and not get away with just going about their business. We talk a lot about the savior mentality. We talk about how as soon as you get comfortable you know you're doing something wrong. You need to stay uncomfortable to be doing it well. Keeping people on track is a full-time job! I think we do that pretty well, but it's really hard sometimes.

NISHANT: I had no idea that that was part of your job.

JORDAN: I mean other things I do is a lot of leadership development, across the board with all sorts of people. I do a lot of work around nonviolent direct action training. I also do a lot of work around campaign building and helping people get clear about what we want, who can give it to us, and how we want to apply pressure to get there. We also do a lot of legislative work at the federal level for immigration reform, and at the state level it's all over the map, from trying to prevent collusion between police and ICE, doing a lot of work around the detention center, and conditions inside the detention center.

NISHANT: That's a lot of amazing work! Can you share some of the victories you've had over the years?

JORDAN: For sure. In 2013, there was a very large coalition of people who were able to pass in-state tuition for undocumented students. It took eleven years to get that passed. For ten of those years, we would send young people back home at the end of the day being sorry. It was really tough. But when we finally got it, hundreds of young people and their families came to see the signing of the bill. The legislative win was a really huge thing. I know this in some ways fixes some things but leaves the whole bunch of things open that still need to be fixed. But it's still a victory!

I think every time we're able to get a queer and trans person out of the detention center and into a safer situation it feels like a huge victory. But you know it's messy sometimes. For folks inside detention centers sometimes it is a better outcome for your immigration case if you stay in detention. That is really hard because of suicidal ideation, depression, and, for the last few years, COVID-19. It can be really hard to say that you need to stay there for the best possible outcome. Sometimes we're able to get people out right away. It feels really good when we're able to get someone out and they're able to be united with a family member, or just take them out for pizza, etc. It feels really good to have some of these victories.

Sometimes, it is really hard for trans women when they come out of detention. When they are in detention, they have a support system in terms of a social worker or a pen pal or somebody like me who puts money in their books. So sometimes when they leave detention, they can experience a little bit of a free fall if they don't have a support system.

It also is a really big victory when we hear from these women later and they say that $200–$300 that we gave them got them to their relative's house or they're able to be on their own now. Not only do they get to leave detention, but they have kind of a landing strip. When folks are able to say this made a difference, it feels really good. But sometimes it doesn't work out, and we give them another $600 and see what happens.

Amongst other victories, in 2013 we were able to get driver's licenses for undocumented folks in Colorado. Totally imperfect because the stipulation for the driver's license was that you did not have SSN. So DACA-mented people couldn't get driver's licenses because they had SSN. We had to go back to the legislature and fix that. But that felt really big when, you know, parents could have a driver's license and be able to drive to school to pick up their kids, and when people running small businesses were able to get insurance, it opened up the world.

NISHANT: Those are all very significant victories. Thank you for sharing them. Can we talk more about queer and trans migrant justice work? What are some of the challenges that queer and trans migrants face? And why is it important to center their voices in migrant justice work?

JORDAN: Totally, I want to start with the second piece, and then work backwards a little bit. It's just so important to center queer and trans perspectives in migrant justice work because if we can get justice for these people, for our people, everything will improve for everyone. One of the things we talk about is that no one belongs in a detention center; it's just not a place to keep people in.

Queer and trans people are significantly more likely to experience sexual assault, depression, anxiety, eating disorders, and malnutrition. When we're able to say explicitly that what these people are experiencing shines a light on the whole system and how broken it is. It's just not okay that anybody should be treated that way and that anyone should have to enter those kinds of circumstances.

It is also true that queer and trans folks are disproportionately victimized and targeted by the border patrol. When we're able to point out that many queer and trans people are seeking asylum and this is how they're treated, it really shines a light on the fact that asylum seekers from all over the world are treated this way. I do believe that it's really important to center the stories and experiences of queer and trans folks because it highlights what's wrong with the system.

There are two places in the United States where trans folks are detained: Tacoma, Washington, and Aurora, Colorado. These are trans-designated pods. In these detention centers what we've found is that overwhelmingly trans folks will create community with each other. In one of these facilities, there was this trans woman from El Salvador who was deaf. In that facility, all other trans women learned sign language so that they could better communicate with her, which is beautiful! Often there are some women who are prediabetic, so everyone else shares food and makes sure that they would get commissary food to supplement the nutrition that they weren't getting inside from the official menu. The official menu, there aren't enough calories or protein. So, the women in the facility create this community to take care of each other.

We need to center and lift up the stories of these trans women, their resilience, and their ability to build community wherever they are. It's really incredible to watch and experience. It does give us hope, and it really highlights people's humanity. This is something we can build on, right? So that when people are outside of detention centers they can support each other, care for each other, and check up on each other in the same ways. It's the kind of thing you want to protect really fiercely!

NISHANT: Thank you for sharing these stories. Do you think the larger migrant justice and immigrant rights movements center queer and trans perspectives in their organizing?

JORDAN: When I started at AFSC years ago, queer and trans folks were a little bit of a subtext. But nowadays it's really changed! Recently, there was a national gathering with three panel discussions. One panel discussion was all Black migrants, another was people who won their cases out of detention, and the third was all trans women migrants. All trans women were pretty incredible and impressive!

Our immigrant leaders are all for it. They're not using a lot of super savvy jargon, but they are 100 percent behind this. They see that trans women are leaders in their own right. They're leading their own kind of movement within a movement. I think because so many trans people seek asylum, there is maybe a higher percentage of trans folks that are immigrants. So, in the general population, they represent a larger part of the immigrant rights movement.

I think that's interesting, and I don't think it used to be that way ten years ago, or even five years ago. It feels very much on top now. It's cool that our movement is seeing the leadership there. It's imperfect for sure. For instance, at national immigrant rights gatherings, nobody will think about how much harder it is for a trans person to be traveling with documents that match or don't match their identity. Nobody will think that it's a shame and something we should work on. But nobody would even consider not having trans people at the gathering. Which is great! Certainly, there's plenty of homophobia and transphobia within the immigrant community generally, but it's really different than it was ten years ago, which is just wild!

NISHANT: What do you think made that shift?

JORDAN: Oh, I think we won't shut up! These stories are important as they highlight what needs to change, and we'll just keep telling those stories. I think trans immigrants have really led the detention world, calling for just treatment inside these facilities. I think sometimes what happens in detention centers is that people will think the best way to get through this is to keep my head down. But trans folks are often not keeping their heads down. For them this is atrocious, this is inedible food, this is substandard health care, and that's not okay! They often say, I can't keep my head down about it! So, they tend to be the ones who will say, absolutely not, this is not okay!

A lot of immigrants who are in detention, they're in there for an average of sixty to ninety days. But trans folks are often there for two years or more. So, for them there's no keeping the head down and no bearing through it. I think that's really important to keep in mind, and I think that leadership is there from trans folks.

NISHANT: What's been some of the work that you're doing locally to center trans migrant voices?

JORDAN: There's a range. Some of the work has been to collect money, so that we can provide for the people inside the detention center. To have money on their commissary books and money on their phones; phones so they can call out, they can receive calls, they can listen to music, they can watch TV shows on tablets, etc. The food that is served is often frozen, rotten, and inedible. So, folks inside rely on their commissary to supplement their nutrition. When we are able to put money on people's books for commissary, it makes a huge impact on their quality of life inside the detention center. We have to use these really clunky systems to put money on their books, but that feels important to do.

The work that we do around putting money on people's books is very grassroots. It's quite literally a GoFundMe that goes to a friend's bank account, and then goes back out of that same account to provide for people. It's not a super hard thing to do. If you are thinking about doing it in your own city, you should try it.

When trans women are leaving the detention center we provide them with a bag of makeup. Some people question us for providing a bag of makeup. Why bother giving every woman who comes out of detention a bag of makeup? For trans women it's exciting, and it's anxiety, depression, and suicidal ideation prevention. In addition, sometimes it's about passing and not passing. For us it's a way that we can keep people safe, keep people feeling in their bodies, keep people feeling cared for and seen. We usually also give them shampoo and bath bombs, which sometimes they can or cannot use right away. But they feel a little bit pampered, and that feels important to us.

We also work really closely with some of the other organizations that do post-release support. A lot of the folks who come out of the detention center will fly to family members around the country, they don't necessarily stay in Denver. We will work to make sure that they've got jackets that match their gender, and their size. A lot of people come from South America, and are headed to New York with sandals. We don't want that, so we make sure we've got boots, jackets, and appropriate and gender-affirming clothing.

We'll help to get them to the airport and get through TSA. Our volunteers have special training to help them advocate for somebody whose identity may be different than what their documents say. So, speaking the right language to TSA but also speaking the right language to the person to say, "I've got your back." We act as a bridge for their next steps and are able to step into what comes next with some dignity. After spending so much time in a detention center, which systematically and intentionally strips you of your dignity, to be able to be in community once you're out and get some of that dignity back feels really important.

Aside from this direct service, we do a lot of organizing to get the message out that detention is deadly and we need to free them all! We need to fight these facilities who are profiting from pain. We had several trans women who spoke with members of Congress about the cleaning solvents that they were forced to use inside the detention center. They were causing not just headaches and nausea but also bleeding gums and sores. It was a pesticide-level cleaning agent that was not intended to be used inside. But they were making the women clean the facility with it. We had trans women share with Congressman Jason Crow about that practice. And he, you know, put a stop to it. When he puts a stop to it then that changes for the whole facility. The practice of using these pesticide-grade cleaning solutions became part of a study and came under great scrutiny. This went nationwide.

It is a huge impact that these women are making! These are women who are sticking their necks out and talking about their experiences. It improves conditions for everyone at the whole facility!

NISHANT: This is all such amazing work! Is there any organizing work happening in other places across the country that you would like to highlight?

JORDAN: A lot of the amazing work is happening in powerhouses likes the Familia: Trans Queer Liberation Movement and Trans Latin@ Coalition. There is also lots of amazing work happening outside of these organizations. A lot of what folks are working on right now is what we need: a just and fair humane immigration system. We need Congress to get off their ass. What that has looked like for trans and queer folks is highlighting the injustices and sharing their stories. They've done that in a bunch of different ways.

This is weird, but because of COVID so much of this has gone virtual. Instead of having to get a bunch of congresspeople in the same room physically, you can get them in the same room virtually. Then you can have them basically listen to people's stories. Those stories highlight exactly what needs to change in our legislative work. There's been many such congressional briefings, where it's basically six trans women on a panel sharing their stories. More recently, it was three trans women and three trans men. Each of them had a different story that highlighted a different piece of the work that needed changing, and that was really cool!

You know leadership development and work that has to happen around coalescing a vision, that kind of work is happening at the national level right now. There's been some pretty amazing direct actions that highlight the change that needs to happen. There was a facility in Santa Ana, California, that was particularly egregious and that got shut down. And there have been a bunch of really beautiful, creative, bold, and courageous direct actions that involved drag! There have been other actions like occupying the spaces. The national scene has been pretty cool!

NISHANT: Those are really good examples! So, the final question: what do you envision for trans abolitionist futures?

JORDAN: I would say: free them all! Nobody belongs in a detention center. I believe that's true not just for immigrants in detention centers but for all people in all cages. Cages are not the solution. They don't keep us any safer. I think fewer and fewer people every day think that anymore.

And I do think that it will be hard, we have to figure out how to address harm, and I think we can do that! The more people we have thinking about how we do that in more creative, more courageous, and more bold ways, we will come up with better solutions to address harm. But most importantly, I want the people who are inside detention centers and prisons to be part of that conversation in real ways. That's why we need them out! So that they can contribute to these conversations, so that we can come up with the best solutions. I'm kind of a hard-line abolitionist. People always come back with, what about the rapists and murderers? That's fine, you can have those conversations. But I do think it's a bigger conversation around prevention.

NISHANT: Thank you for sharing these stories and insights!

20

RESISTANCE ARCHIVING

Reflections on the IMM Print Detention Stories Project

TINA SHULL AND JAMILA HAMMAMI

OUTSIDE OF THE THEO LACY Jail in Orange County, California, a crowd gathered on a sunny November day in 2016 to protest the U.S. Immigration and Customs Enforcement (ICE) detention of community members at the jail, and the horrific conditions facing all who were imprisoned there. Wielding signs reading "ICE out of OC" and "#Not1More Deportation," local immigrant and LGBTQ+ rights organizations, lawyers, and family members chanted demands to speak with the facility's deportation officer, and called for the release of their loved ones (figure 20.1). Several news vans arrived in time for a planned press conference; gaining media attention was part of the strategy. A young woman named Andrea, whose brother was detained at the jail and facing deportation, held a written statement she had prepared.[1] But when a local television news anchor put a microphone before her and asked, "What did your brother do to get arrested?" Andrea froze. Her hands began to tremble, and the anchor moved on to speak to someone else. Consoling Andrea afterward, an advocate said, "This is why we need to make our own media."

This interaction is one example of how communities facing immigration enforcement can experience trauma when sharing their stories with the public. The reporter's question also shows how presumptions of criminality permeate discourse on immigration and shape legacy media reporting. One week after the protest at Theo Lacy, Donald Trump was elected president on a platform of hate, and community members' fears of speaking out, as well as retaliatory conditions in detention, worsened.

As abolitionist scholars and organizers, we reflect in this essay on our efforts in resistance archiving, defined here as the intentional practice of documenting stories that counter the violent logics of prisons and borders, during the Trump era. Through a discussion of the creation of IMM Print, a digital archive of immigration detention stories launched by Tina during her time as a Soros Justice Fellow at Freedom for Immigrants in 2016–18—and drawing also on Jamila's work as founder and former executive director of the Queer Detainee Empowerment Project (QDEP)—we reflect on the challenges of resistance archiving within the "cramped political spaces" of the immigrant rights movement and the process of navigating the continuities and ruptures of Trump-era enforcement violence.[2]

A report by Freedom for Immigrants found that although media coverage of immigration detention tripled between 2010 and 2017, migrant voices remained largely missing.[3] Instead, news reporting has privileged the perspectives of ICE, other officials, and U.S. citizen actors, who often get both the first and last word. More egregiously, respectable news outlets continue to cite anti-immigrant organizations such as the Center for Immigration Studies (CIS), which has been designated a hate group by the Southern Poverty Law Center and immigration scholars.[4] Even coverage that is sympathetic to migrants focuses primarily on abuses that take place within the detention system. Although accurate, such reporting centers on themes of suffering, victimhood, and dependence, rather than on the agency of affected communities and the alternatives to incarceration they advocate for.

In a landscape rife with trauma and retaliation, documenting stories from detention is a fragmented and dangerous process. Stories are critiqued for foregrounding their singularity, and for sensationalizing trauma as "tragedy porn," contributing to tropes of migrant victimization. As Sujatha Fernandes cautions, stories can also fuel neoliberal agendas, especially if "reconfigured on the model of the market to produce entrepreneurial, upwardly mobile subjects." And individual stories lacking context can "shift the focus away from structurally defined axes of oppression and help to defuse the confrontational politics of social movements."[5] In effect, they can detract from systemic understandings of state-sanctioned border and carceral violence. Speaking out can also mean retaliation, persecution, and even death—effects that fall disproportionately on illegalized, racialized, and criminalized groups, especially Black, Indigenous, queer, or trans people, as well as women and children. Even if done anonymously or in relative safety, telling one's story often exacts a toll by reanimating trauma.

However, as prison abolitionist Mariame Kaba argues, "The work of abolition insists that we foreground the people who are behind the walls—that we listen to them, that we take their ideas seriously."[6] First-hand stories from detention illustrate anatomies of migrant detention and escalating state violence under Trump: isolation from communications with the outside; routine denials of due process, medical care, and adequate nutrition; physical and psychic assaults; and retaliation against resistance inside and out. Despite the challenges surrounding storytelling, IMM Print and other efforts in resistance archiving can help map abolitionist imaginaries—alternatives to escalating border and carceral violence in the Trump era and beyond.[7]

Conceived and launched as the Trump administration took office in 2017, IMM Print is "a publication by and for people affected by immigration detention." It is produced through inside-outside organizing, a strategy prioritizing the leadership and knowledge of incarcerated people with support from collaborators on the outside.[8] This chapter culminates in a series of short stories and artwork from detention—an archive in itself—to illustrate how IMM Print became a platform for mobilizing freedom campaigns and actions countering the violence and retaliation endemic in the U.S. carceral state, and the Trump administration's escalating war on migrants.

SOWING HATE AND FEAR: ORIGINS OF TRUMP'S WAR ON MIGRANTS

Today, migrant detention has become fully entrenched within the landscape of racially targeted mass incarceration in the United States. Originating in nineteenth-century exclusionary violence targeting Asian and Latinx migrant groups, detention's foundational logic has become normalized, especially since Ronald Reagan's administration.[9] We assert that detention must be understood as a function of U.S. imperialism, a mechanism of white nationalist state-making at the intersections of processes of policing, criminalization, and terror, which play out both within and beyond U.S. state borders. A core feature of detention is its retaliatory nature, its operation as a form of counterinsurgency waged against those deemed enemies of the state, meant to render migrants—and their voices—invisible.[10]

In *The Borders of AIDS*, Karma R. Chávez defines a "logic" as "a structure of thinking that thereby structures expression," whereas alienizing logic is "a structure of thinking that insists that some are necessarily members of a community and some are recognized as not belonging, even if they physically reside there." Chávez lists the myriad manifestations of alienizing logic throughout U.S. history: "genocide, lynching, the plantation, the reservation, the ghetto, the internment camp, the prison, the hospital, quarantine, ban, or deportation."[11] This section traces important precursors to Trump-era immigration enforcement violence, focusing especially on their narrative and rhetorical attendants.

THE TANTON NETWORK

In the 1980s and 1990s, a hostile public sphere of propaganda accompanied immigration enforcement violence, targeting immigrants in the United States. Anti-immigrant advocates had become more sophisticated in their media strategies and tactics by this time, and they sought to strip undocumented Latinx migrants of their social, political, and civil rights. In the late 1970s and early 1980s, John Tanton was a major force behind the rise of anti-immigrant sentiment and propaganda in the United States.[12] Tanton strongly shifted public perception of immigrants, laws, and policies in the country.

Tanton, an ophthalmologist from upstate Michigan and founder of the Tanton Network, sought strict migration reform to build his goal of a white United States. He launched a slew of restrictionist immigration think tanks and lobbying groups, now deemed hate groups by the Southern Poverty Law Center. These include CIS, the Federation for American Immigration Reform (FAIR), the Immigration Reform Law Institute, and NumbersUSA.

In a letter to Roy Beck, executive director of NumbersUSA, dated January 1996—the same year that Bill Clinton's administration passed a sweeping set of new laws criminalizing migration and expanding detention—Tanton wrote: "I have no doubt that individual minority persons can assimilate to the culture necessary to run an advanced society but if through mass migration, the culture of the homeland is transplanted from Latin America to California, then my guess is we will see the same degree of success with governmental and social institutions that we have seen in Latin America."[13] Seeing the Latinx migrant community as a racial and cultural threat to the U.S. nation-state, Tanton built an anti-immigrant machine via his network of dozens of organizations, which were generously funded by some of the wealthiest people in the United States, including Mellon heiress Cordelia Scaife May. Tanton and May also frequently asserted that immigrants threatened the environment, citing fears of overpopulation in the United States.[14] According to Reece Jones, "even as the Tanton Network of anti-immigrant groups including FAIR, CIS, and Numbers USA eventually distanced themselves from Tanton's racist writings and affiliations, . . . May's funding dramatically increased their influence in Washington, DC, and around the country."[15] Through the anti-immigrant narrative of the Tanton Network in the 1980s and 1990s, immigrants were effectively scapegoated as a threat to the economic, environmental, cultural, and national security of the United States.

Posing as a credible think tank, CIS has strategically infiltrated media narratives over the past four decades to sow disinformation and skewed statistics linking migration to crime and taxpayer expenditures, effectively pulling the immigration debate further to the right. Lacking in scholarly credentials, CIS director Mark Krikorian has become a frequent immigration commentator and is often featured in left-leaning news outlets ranging from PBS to the *Los Angeles Times*.[16] During the Trump administration, Tanton Network organizations enjoyed exceptional access to White House policymaking, including the appointment of Julie Kirchner, former executive director of FAIR, as U.S. Citizenship and Immigration Services (USCIS) ombudsman.[17]

FROM OBAMA TO TRUMP

New mandates for detention put in place by the George W. Bush administration, as well as Barack Obama's compromising approach to immigration politics and recommitment to enforcement, caused detention numbers to swell under the Obama administration.[18] After 9/11, the war on terror reframed migration control as a national security issue, as seen in the formation of the U.S. Department of Homeland Security (DHS) and its immigration enforcement arms: ICE, USCIS, and Customs and Border Protection (CBP). As Leisy J. Abrego and Genevieve Negrón-Gonzales conclude, "While credited with the passage of DACA, [Obama] also oversaw a period of mass deportations that both rivaled those of previous administrations and created the institutional infrastructure that laid the groundwork for Trump's immigration enforcement machine."[19] According to a 2014 report by the Center for Migration Studies, in the five years since the Obama administration had announced its 2009 detention reform initiative, the number of noncitizens detained by DHS each year had increased by nearly 25 percent.[20] Obama's expansion of immigration detention included a return to detaining families in response to a Central American child migration "crisis" in 2014 and, importantly, a reassertion of the long-standing trope of the "criminal immigrant," whose legacy carried into the Trump era and continues under Joe Biden's administration.[21]

In the first six years of Obama's presidency, he built on growing crimmigration trends (the melding of criminal and immigration enforcement systems) by expanding his predecessor's Secure Communities and 287(g) programs, heightening local law enforcement cooperation with ICE, and using detainers to feed those with criminal charges or convictions into the deportation pipeline. The overcriminalization of Black people throughout the rise of racially targeted mass incarceration in the modern era also resulted in an explosive number of Black migrants being subjected to detention and deportation under Obama.[22] As Jack Herrera recounts: "Decades of overcriminalization of Black communities had resulted in higher rates of conviction for Black people, which, when paired with Obama's emphasis on people with criminal records, led in turn to higher rates of deportation for Black migrants."[23] When Obama left office, he had deported more people than any other president in the history of the United States—in fact, his total numbers would exceed those of the four years of the Trump administration.

However, as Carolina Valdivia argues, the Trump era also ushered in a "new historic reality," with "changes in immigration policy and enforcement that yield a qualitatively different experience of what it means to be undocumented in the United States."[24] With violence and white supremacy emboldened, hate crimes against immigrants and new attacks on queer and trans people began to escalate.[25] In our work, we also noted a rollback of the narrative progress made by the immigrant rights movement in recent years, with the term "illegal immigration," for example, becoming common in public discourse. Heighted enforcement violence was accompanied by an increase in media reporting on immigrants being forced "back into the shadows."[26]

The Trump administration quickly defined the "bad immigrant" that the U.S.-Mexico border wall would "protect Americans" from. On the campaign trail, Trump openly named Latinx people affected by migration restrictions as "rapists" and "criminals." Upon taking office, Trump issued two executive orders signaling heightened crimmigration. The first, "Border Security and Immigration Enforcement Improvements," on January 25, 2017, included a mandate for new U.S.-Mexico border wall construction. Days later, Trump signed the so-called Muslim Ban, an executive order banning foreign nationals from seven predominantly Muslim countries from visiting the United States, heightening anti-Blackness and Islamophobia.[27] In effect, Trump's anti-immigrant rhetoric made every migrant a target.

Broadening the criminalization of all people who migrated over the U.S.-Mexico border as well as those living without papers across the United States, the Trump administration picked up where Obama left off and moved to rapidly expand the detention system, including family and private contract facilities. By early 2020, detention levels reached an all-time high, with nearly sixty thousand in detention on any given day. Trump's plans to continue detention expansion were curbed only by the advent of the COVID-19 pandemic.[28]

As COVID-19 tore through prison and detention sites over the next two years and exacerbated already extreme conditions of medical neglect, death rates in detention grew even as detention numbers decreased.[29] In early 2021, detention numbers reached their lowest in two decades, but they have been rebounding under the Biden administration in tandem with a sharp and disturbing rise in e-carceration—new forms of digital surveillance including the use of ankle monitors and geolocation tracking.[30] The pandemic also prompted a new spate of hunger strikes and uprisings across detention sites, and calls for abolition. Echoing past exclusions based on perceived public health risks, such as the 1882 Chinese Exclusion Act and the HIV/AIDS immigration ban (1987–2010), the Trump administration weaponized Title 42, an aspect of U.S. health law, to target and exclude at the U.S.-Mexico border asylum-seeking migrants deemed a "health risk." Haitians, who largely migrate through the El Paso–Juárez and San Diego–Tijuana ports of entry and who have historically faced exceptional exclusion, especially during the HIV/AIDS crisis, have again been targeted by Title 42—which the incoming Biden administration kept in place until May 2022. According to a report by the Haitian Bridge Alliance, the Quixote Center, and the UndocuBlack Network, more Haitians were deported under Title 42 in the first month of the Biden administration than in all of 2020.[31] Under Trump and now Biden, Haitians have been continually deported into a growing political and ecological crisis in Haiti. Although deportation rates declined under the Trump administration, Trump's expanded use of detention and legacy of hateful rhetoric continue as many Trump-era enforcement policies remain in place.

DREAMS AND DESERVINGNESS

Although some organizers hold radical anticapitalist, abolitionist, or antistatist political views, narrative tactics have varied across the immigrant rights movement. As Austin Kocher and Angela Stuesse argue, deportation defense campaigns (DDCs) have had to grapple with "questions about when and how to challenge dominant discourses and institutions while also achieving short-term goals."[32] The sanctuary movement of the 1980s, as well as the new sanctuary movement that emerged in the late 2010s, has also grappled with movement strategy and the divisiveness caused by narratives of immigrant "deservingness."[33] This narrative framing has been largely shaped by the Democratic-led fight for comprehensive immigration reform, and especially the Development, Relief, and Education for Alien Minors (DREAM) Act—first introduced in 2001 but yet to become enacted as legislation. The DREAM Act would provide permanent protection from deportation for certain immigrants, primarily those who came to the United States as children, attended school, and do not have a criminal record.

These campaigns have generated a narrative binary, in which immigrants are either good/deserving or bad/undeserving. R. A. Moffitt specifies, "in the eyes of the American voter, those who are deserving are those who work, who are married or at least widowed, and who have children. Those who are undeserving are those who do not work, who are single parents, and who do not have children."[34] This binary causes substantial harm to those deemed the "bad immigrant," who are often Black, Muslim, poor, queer, or trans, or of a criminalized community in the United States. Below, we discuss how we have unfortunately witnessed and navigated tensions surrounding this narrative binary in participating DDCs and storytelling work.

Dylan Rodríguez argues that the rise of the U.S. prison-industrial complex has been "enabled and complemented" by a growing nonprofit-industrial complex, defined as "the industrialized incorporation of pro-state liberal and progressive campaigns and movements into a spectrum of government-proctored non-profit organizations." Fueled by an "industry of fear," many nonprofit organizations' reluctance to critique the state (and its foundational logics) head-on, and their need to obtain operational funding, has led to the promotion of legislative reforms that proliferate new modes of state surveillance, policing, and incarceration.[35] The "good immigrant" narrative has been utilized by the so-called Beltway immigrant rights movement, which has coalesced around a goal of advocating in Washington, D.C., for legislative reform. However, as Abrego and Negrón-Gonzales argue, "the nonprofit industrial complex, DC lobbying groups, journalists, and researchers" have also played a role in solidifying this binary.[36]

Advocacy for the DREAM Act adopted a narrative strategy with a "tight discursive frame," emphasizing American values of hard work and economic contribution, assimilation, and pure innocence. This strategy aimed to make this small group of undocumented youth deserving of remaining in the United States, and, according to Walter Nicholls and Tara Fiorito, to "exonerate them of their 'illegality' by stressing their status was 'no fault of their own.'"[37] In 2015, Obama invited six DREAMers, undocumented youth held up as exceptionally deserving, to visit him at the White House.[38]

Not acknowledging the material conditions for the most marginalized people seeking to migrate to or live in the United States, the narrative of the deserving immigrant is steeped in anti-Blackness, racism, classism, Islamophobia, queerphobia, and transphobia. Ultimately, those excluded by race, class, and gender identity experience the violence of border enforcement disproportionately. By holding up this binary, the Obama administration effectively scapegoated marginalized and overpoliced migrant communities to justify ICE and CBP violence against those who were criminalized or deemed undeserving of citizenship privileges. In 2014, in part as a way to deflect criticism of the administration's return to the use of family detention, Obama infamously announced a change in enforcement priorities with his "Felons not Families, Criminals not Children" reform speech, in which he falsely claimed that ICE would focus only on deporting migrants deemed to have been guilty of serious crimes.[39] The Obama administration's "felons, not families" enforcement guidelines still led to the deportation of three million people.

DESERVINGNESS IN THE QUEER AND TRANS IMMIGRANT RIGHTS MOVEMENT

The queer and trans immigrant rights movement's resistance has always been openly abolitionist, long before the rise of the Beltway movement. Queer and trans organizing has pushed the boundaries of respectability politics with demands that were often deemed "too radical," making it a critical piece of this history. Notably, grassroots queer and trans groups were a part of the #Not1More campaign, which later grew into the call to #AbolishICE.[40] However, in the Obama and Trump eras, DDCs, bond campaigns, and letters of support to ICE proving people's deservingness became a "necessary evil": this work meant engaging in exploitative systems and narratives, but it was a way to free people from immigrant prison, to obtain community and governmental support, and to acquire funds to keep the work moving forward. In this section, we reflect on strategies employed during the Obama and Trump eras to demand the freedom of those incarcerated in immigrant prisons, and the multiple problematic facets these strategies had, including pinkwashing, which is the propping up of gay rights in ways that deflect from other harmful practices.

It is critical to maintain an understanding of the material conditions for queer and transgender people in the U.S. nation-state. Queer and trans people are still rendered as "alien" and thus "undeserving" in the U.S. public sphere, and they face deep-seated homophobia, transphobia, and pos-phobia (a fear of people who are HIV positive).[41] Queer and trans folks who migrate to the United States experience layered alienation, Othering, and perceived undeservingness. Many detained migrants who are queer and transgender are also BIPOC, and sometimes HIV positive. The U.S. nation-state was constructed and bolstered to exterminate and exclude the Other, those who do not exemplify whiteness, heteronormativity, or citizenship, all that is the American dream. Labeling this phenomenon in the U.S. public sphere as alienizing logic, Chávez asserts that "disease becomes one of many opportunities."[42] Since the Reagan era, those who are HIV positive have been depicted as less deserving. It is no coincidence that U.S. responses to the HIV/AIDS crisis, including the HIV-positive immigration ban and the confinement of Haitian migrants suspected of being HIV positive in quarantine camps at Guantanamo Bay in the 1990s, helped facilitate the expansion of the modern detention system.

Unfortunately, the use of narratives of deservingness often became necessary to ensure the freedom of those inside the walls and to stop deportations—and to be clear, queer and transgender people do deserve freedom and a place in the United States. As a result, many queer rights campaigns reinforce such narratives, like that surrounding advocacy for DREAMers. While our discussion here does not take away from the radical impacts and contributions of these movements, it is crucial to reflect on how these narratives prevail and why they are deemed necessary.

First, messaging that focuses on the deservingness of freedom from the grips of ICE for queer and trans folks has resulted in local and national campaigns that played into the alarming nature of "tragedy porn." Tragedy porn can be defined as narratives that emphasize harms endured to prove why people should be freed from ICE custody and "allowed" to exist in the U.S. nation-state. It is commonplace for mainstream queer and trans immigrant rights organizations to disclose and highlight childhood, intimate partner, and adult sexual violence, as well as childhood abandonment, substance misuse, "criminal" charges, trafficking, and HIV status, to expound on the deservingness of specific individuals to merit release.

Second, the ways in which the mainstream immigrant rights movement plays into heteronormative U.S. family values has also become part of the strategy. This includes campaigns that emphasize monogamous romantic relationships, nuclear family ties, and notions of "home" that prop up citizenship rights in the U.S. nation-state as a legitimate form of protection for queer and trans people—even as homophobic violence across U.S. society has continued to escalate. As the Obama administration ended, GLAAD reported that 2016 was the deadliest year thus far for transgender people in the United States.[43]

Finally, mainstream immigrant rights organizations working on queer and transgender migration have often refrained from discussing the legacies and reality of Western evangelical Christian colonialism, militarism, or U.S. global imperialism—in sum, the root causes of migration. Although people frequently flee countries that have a long history of U.S. state and capitalist intervention, Beltway organization messaging has primarily focused on propping up the U.S. nation-state as a place of freedom. The negation of the material conditions that result in legislation and violence against the queer and transgender community and forced migration is also a negation of the lived experiences of many queer and trans people locked in ICE prisons, and has been a disservice to the movement.

Over the past decade (since the early 2010s), Democrats have picked up the cause of gay rights across the country, posturing support for the queer and trans movement, such as through congressional briefings on ending transgender detention, for which large immigrant rights organizations partnered with grassroots queer and trans organizations. However, in the end few tangible gains have been made. Time and time again, we have found compromises to be necessary for ICE engagement, digital organizing campaigns, foundation funding, accountability reports to individuals who wanted to support the work, legislative attention, and, later, the creation by ICE of gay, bisexual, and transgender (GBT) detention pods at such sites as the Santa Ana Jail in California and Cibola in Arizona. As Chávez argues, identity-based appeals that demand review and accountability within the detention system's existing structures— such as a 2011 petition by the National Immigrant Justice Center on behalf of thirteen detained queer and trans individuals—may divert resources away from abolition and toward pinkwashing reform efforts such as the GBT pods.[44]

Narratives of tragedy porn and family values have also leaked into smaller, grassroots trans and queer organizing, such as that of the Queer Detainee Empowerment Project. Often, our digital messaging on Twitter and Facebook focused on the tragic realities of the violence that people were forced to endure, and their deservingness to remain in the United States. Although resisting narrative frames of respectability remained a priority for many organizers, this work often unintentionally played into narratives of criminality and heteronormativity. For example, the display of brutal physical, sexual, and psychological violence in immigrant prison, along with an appeal to family values, was critical to what we will call here the #FreeVeronica campaign.[45]

Focusing on Veronica, a transgender woman incarcerated by ICE, the #FreeVeronica campaign highlighted the sexual violence she was forced to endure to demonstrate that she needed to be freed. The dynamic fed into the tragedy porn narrative, took away her humanity, and contradicted organizers' beliefs that no one should be locked in a cage by the carceral state. News media headlines and the digital messaging of organizations involved in the campaign stated language such as, "Trans immigration detainee and rape survivor deserves safety," "petition launched to . . . [free] a trans immigration detainee raped in custody," and "transgender woman raped . . . ICE refuses to ensure her safety," and often included images of Veronica. The campaign also highlighted the fact that ICE demanded that she sign a release form claiming that the rape was consensual. When she refused to do so, she was forced into solitary confinement as punishment for the physical and sexual violence that she had been forced to bear.

The #FreeVeronica campaign was ultimately successful, but this messaging and digital activism enforced two problematic narratives. First, the campaign's demands that ICE provide "safety" for Veronica contradicted organizers' beliefs that no cage could ever conceivably protect anyone, and that ICE exists only to continue the colonial violence of borders through punishment and terror. And second, media headlines associating trans migrants with sexual violence furthered public notions that people in immigrant prisons are violent, negating the reality that the violence of border enforcement and prisons themselves manifest violent material conditions for those subjected to them. #FreeVeronica narratives focusing on violence and victimhood were attempts to achieve due process and basic human rights through claims to deservingness, yet at the same time they also reinforced notions of criminality and sexual deviance affirmed by Obama's stated intent to target "felons" and Trump's claims that people who had migrated to the United States from Latin

America were "rapists."[46] As Mariame Kaba puts it, "the contradictions of demanding protection from the state that also targets and kills us have proved irreconcilable."[47]

The alienizing logic of the U.S. nation-state has created a dynamic of having to overly prove the deservingness of queer and trans people through DDCs, bond campaigns, letters of support, and fundraising work. The reproduction of such portrayals in varying forms (for example, in annual reports for foundations and donors' consumption) is a problematic dance: if we do not present these narratives and imagery, people may not be released and could be subjected to expulsion, and there would be no way to pay for our work. At the same time, discussing such personal and intimate details about people's lives, even with their consent, remains exploitative.

In some ways, annual reports exist as their own form of resistance archive. But the goal of annual reports is to ensure funding to continue the work; they don't just highlight organizing and campaign victories, they discuss personal and intimate details about people's lives. Even with the consent of folks, they are exploitative. To mitigate this harm, some organizational approaches to annual reports have shifted from merely writing "about" people and their tragedies, to allowing people to write their own letters and provide their own images.[48]

VULTURE JOURNALISTS AND RESEARCHERS

Another strategy to sidestep the gaze of the nonprofit-industrial complex has been to seek more direct access to legacy media outlets for people in and affected by detention, including through the publishing of op-eds. However, although many journalists and researchers covering immigration proceed with trauma-informed approaches and expressions of movement solidarity, many others have often acted as vultures, regularly expecting access to those affected by migration restrictions and the horrors of U.S. immigrant prisons. Reporters and scholars seeking to profit, either financially or professionally, from people's trauma need to proceed with awareness of the harms this can cause. Regularly, we have found ourselves playing interference, demanding compensation from predatory journalists for the labor, time, and renewed trauma for those incarcerated by the state. This became our way of attempting to ensure people could maintain agency over their stories and their lives. Journalists would frequently refuse, arguing that they did not have to compensate anyone in the past, so why should they now?

The ongoing struggle to explain to journalists that the time, emotional labor, and trauma of people incarcerated in immigrant prisons did not exist for their consumption became a constant conversation that ended in a statement by us that "you are not entitled to someone else's trauma." Such arguments with vulture journalists clearly illustrate that many journalists see those who have migrated to the United States and been incarcerated as not equal to the rest of the U.S. population and not deserving of agency. Mainstream journalism demonstrates the necessity for platforms for people in detention to tell their stories in ways that provide them with agency and autonomy.

Several questions arise from these configurations of resistance archiving: Do people feel that they have options in when and how to tell their stories? Do people feel they could say no, or do they fear not having access to services or support if they refuse? Is it truly consent? Reflecting, we feel that many storytelling efforts, DDCs, bond campaigns, letters of support, and even annual reports that play into tragedy porn tropes to prove deservingness can be a form of coercion that is at best regrettable. Therefore, as an open-access forum for people affected by migration restrictions to tell their own stories, IMM Print also created a digital archive of critical systemic analysis to accompany stories in a way that did not exist anywhere else in the immigrant rights movement.

RESISTANCE ARCHIVING

IMM Print originated with the primary purpose of providing a space for people in detention to share their experiences of displacement, incarceration, and survival on their own terms, without mediation. A secondary purpose was for their stories to be preserved under community rather than institutional ownership, kept in a digital format so as to be editable upon request, as storytellers' wishes and personal and political circumstances change over time (although their being housed within a nonprofit organization yields its own set of challenges and critiques). In line with emerging praxis in critical refugee studies, our small team of visitor volunteers, students, and community members adopted a participatory approach, employing a process of informed consent to center the direct knowledge and expertise of people in detention.[49] Our aim has been to shift narrative focus from damage to desire, so as to move beyond suffering to what happens next: survival, political education, the building of communities of care, and liberation.[50]

Our conception of resistance archiving builds on histories of radical resistance through community-based storytelling. Ranging from the feminist collective newspaper *Off Our Backs* and sanctuary movement newsletters such as *Basta!* to the DIVA TV video documentary project by queer rights group AIDS Coalition to Unleash Power (ACT UP) protesting HIV-positive Haitian incarcerations in New York and at Guantanamo Bay, "marginalized communities have always created their own media to tell stories about themselves from their own perspectives," as Chávez asserts.[51] Through inside-outside organizing and with the support of collaborators on the outside, detention storytelling efforts have had both problematic and liberatory results.

Reflecting on the importance of "participatory" defense campaigns, Mariama Kaba urges for storytelling efforts to be guided by an ethic of care and conducted in solidarity with incarcerated people. Defense campaigns are "essential for educating the public, including prison reformers and abolitionists, about the racial and gendered terror of criminalization and incarceration," and "necessary for popular education to strengthen our movements: both by informing and improving overall movement strategies, and by challenging false binaries."[52] However, Kaba continues, individual, short-term campaigns are "most effective as abolitionist strategies when they are framed in a way that speaks to the need to abolish prisons in general . . . individual cases should be framed as emblematic of the conditions faced by thousands or millions who should also be free." In other words, discussions of interpersonal violence should be accompanied by a discussion of state violence—without a critique of state power and capitalism, stories are "at best incomplete and at worst reifications of oppressive structures that are constitutive of interpersonal violence."[53]

IMM Print attempts to achieve this by inviting affected community members, historians, and other scholars to participate in a collaborative and self-reflective process to place stories in an expanding digital archive, alongside other crowd-sourced educational materials such as the

#ImmigrationDetentionSyllabus.[54] While IMM Print runs into some of the same narrative challenges as nonprofit reporting, legacy journalism, and DDCs, its sole purpose is for firsthand accounts to exist outside of these institutional constraints, to be stored long term, and to be shared without mediation. It is also a platform for political and public education, with a tandem end goal of liberation for individuals, and the abolition of systems of abuse and exploitation.

IMM Print's digital format is inspired by the long-standing power of creative online activism within the immigrant rights and prison abolition movements. Digital organizing and activism have been crucial means to win campaigns across movements, from the Zapatistas, who used the internet in the 1990s to coordinate their protest in Chiapas against the North American Free Trade Agreement (NAFTA), to United We Dream, which has used it in the 2000s to form the largest undocumented immigrant youth movement in history.[55]

Another crucial campaign leading the immigrant rights movement into the Trump era, as discussed above, was the #Not1More campaign, which later became the #AbolishICE movement. In 2014, when #Not1More sprang up, it was abolitionist to its core. Tania Unzueta recounts that #Not1More "was a direct challenge to the strategy, even then, to continue to focus on lobbying Congress and not anger the President with our demands."[56] #Not1More grew into #AbolishICE, alongside the rise of the Black Lives Matter movement, with the shared goals of unveiling and diminishing the prison-industrial complex in its varying forms, fighting police violence, and abolishing government agencies that terrorize and harm BIPOC communities. The resistance of the movement was crucial, shifting away from the "deservingness" strategy to focus on those most vulnerable to the brutality of the deportation machine: criminalized people living with migration restrictions.

A combination of digital formats—hypertextual, hypernarrative, and archival—connects IMM Print to broader audiences by encouraging exploration throughout the site and offering a range of ways to engage. Users are guided to move through story content in the ordering of blog posts. While any arrangement choice forms its own argument, site visitors are also free to navigate as they see fit and come to their own conclusions. Our use of hyperlinks within stories that link to archived content in original and long formats (useful for students, researchers, or anyone seeking more information), as well as to relevant community discussion and educational materials, allows users to jump around or home in on topics of their choosing. These materials also encourage audiences to engage with project content in various public educational and community settings. As an archive, the project is designed to be preserved and ever-expanding, but stories can also be taken down or edited upon request. We also include a space on the site for visitors to contact us and contribute their own stories and media, along with guidance for doing so.

Other challenges that we have continued to face include navigating the impacts of trauma on communities (and in many cases, the impacts of vicarious trauma on ourselves), obtaining funding to maintain the project and compensate storytellers, and meeting deep needs in communities in which we work.[57] Another lingering tension inherent in all digital history projects—a tension that is both scholarly and political—is the question of shaping and presenting an argument versus honoring the words and narratives that people wish to share in their own right. In other words, what should you do when you disagree with narratives you are presenting? For example, in conversation, people in and affected by immigration detention often liken their experiences to being treated "like a criminal" or make an appeal along the lines of, "I am not a criminal." Narratives also often appeal to themes of deservingness: a sense of national belonging, patriotism, sacrifice, hard work, heteronormativity, and compliance. These narratives are divisive—harmful to communities who are criminalized and illegalized—and they run counter to the project's larger aims. We have tried to address these tensions in a variety of ways: through conversing with storytellers, editing or making omissions (which is problematic in itself), presenting stories with annotation and disclaimers, and including a mission and values statement on the IMM Print "About" page.

IMM PRINT

The following is a series of abridged stories posted to IMM Print during the Trump administration—a resistance archive in itself—to illustrate the pitfalls and potentials of resistance archiving, and to reflect on how we attempted to navigate the changing terrains of resistance and state retaliation during these years. These stories range from individual deportation defense and bond campaigns, to friendships and solidarities built through pen pal programs, art, and newsletters, to collaborations with allied journalists to support hunger strikes and to abolish a local ICE contract; we also note where IMM Print provided space for full stories to be told and for critical systemic analysis.

DEPORTATION DEFENSE AND BOND CAMPAIGNS

When a community member was re-detained by ICE in Orange County, California, in November 2016, the same month Trump was elected, advocates launched the #FreeKapi campaign (figure 20.1). We staged actions outside the Theo Lacy Jail, and collaborated with Kapi while he was detained to publish an op-ed written by him in a local newspaper, in which he emphasized his contributions to his community and called detention the "shame of America."[58] Kapi was aware of the risks of retaliation he faced and we acted at his direction, although after Trump's election we witnessed an escalation of retaliation that tragically resulted in Kapi's deportation.

Figure 20.1. A protest at the Theo Lacy Jail in California, November 2016. Signs read "Free Kapi Now" and "Department of Homeland Security Out of OC." Photo posted by Salvador Sarmiento (@sg_chambita), "Protests erupt," Twitter, November 3, 2016. Image courtesy of Salvador Sarmiento.

IMM Print also became a platform for people to share their own stories in support of bond campaigns to free them. Individuals shared photos of themselves, personal hopes, and creative writing. Here, J. writes about his childhood in Namibia and the bullying he faced for being different:

> My neighborhood could be volatile. It was a scary place for me at times and for various reasons too, but here in particular some kids our age were desperate for a way to pass time like having a human punching bag; I'm talking about bullies.
>
> So being a *zoba,* an outcast or nerd, I was a pretty good bully magnet—did I mention I named my dog after a cartoon character? I was pretty different. I was sensitive, even delicate at times. I really couldn't rely on any ability to *rwana,* fight, or *duka,* run.[59]

In support of his own bond campaign, Victor Perez shared his story and image on IMM Print. We shared these across Twitter and social media to successfully raise money to bond him out of the Adelanto Detention Facility after three and a half years in detention. "I'm the One Who's Been Here the Longest," he said, and wrote about combating the stigma of mental illness and drawing pictures to cope with incarceration.[60]

PEN PAL PROGRAMS, ART, NEWSLETTERS

Detention visitation and pen pal programs, the sharing of artwork, and the production and dissemination of newsletters created by detained migrants were all ways to combat the isolation and barriers to communication with the outside world that people in detention faced, and to express friendship and solidarity. IMM Print, in collaboration with visitation programs like the QDEP, also provided critical analysis alongside stories.

In response to the Trump administration's creation of a new agency, VOICE (Victims of Immigration Crime Engagement), intended to distort crime statistics and encourage the public to report on undocumented immigrants, IMM Print launched a series of stories called "VOICE: Victims of ICE" to flip the narrative and call out crimes committed by ICE, "the real perpetrator of human and civil rights violations," against people in detention. Tina also published an op-ed in *Truthout,* a publication

Figure 20.2. A drawing of conditions of solitary confinement at the Theo Lacy Jail in California, sent by Adolfo to Freedom for Immigrants, 2017. Freedom for Immigrants, "VOICE: Victims of ICE," IMM Print.

allied with IMM Print's mission, to amplify the story and provide historical context to the Trump administration's lies.[61] We included the artworks in figures 20.2 and 20.3 in a piece on solitary confinement. Artwork exchanged with us via visitation pen pal programs shows how people experienced solitary confinement, as well as how they envisioned freedom. A group of migrants detained at Adelanto in 2017 also mailed Freedom for Immigrants a newsletter they created, *Breaking Chains Ministries*, with hand-drawn artwork by Bad Boy Art. Upon their request, we formatted the newsletter and mailed copies to the prison (figure 20.4). With people detained at Adelanto as the newsletter's only intended audience, we did not publish *Breaking Chains* online.

IMM Print also made space for grassroots and radical organizations on the outside to provide critical analysis in response to Trump's escalating war on queer and trans people. In response to Trump's transgender military ban, Jamila wrote an open letter on behalf of QDEP to critique the public discourse of deservingness that normalizes war and U.S. empire. Clarifying QDEP's antiwar, anti-imperial stance, they write, "the US Military Machine has resulted in the forced migration of our people;

Figure 20.3. A drawing of a red rose with the inscription "Thanks for Being A Friend." Sent by Lalo at the Adelanto Detention Facility to Freedom for Immigrants, 2017. Freedom for Immigrants, "VOICE: Victims of ICE," IMM Print.

why support pitting oppressed people against other oppressed people?" The letter, posted to IMM Print, continues: "The number of LGBTQ/ HIV+ immigrants that we work with that are detained in immigration detention and that are refused asylum is huge. It's telling of a larger issue of refusing some of the most marginalized people in this world seeking safety after their long journey to the United States, where they are held in cages and experience medical neglect, physical violence, sexual violence, and deplorable conditions, in the 'Free World.'"[62]

Figure 20.4. *Breaking Chains Ministries*, a newsletter created by migrants detained at Adelanto and mailed to Freedom for Immigrants. The newsletter included hand-drawn artwork by Bad Boy Art. June/July 2017. Photo by Tina Shull.

WORKING WITH ALLIED JOURNALISTS: HUNGER STRIKES AND JAIL CLOSURES

IMM Print also published lists of demands shared by migrants waging a wave of hunger strikes at the Adelanto Detention Facility in Southern California. Many of these migrants had traveled with refugee caravans in the spring of 2017 and throughout 2018. In addition to reporting on abuses happening inside Adelanto in real time and helping raise funds to support the Adelanto Bond Fund, IMM Print coordinated with supportive journalists to serve as an archive of organizational press releases and complaint documents that legacy reporting would not publish in full but could cite (figure 20.5).[63]

Figure 20.5. Artwork created by Clergy and Laity United for Economic Justice (CLUE Justice) in support of the Adelanto Bond Fund, 2017. Posted by Alex Mensing (@alex_mensing), "Generous donations," Twitter, August 18, 2017. Image courtesy of CLUE Justice and Alex Mensing.

We did this again in the fall of 2017, as IMM Print raised public awareness of the horrific conditions at the West County Detention Facility in Richmond, California, publishing a list of women's complaints in collaboration with media reporting that led to the eventual cancellation of the facility's ICE contract in 2018 (figure 20.6). Allying with journalists who have the right politics and intentions to share news from inside helped support a successful campaign to close a jail.[64]

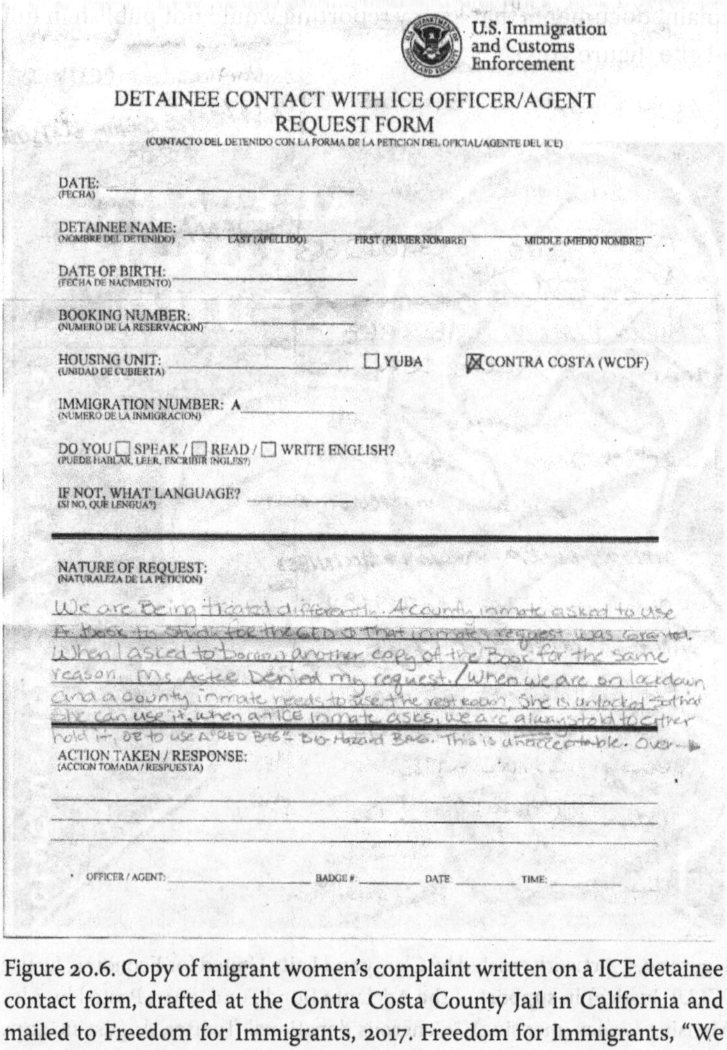

U.S. Immigration and Customs Enforcement

DETAINEE CONTACT WITH ICE OFFICER/AGENT REQUEST FORM
(CONTACTO DEL DETENIDO CON LA FORMA DE LA PETICION DEL OFICIAL/AGENTE DEL ICE)

DATE: (FECHA) ____________

DETAINEE NAME: (NOMBRE DEL DETENIDO) ____ LAST (APELLIDO) ____ FIRST (PRIMER NOMBRE) ____ MIDDLE (MEDIO NOMBRE)

DATE OF BIRTH: (FECHA DE NACIMIENTO) ____________

BOOKING NUMBER: (NUMERO DE LA RESERVACION) ____________

HOUSING UNIT: (UNIDAD DE CUBIERTA) ____________ ☐ YUBA ☒ CONTRA COSTA (WCDF)

IMMIGRATION NUMBER: A ____________ (NUMERO DE LA INMIGRACION)

DO YOU ☐ SPEAK / ☐ READ / ☐ WRITE ENGLISH? (PUEDE HABLAR, LEER, ESCRIBIR INGLES?)

IF NOT, WHAT LANGUAGE? (SI NO, QUE LENGUA?) ____________

NATURE OF REQUEST: (NATURALEZA DE LA PETICION)

We are Being treated differently. A county inmate asked to use A Book to Study for the GED & That inmate's request was granted. When I asked to borrow another copy of the Book for the same reason. Ms Astee Denied my request. / When we are on lockdown and a county inmate needs to use the rest room, She is unlocked so that she can use it, when an ICE inmate asks, we are always told to either hold it, or to use a "RED BAG" Bio-Hazard BAG. This is unacceptable. Over ▸

ACTION TAKEN / RESPONSE: (ACCION TOMADA / RESPUESTA)

OFFICER / AGENT: ____________ BADGE #: ______ DATE ______ TIME: ______

Figure 20.6. Copy of migrant women's complaint written on a ICE detainee contact form, drafted at the Contra Costa County Jail in California and mailed to Freedom for Immigrants, 2017. Freedom for Immigrants, "We Are Being Treated Differently," IMM Print.

NOTES

1. These events are recounted from author Shull's witnessing. Andrea's name has been changed to protect her identity.
2. Kocher and Stuesse, "Undocumented Activism and Minor Politics."
3. Shull, *Immigration Detention in the Media.*
4. Southern Poverty Law Center, "Center for Immigration Studies." For more on the history of CIS (as well as the Tanton Network, to which it belongs, and which is discussed later in this chapter), see Jones, *White Borders*; Denvir, *All-American Nativism*; Goodman, "Unmaking the Nation of Immigrants."
5. Fernandes, *Curated Stories*, 3–4.
6. Kaba, "Towards the Horizon of Abolition."
7. Shull, "QTGNC Stories from US Immigration Detention and Abolitionist Imaginaries, 1980–Present."
8. IMM Print, "About Us."
9. D. Hernández, "Carceral Shadows."
10. Shull, "Reagan's Cold War on Immigrants," 5–7.
11. Chávez, *The Borders of AIDS*, 5, 4.
12. C. Goodman, "Unmaking the Nation of Immigrants."
13. Southern Poverty Law Center, "John Tanton."
14. Denvir, *All-American Nativism*, 33. Daniel Denvir discusses the broad societal influence of Paul R. Ehrlich and Anne Erlich's 1968 book *The Population Bomb*, which itself draws on 1920s-era eugenicist white supremacist ideology.
15. Jones, *White Borders*, 8.
16. See, e.g., Do, "For Asians in the US Illegally, 'There Is More Shame and More Quiet.'"
17. Plot Against Immigrants, home page; Ndulue et al., *The Language of Immigration Reporting.*
18. A growing body of historical scholarship traces continuities across presidential administrations in the post–World War II rise of immigration enforcement and detention in the United States, as well as the way exclusionary measures were shaped by notions of race, class, gender, political ideology, and dis/ability. See Cullison, "Valley of Caged Immigrants"; A. Goodman, *The Deportation Machine*; Lindskoog, *Detain and Punish*; Ordaz, *The Shadow of El Centro*; Shull, *Detention Empire*; Young, *Forever Prisoners.*
19. Abrego and Negrón-Gonzales, introduction, 16.
20. Center for Migration Studies, "Immigration Detention."
21. For more on historical conceptions of the "criminal alien," see K. Hernández, *Migra!*; A. Goodman, *The Deportation Machine*; Young, *Forever Prisoners*; Ordaz, *The Shadow of El Centro.*
22. State of Black Immigrants, home page.
23. Herrera, "Black Immigrants Matter."
24. Valdivia, "Undocumented Young Adults' Heightened Vulnerability in the Trump Era," 128.

25. Okeowo, "Hate on the Rise After Trump's Election"; Southern Poverty Law Center, "Ten Days After."

26. Arroyo, "In the Age of Trump."

27. Trump, "Border Security and Immigration Enforcement Improvements"; Trump, "Protecting the Nation from Foreign Terrorist Entry into the United States."

28. Zukowska, "The Cost of Freedom."

29. Terp et al., "Deaths in Immigration and Customs Enforcement (ICE) detention."

30. Just Futures Law, "ICE Digital Prisons." As of July 2023, just over thirty-one thousand people were being held in ICE detention; see Transactional Records Action Clearinghouse, "Immigration Detention Quick Facts."

31. N. Phillips and Ricker, *The Invisible Wall*.

32. Kocher and Stuesse, "Undocumented Activism and Minor Politics," abstract.

33. Shull, "Reagan's Cold War on Immigrants," 27–28; Yukich, "Constructing the Model Immigrant"; Paik, "Abolitionist Futures and the US Sanctuary Movement."

34. Moffitt, "The Deserving Poor, the Family, and the U.S. Welfare System," 745.

35. Rodríguez, "The Political Logic of the Non-Profit Industrial Complex," 21. See also Davis, *Are Prisons Obsolete?*

36. Abrego and Negrón-Gonzales, *We Are Not Dreamers*, 9.

37. Nicholls and Fiorito, "Dreamers Unbound."

38. Holst, "Meet the 6 DREAMers the President Met with in the Oval Office Yesterday."

39. Obama, "Address to the Nation on Immigration Reform."

40. Unzueta, " We Fell in Love in a Hopeless Place."

41. Hammami, "Bridging Immigration Justice and Prison Abolition."

42. Chávez, *The Borders of AIDS*, 43.

43. Schmider, "2016 Was the Deadliest Year on Record for Transgender People."

44. Chávez, "Protecting LGBT Immigrant Detainees."

45. Veronica's name has been intentionally anonymized to not continue the disclosing of survivors' tragedies for the consumption of others.

46. A. Phillips, "They're Rapists."

47. Kaba, *We Do This 'Til We Free Us*, 113.

48. Queer Detainee Empowerment Project, *Queering the Immigration Dialogue*.

49. "The Critical Refugee Studies Collective believes that refugee storytelling allows for new forms of knowledge to be produced." See Critical Refugee Studies Collective, home page.

50. Tuck, "Suspending Damage."

51. Chávez, *The Borders of AIDS*, 54.

52. Kaba, *We Do This 'Til We Free Us*, 116.

53. Kaba, 111, 117.

54. Freedom for Immigrants, "The #ImmigrationDetentionSyllabus."

55. Daly, *Humans R Social Media*, chap. 6, "Activism"; United We Dream, home page.

56. Unzueta, "We Fell in Love in a Hopeless Place."

57. Lipsky, *Trauma Stewardship*; Brown, *Emergent Strategy*.
58. Kapijimpanga, "Kapijimpanga."
59. J., "Stand By or Cry?"
60. Perez, "I'm the One Who's Been Here the Longest."
61. Freedom for Immigrants, "VOICE: Victims of ICE"; Shull, "Why Trump's Agency, 'VOICE,' Should Stand for 'Victims of ICE.'"
62. Hammami, "A Letter from QDEP's Executive Director on Trump's Transgender Military Ban."
63. Freedom for Immigrants, "Private Prison Guards Threaten Women in Immigration Detention"; Freedom for Immigrants, "#Adelanto9 Launch Hunger Strike in California."
64. Freedom for Immigrants, "We Are Being Treated Differently." See also Knoebel, "Spotlight"; Van Niekerken, "Contra Costa Immigration Uproar."

BIBLIOGRAPHY

Abrego, Leisy J., and Genevieve Negrón-Gonzales. Introduction to *We Are Not Dreamers: Undocumented Scholars Theorize Undocumented Life in the United States*, edited by Leisy J. Abrego and Genevieve Negrón-Gonzales, 1–22. Durham, N.C.: Duke University Press, 2020.

Arroyo, Lorena. "In the Age of Trump, Fear Drives Some Undocumented Immigrants Back into the Shadows." *Univision News*, February 11, 2017. https://www.univision.com/univision-news/immigration/in-the-age-of-trump-fear-drives-some-undocumented-immigrants-back-into-the-shadows.

Brown, Adrienne Maree. *Emergent Strategy: Shaping Change, Changing Worlds*. Chico, Calif.: AK Press, 2017.

Center for Migration Studies. "Immigration Detention: Behind the Record Numbers." February 13, 2014. https://cmsny.org/immigration-detention-behind-the-record-numbers/.

Chávez, Karma R. *The Borders of AIDS: Race, Quarantine, and Resistance*. Seattle: University of Washington Press, 2021.

Chávez, Karma R. "Protecting LGBT Immigrant Detainees: The Rhetoric of Identity and the Expansion of the Prison-Industrial Complex." In *The Rhetorics of US Immigration: Identity, Community, Otherness*, edited by E. Johanna Hartelius, 70–90. State College: Pennsylvania State University Press, 2015.

Critical Refugee Studies Collective. Home page. Accessed May 15, 2023. https://criticalrefugeestudies.com/.

Cullison, Jennifer. "Valley of Caged Immigrants: Punishment, Protest, and the Rise of the Port Isabel Detention Center." *Tabula Rasa*, no. 33 (2020). https://doi.org/10.25058/20112742.n33.09.

Daly, Diana. *Humans R Social Media*. University of Arizona, winter 2022. https://opentextbooks.library.arizona.edu/hrsmwinter2022/.

Davis, Angela. *Are Prisons Obsolete?* New York: Seven Stories Press, 2003.

Denvir, Daniel. *All-American Nativism: How the Bipartisan War on Immigrants Explains Politics as We Know It*. London: Verso, 2020.

Do, Ahn. "For Asians in the US Illegally, 'There Is More Shame and More Quiet.'" *Los Angeles Times*, December 17, 2016.

Fernandes, Sujatha. *Curated Stories: The Uses and Misuses of Storytelling*. Oxford: Oxford University Press, 2017.

Freedom for Immigrants. "#Adelanto9 Launch Hunger Strike in California." IMM Print, June 12, 2017. https://imm-print.com/adelanto9-launch-hunger-strike-in -california-e189bbcdc26b/.

Freedom for Immigrants. "The #ImmigrationDetentionSyllabus." Accessed March 1, 2022. https://www.freedomforimmigrants.org/immigration-detention-syllabus/.

Freedom for Immigrants. "Private Prison Guards Threaten Women in Immigration Detention with Pepper Spray and Solitary Confinement." IMM Print, June 14, 2017. https://imm-print.com/private-prison-guards-threaten-women-in-immigration -detention-with-pepper-spray-and-solitary-e284b25479ec/.

Freedom for Immigrants. "VOICE: Victims of ICE." IMM Print, March 26, 2017. https://imm-print.com/voice-victims-of-ice-2bc417352abd/.

Freedom for Immigrants. "We Are Being Treated Differently. We Only Want to Be Treated with Respect." IMM Print, November 9, 2017. https://imm-print.com/ we-are-being-treated-differently-we-only-want-to-be-treated-with-respect -176c529ac126/.

Goodman, Adam. *The Deportation Machine: America's Long History of Expelling Immigrants*. Princeton, N.J.: Princeton University Press, 2020.

Goodman, Carly. "Unmaking the Nation of Immigrants: How John Tanton's Network of Organizations Transformed Policy and Politics." In *A Field Guide to White Supremacy*, edited by Kathleen Belew and Ramón A. Gutiérrez, 203–19. Berkeley: University of California Press, 2021.

Hammami, Jamila. "A Letter from QDEP's Executive Director on Trump's Transgender Military Ban." IMM Print, July 29, 2017. https://imm-print.com/a -letter-from-qdeps-executive-director-on-trump-s-transgender-military-ban -4616dbf0d622/.

Hammami, Jamila. "Bridging Immigration Justice and Prison Abolition." In *Queer and Trans Migrations: Dynamics of Illegalization, Detention, and Deportation*, edited by Eithne Luibhéid and Karma R. Chávez, 133–35. Urbana: University of Illinois Press, 2020.

Hernández, David Manuel. "Carceral Shadows: Entangled Lineages and Technologies of Migrant Detention." In *Caging Borders and Carceral States: Incarcerations, Immigration Detentions, and Resistance*, edited by Robert T. Chase, 57–92. Chapel Hill: University of North Carolina Press, 2019.

Hernández, Kelly Lytle. *Migra! A History of the U.S. Border Patrol*. Berkeley: University of California Press, 2010.

Herrera, Jack. "Black Immigrants Matter." *Nation*, March 24, 2021.

Holst, Lindsay. "Meet the 6 DREAMers the President Met with in the Oval Office Yesterday." White House blog (archived website), February 5, 2015. https:// obamawhitehouse.archives.gov/blog/2015/02/05/meet-6-dreamers-president -met-oval-office-yesterday.

IMM Print. "About Us." Accessed February 28, 2022. https://imm-print.com/about -us.

J. "Stand By or Cry? Everybody Can Redeem Themselves, Even Dogs." IMM Print, November 18, 2017. https://imm-print.com/stand-by-or-cry-everybody-can -redeem-themselves-even-dogs-72f92fbad4e5/.

Jones, Reece. *White Borders: The History of Race and Immigration in the United States from Chinese Exclusion to the Border Wall.* New York: Penguin Random House, 2021.

Just Futures Law. "ICE Digital Prisons." Accessed May 15, 2023. https://justfutureslaw .org/ice-digital-prisons/.

Kaba, Mariame. "Towards the Horizon of Abolition: A Conversation with Mariame Kaba." Interview by John Duda. Next System Project, November 9, 2017. https://thenextsystem.org/learn/stories/towards-horizon-abolition-conversation -mariame-kaba.

Kaba, Mariame. *We Do This 'Til We Free Us: Abolitionist Organizing and Transforming Justice.* Chicago: Haymarket Books, 2021.

Kapijimpanga, Casey. "Kapijimpanga: The U.S. is Trying to Deport Me, But You Can't Deport My Story." *Voice of OC* (blog), June 21, 2017. https://voiceofoc.org/2017/ 06/kapijimpanga.

Knoebel, Cindy. "Spotlight: West County Detention Visitation Group." IMM Print, December 16, 2017. https://imm-print.com/spotlight-west-county-detention -facility-visitation-group/.

Kocher, Austin, and Angela Stuesse. "Undocumented Activism and Minor Politics: Inside the Cramped Political Spaces of Deportation Defense Campaigns." *Antipode* 53, no. 2 (2021): 331–54.

Lindskoog, Carl. *Detain and Punish: Haitian Refugees and the Rise of the World's Largest Immigration Detention System.* Gainesville: University of Florida Press, 2018.

Lipsky, Laura van Dernoot. *Trauma Stewardship: An Everyday Guide to Caring for Self While Caring for Others.* Oakland, Calif.: BK Life, 2009.

Moffitt, R. A. "The Deserving Poor, the Family, and the U.S. Welfare System." *Demography* 52, no. 3 (2015): 729–49.

Ndulue, Emily B., Fernando Bermejo, Kristian Ramos, Sarah E. Lowe, Nathaniel Hoffman, and Ethan Zuckerman. *The Language of Immigration Reporting: Normalizing vs. WatchDogging in a Nativist Age.* Define American, October 2019.

Nicholls, Walter, and Tara Fiorito. "Dreamers Unbound: Immigrant Youth Mobilizing." *New Labor Forum*, January 2015. https://newlaborforum.cuny.edu/2015/01/ 19/dreamers.

Obama, Barack. "Address to the Nation on Immigration Reform." November 20, 2014. American Presidency Project. https://www.presidency.ucsb.edu/node/308498.

Okeowo, Alexis. "Hate on the Rise After Trump's Election." *New Yorker*, November 17, 2016.

Ordaz, Jessica. *The Shadow of El Centro: A History of Migrant Incarceration and Solidarity*. Chapel Hill: University of North Carolina Press, 2021.

Paik, A. Naomi. "Abolitionist Futures and the US Sanctuary Movement." *Race and Class* 59, no. 2 (2017): 3–15.

Perez, Victor. "I'm the One Who's Been Here the Longest." IMM Print, May 23, 2017. https://imm-print.com/im-the-one-who-s-been-here-the-longest-ef80a89ae139/.

Phillips, Amber. "'They're Rapists': President Trump's Campaign Speech Two Years Later, Annotated." *Washington Post*, June 16, 2017.

Phillips, Nicole, and Tom Ricker. *The Invisible Wall: Title 42 and Its Impact on Haitian Migrants*. Haitian Bridge Alliance, the Quixote Center, and the UndocuBlack Network, March 2021.

Plot Against Immigrants. Home page. Accessed May 15, 2023. https://plotagainstimmigrants.com/.

Queer Detainee Empowerment Project. *Queering the Immigration Dialogue: Queer Detainee Empowerment Project 2016 Annual Report*. 2016.

Rodríguez, Dylan. "The Political Logic of the Non-Profit Industrial Complex." In *The Revolution Will Not Be Funded: Beyond the Non-Profit Industrial Complex*, by INCITE!, 21–40. Durham, N.C.: Duke University Press, 2017.

Schmider, Alex. "2016 Was the Deadliest Year on Record for Transgender People." GLAAD, November 9, 2016. https://www.glaad.org/blog/2016-was-deadliest-year-record-transgender-people.

Shull, Tina (Kristina). *Detention Empire: Reagan's War on Immigrants and the Seeds of Resistance*. Chapel Hill: University of North Carolina Press, 2022.

Shull, Tina (Kristina). *Immigration Detention in the Media: Missing Migrant Voices and the Need for Humanistic Storytelling*. Edited by Christina Fialho. With Lauren Anderson and Angelica Victoria Camacho. Community Initiatives for Visiting Immigrants in Confinement, 2017.

Shull, Tina. "QTGNC Stories from US Immigration Detention and Abolitionist Imaginaries, 1980–Present." In *Abolition Feminisms*, vol. 1, *Organizing, Survival, and Transformative Practice*, edited by Alisa Bierria, Jakeya Caruthers, and Brooke Lober, 159–89. Chicago: Haymarket Books, 2022.

Shull, Tina (Kristina). "Reagan's Cold War on Immigrants: Resistance and the Rise of a Detention Regime, 1981–1985." *Journal of American Ethnic History* 40, no. 2 (2021): 5–51.

Shull, Tina. "Why Trump's Agency, 'VOICE,' Should Stand for 'Victims of ICE.'" *Truthout*, April 6, 2017. https://truthout.org/articles/why-trump-s-agency.

Southern Poverty Law Center. "Center for Immigration Studies." Accessed May 15, 2023. https://www.splcenter.org/fighting-hate/extremist-files/group/center-immigration-studies.

Southern Poverty Law Center. "John Tanton." Accessed March 1, 2022. https://www
.splcenter.org/fighting-hate/extremist-files/individual/john-tanton.

Southern Poverty Law Center. "Ten Days After: Harassment and Intimidation in
the Aftermath of the Election." November 29, 2016. https://www.splcenter.org/
20161129/ten-days-after-harassment-and-intimidation-aftermath-election.

State of Black Immigrants. Home page. Accessed May 15, 2023. https://
stateofblackimmigrants.com/.

Terp, Sophie, Sameer Ahmed, Elizabeth Burner, Madeline Ross, Molly Grassini, Briah
Fischer, and Parveen Parmar. "Deaths in Immigration and Customs Enforcement
(ICE) Detention, FY 2018–2020." *AIMS Public Health* 8, no. 1 (2021): 81–89.

Transactional Records Action Clearinghouse. "Immigration Detention Quick Facts."
Data for July 16, 2023. https://trac.syr.edu/immigration/quickfacts.

Trump, Donald J. "Border Security and Immigration Enforcement Improvements."
Exec. order 13767, January 25, 2017. American Presidency Project. https://www
.presidency.ucsb.edu/node/322155.

Trump, Donald J. "Protecting the Nation from Foreign Terrorist Entry into the United
States." Exec. order 13769, January 27, 2017. American Presidency Project. https://
www.presidency.ucsb.edu/node/322204.

Tuck, Eve. "Suspending Damage: A Letter to Communities." *Harvard Educational
Review* 79, no. 3 (2009): 409–27.

United We Dream. Home page. Accessed May 15, 2023. https://unitedwedream.org/.

Unzueta, Tania. "We Fell in Love in a Hopeless Place: A Grassroots History from
#Not1More to Abolish ICE." *Medium*, June 29, 2018. https://medium.com/
@LaTania/23089cf21711.

Valdivia, Carolina. "Undocumented Young Adults' Heightened Vulnerability in the
Trump Era." In *We Are Not Dreamers: Undocumented Scholars Theorize Undocu-
mented Life in the United States*, edited by Leisy J. Abrego and Genevieve Negrón-
Gonzales, 127–45. Durham, N.C.: Duke University Press, 2020.

Van Niekerken, Bill. "Contra Costa Immigration Uproar." *San Francisco Chronicle*,
July 10, 2018. https://projects.sfchronicle.com/2018/ice-timeline/.

Young, Elliott. *Forever Prisoners: How the United States Made the World's Largest
Immigrant Detention System*. Oxford: Oxford University Press, 2021

Yukich, Grace. "Constructing the Model Immigrant: Movement Strategy and Immigrant Deservingness in the New Sanctuary Movement." *Social Problems* 60, no.
3 (2013): 302–20.

Zukowska, Marzena. "The Cost of Freedom." In *Asylum for Sale: Profit and Protest in
the Migration Industry*, edited by Siobhán McGuirk and Adrienne Pine, 181–92.
Oakland, Calif.: PM Press, 2020.

AFTERWORD

AS YOU REACH THE CONCLUSION of this powerful volume, I suspect you're uncomfortably residing in the dread that, for many, characterized our experience of the four years of the Trump presidency. That dread is important for all of us, for it should function as a palpable, affective catalyst to our collective political action against what Trump made plain about politics in these alleged united states and beyond. Because this is the book's afterword, the moment in your reading when you've assimilated in great detail the many tragedies Trump's presidency perpetrated, as well as the tremendous ways so many resisted, this is your opportunity to reflect on what you will do with what you know.

Resistance and Abolition in the Borderlands: Confronting Trump's Reign of Terror is a powerful and dynamic historical account of the years following Trump's 2016 election, an election that as others have noted in the volume, began with an indictment of Mexican migrants as rapists and murderers. Trump, thus, never shied away from making clear his repugnant views. My worry now, two years into the Biden administration, is the same worry I had during the Obama administration: what about those who are less transparent in their views about migration and borders? Put differently, I want us to reflect on the eras before and after Trump, eras that materially, even if not always rhetorically, have been and continue to be brutally violent against migrants, women, queer and trans folks, the environment, poor people, the disabled, religious minorities, and BIPOC communities. This post-Trump moment invites us to consider how it is not merely white supremacist, anti-trans, misogynist, Zionist zealotry that we must be concerned with. We must also take a hard look at those whose work against our communities is perhaps more subtle.

As discussed in this volume, in late 2021, in the United States, we were inundated with harrowing images of border patrol agents and Texas Rangers on horseback rounding up Haitian asylum seekers near Del Rio, Texas, and reportedly using whips to do so, despite U.S. Border Patrol's insistence that no one was ever struck by an agent.[1] In a country founded on slavery, even the appearance of U.S. officials whipping Black people should give anyone pause. But these particular Black people are being targeted by the Biden administration using a March 2020 Trump-era order from the U.S. Centers for Disease Control and Prevention (CDC), allowing the use of Title 42 of the U.S. Code. In Title 42, section 265, the federal government, and specifically the CDC, is allowed during threat of "communicable disease" to "prohibit, in whole or in part, the introduction of persons and property from such countries or places as he shall designate in order to avert such danger, and for such period of time as he may deem necessary for such purpose."[2] By April 2022, Title 42 had been utilized 1.7 million times in just two years to expel migrants.[3]

Trump, and now Biden, chose to apply this to anyone arriving from Mexico or Canada because such people would arrive at ports of entry in ways that would introduce them to a "congregate setting." Trump, and now Biden, reasoned that such settings put migrants in a situation in which spread of COVID-19 would be imminent, even while public health officials outside of the government have repeatedly said that applying public health principles like masks and social distancing, or processing people outdoors or in spaces with good ventilation, would make better public health sense than deporting people, many with a credible fear of future political persecution. In a September 2021 interview, U.S. Department of Homeland Security secretary Alejandro Mayorkas defended the Biden administration, stating, "It is currently our government's intention to continue to exercise our Title 42 authority in light of the public-health imperative as determined by the Centers for Disease Control."[4] Although many have only heard about Title 42 for this first time in recent years, Title 42 is the same provision that led to the imprisonment of HIV-positive Haitian refugees from 1991 to 1993 in a concentration camp at Guantanamo Bay, Cuba, under both Presidents Bush and Clinton.

Many activists have decried the fact that Biden, a liberal, hasn't adequately tried to stop the use of Title 42 and instead has, in significant ways, leaned into his predecessor's approach. The Russian war against Ukraine forced the administration's hand as within weeks of the start of the war, hundreds of blond-haired and blue-eyed Ukrainians made their way to the U.S.-Mexico border to ask for asylum or at least temporary refuge. Many of these people showed up to the same shelters and made their appeals to the same U.S. officials as Haitians, Nicaraguans, Hondurans, Venezuelans, and any number of other Latin Americans who had been turned away or told to wait in line for months, and maybe even years. Despite the ongoing pandemic, and the ongoing enforcement of Title 42 restrictions, Ukrainians, including those who had no immediate family ties in the United States, were fast-tracked and granted various types of relief by the U.S. government. In fact, barely six weeks into the war, the United States had pledged to receive a hundred thousand Ukrainian refugees and already processed thousands, many within a few short hours of asking for asylum.[5] Immediately, commentators and activists in the United States and Mexico called attention to the double standard.[6] While various political officials reasoned that the immediacy of the war in Ukraine justified the differential treatment, the fact of race and the long-standing preference in U.S. immigration and refugee law for white European migrants could hardly be ignored.

In April 2022, the Biden administration announced an end to Title 42 restrictions. Just a month later, a Louisiana federal judge blocked Biden's efforts to end Title 42 after twenty-four Republican state attorneys general warned that ending it would result in a surge of migrants that would overwhelm state and local resources.[7] The Biden administration publicly denounced the ruling and claimed it would continue to fight it. Nevertheless, in September 2022, reports emerged that the Biden administration had quietly pressured the Mexican government, which already accepts immediately deported migrants from Honduras, El Salvador, and Guatemala, to also accept immediate deportations from Cuba, Venezuela, and Nicaragua.[8]

As of the time of this writing, December 2022, a federal judge has ruled that border officials must stop using Title 42 on December 21, 2022. This ruling has already caused concerns among some Democrats about what the Biden plan will be to manage migration, since currently 40 percent of removals at the U.S.-Mexico border occur through Title 42.[9] It is not hard to deduce that lawmakers' concerns are with Latin American and Caribbean migrants. Meanwhile, as of November 21, 2022, Ukrainians in the United States under the Uniting for Ukraine program are now employment eligible.[10] The United States should absolutely accept Ukrainian asylum seekers, and they should have the right to work! But even if we already know the answers, we must demand direct answers to the questions: What differentiates Ukrainians from Latin Americans and Caribbeans? Why are there open borders for Europeans and not for those from south of the U.S. border?

Whether in the era of HIV/AIDS or COVID, Title 42 provisions did little to nothing in preventing the spread of disease. Instead, in both instances, Democrats and Republicans used disease as an opportunity to express what I have called the U.S. state's alienizing logic. "Alienizing logic" refers to "a structure of thinking that insists that some are necessarily members of a community and some are recognized as not belonging, even if they physically reside there."[11] Because the U.S. nation-state is born of genocide and slavery, built by racialized migrant labor, reproduced by wealthy, able-bodied, white women, and protected by their husbands, it's pretty clear who belongs and who doesn't. When it comes to immigration and border policy, as this volume makes clear, the telos is to protect and maintain the white, able-bodied, wealthy, Christian, heteropatriarchal character of the U.S. nation-state. This telos is reinforced by our "friends" and our foes alike. What are we to do?

This book ends with abolitionist dreams, and I want to conclude by reiterating the importance of a telos of abolition in our scholarship and political work.[12] If our telos is the abolition of borders and bordering regimes, then we give ourselves a compass with which to navigate all our work, no matter who is in power. After all, as *Resistance and Abolition in the Borderlands: Confronting Trump's Reign of Terror* starkly reveals, Trump reminded us of who "we" are, foundationally, as U.S. American people. Trump reminded us of what "we" are capable of, and fundamentally what "we" believe. But he's a symptom, not the root cause, and the work of abolition remains before us.

Karma R. Chávez
University of Texas at Austin

NOTES

1. McMenamin, "Haitian Migrants Subject to Border Patrol Whips at Texas Border."
2. Suspension of Entries and Imports from Designated Places to Prevent Spread of Communicable Diseases, 42 U.S.C. § 265 (1944).
3. García, "Texas Sues to Block Biden Administration from Lifting Title 42."
4. Downey, "Mayorkas Defends Biden Administration's Use of Title 42 Expulsions for Migrants."
5. Montoya-Galvez, "US Officials Processed 9,926 Undocumented Ukrainians in Last Two Months."
6. Hammami, "The US Must Acknowledge the Role Racism Plays in Migration Policies."
7. Alvarez, "Federal Judge Blocks Biden Administration from Lifting Title 42 for Now."
8. Hesson, Graham, and Pamuk, "Exclusive."
9. Moore, "Democratic Senators Express 'Deep Concerns' over Biden Ending Title 42."
10. Wilck, "Work Authorization for Ukrainians."
11. Chávez, *The Borders of AIDS*, 5. See also Tina Shull and Jamili Hammami's chapter in this volume.
12. Cisneros, "Free to Move, Free to Stay, Free to Return."

BIBLIOGRAPHY

Alvarez, Priscilla. "Federal Judge Blocks Biden Administration from Lifting Title 42 for Now." *CNN*, May 20, 2022. https://www.cnn.com/2022/05/20/politics/title-42 -biden-us-mexico-border/index.html.

Chávez, Karma R. *The Borders of AIDS: Race, Quarantine, and Resistance.* Seattle: University of Washington Press, 2021.

Cisneros, Josue David. "Free to Move, Free to Stay, Free to Return: Border Rhetorics and a Commitment to Telos." *Communication and Critical/Cultural Studies* 18, no. 1 (2021): 94–101.

Downey, Caroline. "Mayorkas Defends Biden Administration's Use of Title 42 Expulsions for Migrants." *Yahoo! News*, September 21, 2021. https://news.yahoo.com/ mayorkas-defends-biden-administration-title-015502308.html.

García, Uriel J. "Texas Sues to Block Biden Administration from Lifting Title 42, A Pandemic-Era Health Rule Used to Expel Migrants." *Texas Tribune*, April 22, 2022.

Hammami, Jamila. "The US Must Acknowledge the Role Racism Plays in Migration Policies." *Common Dreams*, August 16, 2022. https://www.commondreams.org/ views/2022/08/16/us-must-acknowledge-role-racism-plays-migration-policies.

Hesson, Ted, Dave Graham, and Humeyra Pamuk. "Exclusive: Biden Urges Mexico to Take Migrants Under COVID Expulsion Order He Promised to End." Reuters, September 15, 2022. https://www.reuters.com/world/americas/exclusive-biden -urges-mexico-take-migrants-under-covid-expulsion-order-he-2022-09-14/.

McMenamin, Lexi. "Haitian Migrants Subject to Border Patrol Whips at Texas Border." *Teen Vogue*, September 21, 2021. https://www.teenvogue.com/story/haiti -border-patrol-whips-refugees.

Montoya-Galvez, Camilo. "US Officials Processed 9,926 Undocumented Ukrainians in Last Two Months, Data Show." *CBS News*, April 11, 2022. https://www.cbsnews .com/news/immigration-ukraine-us-mexico-border/.

Moore, Mark. "Democratic Senators Express 'Deep Concerns' over Biden Ending Title 42." *New York Post*, November 29, 2022.

Wilck, Ryan A. "Work Authorization for Ukrainians—Uniting Ukraine Program." Reddy and Neumann, P.C., November 22, 2022. https://www.rnlawgroup.com/ work-authorization-for-ukrainians-uniting-for-ukraine-program/.

CONTRIBUTORS

Arturo J. Aldama, born in Mexico City and raised in Sacramento, California, serves as associate professor and chair of ethnic studies at the University of Colorado Boulder. He received his PhD in ethnic studies from the University of California, Berkeley, in 1996. Select publications include *Disrupting Savagism: Intersecting Chicana/o, Mexican Immigrant, and Native American Struggles for Representation* and *Violence and the Body: Race, Gender, and the State*. He served as co-specialist editor of the *Encyclopedia of Latino Popular Culture*, a 400,000-word, multivolume project that is the first of its kind. He served as editor or co-editor of *Decolonial Voices: Chicana and Chicano Cultural Studies in the 21st Century, Enduring Legacies: Ethnic Histories and Cultures of Colorado, Performing the US Latina and Latino Borderlands*, and *Comparative Indigeneities of the Américas: Toward a Hemispheric Approach*. His most recent book, *Decolonizing Latinx Masculinities*, co-edited with his brother Frederick Luis Aldama, was named runner-up for best nonfiction by Empowering Latino Futures.

Rebecca Avalos focuses on the meeting point of critical legal studies, racial formation, Latinx studies, white supremacy, and presidential rhetoric. Rebecca received her PhD at the University of Colorado Boulder in rhetoric and culture. Before her years of residence at the University of Colorado Boulder, Rebecca received her MA in communication studies with a focus on social movement rhetorical theory at California State

University, Fullerton, and she holds a BA in communication studies and a BA in Chicano and Latino studies from California State University, Long Beach. Raised in South East Los Angeles, Rebecca has a deep and unwavering commitment to the pursuit of justice.

Cynthia Bejarano, a native of the southern New Mexico border, is Regents Professor in the Gender and Sexuality Studies program at New Mexico State University (NMSU) and the College of Arts and Sciences Stan Fulton Endowed Chair. Her research, advocacy/activism, and scholarship center on migrant, immigrant, and farmworker advocacy; gender-based violence and feminicides; and the militarization/securitization of the border and its impact on local people. Since 2002, she has worked as the principal investigator for the U.S. Department of Education's College Assistance Migrant Program at NMSU, serving six hundred first-year farmworker students. Her publications include several peer-reviewed articles, chapters, creative works, and books like *¿Qué ònda? Urban Youth Culture and Border Identity, Terrorizing Women: Feminicide in the Americas* with co-editor Rosa-Linda Fregoso, and the forthcoming *Frontera Madre(hood): Brown Mothers Challenging Oppression and Transborder Violence at the U.S.-Mexico Border* with co-editor Cristina Morales.

Tria Blu Wakpa is assistant professor of dance studies in the Department of World Arts and Cultures/Dance at the University of California, Los Angeles (UCLA). She is a scholar, poet, and practitioner of Indigenous dance, Indigenous sign language, martial arts, and yoga. Her first book project historically and politically contextualizes Native American choreographies at four sites of confinement on Lakota lands: a former Indian boarding school, men's and women's prisons, and a tribal juvenile hall. Professor Blu Wakpa is also affiliated with UCLA's American Indian Studies Center and Center for Community Engagement.

Renata Carvalho Barreto is a Brazilian historian and filmmaker. Her work as an experimental artist concerns the re-placement of the audiovisual archive, giving emphasis to African and Indigenous records. As a historian, she subverts the fabrications of power that permit the existence of a linear hegemonic historiography, with writings and lectures in critical art history, history of media, and art practice. Her work as an interdisciplinary scholar is framed by radical pedagogy, decolonial praxis, nonprofit art theory, and cultural studies. She holds a BA in history (Universidade de Brasília) and an MFA in film, video, animation, and new genres (University of Wisconsin–Milwaukee). Born and raised in Brasília, Renata has extensive experience in public education, aiming at inclusive pedagogy methods.

Karma R. Chávez is the Bobby and Sherri Patton Professor of Mexican American and Latina/o Studies and department chair at the University of Texas at Austin. Select publications include *The Borders of AIDS: Race, Quarantine, and Resistance, Palestine on the Air, Queer Migration Politics: Activist Rhetoric and Coalitional Possibilities,* and *Queer and Trans Migrations: Dynamics of Illegalization, Detention, and Deportation* (co-edited).

Leo R. Chavez is distinguished professor of anthropology at the University of California, Irvine, and author of *The Latino Threat: Constructing Immigrants, Citizens, and the Nation* and *Anchor Babies and the Challenge of Birthright Citizenship.*

Jennifer Cullison, assistant professor and native of the San Francisco Bay Area, earned her PhD in history from the University of Colorado Boulder and joined the Department of History at California State University, Stanislaus, in 2022. She teaches classes in U.S. history, ethnic and immigration history, and public and oral history. Her research focuses on U.S. immigration policy history and the human experience of, especially, undocumented immigrants and people detained by U.S. immigration regimes in the postwar era. Key to her work has been the use of international archives, interviews, digital humanities, and oral histories. She has volunteered with Casa de Paz, La Posada Providencia, Detention Watch Network, and the ICEonTrial campaign. She recently coordinated a twenty-interview collection called the Realities of Undocumented Immigrants Oral History Project, available now at the University of Nevada, Reno.

Jasmin Lilian Diab is a scholar and expert in migration, gender, and conflict studies. She is the director of the Institute for Migration Studies at the Lebanese American University, where she also serves as assistant professor and coordinator of migration studies. In 2022, she became the UN University Centre for Policy Research's first-ever global fellow on migration and inequality. She is a research affiliate at the Centre for Refugee Studies at York University and a global fellow at Brown University's Center for Human Rights and Humanitarian Studies, as well as a visiting fellow at the University of Cambridge, supporting the Centre for Lebanese Studies' British Academy bilateral research chair on education in conflict. She is a former visiting professor at the UN-mandated University for Peace in the Department of Peace and Conflict Studies, and has served as a senior guest lecturer at the University of Palermo, University Institute of Lisbon, and McGill University.

Allison Glover has been a volunteer through the Berkshire Immigrant Center (Massachusetts), the Dilley Pro Bono Project (Texas), and Casa de Paz and Rocky Mountain Immigrant Advocacy Network (Colorado), interpreting, translating, and advocating for Spanish speakers in immigration proceedings. Currently, she is the director of community engagement at Colorado Hosting Asylum Network, a nonprofit organization that welcomes the newly arrived and helps asylum seekers pursue their claim in immigration court.

Jamila Hammami is a Texan abolitionist cross-movement grassroots organizer, political strategist, archivist, writer, researcher, trainer, facilitator, and educator. For nearly twenty years, their organizing work has focused on racial, migratory, and queer justice, bridging the anti-imperialist, prison-industrial complex, and border abolition movements. Jamila's writing and research focus on race, empire, fascism, surveillance, political economy, labor, community organizing, resistance, border, and carceral studies. Jamila is a steering committee member of the international Open Borders Conference, the former founding executive director of the Queer Detainee Empowerment Project, and a Frederick Douglass 200 bicentennial abolitionist honoree.

Alexandria Herrera is a dual-title PhD candidate in Latin American history and women's, gender, and sexuality studies at Pennsylvania State University, where she also received her dual-title master's degree. She received bachelor's degrees in history and Spanish literature from the

University of Arizona. Herrera is primarily a historian of public health and medicine in nineteenth- and twentieth-century Guatemala. She grew up in Tucson, Arizona, a fact that has greatly shaped her academic interests and activism on border policy, immigration, gender, violence against women, and Guatemalan Indigenous peoples' experiences along the U.S.-Mexico border. Herrera's research has been funded by the U.S. Department of Education's Foreign Language and Area Studies (FLAS) Fellowship program, Pennsylvania State University's Center for Humanities and Information, and the Fulbright-Hays Doctoral Dissertation Research Abroad (DDRA) program.

Diana J. López was born in El Paso, Texas, and raised in Sunland Park, New Mexico, and Ciudad Juárez. She is a PhD student in the history of the borderlands at the University of Texas at El Paso. Her dissertation research centers the oral histories of border women in Ciudad Juárez and El Paso to illustrate *transfronteriza* solidarities in response to gender-based violence, surveillance, and policing from 1965 to 2015. She received bachelor's degrees in psychology, Spanish, and gender and sexuality studies from New Mexico State University. She earned an MS in Mexican American studies from the University of Arizona. Diana is a junior researcher for the Crossing Latinidades Humanities Research Initiative through the Mellon Foundation. As a researcher invested in public-facing scholarship, Diana is currently a Latino Museum Studies Program fellow for the National Museum of the American Latino in Washington, D.C.

Sergio A. Macías is associate teaching professor in the Department of Spanish Language, Literary, and Cultural Studies, and affiliated faculty in the Critical Race and Ethnic Studies Department, the Gender and Women's Studies program, and the Center for World Languages and Cultures at the University of Denver (DU). He obtained his PhD from the University of Colorado Boulder, after earning his MA in Spanish with an emphasis in peninsular literature from that same institution. He actively participates in interdisciplinary community outreach programs, such as DU's Immigration Cluster, funded and supported by the Mellon Foundation and the Center for Community Engagement to Advance Scholarship. He offers service-learning courses that facilitate student volunteer opportunities with Casa de Paz, a nonprofit organization that supports undocumented immigrants recently released from detention centers.

Cinthya Martinez is a first-generation Mexican scholar and community organizer focusing on migrant detention, state sexual violence, and feminist abolition theory/praxis. She received her PhD in ethnic studies from the University of California, Riverside, and is currently a postdoctoral fellow in the Department of Latin American and Latino Studies at the University of California, Santa Cruz. Cinthya's research focuses on sexual violence and reproductive (in)justice in ICE detention facilities, while examining how affected communities, and migrant activists more broadly, are forging geographies of abolition through confronting the connections between carceral and border regimes.

Alexis N. Meza is a postdoctoral fellow in the Department of Social and Cultural Analysis at New York University. Her research focuses on the Central American diaspora, memory, and radical politics. As a scholar of critical refugee and migration studies, she has used her academic training to collaborate with grassroots movements to defend asylum and to end the practice of immigration detention.

Roberto A. Mónico is assistant professor in the Department of Critical Race, Gender, and Sexuality Studies at California State Polytechnic University, Humboldt. He focuses on the criminal legal system and on the way that political ideology produces criminality aimed at nonwhite working-class communities.

José Enrique Navarro is associate professor of Spanish at Wichita State University. His research and teaching focus on contemporary Spanish American fiction, Latinx studies, and graphic novels. He is co-author of *Mexican Americans of Wichita's North End*, named best history book at the 2022 International Latino Book Awards. Previous publications have appeared in *Revista Canadiense de Estudios Hispánicos*, *Hispanic Issues On Line*, and *Symposium: A Quarterly Journal in Modern Literatures*, among other venues.

Jessica Ordaz is assistant professor of ethnic studies at the University of Colorado Boulder. She grew up in Northern California to Mexican parents from Purépero, Michoacán. She received her doctorate from the University of California, Davis, in American history. During the 2017–18 academic year, Ordaz was the Andrew W. Mellon Sawyer Seminar post-doctoral fellow at the University of Washington, with a focus on comparative racial capitalism. Her first book was titled *The Shadow of El Centro: A History of Migrant Incarceration and Solidarity*. Her second project will explore the multifaceted history of veganism and plant-based foods throughout the Americas, focusing on colonization, food politics, and social justice.

Eliseo Ortiz is a media artist, filmmaker, and scholar working in the interstices between Mexico and the United States. Dr. Ortiz is assistant professor in digital technology and culture at Washington State University and previously served as head of the Arts Department at the University of Monterrey in Mexico. His artistic work has been presented in *Mono No Aware*, Centro Cultural Tlatelolco, and Currents New Media. His writing has appeared in *Poetry, InVisible Culture: An Electronic Journal for Visual Culture, You Are Here: The Journal of Creative Geography*, and *Flat Journal*. Dr. Ortiz was a Fulbright fellow, has received support from the National Fund for Culture and the Arts of Mexico, and was a research fellow at the Media Archaeology Lab at the University of Colorado Boulder.

Kiara Padilla is a Chicana feminist abolitionist born and raised in the San Fernando Valley of greater Los Angeles. She is a PhD candidate in American studies at the University of Minnesota, Twin Cities, and teaches undergraduate courses on race and incarceration and on Latinos and citizenship in the United States. Her interdisciplinary work draws from critical carceral studies, Chicanx and Latinx studies, and women of color feminisms to study abolitionisms in and from the U.S.-Mexico borderlands.

Leslie Quintanilla organizes around the goal of autonomy beyond borders and seeks decolonial possibilities with a network of grassroots organizations, including the Center for Interdisciplinary Environmental Justice and Free Them All San Diego. She received her PhD in ethnic studies, with a certificate in critical gender studies, from the University of California, San Diego, and is currently an assistant professor at San

Francisco State University in the Department of Women and Gender Studies.

J-M Rivera is professor of English at the University of Colorado Boulder. His first book, *The Emergence of Mexican America*, won the Thomas J. Lyon Book Award. His second book, *Undocuments*, recently won the Kayden and E. Pope Awards. He has edited, introduced, and translated two books for the Recovering the US Hispanic Literary Heritage Project and has published widely in scholarship, essays, memoir, creative nonfiction, and poetry. He was the curator of El Laboratorio, a literary space for Latinx writers, and cocreator of CrossBorders, an international collective of writers and artists engaging borders in their art practices. He teaches creative nonfiction, Latinx studies, nineteenth-century American literature and culture, and documentary studies. He is currently working on a hybrid-genre book entitled "Recoil," which explores how the quantitative turn forges guns, populism, and race into a monument of American nationalism and masculinity.

Heidy Sarabia was born and raised in Mexico City and migrated to Sacramento, California, in the 1990s with her family. She is now associate professor in the Department of Sociology at California State University, Sacramento. Her research focuses on globalization processes such as global stratification, borders and borderlands, border violence, transnational social change, and immigrant adaptation and incorporation in the United States. She received her PhD from the University of California, Berkeley, and holds a BA from the University of California, Los Angeles. She was a postdoctoral fellow at the University of Pennsylvania. Her current research projects examine experiences among Latinx faculty, staff, and students in Hispanic-serving institutions (HSI), college engagement among undocumented college students and first-year college students, and experiences of migrants who change legal status.

Tina Shull is associate professor and director of Public History at the University of North Carolina at Charlotte. She is a historian of race, empire, war, climate migration, mass incarceration, environmental justice, and feminist abolitionist movement-building in the modern United States and world. She is the creator of the IMM Print detention stories archive and Climate Refugee Stories, a digital history project about migration, borders, and the fight for climate justice. She is the author of *Detention Empire: Reagan's War on Immigrants and the Seeds of Resistance* and a 2016 Soros Justice Fellow.

Nishant Upadhyay is assistant professor in the Department of Ethnic Studies at the University of Colorado Boulder. Their research focuses on intersections of race, indigeneity, caste, gender, and sexuality. Their book manuscript, "Indians on Indian Lands: Transnational Intersections of Race, Caste, and Indigeneity," studies the formation of dominant-caste Hindu Indian diasporas in North America and Indian diasporic complicities in processes of settler colonialism, racial capitalism, anti-Blackness, heteronormativity, Brahminical supremacy, and Hindu nationalism. The manuscript is under advance contract with the University of Illinois Press. Their scholarship has been published in *Cultural Studies, Interventions, Journal of Critical Ethnic Studies, Feminist Studies, WSQ,* and other journals, anthologies, and online spaces. They edited a special issue of *Sikh Formations: Religion, Culture, Theory* on the Ghadar movement, and co-edited a special issue of *Feral Feminisms* on transnational feminist analysis of settler colonialism.

Maria Vargas was born in Santa Clara, California, and raised in East Palo Alto, a predominantly working-class and immigrant Bay Area neighborhood. She is the proud daughter of Mexican immigrants and graduated from the University of Maryland, College Park, with her PhD in American studies. She lectured in the Department of Latina/Latino Studies at San Francisco State University and is now assistant professor in the Ethnic Studies Department at California State University, Sacramento, where she teaches introductory courses in Chicanx/Latinx and ethnic studies as well as on race in Latin America and the Caribbean. Her work focuses on transnational and decolonial approaches that challenge the impunity of racialized feminicides or hypersexualized racial violence toward Indigenous women in Guatemala. Her areas of specialization include Central American studies, women and gender studies, and decolonial studies.

Antonio Vásquez teaches courses in the Department of Mexican American and Latina/o Studies at the University of Texas at Austin. He holds a PhD in Chicano/Latino studies and American studies and an MA in international relations.

INDEX